CW01081682

POETRY FOCUS

2012
LEAVING CERTIFICATE POEMS AND NOTES FOR ENGLISH HIGHER LEVEL

Martin Kieran & Frances Rocks

GILL & MACMILLAN

Gill & Macmillan Ltd
Hume Avenue
Park West
Dublin 12
with associated companies throughout the world
www.gillmacmillan.ie

Design by Liz White Designs
Print origination in Ireland by O'K Graphic Design, Dublin

The paper used in this book is made from the wood pulp of managed forests. For every tree felled, at least one tree is planted, thereby renewing natural resources.

PICTURE CREDITS
For permission to reproduce photographs, the author and publisher gratefully acknowledge the following:

© Alamy: 161, 248, 342, 349, 373, 387, 395, 405, 409, 418, 423, 427; © Corbis: 383; © Faber & Faber Ltd: 113; © Getty: 5, 116, 121, 126, 142, 166, 170, 253, 277, 292, 300, 305, 309, 324, 330, 335, 364, 369, 391, 414; © Imagefile: 132, 157, 258, 263, 283, 401; © Lebrecht: 270; © Mary Evans: 355; © Press Association: 245; © RTÉ: 360; © Topfoto: 137, 148, 152, 175, 321.

The authors and publisher have made every effort to trace all copyright holders, but if any has been inadvertently overlooked we would be pleased to make the necessary arrangement at the first opportunity.

CONTENTS

Introduction

Poetry Focus is a new, modern poetry textbook for Leaving Certificate Higher Level English. It includes all the prescribed poems for 2012 as well as succinct commentaries on each one. In addition, there are sample student paragraphs on each poem, sample question plans and full graded sample essays. Well-organised and easily accessible study notes provide all the necessary information to allow students to explore the poems and to develop their own individual responses.

- **Explorations** (a series of short questions) follow the text of each poem. These allow students to make initial responses before any in-depth study or analysis. Exploration questions provide a good opportunity for written and/or oral exercises.

- **Study notes** highlight the main features of the poet's subject matter and style. These discussion notes will enhance the student's own critical appreciation through focused group work and/or written exercises. Analytical skills are developed in a coherent, practical way to give students confidence in articulating their own personal responses to the poems and poets.

- **Graded sample paragraphs** aid students in fluently structuring and developing valid points and in using relevant quotations and reference in support.

- **Key quotes** encourage students to select their own individual combination of references from a poem and to write brief commentaries on specific quotations.

- **Sample essay plans** on each poet's work illustrate how to interpret a question and recognise the particular nuances of key words in examination questions. Evaluation of these essay plans increases student confidence in working out clear responses for themselves.

- **There is no single 'correct' approach** to answering the poetry question. Candidates are free to respond in any appropriate way that shows good knowledge of and engagement with the prescribed poems.

- **Full sample Leaving Certificate essays**, graded and accompanied by experienced examiners' comments, show the student exactly what is required to achieve a successful A grade in the Leaving Cert exam and to develop a real enthusiasm for English poetry. This is essential in identifying the task as required by the PCLM marking scheme.

HOW IS THE PRESCRIBED POETRY QUESTION MARKED?

Marking is done (ex. 50 marks) by reference to the PCLM criteria for assessment:

- Clarity of purpose (P): 30% of the total (i.e. 15 marks).
- Coherence of delivery (C): 30% of the total (i.e. 15 marks).
- Efficiency of language use (L): 30% of the total (i.e. 15 marks).
- Accuracy of mechanics (M): 10% of the total (i.e. 5 marks).

Each answer will be in the form of a response to a specific task requiring candidates to:

- Display a clear and purposeful engagement with the set task. (P)
- Sustain the response in an appropriate manner over the entire answer. (C)
- Manage and control language appropriate to the task. (L)
- Display levels of accuracy in spelling and grammar appropriate to the required/chosen register. (M)

GENERAL

'Students at Higher Level will be required to study a representative selection from the work of eight poets: a representative selection would seek to reflect the range of a poet's themes and interests and exhibit his/her characteristic style and viewpoint. Normally the study of at least six poems by each poet would be expected.' (DES English Syllabus, 6.3)

The marking scheme guidelines from the State Examinations Commission state that in the case of each poet, the candidates have **freedom of choice** in relation to the poems studied. In addition, there is **not a finite list of any 'poet's themes and interests'**.

Note that in responding to the question set on any given poet, the candidates must refer to the poem(s) they have studied but **are not required to refer to any *specific* poem(s), nor are they expected to discuss or refer to all the poems they have chosen to study**.

In each of the questions in **Prescribed Poetry**, the underlying nature of the task is the invitation to the candidates to **engage with the poems themselves**.

EXAM ADVICE

- You are not expected to write about any **set number of poems** in the examination. You might decide to focus in detail on a small number of poems, or you could choose to write in a more general way on several poems.

- Most candidates write one or two well-developed **paragraphs** on each of the poems they have chosen for discussion. In other cases, a paragraph will focus on one specific aspect of the poet's work. When discussing recurring themes or features of style, appropriate cross-references to other poems may also be useful.

- Reflect on central **themes** and viewpoints in the poems you discuss. Comment also on the use of language and the poet's distinctive **style**. Examine imagery, tone, structure, rhythm and rhyme. Be careful not to simply list aspects of style, such as alliteration or repetition. There's little point in mentioning that a poet uses sound effects or metaphors without discussing the effectiveness of such characteristics.

- Focus on **the task** you have been given in the poetry question. An awareness of audience is important. Are you meant to be writing a letter to the poet? Perhaps you are giving a talk about the poet or writing an article, a review or an introduction to a new collection of the poet's work. If your poetry answer has the appropriate tone and register, it will have an authentic feel and be more convincing.

- Always root your answers in the text of the poems. Support the points you make with **relevant reference and quotation**. Make sure your own expression is fresh and lively. Avoid awkward expressions, such as 'It says in the poem that...'. Look for alternatives: 'There is a sense of...', 'The tone seems to suggest...', 'It's evident that...', etc.

- Neat, **legible handwriting** will help to make a positive impression on examiners. Corrections should be made by simply drawing a line through the mistake. Scored-out words distract attention from the content of your work.

- Keep the emphasis on why particular poets **appeal to you**. Consider the continuing relevance or significance of a poet's work. Perhaps you have shared some of the feelings or experiences expressed in the poems. Avoid starting answers with prepared biographical sketches. Details of a poet's life are better used when discussing how the poems themselves were shaped by such experiences.

- Remember that the examination encourages **individual engagement** with the prescribed poems. Poetry can make us think and feel and imagine. It opens our minds to the wonderful possibilities of language and ideas. Your interaction with the poems is what matters most. Study notes and critical interpretations are all there to be challenged. Read the poems carefully and have confidence in expressing your own personal response.

'Poetry begins – as all art does – where certainties end.'

Eavan Boland

(1944–)

Eavan Boland has been one of the most prominent voices in Irish poetry. Born in Dublin but raised in London, she had early experiences with anti-Irish racism that gave her a strong sense of heritage and a keen awareness of her identity. She later returned to attend school and university in Dublin, where she published a pamphlet of poetry after her graduation. Boland received her BA from Trinity College in 1966. Since then she has held numerous teaching positions and has published poetry, books of criticism and articles. She married in 1969 and has two children. Her experiences as a wife and mother have influenced her to explore the beauty and significance of everyday living. Boland writes plainly and eloquently about her experiences as a woman, mother and exile. The author of many highly acclaimed poetry collections, Eavan Boland is Professor of English at Stanford University, California, where she directs a creative writing course.

PRESCRIBED POEMS (HIGHER LEVEL)

1 'The War Horse' (p. 4)

A runaway horse in a quiet suburban estate is the starting point for Boland's explorations of attitudes to warfare and violence throughout Irish history.

2 'Child of Our Time' (p. 9)

Written in response to a newspaper photograph of a child killed in the 1974 Dublin bombings, the poem tries to draw some kind of meaning from the tragedy.

3 'The Famine Road' (p. 13)

The poet dramatically recreates a tragic period in Irish history. Boland also links the Famine with another traumatic experience, the story of a woman diagnosed as infertile by her doctor.

4 'The Shadow Doll' (p. 18)

Boland considers the changing nature of marriage since Victorian times. The silence and submission of women are signified by the porcelain doll in its airless glass dome.

5 'White Hawthorn in the West of Ireland' (p. 22)

The poet's journey into the West brings her into contact with a wildly beautiful landscape where she can explore Irish superstitions and a strange, unspoken language.

6 'Outside History' (p. 26)

Another poem addressing the experience of the marginalised ('outsiders') and reflecting Boland's own humanity as a female Irish poet.

7 'The Black Lace Fan My Mother Gave Me' (p. 31)

This poem was inspired by the first gift given by Boland's father to her mother back in 1930s Paris. The souvenir is a symbol of young love and the mystery of changing relationships.

8 'This Moment' (p. 36)

In this short lyric, Boland unobtrusively captures the mystery and magic of the natural world and the beauty of loving relationships.

9 'The Pomegranate' (p. 40)

Another personal poem in which Boland uses mythical references to examine the complexity of feelings experienced in mother–daughter relationships.

10 'Love' (p. 45)

This reflective poem is addressed to the poet's husband and considers the changing nature of romantic love. In developing her themes, Boland draws on Greek mythology.

Eavan Boland

Eavan Boland

The War Horse

This dry night, nothing unusual
About the clip, clop, casual

Iron of his shoes as he stamps death
Like a mint on the innocent coinage of earth.

I lift the window, watch the ambling feather   5
Of hock and fetlock, loosed from its daily tether

In the tinker camp on the Enniskerry Road,
Pass, his breath hissing, his snuffling head

Down. He is gone. No great harm is done.
Only a leaf of our laurel hedge is torn –   10

Of distant interest like a maimed limb,
Only a rose which now will never climb

The stone of our house, expendable, a mere
Line of defence against him, a volunteer

You might say, only a crocus, its bulbous head   15
Blown from growth, one of the screamless dead.

But we, we are safe, our unformed fear
Of fierce commitment gone; why should we care

If a rose, a hedge, a crocus are uprooted
Like corpses, remote, crushed, mutilated?   20

He stumbles on like a rumour of war, huge
Threatening. Neighbours use the subterfuge

Of curtains. He stumbles down our short street
Thankfully passing us, I pause, wait,

Then to breathe relief lean on the sill   25
And for a second only my blood is still

With atavism. That rose he smashed frays
Ribboned across our hedge, recalling days

Of burned countryside, illicit braid:
A cause ruined before, a world betrayed.   30

*'his breath hissing, his
snuffling head'*

EXPLORATIONS

1   Boland felt that 'the daily things I did ... were not fit material for poetry'. Discuss this statement in relation to the poem, with reference to the text.

2   Write your own personal response to the poem, highlighting the impact it made on you.

3   'I wrote the poem slowly, adding each couplet with care.' Consider how the structure and style of the poem emphasise its message.

STUDY NOTES

'The War Horse' was written in 1972 by a newly married Eavan Boland after she had moved to the suburbs at the foothills of the Dublin Mountains. It was an icy winter, and the 'sounds of death from the televisions were heard almost nightly' as the news about the Northern Ireland Troubles was broadcast. In this poem, Boland questions ambivalent attitudes towards war.

This poem is based on a **real event**, the **appearance** of a 'loosed' **Traveller horse**, described in lines 1–9. Boland has said, 'It encompassed a real event. It entered a place in my heart and moved beyond it.' An aural description of the innocuous noise, 'nothing unusual', heralds the arrival of the horse. The horse, a menacing intruder that suggests the opposition between force and formality, wreaked havoc on the neat order of **suburban gardens**. The rigid control of the rhyming couplets mirrors the desire for order in the suburbs.

Onomatopoeia and the alliteration of the hard 'c' vividly describe the horse's walk, like something out of a young child's story: 'clip, clop, casual'. The second couplet counteracts this sense of ordinariness as it describes the damage the horse inflicts. The brutal verb 'stamps' jolts the reader as the garden, 'the innocent coinage of earth', is being destroyed. The simile of a mint, which puts an indelible mark on metal to make coins, is used to describe the destruction. The **consequences of war** are also permanent – people are wounded or killed ('stamps death').

The **poet is an observer**: 'I lift the window, watch'. A detailed description of the horse's leg, 'ambling feather/Of hock and fetlock', belies its capacity for violence. There then follows an explanation of where the horse came from, the 'tinker camp on the Enniskerry Road'. The **random nature of violence** is aptly contained in the verbs 'ambling', 'loosed' and also in the long run-on line 'loosed ... Road'. The sounds the horse makes are vividly conveyed using onomatopoeia: 'hissing', 'snuffling'. The moment of danger passes. 'He is gone.' We can feel the palpable relief: 'No great harm is done'. The colloquial language reduces the event to a trivial disruption.

Lines 10–16 show that the poet has adopted a **sensible approach** as she surveys the **damage**, minimising it with an emphasis on the word 'only': 'only a leaf is torn', 'only a crocus', 'only a rose'. These are all 'expendable'; they can be done without. The language becomes more unsettling as violent descriptions are used to show the mangled blooms: 'like a maimed limb ... which now will never climb', 'Blown from growth'. All describe a world that will never be the same again, potential that will never be realised and life that is cut short. From Boland's perspective, 'the screamless dead' can no longer command attention. And who cares anyway? It is of 'distant interest'. This **apathetic view** can be taken by people as they watch atrocities in other countries. The **language of war** is prominent: 'a mere/Line of defence', 'a volunteer', the head is 'Blown'. The poet's focus has now shifted away from the horse and is **concentrated** on war, its **consequences** and the vulnerability of victims.

In **lines 17–21**, Boland realises that 'we are safe'. War calls for commitment; people must choose to take sides, to fight. This is frightening: 'our unformed fear'. It is there but not expressed, nor given substance or form. Here in this domestic incident is war in miniature, the entry of an intruder who perpetrates damage. The poet asks why the community should care about something so insignificant as a damaged rose or a crushed crocus. She is challenging people who are blasé and examining their **insularity**: 'Why should we care ... corpses, remote, crushed, mutilated?' Are there consequences if people do not care?

Boland criticises her own community in **lines 22–30**, with the neighbours described as hiding behind curtains ('subterfuge'). This 'I don't want to know' attitude reflects the **ambivalence** about the Troubles in the Irish Republic during the 1970s. The tension, 'I pause, wait', is followed by release: 'breathe relief'. At the conclusion, there are two views at the moment of insight. One is the suburban woman's; the other is an Irish person's awareness of connecting with past history. There is an ancestral memory, 'atavism', which associates the smashed rose with the destruction of the Irish. The ribbon trails back to the violence of English colonialism. Boland and her neighbours chose not to confront the horse, just like the Irish did not confront the invaders. The intruder (the horse, the British) destroyed something beautiful and precious (the rose, Irish culture). The mood here is one of loss and regret. Should both intruders have been challenged? How right is it to live so indifferently? The poem **ends on a bleak note**, a lament for 'a world betrayed'.

ANALYSIS

'We are collectively involved in violence which occurs in our land.' Discuss how this poem reflects this statement. Illustrate your response with reference to the poem.

Boland uses an ordinary, domestic incident, the arrival of a tinker's horse into a suburban garden, to explore the ambivalent attitude often prevalent to wars that seem distant. The colloquial phrase 'No great harm is done' and the neighbours who use 'the subterfuge/Of curtains' both illustrate this insular approach. Everything is all right so long as 'we' are safe. The consequences of war are listed as Boland itemizes them: 'maimed limb', 'now will never climb', 'expendable', 'screamless dead'. The vulnerability of the innocent victims is laid bare. Can we afford to be so indifferent? The implicit statement is that we should care. She then conveys the ancestral memory of how Ireland was invaded by the British. The word 'Ribboned' recalls the Ribbonmen, a secret society that was active against the invaders for a while. We are left feeling that perhaps due to the majority of Irish people's indifference and through a lack of commitment, 'A cause' was lost. The poem ends with a lament, 'a world betrayed', with its long echoing 'ay' sound. I think Boland is upset at people's lack of commitment in a time of trouble.

EXAMINER'S COMMENT

Close reading of the poem is evident in the response. Quotations are very well used here to highlight Boland's attitude to people's commitment to war. Expression is also very good. Grade A standard.

CLASS/HOMEWORK EXERCISES

1 Is this poem a private poem, or does it have a wider significance? Use reference to the poem in your answer.
2 Copy the table below into your own notes and use the blank spaces to fill in the missing critical comments about the last two quotations.

Key Quotes

But we, we are safe	Boland explores a detached, insular attitude towards violence.
why should we care/If a rose, a hedge, a crocus are uprooted/Like corpses, remote, crushed, mutilated?	A commonplace incident causes the poet to reflect on our cynical attitude towards war. Assonance emphasises the loss of potential as a consequence of war.
No great harm is done	
recalling days/Of burned countryside, illicit braid	

Child of Our Time

(for Aengus)

Yesterday I knew no lullaby
But you have taught me overnight to order
This song, which takes from your final cry
Its tune, from your unreasoned end its reason;
Its rhythm from the discord of your murder   5
Its motive from the fact you cannot listen.

We who should have known how to instruct
With rhymes for your waking, rhythms for your sleep,
Names for the animals you took to bed,
Tales to distract, legends to protect   10
Later an idiom for you to keep
And living, learn, must learn from you dead,

To make our broken images, rebuild
Themselves around your limbs, your broken
Image, find for your sake whose life our idle   15
Talk has cost, a new language. Child
Of our time, our times have robbed your cradle.
Sleep in a world your final sleep has woken.

Eavan Boland

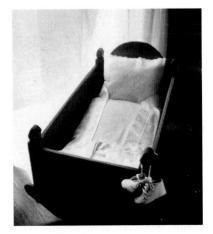

'our times have robbed your cradle'

GLOSSARY

5 *discord*: lack of harmony among people, harsh, confused sounds; conflict.

11 *idiom*: turn of phrase; words which when used together have a different meaning from when used singly.

EXPLORATIONS

1   Boland believes that the 'murder of the innocent' is one of the greatest obscenities. How is this explored in the poem? Write a paragraph in response.

2   Where are the two feelings, tenderness and outrage, evident in the poem? Use reference to the text in your response.

3   What is Boland implying about 'our times'? Is she satisfied or dissatisfied with what is happening? Refer closely to the text in your answer.

STUDY NOTES

'Child of Our Time' was written in 1974 at the height of the Troubles. It was prompted by a harrowing newspaper picture of a fireman tenderly carrying a dead child from the rubble of a bomb explosion in Dublin. It is dedicated to Aengus, the infant son of the poet's friend, who had suffered cot death. This lyric is a response to the sudden and unexpected death of all young children. It also puts an onus on adults to change their ways.

The title of this poem places the little child in a wider context than that of family and town – he is a child of 'our time'. He is our responsibility; he belongs to us. A child should be a **symbol of innocence**, growth, love, potential and the future, but this has been savagely and tragically cut short by 'our time'. Boland did not have children when she wrote this poem ('Yesterday I knew no lullaby'), but in the **first stanza** she describes how she has been taught to sing a lullaby which is different: 'you have taught me overnight to order/This song'. The child's violent and tragic death demands a response, so she will form and order and 'reason' a poem from the child's 'unreasoned end'. It is a song made of harsh sounds, 'discord'. The tone moves from tender compassion ('lullaby') to indignation ('the fact you cannot listen'). There is no escaping the finality of death, yet the poet is a balanced, reasonable person trying to make **order out of disorder** in a poem that is carefully arranged in three stanzas.

The poem is charged with both **sadness and awareness**. The compassionate voice of the poet is heard in 'rhythms for your sleep,/Names for the animals you took to bed'. However, she is aware of the awfulness of the event: 'final cry', 'end', 'murder'. The language is formal, as befits such a solemn occasion: 'We who should have known', 'Child/Of our time'. This poem has elements of an **elegy** (a poem for the dead): it laments, praises and consoles. The poem's many half rhymes mimic this discordant time: 'idle'/'cradle', 'order'/'murder'.

The collective 'we' in the second stanza is used to show the true context of the little child as a member of the human family. **It is 'we' who are responsible** for not making society safer so that childhood could consist of 'Tales to distract, legends to protect'. The repetitive sound of 'rhymes' and 'rhythms' imitates the rocking sound of a mother nursing her child. Boland's aim is clear: we must learn from our mistakes and reconstruct a better world out of 'our broken images'.

In the third stanza, the poet is insistent that **society takes on this responsibility**, that we 'find ... a new language'. We have to engage in dialogue, not 'idle/Talk', so that we can deliver a safer society for our children. Ironically, it is the little child, who 'our time' has 'robbed' from his cradle, who will form the scaffold around which we can build a new and better society: 'rebuild/Themselves around your limbs'. The final line of the poem is a **prayer and a hope**: 'Sleep in a world your final sleep has woken.' It is a wish that the little child be at rest now and that the world may be woken to its senses by his death.

ANALYSIS

Boland is a 'sensitive poet' who is 'rarely thrown off balance by anger'. Discuss this view of the poet in relation to the poem 'Child of Our Time'. Use references from the poem in your response.

SAMPLE PARAGRAPH

'Child of Our Time' is an example of Boland's control in the face of what must be the most horrific event that humanity can witness: the brutal and senseless murder of an innocent child. The poem is carefully ordered into three stanzas that act as balanced paragraphs in an argument. The first stanza emphasises the meaningless atrocity of 'your unreasoned end'. The second stanza places responsibility where it belongs, on the adult society that should have known how to provide a safe environment for the young: 'We who should have known'. The third stanza urges the adults to do something now, to 'find for your sake whose life our idle/Talk has cost, a new language'. The language is formal and controlled, as befits an elegy. When I listen to Ravel's 'Pavane for a Dead Infant', I hear the same stately rhythm. There are just four sentences in this lyric. The child has taught the poet a lullaby with his death. The adults must learn from this tragedy – they have to learn to talk. May the child awake the world to a new time on account of his tragic death. The balance is impressive, as the poet makes order out of disorder rather than letting her anger explode. The poem lacks sentimentality or even spiritual consolation. Instead, the quiet, insistent voice states that 'we' 'must learn'. Sometimes a soft voice delivers a more powerful message. Boland sensitively deals with a tragic event with an absence of anger and with an insistence that, as a result, lessons must be learned. The poet has learned well from the dead child 'to order/This song'.

EXAMINER'S COMMENT

Boland's careful patterning is explored in this answer to advance the argument that the poet explores the tragic event in a sensitive and controlled way. The comment relating to music shows good personal engagement. Effective use of accurate quotation enhances the response. Grade A.

CLASS/HOMEWORK EXERCISES

1   There is a 'difficult sort of comfort' in literature. Discuss this statement in relation to the poem. Support the points you make with reference to the text.

2   Copy the table below into your own notes and use the blank spaces to fill in the missing critical comments about the last two quotations.

Key Quotes

But you have taught me overnight to order/ This song	The dead child's tragic end has given the poet the inspiration to create this poem.
Tales to distract, legends to protect	These are the appropriate nursery elements of childhood: rhymes, fairytales and myths. The poet sees language as a form of protection against danger.
find for your sake whose life our idle/Talk has cost, a new language	The adults must learn to engage in dialogue, as the child has paid the price for their useless words.
rebuild/Themselves around your limbs	
Sleep in a world your final sleep has woken	

The Famine Road

'Idle as trout in light Colonel Jones
these Irish, give them no coins at all; their bones
need toil, their characters no less.' Trevelyan's
seal blooded the deal table. The Relief
Committee deliberated: 'Might it be safe,   5
Colonel, to give them roads, roads to force
from nowhere, going nowhere of course?'

> *one out of every ten and then*
> *another third of those again*
> *women – in a case like yours.*   10

Sick, directionless they worked fork, stick
were iron years away; after all could
they not blood their knuckles on rock, suck
April hailstones for water and for food?
Why for that, cunning as housewives, each eyed –   15
as if at a corner butcher – the other's buttock.

> *anything may have caused it, spores,*
> *a childhood accident; one sees*
> *day after day these mysteries.*

Dusk: they will work tomorrow without him.   20
They know it and walk clear. He has become
a typhoid pariah, his blood tainted, although
he shares it with some there. No more than snow
attends its own flakes where they settle
and melt, will they pray by his death rattle.   25

> *You never will, never you know*
> *but take it well woman, grow*
> *your garden, keep house, good-bye.*

'It has gone better than we expected, Lord
Trevelyan, sedition, idleness, cured   30
in one; from parish to parish, field to field;
the wretches work till they are quite worn,

then fester by their work; we march the corn
to the ships in peace. This Tuesday I saw bones
out of my carriage window. Your servant Jones.'   35

Barren, never to know the load
of his child in you, what is your body
now if not a famine road?

'the wretches work till they are
quite worn'

During the Irish Famine of 1945–48, the British authorities organised various relief schemes. The hungry were given a small wage to buy food for participating in road building and other community projects. Many of the new roads were constructed in remote areas and served little purpose other than controlling the starving population.

1 *Colonel Jones*: army officer and Chairman of the Board of Works.

3 *Trevelyan*: Charles Trevelyan, a senior civil servant in overall charge of famine relief.

4 *Relief Committee*: groups usually consisting of landlords, the clergy and influential people were set up to distribute food.

5 *deliberated*: considered, discussed.

17 *spores*: germs.

22 *typhoid pariah*: someone shunned because of this deadly blood disease.

25 *death rattle*: last sound of the dying.

30 *sedition*: subversion, treachery.

33 *corn/to the ships*: throughout the famine years, corn was exported from Ireland.

EXPLORATIONS

1   Describe the tone of voice in the opening stanza, using close reference to the text.

2   The poet links the abuse of famine victims with the mistreatment of women in modern society. Is this convincing? Explain your answer.

3   In your view, how chillingly pessimistic are the last three lines of the poem? Give reasons for your answer.

STUDY NOTES

The poem raises interesting questions about marginalised people, a favourite theme in Boland's work. Here she makes a connection between a famine road in the 1840s and an infertile woman in modern times. Boland presents the poem as a series of dramatic moments featuring a variety of characters.

Stanza one begins with the voice of Colonel Jones, a British official, reading from a letter written by Lord Trevelyan, who had overall responsibility for famine relief. The boorish tone of the opening comments about 'these Irish' is explicitly offensive. Trevelyan's generalised insults reflect the **depth of prejudice and suspicion** felt towards an entire population, who are 'Idle as trout in light'. Such ruthless disregard is further underlined by the image of the official blood-red seal. The proposed solutions – 'toil' or hard labour building roads 'going nowhere' – could hardly be more cynical and are all the more ironic coming from the 'Relief Committee'.

Stanza two (like stanzas four and six) is italicised and introduces another speaker, the authoritative voice of a consultant doctor. The unidentified voice quoting statistics to an unnamed woman is casually impersonal. The situation becomes clearer as the poem continues: the medical expert is discussing the woman's failure to have children. Boland portrays him as insensitive and patronising: 'anything may have caused it'. His tone becomes increasingly **unsympathetic as he dismisses her disappointment**: 'You never will, never you know'. He almost seems to take delight in repeating the word 'never'. The doctor's final comments are as severe as some of the remarks made by any of the British officials: 'take it well woman, grow/your garden, keep house'.

In stanza three, the poet herself imagines the terrible experiences of the famine victims. The language used to describe their struggle is disturbing: 'Sick, directionless they worked fork'. Prominent **harsh-sounding consonants**, especially 'c' and 'k' in such phrases as 'blood their knuckles on rock', emphasise the suffering. The alarming suggestion of cannibalism ('each eyed – /as if at a corner butcher – the other's buttock') is a reminder of how people were driven beyond normal standards of human behaviour.

Stanza five focuses on the prevalence of death throughout the long famine years. Attitudes harden as widespread disease becomes commonplace. The poet's direct description, steady rhythm and resigned tone combine to reflect the awful reality of the times: 'they will work tomorrow without him'. Boland illustrates the **breakdown of communities** with the tragic example of one 'typhoid pariah' abandoned to die a lonely death without anyone to 'pray by his death rattle'.

This great human catastrophe is made all the more pathetic in stanza seven, which begins with an excerpt from Colonel Jones's response to Trevelyan: 'It has gone better than we expected'. **The offhand tone is self-satisfied** as he reports that the road-building schemes have succeeded in their real purpose of controlling the peasant population ('the wretches'). The horrifyingly detached admission – without the slightest sense of irony – of allowing the starving to 'fester' while 'we march the corn/to the ships' is almost beyond comprehension. The colonel's matter-of-fact comment about seeing 'bones/out of my carriage window' is a final reminder of the colossal gulf between the powerful and the powerless.

In the final stanza, **Boland's own feelings of revulsion** bring her back to the present when she sums up the 'Barren' reality of the childless woman 'never to know the load/of his child'. The famine road is reintroduced as a common symbol for the shared tragedies of both the victims of mass starvation and infertility. The final rhetorical question leaves us to consider important issues of authority and the abuse of power, whatever the circumstances.

ANALYSIS

How effective is the central symbol of the famine road in this poem? Support your points with reference or quotation.

SAMPLE PARAGRAPH

Eavan Boland's famine road represents the terrible futility of all the poor, unfortunate people who perished from starvation. The English government cruelly forced Irish peasants to build roads for no reason other than to keep them from rebelling. In their own words, these roads were 'going nowhere'. In a way, the roads are also a giveaway sign of the colonial administration in Ireland. Their policies had caused the famine to some extent in the first place. But the poet also uses the same symbol to stand for the infertile woman: 'What is your own body now if it's not a famine road?' She also suffers terrible frustration and must consider her life to be pointless. This symbol is very dramatic. It links the two themes of the poem together and makes us think about how the woman listening to the consultant is like a powerless modern day version of the famine sufferer.

EXAMINER'S COMMENT

There are a number of strong points here, with the answer remaining focused on symbolism throughout both strands of the poem. The dramatic significance is not developed. Overall, the language is reasonably well controlled, except for the slightly inaccurate quotation. A solid C grade.

CLASS/HOMEWORK EXERCISES

1   To what extent does 'The Famine Road' show Eavan Boland's sympathies for the outsiders and the marginalised in society? Refer to the text in your answer.

2   Copy the table below into your own notes and use the blank spaces to fill in the missing critical comments about the last two quotations.

Key Quotes

Idle as trout in light Colonel Jones/ these Irish, give them no coins at all	Boland highlights the callous view of the British administration towards the suffering of famine victims.
Trevelyan's/seal blooded the deal table	Vivid imagery indicates the suffering of the people and the brutality of the administration.
but take it well woman, grow/your garden, keep house, good-bye	The arrogance of the doctor's tone emphasises a dismissive attitude to his female patient.
It has gone better than we expected	
What is your body/now if not a famine road?	

The Shadow Doll

Eavan Boland

They stitched blooms from the ivory tulle
to hem the oyster gleam of the veil.
They made hoops for the crinoline.

Now, in summary and neatly sewn –
a porcelain bride in an airless glamour –   5
the shadow doll survives its occasion.

Under glass, under wraps, it stays
even now, after all, discreet about
visits, fevers, quickenings and lusts

and just how, when she looked at   10
the shell-tone spray of seed pearls,
the bisque features, she could see herself

inside it all, holding less than real
stephanotis, rose petals, never feeling
satin rise and fall with the vows   15

I kept repeating on the night before –
astray among the cards and wedding gifts –
the coffee pots and the clocks and

the battered tan case full of cotton
lace and tissue-paper, pressing down, then   20
pressing down again. And then, locks.

*'They stitched blooms from the ivory tulle/
to hem the oyster gleam of the veil'*

Eavan Boland

A shadow doll was sent to the bride-to-be in Victorian times by her dressmaker. It consisted of a Victorian figurine under a dome of glass modelling the proposed wedding dress.

1 *tulle*: fine net fabric.
2 *oyster*: off-white colour.
3 *crinoline*: hooped petticoat.

8 *discreet*: careful to avoid embarrassment by keeping confidences secret; unobtrusive.
9 *quickenings*: sensations; a woman's awareness of the first movements of the child in the womb.
12 *bisque*: unglazed white porcelain.
14 *stephanotis*: scented white flowers used for displays at both weddings and funerals.

EXPLORATIONS

1 What type of language is used to describe the doll? Do you consider it beautiful or stifling, or both? Illustrate your response with reference to the poem.

2 Do you think marriage has changed for the modern bride? Refer to the last two stanzas in your answer.

3 Choose two phrases from the poem that you found particularly interesting. Explain the reasons for your choice.

STUDY NOTES

'The Shadow Doll' is from the 1990 collection of poems, *Outside History*. The shadow doll wore a model of the wedding dress for the bride-to-be. Boland uses the doll as a symbol to explore the submission and silence surrounding women and women's issues by placing the late twentieth century and Victorian times side by side.

The first two stanzas describe the doll vividly, with her 'ivory tulle' and 'oyster gleam'. The 'porcelain doll' is a **beautiful, fragile object**, but the 'ivory' and 'oyster' colours are lifeless. Passivity and restriction are being shown in the phrase 'neatly sewn'. The **pronoun 'it'** is used – the woman is seen as an object, not a real flesh-and-blood human being. The community is described in the preparations: 'They stitched', 'They made'. Are they colluding in the constraint? The phrase 'airless glamour' conveys an allure that has been deprived of life-giving oxygen. The occasion of the marriage is long gone, but the doll remains as a reminder, a shadow of what was.

The **language of containment** and imprisonment is continued in stanza three: 'Under glass, under wraps'. The doll is silent and 'discreet'; it knows but does not tell. The bride would have kept the doll throughout her life, so the doll would have been present at all major events such as marriage, childbirth, sickness, longings, 'visits, fevers, quickenings and lusts'. These experiences are not explored in poetry, which is why women and their issues are 'outside history'. They are neither recorded nor commented on.

Stanza four sees the **pronoun change to 'she'** as the poet imagines the Victorian bride considering her own wedding: 'she could see herself/inside it all'. It is as if she becomes like the doll, assuming a mask of 'bisque features' and unable to feel real life: 'holding less than real/stephanotis', 'never feeling/satin rise and fall with the vows'. The only remnant of her life is the silent doll. **Stanza five** ends with the word **'vows'**, and this is the link into the next stanza, which is a view from the twentieth-century bride where the pronoun changes to 'I'.

The poet is 'repeating' the same vows as the Victorian bride. Are these entrapping and imprisoning women? Like the Victorian bride, the modern bride is surrounded by things ('cards and wedding gifts'), yet she is 'astray' (**stanza six**), with the same **sense of disorientation** coming over her. Is she feeling this because she is losing her individual identity as she agrees to become part of a couple?

Stanza seven increases the **feelings of restriction** when the suitcase is described as 'battered', and there is the added emphatic repetition of 'pressing down'. Finally, the single monosyllable **'locks'** clicks the poem to an end. The **onomatopoeic sound** echoes through the years as Boland voices the silence in the depressing ending. Little has changed from Victorian times for women.

ANALYSIS

'Boland's poems often end on a bleak note.' Discuss how 'The Shadow Doll' reflects this statement. Illustrate your response with reference to the text.

SAMPLE PARAGRAPH

The onomatopoeia of the monosyllabic word 'locks' echoes with frightening intensity at the end of the poem 'The Shadow Doll'. It suggests to me the clang of a prison door as the prisoner is locked in and denied freedom. This poem explores the nature and meaning of marriage for women. It starts with the description of the Victorian doll with its wedding dress, which seems to become a stifling mask fitted on a living, breathing woman, 'airless glamour', 'Under glass', 'under wraps'. The modern bride is 'astray'. Marriage is shown as confining and silencing, 'discreet'. The repetition of the phrase 'pressing down' has an almost nightmarish sense of claustrophobia. Both the Victorian bride and the modern bride are surrounded by objects, 'seed pearls', 'stephanotis', 'the cards and wedding gifts'. I find it strange that there is no mention of the prospective groom, or friends or families. Instead there is a growing sense of isolation and intimidation culminating in the echoing phrase 'And then, locks'. What is locked in? What is locked out?

EXAMINER'S COMMENT

The response carefully considers the effect of the ending and Boland's exploration of the theme of marriage as a repressive and restricting force on women. The candidate also touches on interesting questions about the narrow views expressed in the poem. A real sense of individual engagement is evident. Grade A standard.

CLASS/HOMEWORK EXERCISES

1   'In her poetry, Boland examines concrete images to explore themes.' In your opinion, how valid is this statement? Use reference to 'The Shadow Doll' in your answer.
2   Copy the table below into your own notes and use the blank spaces to fill in the missing critical comments about the last two quotations.

Key Quotes

a porcelain bride in an airless glamour	The Victorian doll is beautiful but stifled. This is used as a symbol for women in marriage.
discreet about/visits, fevers, quickenings and lusts	The doll is a silent witness to the life of the Victorian bride.
the vows/I kept repeating on the night before	The same promises are made by both brides. For Boland, marriage can still trap women.
astray among the cards and wedding gifts	
And then, locks	

White Hawthorn in the West of Ireland

Eavan Boland

I drove West
in the season between seasons.
I left behind suburban gardens.
Lawnmowers. Small talk.

Under low skies, past splashes of coltsfoot   5
I assumed
the hard shyness of Atlantic light
and the superstitious aura of hawthorn.

All I wanted then was to fill my arms with
sharp flowers,   10
to seem, from a distance, to be part of
that ivory, downhill rush. But I knew,

I had always known
the custom was
not to touch hawthorn.   15
Not to bring it indoors for the sake of

the luck
such constraint would forfeit –
a child might die, perhaps, or an unexplained
fever speckle heifers. So I left it   20

stirring on those hills
with a fluency
only water has. And, like water, able
to re-define land. And free to seem to be –

for anglers,   25
and for travellers astray in
the unmarked lights of a May dusk –
the only language spoken in those parts.

'the custom was/not to touch hawthorn'

GLOSSARY

Hawthorn is a flowering shrub that blossoms in springtime. It is associated with fairytales and superstitions in Irish folklore. People believed that it was unlucky to cut hawthorn or to keep it indoors.

2 *the season*: between spring and summer.

5 *coltsfoot*: wild plant with yellow flowers.

6 *assumed*: became part of.

7 *Atlantic light*: unsettled weather causes the light to vary.

8 *superstitious aura*: disquiet associated with hawthorn stories.

20 *heifers*: cows which have not yet had calves.

EXPLORATIONS

1 Describe the poet's changing mood as she travels from her suburban home to the West. Refer to the text in your answer.

2 There are many beautiful images in the poem. Choose two that you find interesting and briefly explain their appeal.

3 What is the significance of the white hawthorn? What might it symbolise? Refer closely to the poem in your answer.

STUDY NOTES

In this poem, the folklore associated with hawthorn in rural Ireland is seen as symbolic of an ancient 'language' that has almost disappeared. Boland structures her themes around the image of a journey into the West. It seems as though she is hoping to return to her roots in the traditional landscape of the West of Ireland.

The poem opens on a conversational note. Boland's clear intention is to leave the city behind: 'I drove West/in the season between seasons'. Her tone is determined, dismissing the **artificial life of suburbia** ('Lawnmowers. Small talk.') in favour of the freedom awaiting her. **Stanza one** emphasises the poet's strong desire to get away from her cultivated suburban confines, which seem colourless and overly regulated. The **broken rhythm** of line 4 adds to the abrupt sense of rigidity.

This orderly landscape is in stark contrast with the world of 'Atlantic light' she discovers on her journey. **Stanzas two** and **three** contain **striking images of energy and growth**. The 'splashes of coltsfoot' suggest a fresh enthusiasm for the wide open spaces as Boland becomes one with this changing environment. The prominent sibilant 's' underpins the rich stillness of the remote countryside.

She seems both fearful and fascinated by the hawthorn's 'superstitious aura'. The experience is similar to an artist becoming increasingly absorbed in the joy of painting. Run-on lines and the frequent use of the pronoun 'I' accentuate our appreciation of the **poet's own delight** in 'that ivory, downhill rush'.

Stanzas four and **five** focus on the mystery and superstition associated with hawthorn in Irish folk tradition. Boland's awareness of the **possible dangers** check her eagerness as she considers the stories: 'a child might die, perhaps'. The poet is momentarily caught between a desire to fill her arms with these wild flowers and her own disquieting belief in the superstitions. Eventually, she decides to follow her intuition and respect the customs of the West: 'So I left it'.

The **personification** ('stirring') of the hawthorn in stanza six reinforces Boland's regard for this unfamiliar landscape as a living place. The poet's imagination has also been stirred by her journey. In comparing the hawthorn to water, she suggests its elemental power. Both share a natural 'fluency' which can shape and 're-define land'.

The poet links the twin forces of superstition and landscape even more forcibly in stanza seven. They defy time and transcend recorded history. The hawthorn trees give the poet a **glimpse of Ireland's ancient culture**. Although nature remains elusive, Boland believes that for outsiders like herself – visiting 'anglers' and tourists – it is 'the only language spoken in these parts'. The poet's final tone is one of resignation as she accepts that she can never fully understand Ireland's unique landscape or the past.

ANALYSIS

How well does Boland contrast suburban life with the natural primitiveness of the country in this poem? Refer to the text in your answer.

SAMPLE PARAGRAPH

Eavan Boland uses contrasts very effectively. The poem begins out in the suburbs – 'suburban gardens'. The image she gives is of a neat, stifling show-house. It is stifling. The small talk between neighbours is just being polite. Everything changes when she drives to the West coast. The images are much more vivid – 'hard shyness of Atlantic light'. This suggests the mystery of the West coast of Ireland. Unlike the false lawns and neatly trimmed gardens, the West has sharp weeds and coltsfoot. Nature is untamed. Even the punctuation in the poem distinguishes the two different places. There are fewer breaks when Boland is describing the areas where the hawthorn grows wild. She uses breaks at the start – 'I left behind suburban gardens./Lawnmowers. Small talk'.

EXAMINER'S COMMENT

This is a solid C grade response to the question. Suitable reference is used to highlight the two 'worlds' within the poem. The point about punctuation is also relevant. However, the expression wavers at the start and the language lacks fluency at times.

CLASS/HOMEWORK EXERCISES

1   What do you think Eavan Boland has learned from her journey to the West of Ireland? Refer to the poem in your answer.
2   Copy the table below into your own notes and use the blank spaces to fill in the missing critical comments about the last two quotations.

Key Quotes

I assumed/the hard shyness of Atlantic light	Boland celebrates the natural beauty and ancient culture in the West of Ireland.
I left behind suburban gardens./ Lawnmowers. Small talk	The poet contrasts the confining urban lifestyle with nature's unrestricted wildness.
Under low skies, past splashes of coltsfoot	Lively visual and aural images suggest the mystery and freedom of the countryside.
that ivory, downhill rush	
the only language spoken in those parts	

Outside History

There are outsiders, always. These stars –
these iron inklings of an Irish January,
whose light happened

thousands of years before
our pain did: they are, they have always been   5
outside history.

They keep their distance. Under them remains
a place where you found
you were human, and

a landscape in which you know you are mortal.   10
And a time to choose between them.
I have chosen:

out of myth into history I move to be
part of that ordeal
whose darkness is   15

only now reaching me from those fields,
those rivers, those roads clotted as
firmaments with the dead.

How slowly they die
As we kneel beside them, whisper in their ear.   20
And we are too late. We are always too late.

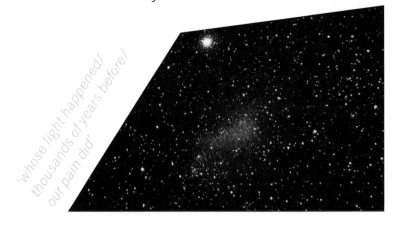

'whose light happened/
thousands of years before/
our pain did'

GLOSSARY

2 *inklings*: slight idea or suspicion; clues.
6 *history*: record or account of past events and developments; the study of these.
13 *myth*: tale with supernatural characters; untrue idea or explanation; imaginary person; story with a germ of truth in it.
17 *clotted*: soft, thick lumps formed.
18 *firmaments*: sky or heavens.

EXPLORATIONS

1 How are the stars 'outsiders'? Do you think they are an effective symbol for those who are marginalised and regarded as of no importance? Discuss, using reference from the poem.

2 Has the poet succeeded in moving 'to be/part of that ordeal'? Look carefully at the imagery and language in the poem.

3 Explain the significance of the last stanza of the poem: 'How slowly they die/As we kneel beside them, whisper in their ear./And we are too late. We are always too late'. In your opinion, has the poet's dilemma been resolved?

STUDY NOTES

'Outside History' was written in 1990 as part of a collection of poems that were arranged to reflect the changing seasons. This poem is set in January. Boland believes that it is important to remember the experiences of those who have not been recorded in history. These are the outsiders, 'the lost, the voiceless, the silent' to whom she gives a hauntingly beautiful voice.

Lines 1–6

The poem opens with an **impersonal statement**: 'There are **outsiders, always**'. The poet is referring to those who have not been recorded in history. The stars are also outsiders, standing outside and above human history. At their great distance, they are shown as cold and distant ('iron', 'Irish January'). They have a permanence and longevity that are in contrast to human life: 'whose light happened/thousands of years before/our pain did'. The run-on line imitates the light that travels thousands of years to reach us. The phrase 'outside history' is placed on its own to emphasise how the stars do not belong to human history.

Lines 7–10

The poet stresses **the aloneness of the stars**: 'They keep their distance'. They don't want to be involved. Now she turns to 'you', a member of the human race, and places 'you' in context with the words 'place' and 'landscape'. This is where 'you found/you were human' and 'mortal'. 'You' are not like the permanent, icy, aloof stars; 'you' are a suffering member of the human race who is subject to ageing and death. The line 'And a time to choose between them' could refer to choosing between the perspective of the stars, i.e. remaining at an uninvolved distance, or the perspective of a member of the human race, i.e. involved and anguished.

Lines 11–18

The phrase 'I have chosen' marks a **turning point** in the poem. Boland has made a deliberate decision, **moving away from 'myth'** and tradition. She felt that myth obscures history. She regarded figures like Caitlin Ni Houlihan and Dark Rosaleen, female symbols for Ireland, as 'passive', 'simplified' and 'decorative' emblems in male poems. She felt that history was laced with myths, which, in her opinion, were as unreal, cold and distant as the stars are from reality. She regarded these mythic emblems as false and limiting, 'a corruption'. Boland is trying to achieve a sense of belonging and wholeness by unwinding the myth and the stereotype. She wanted reality rather than the glittering image of the stars: 'out of myth into history I move to be/part of that ordeal'.

Just as the stars' light travelled vast distances to reach us, so the darkness of unwritten history is travelling to reach her 'only now'. The run-on stanza again suggests great distances that had to be covered for the poet to connect with past history. There follows a description that suggests the **Irish famine**: 'those fields', 'those rivers', 'those roads' which were covered with 'the dead'. The paradoxical phrase 'clotted as/firmaments' uses the language of the stars to describe the numberless bodies strewn everywhere as a result of the famine. This condensed image evokes a poignant sense of the soft mounds of victims lying as numberless as the stars. The full stop after 'the dead' reinforces the finality of death.

Lines 19–21

The final stanza changes to the collective 'we'. Is this referring to the Irish people accepting responsibility for **honouring the dead** and connecting and being part of history? The rite of contrition is being said: 'as we kneel beside them, whisper in their ear'. It was believed that the person's soul would go to rest in heaven as they had made their peace with God, but the repetition of the last line stresses that the words of comfort have come 'too late'. The people don't know they are being honoured by the poet. However, the poem stands as a testament to them and their unrecorded history. Has she changed her attitude from the beginning of the poem: 'There are outsiders, always'? Has she brought them in from the cold sidelines, including them into history? Or has she and 'we' left it too late?

ANALYSIS

Imagine you have invited Eavan Boland to give a reading of her poems to your class or group. What poems would you ask her to read and why do you think they would appeal to your fellow students?

SAMPLE PARAGRAPH

Fellow students, on behalf of our school, St Dominic's, I would like to welcome the poet Eavan Boland to our assembly. Eavan is going to start this workshop with one of my favourite poems, 'Outside History'. In our modern world with all its affluence and prosperity, there are many marginalised people. This poem starts with 'There are outsiders, always'. It is rather like the statement Christ makes when he states that the poor will always be with us. I found the symbol of the stars very effective as it brought home to me how cold and distant people must feel when they are on the sidelines looking in. It reminded me of the film *In the Shadow of the Moon* which we saw last week. The astronaut was speaking from the perspective of the stars. As he stood on the moon he was able to obliterate the earth with his thumb. From the stars' perspective, human history does not exist. Boland, however, starts to move 'into history', to be 'part of the ordeal'. She makes a conscious decision to do so, 'I have chosen'. The phrase rings with conviction. She does give a voice to those who have not been recorded in history, the poor, the weak, the women. And even though the poem seems to end on a bleak note, 'We are always too late', the poem has honoured those who died in their thousands, on 'those roads clotted as/firmaments'. The human compassion of the poet is there in the lines 'as we kneel beside them, whisper in their ear'. What a stark contrast to the iron passivity of the stars! I feel Boland has brought the outsider in and given them their proper place in history. We now look forward to hearing from the poet herself, a big round of applause for Eavan Boland.

EXAMINER'S COMMENT

As part of a full essay, this response is imaginative, and it is also well rooted in the text. The student's lively sense of individual engagement is evident in the format of a speech to fellow students. Grade A standard.

Eavan Boland

CLASS/HOMEWORK EXERCISES

1   Write a letter to Eavan Boland telling her how you responded to some of her poems on your course. Support the points you make by detailed reference to the poems you have chosen.

2   Copy the table below into your own notes and use the blank spaces to fill in the missing critical comments about the last two quotations.

Key Quotes

There are outsiders, always	Boland's aim is to give a voice to those who are on the margins of society.
They keep their distance	The stars are above and impervious to human history.
out of myth into history I move to be/ part of that ordeal	The poet distrusts myth, with its stereotypical images, and wishes to be part of the reality of history, which is the story of the human race with all its suffering.
those roads clotted as/firmaments with the dead	
We are always too late	

The Black Lace Fan My Mother Gave Me

It was the first gift he ever gave her,
buying it for five francs in the Galeries
in pre-war Paris. It was stifling.
A starless drought made the nights stormy.

They stayed in the city for the summer.   5
They met in cafés. She was always early.
He was late. That evening he was later.
They wrapped the fan. He looked at his watch.

She looked down the Boulevard des Capucines.
She ordered more coffee. She stood up.   10
The streets were emptying. The heat was killing.
She thought the distance smelled of rain and lightning.

These are wild roses, appliquéd on silk by hand,
darkly picked, stitched boldly, quickly.
The rest is tortoiseshell and has the reticent,   15
clear patience of its element. It is

a worn-out, underwater bullion and it keeps,
even now, an inference of its violation.
The lace is overcast as if the weather
it opened for and offset had entered it.   20

The past is an empty café terrace.
An airless dusk before thunder. A man running.
And no way now to know what happened then –
none at all – unless, of course, you improvise:

The blackbird on this first sultry morning,   25
in summer, finding buds, worms, fruit,
feels the heat. Suddenly she puts out her wing –
the whole, full, flirtatious span of it.

Eavan Boland

'And no way now to know what happened'

GLOSSARY

2 *Galeries*: Paris store.
13 *appliquéd*: trimming.
15 *tortoiseshell*: clear decorative
    material.
15 *reticent*: reserved, restrained.

17 *bullion*: treasure.
24 *improvise*: make up, imagine.
28 *flirtatious*: enticing, playful.
28 *span*: extent, measure.

EXPLORATIONS

1 The setting is important in this poem. Briefly explain what it contributes to the atmosphere, referring to the text in your answer.

2 Comment on the effect of the short sentences and irregular rhythms in the first three stanzas.

3 Did you like this poem? Give reasons for your response, referring to the text of the poem in your answer.

STUDY NOTES

Set in pre-war Paris in the 1930s, the incident that occurs is the giving of a gift, a black lace fan that the poet's father gave to her mother. A fan was usually seen as a sign of romantic love and desire. However, its significance here is never entirely explained to us. Maybe this is in recognition of our inability to fully understand other people's relationships or to recall the past and the effect it has on us, although we may attempt to. Boland's poem is one of those attempts.

Stanza one begins on a narrative note as the poet recreates a pivotal moment in her parents' lives back in the 1930s. **The fan was a special symbol of young love** and was important because it was 'the first gift' from her father to her mother. Other details of the precise cost and the 'stifling' weather add to the importance of the occasion. Although the Parisian setting is romantic, the mood is tense. Their courtship is framed in a series of captured moments, as though Boland is flicking through an old photo album.

In stanzas two and three, short sentences and the growing unevenness of the rhythm add to this cinematic quality: 'They met in cafés. She was always early'. The hesitant relationship between the lovers is conveyed repeatedly through their nervous gestures: 'He looked at his watch', 'She stood up'. Boland builds up the tension through references to the heat wave: 'the distance smelled of rain and lightning'. The image might also suggest the **stormy nature of what lay ahead** for the couple.

Stanzas four and five focus on the elegant lace fan in **vivid detail**. Boland notes its decorative qualities, carefully embroidered with the most romantic 'wild roses' and fine 'tortoiseshell'. She seems fascinated by the painstaking craft ('stitched boldly') involved in creating this beautiful token of love. But the **poet's appreciation for the fan becomes diminished** with guilt. The tortoiseshell has suffered 'violation' at the expense of the gift. In Boland's mind, the delicate colours decorating the fan came from 'a worn-out, underwater bullion'. The tone is suddenly downbeat as the thought casts a shadow ('the lace is overcast') on her parents' relationship.

In stanza six, the poet returns to the romantic Parisian drama of 'the empty café terrace', but admits that she can never know what really happened that fateful evening in the 'airless dusk before thunder'. Instead, she must 'improvise' it. But at least the romantic moment is preserved in her imagination. Not for the first time, however, there is an underlying suggestion of the reality of relationships over time, and the balance of joy and disappointment that is likely. For Boland, the fan is only a small part of her parents' story. Perhaps she realises that **the past can never be completely understood**.

The striking image of a blackbird dominates the final stanza. The poet returns to the present as she observes the bird 'in summer, finding buds'. The movement of the blackbird's wing is an unexpected link with the black lace fan all those years ago. While the souvenir is old, its significance as a symbol of youthful romance can still be found elsewhere. For the first time, **Boland now seems to understand the beauty of her parents' love** for each other. The last lines are daring and appear to describe both the blackbird and her mother as a young girl holding her new gift: 'Suddenly she puts out her wing –/the whole, full, flirtatious span of it'. The energetic pace of the lines combine with the alliterative sounds and sibilant music to produce a real sense of celebration at the end.

ANALYSIS

It has been said that this is a very unusual love poem. Do you agree with this view? Give reasons for your answer by referring to the text.

SAMPLE PARAGRAPH

'The Black Lace Fan My Mother Gave Me' is not a typical love poem. It is out of the ordinary in ways, e.g. Eavan Boland does not try to glorify the relationship between her parents when they first met. Indeed, they seem unsure of each other. The poet tries to work out the story behind their courtship from looking at the lace fan. She imagines the intense heat of that summer in Paris. 'It was stifling.' References to the weather hint at an uncomfortable relationship, 'The heat was killing.' Boland might be referring indirectly to the future problems in the couple's marriage over the years. The fact that the Second World War was about to break out is also a bad sign. Having said that, the gift of the fan is a symbol of the attraction the couple felt. It is a traditional image of true romance. Unlike other love poems, this is a balanced, unsentimental view of how her parents behaved. There was nervousness and excitement when they were first infatuated with each other, but their love was to change over time. She also compares the fan to a blackbird's wing which excites the poet. This gives us a final impression that Boland is happy to imagine the excited love between her parents back in the 1930s. In a way, the poem is as much about the love Boland herself feels for her parents as about their love.

EXAMINER'S COMMENT

This paragraph focuses well on the way love is presented in the poem. Suitable quotations support the discussion on the way Boland takes a realistic view of her parents. The final point is very interesting and would have been worth developing. A good B grade standard.

CLASS/HOMEWORK EXERCISES

1   Comment on Eavan Boland's use of symbolism in this poem, referring to the text in your answer.

2   Copy the table below into your own notes and use the blank spaces to fill in the missing critical comments about the last two quotations.

Key Quotes

They stayed in the city for the summer. / They met in cafés	The poet focuses on the nature of the relationship between her mother and father.
A starless drought made the nights stormy	The sultry summer in pre-war Paris is conveyed through sensuous imagery.
These are wild roses, appliquéd on silk by hand, / darkly picked	The fan symbolises the early courtship and love between the poet's parents.
The past is an empty café terrace	
the whole, full, flirtatious span of it	

This Moment

Eavan Boland

A neighbourhood.
At dusk.

Things are getting ready
to happen
out of sight.   5

Stars and moths.
And rinds slanting around fruit.

But not yet.

One tree is black.
One window is yellow as butter.   10

A woman leans down to catch a child
who has run into her arms
this moment.

Stars rise.
Moths flutter.   15
Apples sweeten in the dark.

'this moment'

GLOSSARY   7 *rinds*: peels.

EXPLORATIONS

1   What senses does the poet appeal to in her description of the scene?
    Support your answer by referring to the text.
2   Comment on how Boland manages to create drama within the poem.
3   What do you think is the central theme in the poem? Refer closely to the
    text in your answer.

STUDY NOTES

**In this short lyric poem, Boland captures the experience of a passing
moment in time. It is clear that Boland is moved by the ordinariness of
suburban life, where she glimpses the immeasurable beauty of nature
and human nature. The occasion is another reminder of the mystery and
wonder of all creation, as expressed by the American poet Walt
Whitman, who wrote, 'I know of nothing else but miracles'.**

The poem's opening lines introduce a suburban area in any part of the world.
Boland pares the scene down to its essentials. All we learn is that it is dusk, a
time of transition. The atmosphere is one of quiet intensity. Full stops break
the rhythm and force us to evaluate what is happening. Although we are
presented with an **anonymous setting**, it seems strangely familiar. The late
evening – especially as darkness falls – can be a time for reflecting about the
natural world.

The stillness and dramatic anticipation intensify further in lines 3–8.
Something important is about to happen 'out of sight'. Boland then considers
some of nature's wonders: 'Stars and moths'. In the twilight, everything seems
mysterious, even 'rinds slanting around fruit'. The poet's eye for detail is like
that of an artist. The rich, sensory image of the cut fruit is exact and tactile. She
uses simple language precisely to create a **mood of natural calmness** that is
delayed for a split second ('But not yet').

There is time for two more **vivid images** in lines 9–10. The startling colour
contrast between the 'black' tree and the window that is 'yellow as butter' has
a cinematic effect. The simile is homely, in keeping with the domestic setting.
The repetition of 'One' focuses our attention as the build-up continues. Again,
Boland presents the sequence of events in a series of brief glimpses. It is as if
she is marking time, preparing us for the key moment of revelation.

This occurs in lines 11–13. The central image of the mother and child
intuitively reaching out for each other is a powerful symbol of unprompted

love. It is every bit as wonderful as any of life's greatest mysteries. The three lines become progressively condensed as the child reaches her mother. The syntax suggests their eagerness to show their love for each other. Boland's decision to generalise ('A woman' and 'a child') emphasises the **universal significance** of 'this moment'. The crucial importance of people's feelings transcends time and place.

There is a slight tone of anti-climax about the last three lines. However, Boland rounds off her description of the moment by placing it within a wider context. The constant expression of family love is in harmony with everything else that is beautiful in nature. This feeling is suggested by the recurring sibilant 's' sounds and the carefully chosen verbs ('rise', 'flutter' and 'sweeten'), all of which celebrate the excitement and **joy of everyday human relationships**.

ANALYSIS

What features of Boland's writing style are most evident in this poem? Refer closely to the text in your answer.

SAMPLE PARAGRAPH

Some people have described Eavan Boland's poetry as painterly. Her mother was a famous artist. The images she uses to help readers imagine the Dublin suburb are very colourful:

> One tree is black.
> One window is as yellow as butter.

This reminds me of a still life painting. Or of a child's simple artwork. Vivid imagery is typical of her writing. It is more dramatic in that it attracts our attention. I can visualise the suburb at dusk very clearly. Clear expression is another feature of Boland's writing that I love. There is nothing difficult about the poem. Again, it suits all ages, even a young child. This is what is best about 'This Moment'. It is just a simple poem about the happiness of a mother and child. Other great mysteries, such as the way 'Stars are rising' are beyond our understanding. But love between two people is also beautiful. I like the way she makes this point in the poem.

EXAMINER'S COMMENT

This paragraph includes two worthwhile points about imagery and clarity in the poem. These are reasonably well supported with reference (although the quotations are not accurate and the expression is stilted). There is also some personal engagement. An average C grade standard.

CLASS/HOMEWORK EXERCISES

1 Comment on the poet's tone in 'This Moment'. Refer to the text in your discussion.
2 Copy the table below into your own notes and use the blank spaces to fill in the missing critical comments about the last two quotations.

Key Quotes

A woman is leaning down to catch a child	The central thought in the poem is the wonder and beauty of ordinary, natural experiences.
One window is yellow as butter	This colourful, sensuous image intensifies our understanding of the moment Boland is describing.
Apples sweeten in the dark	The use of the sibilant 's' appeals to the senses and has a bittersweet effect.
Things are getting ready/to happen	
And rinds slanting around fruit	

The Pomegranate

Eavan Boland

The only legend I have ever loved is
the story of a daughter lost in hell.
And found and rescued there.
Love and blackmail are the gist of it.
Ceres and Persephone the names.   5
And the best thing about the legend is
I can enter it anywhere. And have.
As a child in exile in
a city of fogs and strange consonants,
I read it first and at first I was   10
an exiled child in the crackling dusk of
the underworld, the stars blighted. Later
I walked out in a summer twilight
searching for my daughter at bed-time.
When she came running I was ready   15
to make any bargain to keep her.
I carried her back past whitebeams
and wasps and honey-scented buddleias.
But I was Ceres then and I knew
winter was in store for every leaf   20
on every tree on that road.
Was inescapable for each one we passed.
And for me.
        It is winter
and the stars are hidden.   25
I climb the stairs and stand where I can see
my child asleep beside her teen magazines,
her can of Coke, her plate of uncut fruit.
The pomegranate! How did I forget it?
She could have come home and been safe   30
and ended the story and all
our heart-broken searching but she reached
out a hand and plucked a pomegranate.
She put out her hand and pulled down
the French sound for apple and   35
the noise of stone and the proof
that even in the place of death,
at the heart of legend, in the midst

Eavan Boland

of rocks full of unshed tears
ready to be diamonds by the time   40
the story was told, a child can be
hungry. I could warn her. There is still a chance.
The rain is cold. The road is flint-coloured.
The suburb has cars and cable television.
The veiled stars are above ground.   45
It is another world. But what else
can a mother give her daughter but such
beautiful rifts in time?
If I defer the grief I will diminish the gift.
The legend will be hers as well as mine.   50
She will enter it. As I have.
She will wake up. She will hold
the papery flushed skin in her hand.
And to her lips. I will say nothing.

'my child asleep'

GLOSSARY

The pomegranate (from a French word meaning an apple with many seeds) is a pulpy oriental fruit.

5 *Ceres and Persephone*: mythological figures. Ceres was the goddess of earth and motherhood. Persephone was her beautiful daughter who was forced by Pluto to become his wife and was imprisoned in Hades, the underworld. Ceres was determined to find Persephone and threatened to prevent anything from growing on the earth until she was allowed to rescue her daughter. But because Persephone had eaten sacred pomegranate seeds in Hades, she was condemned forever to spend part of every year there.

9 *city of fogs*: London, where the poet once lived.

18 *buddleias*: ornamental bushes with small purple flowers.

48 *rifts*: gaps, cracks.

49 *defer*: delay.

Eavan Boland

EXPLORATIONS

1   Boland conveys a clear sense of the city of London in this poem. How does she succeed in doing this? Refer closely to the text in your answer.
2   From your reading of this poem, what do you learn about the relationship between the poet and her own daughter? Refer to the text in your answer.
3   Comment on the poet's mood in the last five lines of the poem.

STUDY NOTES

In the poem, narrated as one unrhymed stanza, Boland explores the theme of parental loss by comparing her own experiences as a mother and daughter with the myth of Ceres and Persephone. Although it is a personal poem, it has a much wider relevance for families everywhere.

Boland presents this exploration of the mother–child relationship as a dramatic narrative. In the opening lines, the poet tells us that she has always related to 'the story of a daughter lost in hell'. This goes back to her early experience as 'a child in exile' living in London. Her **sense of displacement** is evident in the detailed description of that 'city of fogs and strange consonants'. Like Persephone trapped in Hades, Boland yearned for home. But the myth has a broader relevance to the poet's life – she 'can enter it anywhere'. Years later, she recalls a time when, as a mother, she could also identify with Ceres, 'searching for my daughter'.

Lines 13–18 express the intensity of Boland's feelings for her child: she was quite prepared 'to make any bargain to keep her'. The **anxious tone** reflects the poet's awareness of the importance of appreciating the closeness between herself and her teenage daughter while time allows. She expresses her maternal feelings through rich natural images: 'I carried her back past whitebeams'. But she is also increasingly aware that both she and her daughter are ageing. This is particularly evident in line 20, as she anticipates an 'inescapable' change in their relationship: 'winter was in store for every leaf'.

Line 24 marks a defining moment ('It is winter') for them both. Observing her daughter asleep in her bedroom, Boland now sees herself as Ceres and the 'plate of uncut fruit' as the pomegranate. This marks the realisation that **her child has become an adult**. The poet imagines how different it might have been had Persephone not eaten the fruit – 'She could have come home' and ended all the 'heart-broken searching'. But Persephone deliberately made her choice, a decision that is emphasised by the repeated mention of her gesture ('she reached/out a hand', 'She put out her hand'). Significantly, Boland is sympathetic: 'a child can be/hungry'.

In line 42, the poet considers alerting her daughter ('I could warn her') about the dangers and disappointments that lie ahead. **Harsh imagery** suggests the difficulties of modern life: 'The rain is cold. The road is flint-coloured'. Boland wonders if 'beautiful rifts in time' are the most a mother can offer. Such delaying tactics may only postpone natural development into adulthood.

In the end, she decides to 'say nothing'. There is a clear sense of resignation in the final lines. The poet accepts the reality of change. Boland's daughter will experience the same stages of childhood and motherhood as the poet herself: 'The legend will be hers as well as mine'. This truth is underlined by the recurring use of 'She will', a recognition that her daughter's destiny is in her own hands. The poem ends on a quietly reflective note as Boland respectfully acknowledges the right of her daughter to mature naturally and make her own way in life.

ANALYSIS

The poet makes many comparisons between the legend of Ceres and Persephone and her own experiences. How effective are these comparisons? Refer to the text in your answer.

SAMPLE PARAGRAPH

In my view, Eavan Boland has been very successful in blending her own life as a child and mother with Persephone and Ceres. The fact that she uses an ancient legend adds a touch of mystery to the theme of mother–daughter relationships. This gives the poem a universal quality. First, she compares herself to Persephone, the exiled child in London where the stars were 'blighted'. This links the grimy city life to the underworld of Hades. But Boland is more concerned with the present and her fears of losing her own daughter who is growing up fast. By describing her fears through the old story of Ceres, she increases our understanding of how anxious she was feeling. Both parents were 'searching' desperately. Together, the legend and the true-life story of the poet and her reluctance to come to terms with her daughter growing up really show how parents have to let go of their children and give them the freedom to make their own mistakes and learn for themselves. Most parents find it hard to give their children freedom. They can't help it.

Eavan Boland

EXAMINER'S COMMENT

There are some very good points here in response to a challenging question. Although the response shows personal engagement, the answer could be rooted more thoroughly in the text. The expression is repetitive in places and one or two sentences are overlong. C grade.

CLASS/HOMEWORK EXERCISES

1   What image of Eavan Boland herself emerges from this poem? Refer closely to the text in your answer.

2   Copy the table below into your own notes and use the blank spaces to fill in the missing critical comments about the last two quotations.

Key Quotes

an exiled child in the crackling dusk	Boland emphasises the sense of loss throughout the poem; it affects individuals at various stages of life.
If I defer the grief I will diminish the gift	The poet cannot shield her daughter from reality. Separation and loss are an unavoidable part of ageing.
The rain is cold. The road is flint-coloured	Bleak imagery and sharp sounds suggest the severity of modern life.
Love and blackmail are the gist of it	
The legend will be hers as well as mine	

Love

Dark falls on this mid-western town
where we once lived when myths collided.
Dusk has hidden the bridge in the river
which slides and deepens
to become the water   5
the hero crossed on his way to hell.

Not far from here is our old apartment.
We had a kitchen and an Amish table.
We had a view. And we discovered there
love had the feather and muscle of wings   10
and had come to live with us,
a brother of fire and air.

We had two infant children one of whom
was touched by death in this town
and spared: and when the hero   15
was hailed by his comrades in hell
their mouths opened and their voices failed and
there is no knowing what they would have asked
about a life they had shared and lost.

I am your wife.   20
It was years ago.
Our child was healed. We love each other still.
Across our day-to-day and ordinary distances
we speak plainly. We hear each other clearly.

And yet I want to return to you   25
on the bridge of the Iowa river as you were,
with snow on the shoulders of your coat
and a car passing with its headlights on:

I see you as a hero in a text –
the image blazing and the edges gilded –   30
and I long to cry out the epic question
my dear companion:

Eavan Boland

Will we ever live so intensely again?
Will love come to us again and be
so formidable at rest it offered us ascension   35
even to look at him?

But the words are shadows and you cannot hear me.
You walk away and I cannot follow.

*'and when the hero/was hailed by his comrades in hell/their mouths
opened and their voices failed'*

1 *mid-western town*: Iowa, a state in the US. Boland attended the prestigious Iowa Writers' Workshop in 1979 and lived there for a while with her family.
2 *myths*: fictitious tales with supernatural characters and events.
6 *hero*: Aeneas was a hero in the *Aeneid*. He visited the underworld by crossing the River Styx where he saw his dead companions, but they could not communicate with him.
8 *Amish*: strict American religious sect that makes functional, practical furniture without decoration.
31 *epic*: great, ambitious.
35 *formidable*: very impressive.

EXPLORATIONS

1   This poem is an open and honest meditation on the nature of love. Write your own personal response to it, referring to the text in your answer.
2   Do you think the use of the Aeneas myth is effective? Give reasons, using the poem as evidence for your point of view.
3   Explain the significance of the last section of the poem: 'But the words are shadows and you cannot hear me./You walk away and I cannot follow'. In your opinion, is this a positive or negative ending?

STUDY NOTES

'Love' is part of a sequence of poems called 'Legends' in which Boland explores parallels between myths and modern life. She records her personal experience of young love in Iowa at a time when tragedy touched the family, when her youngest daughter was seriously ill and came close to death. This is interwoven with the myth of Aeneas returning to the underworld. The narrative poem explores the nature of human relationships and how they change over time. It also shows the similarity of human experience down through the ages.

Lines 1–6

The poem opens in darkness, **remembering the past**. Her personal experience was in 'this mid-western town' in Iowa, and the poem connects this with the myth of Aeneas visiting the underworld. Aeneas crosses the bridge on the River Styx to reach Hades, the land of the Shades ('the hero crossed on his way to hell'). Boland and her husband were also experiencing their own hell as they visited their very sick little girl in hospital.

Lines 7–12

These lines give us a **clear, detailed picture of their external ordinary life**: 'a kitchen', 'an Amish table', 'a view'. The poem is written in loose, non-rhyming stanzas, which suits reminiscences. Their internal emotional life is shown in the **striking metaphor** 'love had the feather and muscle of wings'. Love was beating, alive, vibrant. 'Feather' suggests it could soar to great heights, while 'muscle' suggests it was a powerful emotion. This natural, graceful love was palpable, substantial, elemental, 'a brother of fire and air'.

Lines 13–19

The **personal drama** of the sick daughter who 'was touched by death' is recalled. But Boland did not lose her child. The word 'spared' links us with the myth again. Aeneas is in the underworld, but because his comrades are shadows, they cannot ask the questions they are longing to ask about the life they once shared. The moment of communication is lost: 'there is no knowing what they would have asked'.

Lines 20–36

Now the poet meditates on the **changing nature of love**. The 'we' becomes 'I' – 'I am your wife'. Do they, as husband and wife, communicate as deeply as they did before? 'We speak plainly' suggests they do not. Her tone is crisp and matter of fact, almost **businesslike**. She wants to recapture the intensity of their love and shared times, when she saw her husband as 'a hero in a text'. In her memory of him, he is outlined by the cars' lights as they pass on the bridge. Described as 'blazing' and 'gilded', he is contrasted to the darkness of the night, as Aeneas is contrasted with the darkness of the underworld. She is longing to experience that special time, that transcendence, again.

Rhetorical questions are posed at the end: 'Will we ever live so intensely again?' The inference is no. She can imagine asking these questions about the life they shared together, but she cannot actually articulate them. This is **similar to Aeneas' dilemma** – his comrades long to ask questions about the life they shared with him, but 'their voices failed'. Neither Boland nor the 'comrades' could express their strong feelings; neither can ask the questions they want to ask. The words of the questions remain unformed, unspoken, 'shadows'.

Lines 37–38

The poem ends with a two-line stanza in which she accepts that the **gap cannot be bridged**: 'You walk away and I cannot follow'. There is a real sense of loss and resignation in Boland's final tone.

ANALYSIS

This poem is about memory. How does the poet explore the theme? Refer either to the content or style in your answer. Illustrate your response with reference to the poem.

SAMPLE PARAGRAPH

By blending myth and personal experience, Boland gives her poems a true sense of universality. But she also blends timelines, the past and the present tenses to give a quality of timelessness to her work. In 'Love', the immediacy and freshness of a potent memory is captured by her use of the present tense: 'Dark falls', 'the bridge ... slides and deepens/to become the water', 'here is our old apartment'. The recent past is shown in the past tense as she recalls what they had: 'We had a kitchen and an Amish table./We had a view', 'love ... had come to live with us', 'We had two infant children'. In the past they had a life together which was lived very intensely. Are they missing any of this now? The tense then changes to the present as Boland states her identity: 'I am your wife'. I notice that it is the partnership she is referring to, not her role as mother. Here she honestly and openly explores her concerns about the changing nature of love. Their moment of crisis is over: 'Our child was healed'. She itemises a list: 'We speak', 'we hear'. They 'love each other still'. But a note of longing is heard in 'I want' and the future tense 'Will we?' Realistically she appraises the current situation and notes 'words are shadows', 'you cannot hear me', 'You walk away', 'I cannot follow'. The intense personal nature of their love has changed. Like Aeneas' comrades, she cannot voice her question ('voices failed'), and her husband, like Aeneas, cannot hear. The changing tenses add a timeless quality to the experience of memory, as time shared is recalled. The poem ends with the never-changing realisation that time cannot be relived.

EXAMINER'S COMMENT

An unusual approach is taken as the response features on the use of tenses as a stylistic feature to communicate theme. There is evidence of close reading of the poem and effective use of accurate quotation throughout. Grade A standard.

CLASS/HOMEWORK EXERCISES

1   'When myths collided.' Do you consider Boland's use of myths in her work effective in exploring her themes? Discuss, referring to the poems on your course.

2   Copy the table below into your own notes and use the blank spaces to fill in the missing critical comments about the last two quotations.

Eavan Boland

Key Quotes

But the words are shadows and you cannot hear me. / You walk away and I cannot follow	Both the comrades of Aeneas and Boland herself cannot connect with their respective 'heroes'. They shared life and dangers with these heroes, but they cannot ask them a question.
love had the feather and muscle of wings	This metaphor suggests the dynamic and vibrant love between the young wife and husband. It was both uplifting and strong.
Across our day-to-day and ordinary distances / we speak plainly	Now in later life they converse in an ordinary way, but Boland seems to be longing to return to a time when they communicated in an extraordinary way.
it offered us ascension / even to look at him	
and I long to cry out the epic question	

LEAVING CERT SAMPLE ESSAY

Q **'The appeal of Eavan Boland's poetry.'**

Using the above title, write an essay outlining what you consider to be the appeal of Boland's poetry. Support your points by reference to the poetry of Eavan Boland on your course.

MARKING SCHEME GUIDELINES

Answers to the question must contain clear evidence of engagement with the poetry on the course. Allow that candidates might focus, in part at least, on reasons why the poetry does not appeal to readers. Expect a wide variety of approaches in the candidates' answering.

Some of the following areas might be addressed:

- Her perspective on Irishness, history and myth.
- Her sense of national identity.
- Her siding with victims and the downtrodden.
- Striking love poetry.
- Treatment of the suburbs as a suitable locale for poetry.
- Delicate use of language and imagery, etc.

SAMPLE ESSAY
(The Appeal of Boland's Poetry)

1 When reading Eavan Boland's poetry, an appealing aspect is that a genuine concern for the past is obvious. There is a sense that women are outside history. She has an attractive, sympathetic response to suffering. Her mixture of public and private events and public and private attitudes is also interesting. I also enjoyed her use of language.

2 In 'Outside History', Boland recognises the great women of the past who were ignored: 'There are outsiders, always.' She calls them 'stars', 'iron inklings of an Irish January'. I was delighted that our first woman President, Mary Robinson, quoted this in her inauguration speech. Just as the sky is cluttered with stars that are above and outside man's history, so history is full of these women 'whose darkness is/only now reaching me from those fields'. The contrast between the vastness of the cosmos and the self-importance of the world is striking. Boland's decision to highlight these women is stated strongly in the phrase 'I have chosen'. The use of 'we' shows that Boland has assumed the role of speaking for the Irish people 'As we kneel beside them', almost trying to hear what they have to say. The poem ends bleakly with the realisation that 'We are always too late'.

3 Boland gives a very interesting woman's perspective in her poems. This is often missing in literature, just as Irish women are missing from recorded history. In 'The Famine Road', Boland has absented herself from the poem. She doesn't personalise the poem, but her presence is felt everywhere in her sympathetic response to the suffering: 'after all could/they not blood their knuckles on rock, suck/April hailstones for water and for food?' The wandering lines portray the wandering roads that were 'going nowhere'. The poem begins with a letter being read by Colonel Jones from Trevalyan to a relief committee. The dismissive tone of the letter comes across vividly in the phrases 'Idle as trout' and 'their bones/need toil'. The terrible death sentence is dramatically shown: 'Trevalyan's/seal blooded the deal table'. The wax seal has become a death warrant.

4 Against this public and political world, the world of the nineteenth-century Irish famine is intertwined with another woman's private sorrow. The italicised verse is given no introduction as a doctor coldly judges what is best for another. Cold statistics are quoted: 'one out of every ten'. What consolation is that to the poor woman who will never know 'the load/of his child' in her? Her body will produce nothing, just as the famine road works result in death: 'This Tuesday I saw bones/out of my carriage window'. This poem works on many levels – the private and personal, the public and historical, the male and female, the master and subordinate – but overseeing it all is the compassionate poet who makes us see the pity of it. This is an appealing aspect for readers.

5 This double private–public aspect of Boland's poetry is interestingly shown in 'Child of Our Time'. A child has died in an explosion in Dublin city. This infant has become a 'child of our time', a victim because we, the adults, did not do enough to protect the vulnerable: 'our times have robbed your cradle'. The dedication, 'for Aengus', refers to a friend's baby who had died a cot death. Here again, Boland is intertwining a public tragedy with a personal grief. Is she telling us that we have to realise that all grief is personal? The conclusion hints at the peaceful world the child will sleep in now that our world has done its worst: 'Sleep in a world your final sleep has woken'. It also suggests that we have woken up to what we have both done ('our idle/Talk') and not done ('We who should have known') and hopefully will mend our ways ('find for your sake ... a new language').

6 The parent–child relationship is also given another perspective in 'This Moment'. This poem has a mysterious quality to it. The description of the 'rinds slanting around fruit' conveys the silent, strange world of Nature. Things are happening, but 'out of sight'. The disjointed line pattern echoes this. The domestic atmosphere is increased by the image of the woman leaning down 'to catch a child/who has run into her arms/this moment'. For a mother and child, this is indeed a golden moment. But again, we have the double perspective on an event. 'This Moment' has two very different sides: the child returning after a day's play into the safety of the home, and the changing, growing world of Nature, working to its own rhythm.

7 I found the poetry of Eavan Boland appealing because of her subject matter and the perspectives she gives us as well as the questions she raises. I found her poetic techniques very powerful in conveying her message, either in the italicised doctor's words in 'The Famine Road' or in the disjointed line structure in 'This Moment'. But I found her compassionate voice most appealing of all, as she quietly shows us that we must remember the Irish women who are not recorded in history; we must find 'a new language' to discuss rather than distrust; and we should appreciate the wonder of our beautiful, ordinary yet extraordinary world: 'A neighbourhood./At dusk'. The appeal of Eavan Boland is both as a woman and a poet.

(approx. 900 words)

GRADE: A2		
P	=	13/15
C	=	13/15
L	=	13/15
M	=	5/5
Total	=	44/50

EXAMINER'S COMMENT

The candidate has concentrated her response to an exploration of Boland's double perspective and her compassionate quality. The appeal of the poems is implicitly stated throughout much of the essay. A solid performance, very well illustrated with apt reference and quotation.

Eavan Boland

1   'Eavan Boland deals with issues which are both private and personal, but which also have a universal appeal.' Discuss this statement, supporting your answer with reference to the poems by Boland on your course.

2   Write the text of a talk you would give your class on the merits of Eavan Boland's poetry, referring both to the themes explored and the style of her communication. Illustrate your answer by reference to the poems by Eavan Boland on your course.

3   'Boland, a modern poet dealing with contemporary issues.' How relevant do you think this view of Eavan Boland is? Discuss, using reference to the poetry of hers on your course.

SAMPLE ESSAY PLAN (Q1)

'Eavan Boland deals with issues which are both private and personal, but which also have a universal appeal.' Discuss this statement, supporting your answer with reference to the poems by Boland on your course.

Intro:	A personal response is required; mention both content and style. Both the private and public as well as universal dimensions of her poetry are to be explored.
Point 1:	'Child of Our Time' – personal response to newspaper picture of the dead child given resonance by saying all of us need to use a new language. Tone both compassionate and admonishing.
Point 2:	'The Pomegranate' – deals with the relationship between mother and daughter, particularly the moment of separation when the child has to go, despite the mother's worry of then being unable to protect her. This personal situation is linked to the myth of Persephone and Ceres, giving it a timeless dimension.
Point 3:	'The War Horse' – metaphorical poem about the attitudes to war. Rigid, controlled couplets show

the suburban desire for order, while the epic title widens the appeal of the poem. Contemplates history in a unique fashion; the blending of past and present blurs the boundaries of time.

- *Point 4:* 'This Moment' – a moment in suburbia, at dusk. Emphasis on 'a' suggests it can apply to any child, any neighbourhood. The collective experience is shown.

- *Point 5:* 'Love' – again, a link with a myth gives a unanimous appeal to the poem. Aeneas and the underworld illustrate the frustration of the poet grappling with the changing aspects of love. A treatment of emotion in an honest way.

- *Conclusion:* Boland refers to specific personal moments or events and gives them a widespread interest by linking them with mythology, by changing tones and by her striking visual descriptions. Her poetry transcends the particular to become general.

EXERCISE

Develop one of the above points into a paragraph.

POINT 5 – SAMPLE PARAGRAPH

By interweaving myth with a personal story, Boland creates poetry that becomes universally appealing. She uses this technique in 'The Pomegranate' and also in the poem 'Love'. Here, the story of the hero Aeneas, who goes to the underworld where his dead comrades are, is interwoven with a story of Boland's, when her daughter was seriously ill. In each there is a hero, Aeneas and Boland's husband ('the hero crossed on his way to hell'). Each has their own trauma to deal with. Aeneas cannot hear what 'his comrades in hell' want to ask, as their 'voices failed'. The questions they wanted to ask 'about a life they had shared and lost' will never be known. Similarly, Boland is unable to ask about a life she and her husband had known, as she feels unable to ask the question 'Will we ever live so intensely again?' They had lived in this way when one of their children was 'touched by death in this town/and spared'. Often in times of tragedy people are capable of great things. To Boland, her husband was 'a hero in a text'. Although both are still in love ('We love each other still'), she longs for the love they once shared ('ascension'). It was an almost ecstatic, spiritual experience. But just as Aeneas is never asked questions by his comrades, so her husband is never asked her question. Instead, the 'words are shadows', without substance, silent. He 'cannot hear' her. Yet again, a domestic event is transformed into a wider arena by enmeshing it with a myth, the story of Aeneas crossing the River Styx.

EXAMINER'S COMMENT

As part of a full essay answer, the student has written an impressive A grade paragraph and gives a personal response firmly rooted in the text. The paragraph centres on the use of myth by Boland to explore the wider dimensions of domestic situations. Well supported by quotes.

Last Words

'Eavan Boland's work continues to deepen in both humanity and complexity.'

Fiona Sampson

'Memory, change, loss, the irrecoverable past – such are the shared condition of humankind, with which she scrupulously engages.'

Anne Stevenson

'Poets are those who ransack their perishing mind and find pattern and form.'

Eavan Boland

'A poem begins in delight and ends in wisdom.'

Robert Frost   (1874–1963)

One of the great twentieth-century poets, **Robert Frost** is highly regarded for his realistic depictions of rural life and his command of American colloquial speech. His work frequently explores themes from early 1900s country life in New England, often using the setting to examine complex social and philosophical ideas. Nature is central to his writing. While his poems seem simple at first, they often transcend the boundaries of time and place with metaphysical significance and a deeper appreciation of human nature in all its beauty and contradictions. Despite many personal tragedies, he had a very successful public life. It is ironic that such a calm, stoical voice emerged from his difficult background. At times bittersweet, sometimes ironic, or often marvelling at his surroundings, Frost continues to be a popular and often-quoted poet. He was honoured frequently during his lifetime, receiving four Pulitzer Prizes.

PRESCRIBED POEMS (HIGHER LEVEL)

Robert Frost

Note that Frost uses American spellings in his work.

1 'The Tuft of Flowers' (p. 60)

One of Frost's best-loved works, this poem describes how a simple clump of wild flowers succeeds in uniting two separate people. The poem illustrates Frost's technique of bringing readers through an everyday rustic experience to reveal a universal truth.

2 'Mending Wall' (p. 65)

Repairing a damaged wall between his neighbour and himself, Frost considers the theme of community and fellowship and wonders if 'Good fences make good neighbors'.

3 'After Apple-Picking' (p. 70)

Set on his New England farm at the end of the apple harvest, Frost meditates on the nature of work, creativity and of what makes a fulfilled life. Characteristically, the poem is thought-provoking and open to many interpretations.

4 'The Road Not Taken' (p. 75)

Another of Frost's most popular poems. Using the symbol of a remote country crossroads, the poet dramatises the decisions people face in life – and the consequences of their choices.

5 'Birches' (p. 80)

The sight of some forest birches excites Frost's imagination to associate childhood games of swinging on the trees with the process of writing poetry. The poem has been seen as an expression of Frost's own philosophical outlook on life.

6 'Out, Out—' (p. 85)

This affecting poem is based on an actual story of a serious chainsaw accident. Despite the tragedy, Frost leaves readers in no doubt of life's grim reality: 'It goes on'.

7 'Spring Pools' (p. 90)

In this beautiful lyric poem, the fragile beauty and transience of the pools give Frost an acute awareness of the natural cycle of growth, decay and renewal.

8 'Acquainted with the Night' (p. 93)

This short lyric depicts the dark, alienating side of urban life. Familiar themes include the passing of time and lack of communication. In metaphorical terms, Frost also explores 'the dark night of the soul'.

9 'Design' (p. 98)

Frost's sonnet, depicting nature as volatile and terrifying, addresses the possibility of an underlying plan or design for the universe.

10 'Provide, Provide' (p. 102)

Another poem that deals with some of Frost's favourite themes – time, old age and independence. For Frost, however, the only certainty or constant in life is change.

The Tuft of Flowers

Robert Frost

I went to turn the grass once after one
Who mowed it in the dew before the sun.

The dew was gone that made his blade so keen
Before I came to view the leveled scene.

I looked for him behind an isle of trees;   5
I listened for his whetstone on the breeze.

But he had gone his way, the grass all mown,
And I must be, as he had been—alone,

'As all must be,' I said within my heart,
'Whether they work together or apart.'   10

But as I said it, swift there passed me by
On noiseless wing a bewildered butterfly,

Seeking with memories grown dim o'er night
Some resting flower of yesterday's delight.

And once I marked his flight go round and round,   15
As where some flower lay withering on the ground.

And then he flew as far as eye could see,
And then on tremulous wing came back to me.

I thought of questions that have no reply,
And would have turned to toss the grass to dry;   20

But he turned first, and led my eye to look
At a tall tuft of flowers beside a brook,

A leaping tongue of bloom the scythe had spared
Beside a reedy brook the scythe had bared.

The mower in the dew had loved them thus,   25
By leaving them to flourish, not for us,

Nor yet to draw one thought of ours to him,
But from sheer morning gladness at the brim.

The butterfly and I had lit upon,
Nevertheless, a message from the dawn,   30

That made me hear the wakening birds around,
And hear his long scythe whispering to the ground,

And feel a spirit kindred to my own;
So that henceforth I worked no more alone;

But glad with him, I worked as with his aid,   35
And weary, sought at noon with him the shade;

And dreaming, as it were, held brotherly speech
With one whose thought I had not hoped to reach.

'Men work together,' I told him from the heart,
'Whether they work together or apart.'   40

*'his long scythe
whispering'*

EXPLORATIONS

1 Describe the dominant mood in lines 1–10 of the poem.
2 Choose two images from the poem that you found particularly interesting and effective. Briefly explain your choice in both cases.
3 Would you describe the poem as uplifting? Give reasons for your answer.

STUDY NOTES

The poem describes how a simple, uncut clump of wild flowers can unite two separate people. It is one of Frost's best-loved works and typifies his technique of bringing readers through an everyday rustic experience to reveal a universal truth – in this case about alienation, friendship and communication. The poem consists of 20 rhymed couplets written in strict verse. Frost once remarked that 'writing without structure is like playing tennis without a net'.

The narrative voice in the opening section of the poem is relaxed, in keeping with the unhurried rhythm. Frost's initial tone is low key and noncommittal. The speaker has gone out to turn the grass so that it can dry. Someone else had mowed it earlier 'in the dew before the sun'. Lines 5–6 reveal the speaker's sense of solitude and isolation; the unnamed mower has 'gone his way'. This leads him to consider **the loneliness of the scene and of human experience**. The introspective mood becomes more depressed as the poet searches for his fellow worker. Figurative descriptions of the 'leveled scene' and 'an isle of trees' add to the atmosphere of pessimism as the speaker implies that he must also be 'alone'. For Frost, this is the essential human experience for all, 'Whether they work together or apart'.

The poem's second section is marked by the sudden appearance of a 'bewildered butterfly'. After fluttering 'round and round' looking for the 'resting flower' that gave it such delight the day before, it then flies close to the speaker: 'on tremulous wing came back to me'. The adjective 'tremulous' suggests fragility and a **new sense of excited anticipation in the air**. The butterfly seems to reflect the speaker's 'questions that have no reply'. Perhaps they have both enjoyed great happiness in the past. The butterfly eventually turns and leads the speaker to a 'tall tuft of flowers beside a brook' that have escaped the mower's scythe – not by accident, but because 'he had loved them' and left them to flourish out of 'sheer morning gladness'.

The significance of the meadow flowers and the brook cannot be overlooked, because here the mood suddenly changes to optimism. The presence of the mysterious butterfly establishes communication between the early-morning mower and the narrator. Frost suggests this connection with his vivid description of the spared flowers as 'a leaping tongue of bloom'. In the **final section**, the speaker and the butterfly 'lit upon,/Nevertheless, a message from the dawn'. With images such as the 'wakening birds around' and a 'spirit kindred to my own', we might assume that this 'message' could indeed be one of human friendship and communal love.

The ending is paradoxical: 'Men work together ... Whether they work together or apart'. However, **Frost believed in spiritual presence and was inspired by an overwhelming sense of fellowship**. Although apart, the speaker and the absent mower are working with a shared appreciation of nature's beauty and a common commitment to a better world. The poem could also be interpreted biographically, since Frost had lost several of his loved ones and may well have written it as an emotional outlet. Even though his family members were deceased, he remains close to them in spirit. Whatever the poet's intention, readers should draw their own conclusions from the poem.

ANALYSIS

In your view, is 'The Tuft of Flowers' a dramatic poem? Refer closely to the text in your answer.

SAMPLE PARAGRAPH

I liked Frost's poem 'The Tuft of Flowers' for many reasons – one of which was its dramatic storyline. It has been described as a lyrical soliloquy. The narrative element is there from the start. The first mower mentioned seems a mysterious character who got me wondering. The central character (poet) is obviously close to nature as he goes about his work turning the grass. His inner drama interests me most, as his attitude changes from loneliness at the beginning to happiness and companionship. The two moods contrast dramatically. First, the sadness of 'I looked for him', 'I listened for his whetstone' and 'brotherly speech' and then the more sociable 'Men work together'. The clear, vivid imagery is also dramatic, especially the butterfly's flight – 'On noiseless wing' – and the description of the small outcrop of flowers – 'a leaping tongue of bloom'. Frost sets his poems in the secluded New England landscape and this provides a beautiful setting for what are

Robert Frost

deep meditations about the important questions in life – 'questions that have no reply'. The rhythm or movement of the poem quickens in the final lines as the poet expresses his positive view of life – 'Men work together'. I thought this was the ideal way to end and rounded off this quietly dramatic poem perfectly.

EXAMINER'S COMMENT

A very well controlled answer, focusing on some key elements of drama and demonstrating a close understanding of the poem. Good personal interaction and commentary also. References were handled effectively and points were clearly presented throughout. Grade A.

CLASS/HOMEWORK EXERCISES

1   In your opinion, what is Frost's main theme or message in 'The Tuft of Flowers'? Refer closely to the text of the poem in your answer.
2   Copy the table below into your own notes and fill in critical comments about the last two quotations.

Key Quotes

I went to turn the grass once	Frost's personal narrative voice uses the language of ordinary day-to-day speech.
And I must be, as he had been—alone	Solitude (leading to a revelation or epiphany) is one of the poem's central themes.
sheer morning gladness	The sibilant 's' effect suggests the movement of the scythe as well as the positive mood.
I thought of questions that have no reply	
a message from the dawn	

Mending Wall

Something there is that doesn't love a wall,
That sends the frozen-ground-swell under it
And spills the upper boulders in the sun,
And makes gaps even two can pass abreast.
The work of hunters is another thing: 5
I have come after them and made repair
Where they have left not one stone on a stone,
But they would have the rabbit out of hiding,
To please the yelping dogs. The gaps I mean,
No one has seen them made or heard them made,   10
But at spring mending-time we find them there.
I let my neighbor know beyond the hill;
And on a day we meet to walk the line
And set the wall between us once again.
We keep the wall between us as we go.   15
To each the boulders that have fallen to each.
And some are loaves and some so nearly balls
We have to use a spell to make them balance:
'Stay where you are until our backs are turned!'
We wear our fingers rough with handling them.   20
Oh, just another kind of outdoor game,
One on a side. It comes to little more:
There where it is we do not need the wall:
He is all pine and I am apple orchard.
My apple trees will never get across   25
And eat the cones under his pines, I tell him.
He only says, 'Good fences make good neighbors.'
Spring is the mischief in me, and I wonder
If I could put a notion in his head:
'*Why* do they make good neighbors? Isn't it   30
Where there are cows? But here there are no cows.
Before I built a wall I'd ask to know
What I was walling in or walling out,
And to whom I was like to give offense.
Something there is that doesn't love a wall,   35
That wants it down.' I could say 'Elves' to him,
But it's not elves exactly, and I'd rather

Robert Frost

He said it for himself. I see him there,
Bringing a stone grasped firmly by the top
In each hand, like an old-stone savage armed.   40
He moves in darkness as it seems to me,
Not of woods only and the shade of trees.
He will not go behind his father's saying,
And he likes having thought of it so well
He says again, 'Good fences make good neighbors.'   45

*'Something there is that doesn't
love a wall'*

GLOSSARY

1 *Something there is that doesn't love a wall*: ice and frost dislocate walls (also a pun on the poet's name).
4 *abreast*: side by side.

27 *Good fences make good neighbors*: one reading is that a strong fence protects by keeping people apart.
36 *Elves*: small supernatural beings, often malevolent.

EXPLORATIONS

1 In your opinion, what is it that doesn't love a wall? Support your answer with reference to the poem.

2 There are two speakers in the poem. Which one is the wiser, in your view? Refer to the text in your answer.

3 Point out two examples of humour in the poem and comment on how effective they are in adding to the message of 'Mending Wall'.

STUDY NOTES

This popular poem of Robert Frost's was written in 1913 and appears first in his second collection, **North of Boston**. When the land was being cleared for agriculture, the stones gathered were made into walls. Frost said this poem 'contrasts two types of people'. President John F. Kennedy asked Frost to read this poem to Khrushchev, Russia's leader at the time of the Cuban Missile Crisis, when there was a possibility of another world war. The Berlin Wall was a symbol of the cold relations between Russia and the US. Imagine the leaders listening to the line 'I'd ask to know/What I was walling in or walling out'.

'Mending Wall' was responsible for building a picture of Frost as an ordinary New England farmer who wrote about normal events and recognisable settings in simple language. Line 1 is mysterious: 'Something there is that doesn't love a wall'. **A force is at work to pull down the barriers** people insist on erecting. The speaker repairs the holes in the wall left by hunters: 'I have come after them and made repair'. But there are other holes in the wall, though 'No one has seen them made or heard them made'. In a yearly ritual, 'at spring mending-time', the poet and his neighbour meet to carry out repairs. Each looks after his own property as they walk along: 'To each the boulders that have fallen to each'. But a tone of coldness creeps into the poem amid this neighbourly task, with the repetition of how the wall has separated them at all times: 'set the wall between us', 'keep the wall between us'.

It is a difficult task, as the stones fall off as quickly as they are placed: 'Stay where you are until our backs are turned!' The **good-humoured banter** of the workers comes alive in the humorous remark, and readers feel as if they are there in New England watching the wall being repaired. The light-hearted mood is continued in line 21 as the poet describes the activity as an 'outdoor game'. Then he comments that they don't even really need the wall where it is: 'He is all pine and I am apple orchard'. The poet jokes that his apple trees cannot go over and eat his neighbour's pine cones. His neighbour then speaks: 'Good fences make good neighbors'. He comes across as a serious type, quoting old sayings, in **contrast** to the mischievous poet: 'Spring is the mischief in me'. Frost is allying himself with the turbulent force that is pushing through the land, creating growth and pulling down walls. The neighbour is shown as one who has accepted what has been said without question, one who upholds the status quo.

In line 31, the poet poses questions to himself and wishes he could say to his neighbour, '*Why* do they make good neighbors?' **He then wonders what a wall is keeping in and keeping out.** He also wonders what is pulling down the wall. He mockingly suggests 'Elves', then discounts that. Frost presents his rather uncommunicative neighbour in a series of unflattering images: 'an old-stone savage armed', 'He moves in darkness'. Is the poet saying that we must question received wisdom and not blindly follow what we are told? The neighbor, who accepts, is presented as a figure of repression who 'moves in darkness'. He just repeats 'Good fences make good neighbors' like a mantra. Is the poet suggesting that there are some people who derive comfort from just remaining the same, who do not welcome change ('He will not go behind his father's saying')?

The tone of the poem changes as the easy, neighbourly sociability of a shared task is replaced by a **feeling of tension**, first in the effort to keep the tumbling wall upright, and then in the opposite attitudes of the two neighbours – the mischievous, questioning poet and the taciturn, unquestioning neighbour 'like an old-stone savage'. The desire for human co-operation is often stopped, not by outside circumstances, but by a lack of desire on the part of the people involved. This is the poet commenting on human dilemmas. The easy-going, almost ruminative tone of someone musing to himself is written in blank verse, unrhymed iambic pentameter. The colloquial conversational phrases are all tightly controlled throughout this thought-provoking poem.

ANALYSIS

Frost examines the distances between people in his work. In your opinion, how successfully is this done in the poem 'Mending Wall'?

SAMPLE PARAGRAPH

I think Frost has very successfully given us a picture of two opposite personalities in this poem. The moody neighbour who doggedly walks on his side of the wall, 'We keep the wall between us both as we go', is vividly described. Here is a person who accepts what was told to him without question 'Good fences make good neighbors'. It is as if he is reciting the two-times tables. This is fact. There is no need to question. He is comfortable and secure in his traditional mindset. 'He will not go behind his father's saying'. He almost mindlessly repeats it. The poet describes him in unflattering terms, referring to him as 'an old stone-armed savage'. He also states that he was one who moved 'in darkness'. Frost does not agree with this unquestioning attitude of his neighbour's. It is not only a wall which divides these two, there is a completely different mindset. The poet has a lively personality, making jokes as they work, 'Stay where you are until our backs are turned', regarding the work as a game. However, he is not lightweight, as he asks the fundamental question about any boundary, 'I'd ask to know/What I was walling in or out'. He also asks the rather sensitive question about who he was likely to give offence to, with his wall. The neighbour has no such finer feeling, and is portrayed as someone who keeps on going in the same route as always. This apparently simple poem, written in blank verse, sticks in the reader's mind long after the reading. Frost has written a poem which is hard to get rid of. We are left wondering, are walls natural or necessary? Must we break down barriers to live as good neighbours? What if we are over-run?

EXAMINER'S COMMENT

A solid response. The poem is examined in some detail. The questions at the conclusion are lively and show engagement with the poem. Some quotations are inaccurate and this reduces the overall standard. Grade B.

CLASS/HOMEWORK EXERCISES

1   Comment on Frost's use of imagery. Do you find it effective? Refer closely to the text in your answer.
2   Copy the table below into your own notes and fill in critical comments about the last two quotations.

Key Quotes

Something there is that doesn't love a wall	The unnatural barriers erected by people are often pushed aside by nature.
We keep the wall between us as we go	The two neighbours walk on their own side of the wall as they carry out repair work. It also acts as a metaphor for the barriers erected by people between themselves.
And to whom I was like to give offence	If a wall is erected, is the person who has been excluded entitled to feel offended?
He moves in darkness as it seems to me	
'Good fences make good neighbors'	

After Apple-Picking

Robert Frost

My long two-pointed ladder's sticking through a tree
Toward heaven still,
And there's a barrel that I didn't fill
Beside it, and there may be two or three
Apples I didn't pick upon some bough.   5
But I am done with apple-picking now.
Essence of winter sleep is on the night,
The scent of apples: I am drowsing off.
I cannot rub the strangeness from my sight
I got from looking through a pane of glass   10
I skimmed this morning from the drinking trough
And held against the world of hoary grass.
It melted, and I let it fall and break.
But I was well
Upon my way to sleep before it fell,   15
And I could tell
What form my dreaming was about to take.
Magnified apples appear and disappear,
Stem end and blossom end,
And every fleck of russet showing clear.   20
My instep arch not only keeps the ache,
It keeps the pressure of a ladder-round.
I feel the ladder sway as the boughs bend.
And I keep hearing from the cellar bin
The rumbling sound   25
Of load on load of apples coming in.
For I have had too much
Of apple-picking: I am overtired
Of the great harvest I myself desired.
There were ten thousand thousand fruit to touch,   30
Cherish in hand, lift down, and not let fall.
For all
That struck the earth,
No matter if not bruised or spiked with stubble,
Went surely to the cider-apple heap   35
As of no worth.
One can see what will trouble
This sleep of mine, whatever sleep it is.

Were he not gone,
The woodchuck could say whether it's like his   40
Long sleep, as I describe its coming on,
Or just some human sleep.

'Toward heaven still'

GLOSSARY

7 *Essence*: scent.
10 *glass*: ice.
12 *hoary*: covered in frost.
20 *russet*: reddish-brown.
22 *ladder-round*: a rung or support on a ladder.

34 *stubble*: remnant stalks left after harvesting.
40 *woodchuck*: groundhog, a native American burrowing animal.

EXPLORATIONS

1   Select one image that evokes the hard, physical work of apple-picking. Comment on its effectiveness.
2   What do you understand lines 27–29 to mean?
3   Write a short personal response to this poem.

STUDY NOTES

The poem is a lyrical evocation of apple harvesting in New England. Frost takes an ordinary experience and transforms it into a meditative moment. Harvesting fruit soon becomes a consideration of how life has been experienced fully but with some regrets and mistakes. Frost chose not to experiment but to use traditional patterns, or as he said, he preferred 'the old-fashioned way to be new'. 'After Apple-Picking' is not free verse, but it is among Frost's least formal works, containing 42 lines varying in length, a rhyme scheme that is also highly irregular and no stanza breaks.

The speaker in the poem (either Frost himself or the farmer persona he often adopted) feels himself drifting off to sleep with the scent of apples in the air. He thinks of the ladder he has left in the orchard still pointing to 'heaven'. Is the poet suggesting that his work has brought him closer to God? The slow-moving rhythm and broad vowel sounds ('two-pointed', 'bough', 'drowsing') in the **opening lines** reflect his **lethargic mood**. Although he seems close to exhaustion, he is pleased that the harvest is complete: 'But I am done with apple-picking now'. Ironically, his mind is filled with random thoughts about the day's work. The drowsy atmosphere is effectively communicated by the poet's mesmerising description: 'Essence of winter sleep is on the night'.

This dream-like state releases Frost's imagination and he remembers the odd sensation he felt while looking through a sheet of ice he had removed earlier from a drinking trough. While the memory is rooted in reality, it appears that he has experienced the world differently: 'I cannot rub the strangeness from my sight'. As he is falling asleep, he is conscious that his dreaming will be associated with **exaggerated images of harvesting**: 'Magnified apples appear and disappear' (**line 18**). The poet emphasises the sensuousness of what is happening. The vivid apples display 'every fleck of russet' and he can feel the pressure of the 'ladder-round' against his foot. He hears the 'rumbling sound' of the fruit being unloaded. The images suggest abundance: 'load on load of apples', 'ten thousand thousand'. Frost's use of repetition, both of evocative sounds and key words, is a prominent feature of the poem that enhances our appreciation of his intense dream.

Physically and mentally tired, the poet also relives the anxiety he had felt about the need to save the crop from being 'bruised or spiked with stubble', and not to lose them to 'the cider-apple heap'. In the poem's **closing lines**, which seem deliberately vague and distorted, Frost wonders again about the nature of consciousness: 'This sleep of mine, whatever sleep it is'. Like so many of his statements, the line is rich in possible interpretations. For some critics, the poem appears to be exploring the art and craft of writing. Others take a broader view, seeing it as a metaphor for how human beings live their lives. The poet's own final thoughts are of the woodchuck's winter retreat, before he eventually surrenders to his own mysterious 'sleep'.

'After Apple-Picking' is typical of Frost's work. Despite the apparent cheerfulness of much of the writing, it has **undertones of a more sober vision of life**. As always, there is a thoughtful quality to the poem. The reference to the approach of winter hints at the constant presence of mortality. Frost's question about what kind of sleep to anticipate suggests untroubled oblivion or possibly some kind of renewal, just as the woodchuck reawakens in the springtime after its long hibernation.

ANALYSIS

How would you describe the dominant mood in 'After Apple-Picking'? Refer closely to the poem in your answer.

SAMPLE PARAGRAPH

In his famous dramatic monologue, 'After Apple-Picking', Robert Frost creates a mood of otherworldliness. At the start, his accurate description of the orchard is realistic. But some of the poem seems symbolic – such as the mention of the ladder pointing to heaven which might suggest Frost's religious feelings. The setting is calm and the poet feels tired but satisfied after his demanding physical work – 'there's a barrel that I didn't fill'. But his tiredness soon makes his mood more dreamy – 'Essence of winter sleep is on the night'. The sibilance and slender vowels add to this languid atmosphere. I could trace a growing surreal quality to the poem as Frost drifts in and out of consciousness, remembering flashes of his work picking the apples – 'The scent of apples: I am drowsing off'. He mentions 'sleep' repeatedly, reflecting his deep weariness. The rhythm is slow and irregular, just like his confused thoughts about the apples he harvested or damaged. At times he is troubled, recalling his worries that some of the fruit would be 'bruised'. By the end of the poem, he is in a dream-like state, equally obsessed with apple-picking and his own need for sleep. He even wonders about 'whatever sleep it is'. As he drifts off, he thinks of the animals that sleep through the winter and compares himself to the woodchuck. I think this kind of whimsical mood reflects his great interest in nature and is a characteristic of this great American poet.

EXAMINER'S COMMENT

This is an accomplished answer that ranges widely and shows some good personal engagement with the poem. There is an assured sense of the central mood and this is supported well with apt quotations. The references to Frost's style are also worthwhile. Grade A.

CLASS/HOMEWORK EXERCISES

1   Comment on the effectiveness of the poem's imagery in appealing to the senses. Refer closely to the text in your answer.
2   Copy the table below into your own notes and fill in critical comments about the last two quotations.

Key Quotes

But I am done with apple-picking now	It is ironic that although the harvesting itself has ended, its significance for Frost is just beginning.
I cannot rub the strangeness from my sight	Exhaustion has caused the poet's confusion. The strong sibilant effect adds emphasis to the mood.
Cherish in hand, lift down, and not let fall	The line reminds us of the speaker's care and devotion while harvesting. The punctuation slows down the rhythm, adding to the sense of pride in work.
Magnified apples appear and disappear	
I feel the ladder sway as the boughs bend	

The Road Not Taken

Robert Frost

Two roads diverged in a yellow wood,
And sorry I could not travel both
And be one traveler, long I stood
And looked down one as far as I could
To where it bent in the undergrowth;   5

Then took the other one, as just as fair,
And having perhaps the better claim,
Because it was grassy and wanted wear;
Though as for that, the passing there
Had worn them really about the same,   10

And both that morning equally lay
In leaves no step had trodden black.
Oh, I kept the first for another day!
Yet knowing how way leads on to way,
I doubted if I should ever come back.   15

I shall be telling this with a sigh
Somewhere ages and ages hence:
Two roads diverged in a wood, and I—
I took the one less traveled by,
And that has made all the difference.   20

*'where it bent in the
undergrowth'*

GLOSSARY

1 *diverged*: separate and go in
   different directions.
5 *undergrowth*: small trees and
   bushes growing beneath larger
   trees in a wood.

7 *claim*: assertion that something is
   true.

Robert Frost

EXPLORATIONS

1 In your opinion, is this a simple poem or does it have a more profound meaning? Outline your views, supporting them with relevant quotation.

2 Select one image from the poem that you consider particularly effective or interesting. Briefly justify your choice.

3 Frost has been described as someone who 'broods and comments on familiar country things ... catching a truth in it'. In your view, what is the tone of this poem? Does it change or remain the same?

STUDY NOTES

One of Frost's most popular poems, this is the opening poem from the collection *Mountain Interval* (1916). It was inspired by his friend, the poet Edward Thomas. Frost told Thomas, 'No matter which road you take, you'll always sigh, and wish you'd taken another'. Frost also said he was influenced by an event which happened to him at a crossroads after a winter snowstorm in 1912. He met a figure, 'my own image', who passed silently by him. Frost wondered at 'this other self'. The poem dramatises the choices we make in life and their consequences.

Huge themes are summarised in a simple narrative in this poem. In the first stanza, the speaker stands in a wood in autumn where two roads run off in different directions. He has to make a decision – which one will he take? The roads are 'about the same', so the emphasis is not on the decision, but on the **process of decision-making and its consequences**. The speaker decides that he cannot see where the first road is leading ('it bent in the undergrowth'), so he chooses the other one, though it is unclear why. The reference to the 'yellow wood' suggests that the poet is mature enough to realise the consequences of his decision. He won't have this opportunity again: 'I doubted if I should ever come back'. The beautiful image of the 'yellow wood' conjures up a picture of the autumn in New England, but it also has a deeper meaning and is tinged with regret. A person can't do everything in life; choice is part of the human condition.

Frost has said, 'I'm not a nature poet. There's always something else in my poetry.' Here, in this simple act, he is **exploring what it means to be human** and dramatises the decision-making process. There is the human desire to avoid making a decision ('sorry I could not travel both') and the consideration of the possible choices ('long I stood/And looked down one as far as I could'). The **regular rhyme scheme** mirrors the poet looking this way and that as he tries to decide which to choose (*abaab, cdccd, efeef, ghggh*). The unusual rhyme also underlines the unusual choice made. Frost felt that 'the most important thing about a poem ... is how wilfully, gracefully, naturally entertainingly and beautifully its rhymes are'.

Then, in **stanza two**, **he makes the decision**: he 'took the other one'. Why? Was it because it 'was grassy and wanted wear'? Is this someone who is individualistic and likes to do something different to the crowd? Does this suggest a desire for adventure? Then the poet becomes increasingly mischievous. When he sent the poem to his friend, Edward Thomas, Frost wrote: 'I don't know if you can get anyone to see the fun of the thing without showing them.' After pointing out the difference between the two roads, he now declares that they were not so different: 'the passing there/Had worn them really about the same'.

In the **third stanza**, he continues to **point out the similarity of the two roads**, which 'equally lay'. So is the idea that if you choose the less conventional route in life, you may not end up having adventures? The reader is now as confused as the poet was when trying to decide what to do. The second great truth is then revealed: no matter what we get, we always want what we don't have. The regret is palpable in the emphatic 'Oh, I kept the first for another day!' But there won't be another day, because time marches on and we cannot return to the past; we can only go on, as 'way leads on to way'.

In **stanza four**, the poet realises in **hindsight** that he will tell of this day in the future, 'ages and ages hence', though why 'with a sigh'? Has his choice resulted in suffering? Frost's own personal life was littered with suffering and tragedy. Does the repetition of 'I' and the inclusion of the dash suggest that the poet is asserting his maverick individuality as he resolutely declares: 'I took the one less traveled by,/And that has made all the difference'? Do you think he feels he made the right choice for himself? This common experience of choice and decision-making is caught succinctly in this simple narrative. It sounds like a person thinking aloud; the language seems ordinary. Yet upon closer examination, we become aware of the **musical sound effects**. The repeated 'e' sound, coupled with the sibilant 's' sounds ('it was grassy') and alliteration ('wanted wear') convey a calm, deliberating voice. Here is Frost's 'sound of sense'. This poem is inclusive rather than exclusive, as it invites the reader to share in the poet's decision-making.

ANALYSIS

'Frost uses traditional form not in an experimental way, but adapted to his purpose.' Discuss this statement with reference to 'The Road Not Taken'. Quote in support of your answer.

SAMPLE PARAGRAPH

Frost takes traditional subject matter similar to the Romantics, nature and man's relationship with nature, and tells us, 'There's plenty to be dark about, you know. It's full of darkness.' He forms his poems not in an experimental way, but in a deliberate way which suits his purpose. He uses iambic pentameter, a traditional metre used by Shakespeare, as it most closely resembles the English speaking voice, and it is an ironic, sceptical voice, 'yet knowing how way leads on to way', which resonates in 'The Road Not Taken'. The structure of the poem follows the deliberating process, as first the speaker tries to avoid making a choice, then considers the alternatives, 'long I stood'. The decision is made and almost immediately there is a sense of regret: 'Oh, I kept the first for another day'. The use of an unusual rhyme scheme adds to the excluded feel of the speaker. This is someone to whom individuality and self-sufficiency matters: 'I took the one less traveled by,/And that has made all the difference'. There is a sureness in the tone of the last lines which is like those of the early American pioneers: 'I did it and did it my way'. The rhyme scheme of the first stanza is *abaab*. The unusual rhyme scheme mirrors the unusual choice the poet made. Frost believed in the 'sound of sense', as he tells us that we can know what is going on even through a closed door by the sound, not necessarily the meaning of words. He also says that 'sound is the gold in the ore' of a poem. Consider the line, 'Because it was grassy and wanted wear'. The alliteration and the sibilance suggest an almost idyllic wilderness. So Frost structures the form of his poems for a purpose. In this poem the rhyme scheme mimics the glancing this way and that as the speaker tries to decide what route to take. These are some of the ways Frost uses form for a purpose, rather than experimenting just for its own sake.

EXAMINER'S COMMENT

This thoroughly developed answer shows a deep sense of engagement with both the poem and poet. The well-sustained focus and integrated quoting ensure that the paragraph reached an impressive A grade standard.

CLASS/HOMEWORK EXERCISES

1   Frost's ambition was to 'write a few poems it will be hard to get rid of'. Do you think he succeeded? Refer to the poem 'The Road Not Taken' in your response.

2   Copy the table below into your own notes and fill in critical comments about the last two quotations.

Key Quotes

And sorry I could not travel both/And be one traveler	Frost expresses a universal sorrow that it is not possible to be everyone and do everything.
the passing there/Had worn them really about the same	The poet is admitting that really there was little difference between the roads.
Yet knowing how way leads on to way	Once a course of action is decided upon, there is no going back. The repetition emphasises the decision.
I shall be telling this with a sigh	
I took the one less traveled by,/And that has made all the difference	

Birches

Robert Frost

When I see birches bend to left and right
Across the lines of straighter darker trees,
I like to think some boy's been swinging them.
But swinging doesn't bend them down to stay
As ice storms do. Often you must have seen them   5
Loaded with ice a sunny winter morning
After a rain. They click upon themselves
As the breeze rises, and turn many-colored
As the stir cracks and crazes their enamel.
Soon the sun's warmth makes them shed crystal shells   10
Shattering and avalanching on the snow crust—
Such heaps of broken glass to sweep away
You'd think the inner dome of heaven had fallen.
They are dragged to the withered bracken by the load,
And they seem not to break; though once they are bowed   15
So low for long, they never right themselves:
You may see their trunks arching in the woods
Years afterwards, trailing their leaves on the ground
Like girls on hands and knees that throw their hair
Before them over their heads to dry in the sun.   20
But I was going to say when Truth broke in
With all her matter-of-fact about the ice storm,
I should prefer to have some boy bend them
As he went out and in to fetch the cows—
Some boy too far from town to learn baseball,   25
Whose only play was what he found himself,
Summer or winter, and could play alone.
One by one he subdued his father's trees
By riding them down over and over again
Until he took the stiffness out of them,   30
And not one but hung limp, not one was left
For him to conquer. He learned all there was
To learn about not launching out too soon
And so not carrying the tree away
Clear to the ground. He always kept his poise   35
To the top branches, climbing carefully
With the same pains you use to fill a cup
Up to the brim, and even above the brim.

Then he flung outward, feet first, with a swish,
Kicking his way down through the air to the ground.   40
So was I once myself a swinger of birches.
And so I dream of going back to be.
It's when I'm weary of considerations,
And life is too much like a pathless wood
Where your face burns and tickles with the cobwebs   45
Broken across it, and one eye is weeping
From a twig's having lashed across it open.
I'd like to get away from earth awhile
And then come back to it and begin over.
May no fate willfully misunderstand me   50
And half grant what I wish and snatch me away
Not to return. Earth's the right place for love:
I don't know where it's likely to go better.
I'd like to go by climbing a birch tree,
And climb black branches up a snow-white trunk   55
Toward heaven, till the tree could bear no more,
But dipped its top and set me down again.
That would be good both going and coming back.
One could do worse than be a swinger of birches.

*'birches bend to left
and right'*

1 *birches*: deciduous trees with smooth, white bark.
7 *click*: tapping sound made by the branches when they touch.
9 *crazes their enamel*: cracks the ice on the trees.
10 *crystal shells*: drops of melting ice on branches.
11 *avalanching*: collapsing.
14 *bracken*: fern leaves.
31 *limp*: loose; wilted.
39 *swish*: whoosh.
50 *willfully*: deliberately.

Robert Frost

EXPLORATIONS

1   Choose one image from the poem that you found particularly interesting or effective. Briefly explain your choice.
2   Comment on Frost's use of contrast in the poem.
3   Do you find the poet's overall outlook optimistic or pessimistic? Refer to the text in your answer.

STUDY NOTES

'Birches' was first published in 1915, and like so much of Robert Frost's popular work, there is far more happening within the poem than first appears. The poem has been viewed as an important expression of his philosophical outlook on life. With its formal perfection, its opposition of the internal and external worlds and its occasional dry wit, it is one of the best examples of everything that was interesting and engaging about Frost's poetry.

The opening description of the leaning birches is interesting, as Frost compares them to the 'straighter darker trees'. The scene immediately brings him back to his childhood and he likes to think that 'some boy's been swinging them'. This tension between what has actually happened and what the poet would like to have happened – between the real world and the world of the imagination – runs through much of the poem. Throughout lines 1–20, he wonders why the birches are bent 'to left and right'. He accepts that the true reason is because of the ice weighing them down. The poet's **precise, onomatopoeic language** – particularly the sharp 'c' effect in 'cracks and crazes their enamel' – echoes the tapping sound of the frozen branches. Vivid, sensual imagery brings the wintry scene to life: 'crystal shells', 'snow crust', 'withered bracken'. Frost's conversational tone is engaging: 'You'd think the inner dome of heaven had fallen'. Characteristically, he adds a beautiful simile, comparing the bent branches 'trailing their leaves on the ground' to girls who are drying their cascading hair in the sunshine.

In the poem's second section (lines 21–40), Frost resists the accurate explanation ('Truth') for the bent trees, preferring to interpret the scene imaginatively. He visualises a lonely boy ('too far from town to learn baseball') who has learned to amuse himself among the forest birches. In simple, factual terms, the poet describes the boy as he 'subdued his father's trees'. We are given a sense of his youthful determination to 'conquer' them all until 'not one was left'. His persistence teaches him valuable lessons for later life. Swinging skilfully on the trees, the boy learns 'about not launching out too soon'. Readers are left in no doubt about the rich **metaphorical significance of the birches**. In highlighting the importance of 'poise' and 'climbing carefully', Frost reveals his belief in discipline and artistry as the important elements of a successful life ('to fill a cup/Up to the brim'). Such symbolism is a common feature of his writing.

Lines 41–59 are more nostalgic in tone. Frost recalls that he himself was once 'a swinger of birches' and extends the metaphor of retreating into the world of imagination and poetry. The similarities between climbing birches and writing poetry becomes more explicit: 'I'd like to get away from earth'. However, he stresses that he does not wish for a permanent escape because 'Earth's the right place for love'. Is this what poets do when they withdraw into their imaginations and reflect on reality in an attempt to explore the beauty and mystery of life? They are dreamers, idealists. The birch trees are similarly grounded, but they also reach '*Toward* heaven'. The emphatic image (the italics are Frost's) suggests his continuing aspiration for **spiritual fulfillment through the poetic imagination**: 'That would be good both going and coming back'. Frost ends his poem by stating his satisfaction with overcoming challenges and benefiting from the desire to achieve by writing: 'One could do worse than be a swinger of birches'.

ANALYSIS

Based on your study of 'Birches', comment on the poet's use of detailed description. Refer closely to the text in your answer.

SAMPLE PARAGRAPH

Frost's detailed use of language makes 'Birches' one of the poet's most accessible poems. The simple images and colloquial expression create a natural connection between the poet and his readers. I very much liked the closely observed descriptions of the ice-covered branches: 'the sun's warmth makes them shed crystal shells'. The sibilance here adds to the beauty of the language. There are so many impressive images in the poem. Using onomatopoeia, Frost captures the subtle sounds of the forest in the bitter weather. The trees 'click upon themselves'. The poet obviously loved nature and had a keen eye for its beauty. I also liked his comparison of the trail of leaves to the 'girls on hands and knees that throw their hair'. It was dramatic, fresh and unusual. The boy's movement playing on the trees is dynamic: 'Then he flung outward, feet first, with a swish'. Near the end of the poem, Frost describes a harsher side of the forest when 'your face burns and tickles with the cobwebs'. As someone who spent my childhood in the country, I could relate to this tactile image. For me, Frost is a wonderful writer whose poems give a clear sense of the New England landscape. 'Birches' is a very successful piece of description, mainly due to the poet's precise choice of words and the vivid imagery.

EXAMINER'S COMMENT

This paragraph showed a good knowledge of the text and a clear appreciation of Frost's writing skills. There was a strong sense of personal engagement with the poem and the comments on imagery were very convincing. Grade A.

CLASS/HOMEWORK EXERCISES

1   In your opinion, what is the central theme or message in 'Birches'? Support your answer with reference to the text.
2   Copy the table below into your own notes and fill in critical comments about the last two quotations.

Key Quotes

the stir cracks and crazes their enamel	Onomatopoeia and alliteration combine to echo the wintry atmosphere and bitter, sharp frost.
You'd think the inner dome of heaven had fallen	Colloquial and metaphorical language are used to suggest that the picturesque scene has been destroyed.
Then he flung forward, feet first, with a swish	The punctuation and interrupted rhythm imitate the boy's abrupt movement.
Shattering and avalanching on the snow crust	
Where your face burns and tickles with the cobwebs	

'Out, Out—'

The buzz saw snarled and rattled in the yard
And made dust and dropped stove-length sticks of wood,
Sweet-scented stuff when the breeze drew across it.
And from there those that lifted eyes could count
Five mountain ranges one behind the other   5
Under the sunset far into Vermont.
And the saw snarled and rattled, snarled and rattled,
As it ran light, or had to bear a load.
And nothing happened: day was all but done.
Call it a day, I wish they might have said   10
To please the boy by giving him the half hour
That a boy counts so much when saved from work.
His sister stood beside them in her apron
To tell them 'Supper.' At the word, the saw,
As if to prove that saws knew what supper meant,   15
Leaped out at the boy's hand, or seemed to leap—
He must have given the hand. However it was,
Neither refused the meeting. But the hand!
The boy's first outcry was a rueful laugh,
As he swung toward them holding up the hand,   20
Half in appeal, but half as if to keep
The life from spilling. Then the boy saw all—
Since he was old enough to know, big boy
Doing a man's work, though a child at heart—
He saw all spoiled. 'Don't let him cut my hand off—   25
The doctor, when he comes. Don't let him, sister!'
So. But the hand was gone already.
The doctor put him in the dark of ether.
He lay and puffed his lips out with his breath.
And then—the watcher at his pulse took fright.   30
No one believed. They listened at his heart.
Little—less—nothing!—and that ended it.
No more to build on there. And they, since they
Were not the one dead, turned to their affairs.

'Sweet-scented stuff when the breeze drew
across it'

GLOSSARY

'Out, Out—': phrase from a speech which Macbeth, King of Scotland, made on hearing of the death of his wife and when he was surrounded by enemies. He was commenting on the brevity and fragility of life: 'Out, out brief candle. Life's but a walking shadow' (Shakespeare).

4 *lifted eyes*: reference to Psalm 21 – 'I will lift up mine eyes unto the hills' – but the people here don't. The sunset is ignored.

6 *Vermont*: a state in New England, America.

28 *ether*: form of anaesthetic.

EXPLORATIONS

1 What kind of world is shown in the poem? Consider the roles of adults and children. Use reference from the poem in your response.

2 In your opinion, why does the poet tell the story in chronological order? How does it affect your understanding of the story?

3 Comment on the use of colloquial language in the poem. Refer closely to the text in your answer.

STUDY NOTES

Based on an actual event that occurred in 1910, the poem refers to a tragic accident when the son of a neighbour of Frost's was killed on his father's farm. By chance, he had hit the loose pulley of the sawing machine and his hand was badly cut. He died from heart failure due to shock. The event was reported in a local paper.

This **horrifying subject matter**, the early violent death of a young boy, was, in Frost's opinion, 'too cruel' to include in his poetry readings. The title, which is a reference to a speech from Shakespeare's *Macbeth*, is a telling comment on how tenuous our hold on life is. The scene is set on a busy timber yard: 'a world of actual hard, rattling, buzz saw, snarling action' (Seamus Heaney). In line 1, Frost's rasping onomatopoeic sounds give a vivid sound picture of the noisy, dangerous yard. The **long, flowing, descriptive lines** paint a picture of a place full of menace and physical reality where work has to be done. But there is beauty in the midst of this raw power: 'Sweet-scented stuff when the breeze drew across it'. The soft sibilant 's', the assonance of the long 'e' and the compound word 'Sweet-scented stuff' all go to show the surprising beauty to be found in the midst of the practical 'stove-length sticks of wood'.

The **surroundings are also beautiful**, if only the people would look up. But they, unlike the poet, are unaware of 'Five mountain ranges one behind the other/Under the sunset far into Vermont', as their focus is on the work. The repetition of the verbs 'snarled and rattled, snarled and rattled' mimic the action of the repeated sawing. The detail 'As it ran light, or had to bear a load' shows how the saw pushed through the wood to get it cut, then lightly ran back through the cut. Line 9 tells us that the day was 'all but done'. A **foreshadowing of the impending tragedy** is given in 'I wish they might have said'. This is the only time in the whole poem when the personal pronoun 'I' is used. The poet's compassionate understanding for the young boy is evident as he explains how much it matters to a boy to be given precious time off from such hard work: 'That a boy counts so much'. The colloquial language in line 10, 'Call it a day', brings the reader right into this rural scene, rooting the poem in ordinary day-to-day life. The irony shimmers from the line, for soon there will be no more days for the boy.

A domestic detail adds to the reality of this scene as the boy's sister appears 'in her apron/To tell them "Supper."' In this central episode in line 14, the saw suddenly becomes personified, as if it too 'knew what supper meant'. The **jagged language**, 'Leaped out at the boy's hand, or seemed to leap—', reminds us of the jagged teeth of the saw as it seeks its prey. The mystifying accident is referenced in 'seemed to'. How could it have happened? 'He must have given the hand.' The helplessness of the victim, the boy, is shown: 'Neither refused the meeting'. We are reminded of someone almost paralysed into inaction at the split second of a horrific accident. Was this destiny? Is the poet adversely commenting on the mechanisation of farming, or on the practice of getting a boy to do a man's job? **All the attention is now focused on the hand**: 'But the hand!' The pity of the event is palpable in this climactic phrase.

The boy's reaction is chilling and poignant. He holds up the hand, 'spilling' its life blood. He pathetically asks for help, begging his sister not to let the doctor amputate his hand: 'Don't let him'. Now the poet interjects: 'So'. What more is to be said? It is like a drawn-out breath after the tension of the awful accident. The harsh reality is there for all to see: 'the hand was gone already'. The boy realised this when he 'saw all'. Without the use of his hands, there would be no man's work for him any more: 'He saw all spoiled'.

The closing section in lines 27–31 shows the details of the medical help: the 'dark of ether', the boy's breath 'puffed'. Now **the lines break up into fragments** as the terrible final act of the tragedy unfolds: 'No one believed'. The heartbeats ebbed away: 'Little—less—nothing!' There are echoes of the *Macbeth* speech when Macbeth says, 'It is a tale told by an idiot ... signifying nothing'. The **sober reality hits home**: 'and that ended it'. The realisation that there is now no future for the boy is grasped: 'No more to build on there'. Frost has said that the reality of life is that 'it goes on'. And so the people there, because they were not the one dead, 'turned to their affairs'. No matter what horror happens in life, a new day comes. Neither the people nor the poet are being callous and unfeeling. Seamus Heaney calls it the 'grim accuracy' of the poem's end. The long line length also signals the return to normality.

The tone in this narrative poem shades from the anger and menace of the saw, to the calm of the beautiful rural countryside, to the wistful wishes of the poet and on to the fear and horror of the accident. In the end, Frost's ironic tone gives way to the cold fear of the finality of death, when all is changed forever.

ANALYSIS

Seamus Heaney commented, 'Here was a poet who touched things as they are, somehow.' Discuss this statement with reference to the poem 'Out, Out—'.

SAMPLE PARAGRAPH

This poem touched me deeply, as it reminded me of the Elton John song 'A Candle in the Wind', which he wrote for another young person whose life was as cruelly snuffed out in a terrible accident, just like this young boy. Many people are horrified at the poet and the people at the end of the poem, as they 'turned to their affairs'. Yet this is what life is like; after an accident, people put the kettle on. This does not mean they don't care, it means that the reality of life is, as Frost once said, 'It goes on'. I think it was very brave of the poet to just say things as they are, rather than pretending that life is not dark sometimes. I also felt as if I were actually in the timber yard as the saw 'snarled and rattled' in Vermont. The detail of sound and smell, 'Sweet-scented stuff', brought me there. It reminded me of Kavanagh, our Irish poet, who could see beauty in the most ordinary places. Frost, it seems to me, is also commenting negatively on the practice of having a young boy perform a man's job. The wistful 'I wish they might have said' condemns those who insisted on getting the job finished at the expense of the boy. It was too much to ask of a 'big boy', a 'child at heart'. The reality of the boy's life fading away was vividly captured by the poet in the line 'Little—less—nothing!' The punctuation adds to the effect of the heartbeat becoming weaker and finally stopping. This poet dared to say what life is like. He 'touched things as they are'. He achieved this by his craftsmanship as a poet, and his compassionate eye as a human being.

EXAMINER'S COMMENT

A thoughtful, personal exploration of the poem, using quotations that are well integrated into the answer, which results in an A grade. Contemporary references illustrate the continuing relevance of Frost as a realistic voice.

CLASS/HOMEWORK EXERCISES

1 It has been said that Frost's poems are 'little voyages of discovery'. Write a personal response to this poem, using quotations from the poem to support your answer.

2 Copy the table below into your own notes and fill in critical comments about the last two quotations.

Key Quotes

The buzz saw snarled and rattled in the yard	The harsh reality of farm life is graphically portrayed in this onomatopoeic line.
the saw,/As if to prove saws knew what supper meant	Personification adds to the horror of the accident. It is as though the saw is a predatory animal.
Since he was old enough to know	The boy was old enough to know the meaning of the tragedy that had happened to him; he would no longer be able to do a man's work, now or in the future.
No one believed	
And they, since they/Were not the one dead, turned to their affairs	

Spring Pools

Robert Frost

These pools that, though in forests, still reflect
The total sky almost without defect,
And like the flowers beside them, chill and shiver,
Will like the flowers beside them soon be gone,
And yet not out by any brook or river,   5
But up by roots to bring dark foliage on.

The trees that have it in their pent-up buds
To darken nature and be summer woods—
Let them think twice before they use their powers
To blot out and drink up and sweep away   10
These flowery waters and these watery flowers
From snow that melted only yesterday.

GLOSSARY

2 *defect*: blemish; flaw.
5 *brook*: small stream.
6 *foliage*: plants; undergrowth.

EXPLORATIONS

1 What aspects of the spring pools are conveyed in the first stanza? Refer to the text in your answer.

2 Choose one image from the poem that you found particularly striking. Briefly explain your choice.

3 Write your own personal response to the poem.

'darken nature'

STUDY NOTES

'Spring Pools' captures a moment at the end of winter during which the poet reflects on the natural cycle of growth, decay and renewal. Rain falls from the sky, settles in pools and is then drawn up into the trees. In recalling the origins of this beautiful lyric poem, Frost commented, 'One night I sat alone by my open fireplace and wrote "Spring Pools". It was a very pleasant experience, and I remember it clearly, although I don't remember the writing of many of my other poems.'

The poem's title seems to celebrate new growth and regeneration. Ironically, **stanza one** focuses mainly on the fragility of nature. As always, Frost's **close observation of the natural world is evident** from the start. The clear pool water mirrors the overhead sky 'almost without defect'. While the simple images of the forest and flowers are peaceful, there is no escaping the underlying severity of 'chill and shiver'. The entire stanza of six lines is one long sentence. Its slow-moving pace, repetition and assonant vowels ('pools', 'brook', 'roots') enhance the sombre mood. Pool water will be absorbed by the tree roots to enrich the leaves and create 'dark foliage' and water and flowers will all 'soon be gone'. Frost pays most attention to the interdependence within the natural world and the transience of the beauty around him.

In **stanza two**, the poet addresses the trees directly, warning them to 'think twice before they use their powers'. He personifies them as an intimidating presence, associating them with dark destructiveness and 'pent-up' energy to 'blot out and drink up and sweep away'. Such forceful language combines with a resurgent rhythm to emphasise the power of the trees. The **tone becomes increasingly regretful in the final lines**. We are left with another evocative image of how nature's beauty is subject to constant change: 'snow that melted only yesterday'.

Frost's **poem is typically thought provoking**, touching on familiar themes regarding the mysteries of nature and the passing of time. Some critics interpret 'Spring Pools' as a metaphor for the creative process – water has long been a symbol of inspiration. Frost's own writing is wonderfully controlled, in keeping with the sense of order within the natural world that he describes. Both stanzas mirror each other perfectly and the *aabcbc* rhyme scheme completes the fluency of the lines.

ANALYSIS

How would you describe the dominant mood or atmosphere in 'Spring Pools'?

SAMPLE PARAGRAPH

There is a deep sense of loss going through much of Frost's poem 'Spring Pools'. It struck me first in the negative language of the opening stanza. Frost refers to the perfect sky 'without defect', implying that something might soon destroy the perfection. The peaceful setting of the winter flowers beside the pools is also spoiled when the poet points out that they 'chill and shiver'. The mood is downbeat – everything in nature will end

Robert Frost

inevitably and 'soon be gone'. The image of the trees ('dark foliage') adds to my sense of this depressing feeling. In the second part of the poem, Frost points out the irony of springtime as a season of decay just as much as of growth. To some degree, I think this is a realistic view, but it does take away from the joy of spring. The mood deteriorates as the poem continues. The trees are seen as agents of destruction, drying up the water from the pools and removing the flowers. They 'darken nature' – a dramatic way of summing up the overall mood of this poem.

EXAMINER'S COMMENT

This focused paragraph uses quotations very effectively to communicate the central mood of the poem. Some further discussion of style, particularly tone and rhythm, would have helped the answer. Overall, a basic B grade.

CLASS/HOMEWORK EXERCISES

1   In your view, what is the central theme or message of 'Spring Pools'? Refer closely to the poem in your answer.
2   Copy the table below into your own notes and fill in critical comments about the last two quotations.

Key Quotes

The total sky almost without defect	At the start of the poem, the setting is still and tranquil.
And like the flowers beside them, chill and shiver	Frost introduces a more disturbing element – the vulnerability of nature, as personified by the verbs.
darken nature and be summer woods	The trees in summer will blot out the light on the forest floor – one of the many ironies of the natural cycle.
dark foliage	
These flowery waters and these watery flowers	

Acquainted with the Night

Robert Frost

I have been one acquainted with the night.
I have walked out in rain—and back in rain.
I have outwalked the furthest city light.

I have looked down the saddest city lane.
I have passed by the watchman on his beat   5
And dropped my eyes, unwilling to explain.

I have stood still and stopped the sound of feet
When far away an interrupted cry
Came over houses from another street,

But not to call me back or say good-by;   10
And further still at an unearthly height
One luminary clock against the sky

Proclaimed the time was neither wrong nor right.
I have been one acquainted with the night.

*'I have looked down the
saddest city lane'*

GLOSSARY

12 *luminary clock*: moon; a real clock shining with reflected light; simply passing time.
13 *Proclaimed ... wrong nor right*: this ambiguous message that the clock brings leaves us with more questions than answers. Why is the time neither wrong nor right? For whom is it so? For what is the time neither right nor wrong?

EXPLORATIONS

1   Does the shape of the poem add to or subtract from the poem's message? Comment on how the stanzas are arranged. Refer to the text in your answer.

2   Is there a sense of climax or anticlimax in this poem? Look at the rhyme scheme, the prevalence of end-stopped lines and the repetition. Refer to the text in your answer.

3   Write your own personal response to the poem.

STUDY NOTES

'Acquainted with the Night' is a sonnet from Frost's collection of poetry called **West-Ring Brook** (1928). Unusually for Frost, it is set in a bleak city rather than the countryside. This is one of Frost's darkest poems and portrays a solitary, isolated figure filled with despair. It is reminiscent of the Modernist poets, such as T.S. Eliot, or the American artist Edward Hopper, whose paintings frequently showed a solitary individual.

The twentieth century was a time of huge social upheaval and warfare, and was primarily focused on material progress rather than spiritual awareness. It was the century of the individual, rather than the community. Many people became alienated, lonely and confused. The certainty that institutions bring was lost, moral codes were abandoned and the traditional comforts of extended family and community began to disappear. The poem begins with a declaration: 'I have been one acquainted with the night'. It is a frank statement, rather like the declarations made at an AA meeting. It is also reminiscent of the Old Testament reference to **one who was despised and rejected by men**, a man of sorrows 'acquainted with grief'. The second line in this first stanza shows the direction that the poem will take. There are two journeys: the body travels outwards towards the edge of the city ('I have walked out in rain') while the mind travels inwards to the edge of the psyche ('and back in rain').

This **alienation is echoed in the form of the poem**, which is not a conventional 14-line sonnet (either three quatrains and a rhyming couplet, or an octet and sestet); here there is a terza rima format. The poet uses a three-line rhyming stanza, concluding with a rhyming couplet (*aba, bcb, cdc, ded, ff*). The terza rima was used by the great Italian poet Dante in his famous poem *The Divine Comedy* to describe the descent into hell. Is Frost using this structure in his poem because he is describing his own descent into his own private hell? (His own life had included many personal tragedies.) Is he using this format because nothing is conventional any more? This is a highly personal poem, as it uses 'I' at the beginning of seven of its 14 lines. The rhythm imitates a slow walking movement: 'I have outwalked the furthest city light'. The poet has now gone beyond the last visible sign of civilisation. The use of iambic pentameter is the metre closest to the speaking voice in English, and the measured flow underlines the poet's melancholy mood.

The **solemn, sombre mood** of overwhelming anxiety is shown in the long vowel sounds of the **second stanza**: 'I have looked down the saddest city lane'. The broad vowels 'a' and 'o' lengthen the line and show the world-weariness of one who has seen and experienced too much. Although it is set at night, the traditional time for romance and lovers, we are presented with never-ending rain and gloom. A listless mood is created by the repetition of 'I have'. The run-on line suggests the ongoing trudging of this weary man who is too caught up in his own dark thoughts to even bother communicating with the 'watchman'. He is 'unwilling to explain' and is jealously guarding his privacy. Is this walk symptomatic of his inner state? Can nothing penetrate this extreme loneliness?

The use of the run-on line continues in the **third stanza**. Frost comes to an abrupt stop on his journey as an 'interrupted cry' rings out across the **desolate urban landscape**. Who cried? Why? And why was the cry 'interrupted'? Is something awful happening to someone? We, and the poet, don't know. Can anything be done about it? No. The poet just remarks in the next stanza that it has nothing to do with him, 'not to call me back or say good-by'. This is the chilling aspect of living in a big city: the sense of just being another person nobody cares about. These others have no substance, being reduced to the 'sound of feet' or a 'cry'.

In the **fourth stanza**, the poet speaks of a 'luminary clock'. This could be the moon or a real clock that is reflecting light. Is it symbolic of time passing relentlessly? Why is it at an 'unearthly height'? Is it because time rules the human world and nothing can change this? The **final couplet** proclaims that the 'time was neither wrong nor right'. We are left wondering what the time was neither right nor wrong for – what was supposed to happen? There is a real **sense of confusion** here, and echoes of Hamlet's declaration that 'the time is out of joint'. The poem ends as it begins: 'I have been one acquainted with the night'. We have come full circle, though **nothing has been achieved**. We have experienced the darkness with the poet. There is no sense of comfort or guidance, only the realisation of a hostile world.

ANALYSIS

This poem has been described as a 'dramatic lyric of homelessness'. Do you agree or disagree with this statement? Support your view with references from the text.

SAMPLE PARAGRAPH

The sense of homelessness is palpable in this unconventional sonnet of Robert Frost's. The individual in the poem seems to be always on his own, not connected either with family, friend or acquaintance, a real loner in a big anonymous city. The form of the poem mirrors this individualism. It is a maverick sonnet, just like in the great American tradition of cowboy films or gangster movies: the hero is the loner who never quite fits in. There is no network to comfort this man, no community to offer help and encouragement. This emphasis on self comes at a price. The hero does not want to engage, 'And dropped my eyes'. He wanders through town like the tumbleweed of old, with no roots to hold it still. The poem is like a mini drama as the main character plays out his exterior action: 'I have walked out in rain', and his interior journey, 'unwilling to explain'. The verbs carry the action of this sad man: 'outwalked', 'looked', 'passed by', 'stood', 'stopped'. This man is going nowhere. The setting is vividly realised as the bleak urban landscape is drawn with its endless rain and strange noises. So there is character, action, setting and mood. A lyric is a short musical poem which deals with feelings. The music of this lyrical poem is the rhythm of a slow walk as the steady iambic pentameter tempo steps out a hypnotic beat: 'I have outwalked the furthest city light.' The broad vowels add to this sombre music as the poem grinds on relentlessly: 'I have looked down the saddest city lane'. The regular rhyme scheme adds to the dull, hopeless feeling the character seems to be experiencing. This is indeed dark mood music, as the drawn-out vowel sounds 'lane', 'explain', 'beat' and 'feet' tap out the despair of this lonely man. So, in conclusion, I do agree with the statement that 'Acquainted with the Night' is indeed a dramatic lyric of homelessness.

EXAMINER'S COMMENT

This paragraph addresses the three elements of the question (homelessness, dramatic and lyric). It shows a real appreciation of poetic technique, as the terms are not only explained, but are examined well in relation to the poem. Grade A.

Robert Frost

CLASS/HOMEWORK EXERCISES

1 Seamus Heaney describes this poem as 'dark'. What type of darkness is there? Is it literal or metaphorical or both? Refer to the text in your answer.

2 Copy the table below into your own notes and fill in critical comments about the last two quotations.

Key Quotes

I have been one acquainted with the night	Frost tells us that he has known bad times – in an almost biblical fashion. But we are left with a mystery: what were those bad times?
I have outwalked the furthest city light	There are now no signs of civilisation. The poet has reached a place where there is no guiding light.
I have passed by the watchman on his beat/ And dropped my eyes	It was not just the city's fault that this man was alone. He made no effort to communicate with anyone.
But not to call me back or say good-by	
Proclaimed the time was neither wrong nor right	

Design

Robert Frost

I found a dimpled spider, fat and white,
On a white heal-all, holding up a moth
Like a white piece of rigid satin cloth—
Assorted characters of death and blight
Mixed ready to begin the morning right,   5
Like the ingredients of a witches' broth—
A snow-drop spider, a flower like a froth,
And dead wings carried like a paper kite.

What had that flower to do with being white,
The wayside blue and innocent heal-all?   10
What brought the kindred spider to that height,
Then steered the white moth thither in the night?
What but design of darkness to appall?—
If design govern in a thing so small.

'a dimpled spider, fat and white'

GLOSSARY

The poem's title refers to the argument that the natural design of the universe is proof of God's existence.

1 *dimpled*: indented.
2 *heal-all*: plant (once used as a medicine).

4 *blight*: disease in plants; evil influence.
6 *witches' broth*: revolting recipes used to cast spells.
12 *thither*: to there, to that place.
13 *appall*: horrify (to make pale, literally).

EXPLORATIONS

1   How important a part does the colour white play in this poem? Refer to the text in your answer.
2   Select one comparison from the poem that you consider particularly effective. Briefly explain your choice.
3   Describe the poet's tone in the octave. How does it compare with the tone in the sestet?

STUDY NOTES

'Design' explores our attempts to see order in the universe – and our failure to recognise the order that is present in nature. Frost's sonnet raises several profound questions. Is there a design to life? Is there an explanation for the evil in the world? The poet was fascinated by nature from a philosophical point of view. His choice of the traditional sonnet form allows him to address such an important theme in a controlled way.

In the opening line, Frost describes how he finds a 'dimpled spider, fat and white' on a flower, 'holding up a moth' it has captured. The adjective 'dimpled' usually has harmless connotations far removed from the world of arachnids, but in this context, and combined with the word 'fat', it suggests an unattractive image of venomous engorgement. The colour white (used four more times in this short poem) also tends to have positive overtones of innocence and goodness. But most spiders are brown or black, and purity here quickly gives way to pale ghastliness. Indeed, the **tone becomes increasingly menacing** as the octave proceeds. The unwary moth has been lured to its grizzly death on the 'white heal-all' flower, which makes the situation even more deceitful.

Frost's chilling similes reflect the deathly atmosphere. The hapless moth is held 'Like a white piece of rigid satin cloth'. The 'characters of death' in this grim drama are compared to the 'ingredients of a witches' broth'. Lines 7–8 are particularly ironic. Frost then revises his view of the grotesque scene, seeing the **tragic coincidence** involving the 'snow-drop spider' and 'a flower like a froth'. While the images appear attractive, there is a lingering suggestion of gloom and ferocity.

The focus changes in the **sestet** as the tone grows passionately angry. Frost uses a series of **rhetorical questions demanding an explanation** for what he has witnessed: 'What had that flower to do with being white'? Is this implying that nature isn't so innocent after all? He reruns the sequence of events and wonders what 'steered the white moth thither in the night'. The possibility that such a catastrophic event might be part of a great 'design of darkness' appalls the poet. However, the poem's **final line** ('If design govern in a thing so small') is the most intriguing of all. The word 'if' leaves the possibility that there is no grand plan for the universe, that it is all accidental. Whether predestination or chance is the more terrifying reality is left for readers to consider.

ANALYSIS

In your view, what image of nature does Frost present in his poem 'Design'? Refer closely to the text in your response.

SAMPLE PARAGRAPH

In his poem 'Design', Robert Frost takes an ironic approach to nature. Unlike other poems (e.g. 'The Tuft of Flowers'), where he ends up being reassured by the beauty and mystery of his natural environment, 'Design' is decidedly disquieting. The first few lines describe a repulsive side of nature's basic law – kill or be killed. I found the image of the bloated spider quite revolting: 'fat and white'. The poet cleverly conveys a strong sense of the violence and death that takes place when nature begins 'the morning right'. Dead moths are routine – often in beautiful settings. Nature is full of such contradictions. The image of the moth like a 'white piece of rigid satin cloth' suggested the lining of a coffin and reminded me that we see signs of our own mortality all around us. At the same time, Frost seems to be realistic about nature. Even in violent situations, there are beautiful creatures. The 'dead wings' are compared to a graceful 'paper kite'. Under different circumstances, I could imagine a more attractive 'snow-drop' or the 'wayside blue' of a wild flower. Overall, I think the poet probably shows a less attractive side to nature in the poem, but it is not altogether bleak or depressing. I found his ideas interesting and liked the way he managed simple language to raise deep and disturbing questions about our natural world.

EXAMINER'S COMMENT

The paragraph addressed the question very well. The response was balanced but clear, demonstrating a good understanding of the poem. References and quotations were carefully chosen and used effectively. Varied, confident expression throughout. Grade A.

CLASS/HOMEWORK EXERCISES

1   Sonnets often move from description to reflection ('sight to insight'). To what extent is this true of 'Design'? Refer closely to the poem in your answer.

2   Copy the table below into your own notes and fill in critical comments about the last two quotations.

Key Quotes

I found a dimpled spider, fat and white	Frost takes a matter-of-fact, narrative approach, using his characteristic colloquial diction.
And dead wings carried like a paper kite	The juxtaposition of a disturbing image alongside a childlike simile is a common feature of this poem's ambivalence.
innocent heal-all	Irony plays a central part in this poem. The moth was attracted to its death by the white flowers of a plant that is usually associated with healing.
Assorted characters of death and blight	
design of darkness	

Provide, Provide

The witch that came (the withered hag)
To wash the steps with pail and rag
Was once the beauty Abishag,

The picture pride of Hollywood.
Too many fall from great and good   5
For you to doubt the likelihood.

Die early and avoid the fate.
Or if predestined to die late,
Make up your mind to die in state.

Make the whole stock exchange your own!   10
If need be occupy a throne,
Where nobody can call *you* crone.

Some have relied on what they knew,
Others on being simply true.
What worked for them might work for you.   15

No memory of having starred
Atones for later disregard
Or keeps the end from being hard.

Better to go down dignified
With boughten friendship at your side   20
Than none at all. Provide, provide!

'Was once the beauty Abishag'

3 *Abishag*: beautiful young woman who comforted King David in his old age.

12 *crone*: witchlike; old, withered woman.

17 *Atones*: makes amends (for sin or wrongdoing).

20 *boughten*: bought.

EXPLORATIONS

1 Is the advice given in the poem to be taken seriously or humorously, or a mixture of both? Discuss, using reference from the poem to support your answer.

2 What elements in the poem resemble a fairytale or fable? Pick your favourite element and explain why you like it.

3 What conclusion, if any, does the poem come to? Do you agree or disagree with the view expressed? Refer to the poem to support your view.

STUDY NOTES

This poem was written at the height of Frost's fame, in a collection called *A Further Rage* (1936). It was based on a real woman he had seen cleaning steps. The poem contrasts with most of Frost's work, as the tone is bitter and the emphasis is on material success. The Great Depression, a time of mass unemployment in America, was taking place. Is Frost suggesting that self-sufficiency is the answer?

The first stanza advises us to **plan for the future**. Why? A cold, bleak scene of a withered old woman doing a menial job of washing steps is given as a salutary picture of what happens if you don't provide. This is what happened to Abishag. The reference to the biblical character adds a timeless element – this is a truth for all generations. We don't know what is to be. In this poem, old age equals diminishing beauty and success.

In stanza two, the destructive element of time is stressed as the poem comes to the present, 'Hollywood'. Even in the 'dream factory', beauty does not last. The tone of the poem is one of **addressing a public audience**, as if at an evangelical rally: 'For you to doubt the likelihood'. Fortune is fickle, as we all know.

The poem now offers **mock advice: the only solution is to die young** ('Die early'). Images of icons hover in our minds of tragic, famous deaths of the young and beautiful, such as James Dean and Marilyn Monroe. In the third stanza, **the only other solution is to become wealthy** and 'die in state'. An imperative verb, 'Make', in the fourth stanza shouts at us to grab material success: 'Make the whole stock exchange your own!' The exclamation mark captures the mood of exhortation that pervades this unusual poem of Frost's. The quaint image of the throne adds to the timeless element of this poem, as it is a universal symbol of power and wealth. Only political power, privilege and riches provide protection against the harsh reality of ageing. If 'you' don't want the same fate as Abishag, 'you' must be alert.

Independence was very important to Frost. Now, in stanza six, the poem cautions us that even if our early lives were wonderful, 'having starred', that memory is not a safeguard against the misfortune that might happen later in life. Black humour in the final stanza suggests, with wry, unsentimental honesty, that it is better to **buy friendship** ('boughten') than suffer loneliness at the end of life. Is this cynical view that bought friends are better than none realistic? The poem concludes with great urgency: 'Provide, provide!' Frost did not believe in a benevolent God ruling the universe, but rather takes the view that there is an indifferent God and we are subject to random darkness. This is not an affirmative poem.

Frost favoured **traditional poetic structures**, declaring that he was 'one of the notable craftsmen of this time'. Here the full rhyme of *aaa, bbb, ccc, ddd*, etc. does not seem strained. We hardly notice it in this carefully crafted poem of seven triplets. The rhythmic pattern of blank verse, i.e. four short–long beats, set against the irregular variations of colloquial speech gives this poem its energy. The use of the imperative for the verbs, especially 'Provide, provide', demands that the reader take this message on board. Frost presents **painful ideas** – in this instance a cynical view of fame and success – **in a controlled form**. He has said, 'The poems I make are little bits of order.'

ANALYSIS

'Poetry is a momentary stay against confusion.' Discuss this statement in relation to the poem 'Provide, Provide'. Use references from the poem to support your views.

SAMPLE PARAGRAPH

The bleak, cold situation painted in this poem by Frost is very different from his other poems where a quiet, sensible speaking voice alerts us to the beauties of nature. Here the focus is on 'look out for your old age, as no one is going to want you'. I wonder if Frost was uncomfortable about his decision to commit himself to being famous? Did he, like so many contemporary stars today, find the whole fame business tacky and shallow? He enjoyed giving performances of his poems: 'Words exist in the mouth, not books,' he declared. When he read this poem in public, he usually added a line, 'Or somebody else'll provide for you!/And how'll you like that?' He is condemning those who take 'handouts', social benefits. Frost suffered many emotional tragedies in his long life, and I also wonder if the fact that his father died at 34, and his mother had only eight dollars to bury him contributed to this bleak view of providing for hard times and old age? The poem is stating that change is the only certainty and vehemently exhorts us to get ourselves in order if we don't want to have a miserable time when looks and youth are gone. I like the mock serious tone in which this message is delivered: 'If need be occupy a throne,/Where nobody can call *you* crone'. I think this wry, dry, cynical tone appeals especially to today's reader who is saturated with this 'fame' issue. I also think that humour is very effective in delivering a message, particularly one as unpalatable as this. The airbrushed perfection of the groomed Hollywood stars is captured perfectly in the alliterative phrase: 'The picture pride of Hollywood'. Frost has arranged this line as carefully as the lighting technician has arranged the lighting of a star, so that all seems picture perfect. But the poet knew that this is not how it is – 'the end' is 'hard'. Frost said, 'If you suffer any sense of confusion in life, the best thing you can do is make little poems.' Here is the human's need for order in a terrifying universe. In this poem, Frost has succeeded in 'making a momentary stay against confusion'.

EXAMINER'S COMMENT

This response (to a very challenging question) has taken a ruminative view of Frost's poetry, connecting his views on poetry and life as well as his own personal circumstances into the discussion. However, it over-relies on biographical references and is not sufficiently rooted in the text. B grade.

CLASS/HOMEWORK EXERCISES

1 'A poem begins in delight and ends in wisdom.' Is this a valid statement in relation to the poem 'Provide, Provide'? Use quotation from the poem in your explorations.
2 Copy the table below into your own notes and fill in critical comments about the last two quotations.

Robert Frost

Key Quotes

The witch that came	This is a reference to an old washing woman Frost saw at Harvard University.
Die early and avoid the fate	Mock serious advice given in the poem. Note the imperative tone.
What worked for them might work for you	You can usually learn from the experiences of others. More wry advice.
No memory of having starred/Atones for later disregard	
Better to go down dignified/With boughten friendship at your side/Than none at all	

LEAVING CERT SAMPLE ESSAY

> **Q** **'We enjoy poetry for its ideas and language.'**
>
> **Using the above statement as your title, write an essay on the poetry of Robert Frost. Support the points by reference to the poetry of Robert Frost on your course.**

MARKING SCHEME GUIDELINES

Expect candidates to deal with both elements of the question – ideas and language – but not necessarily separately. Take 'ideas' to mean themes, subjects, attitudes, issues and so on. Take 'language' to mean style, manner, phraseology, appropriate vocabulary, imagery, etc.

The level of engagement with the poetry will serve as an implicit treatment of what 'we enjoy' in the poetry of Robert Frost.

Some of the following areas might provide material for candidates:
- Poet's views on life/experience.
- Habitual concerns in the poems.
- Elegant plainness of his expression.
- Typical patterns of imagery/language.
- Variety of registers in the texts, etc.

SAMPLE ESSAY
(We Enjoy Frost's Poetry for Its Ideas and Language)

1 *How could you not enjoy the work of a man whose favourite book was* Robinson Crusoe? *Here is a quiet, sensible speaking voice dealing with human suffering, isolation, loneliness and our relations with the world around us. No wonder his poems were sent to inspire soldiers in the Second World War, or that he was chosen to speak at the inauguration of JFK. 'Mending Wall' deals with an annual event where two neighbours check and mend their boundary wall ritualistically each spring. The communal activity joins people, but this poem is also about gaps in understanding between people. The speaker delights in mischief, in contrast to his neighbour, who 'walks in darkness' because he is traditional and is content to repeat received wisdom from previous generations without question: 'Good walls make good neighbors'.*

2 Civilisation needs boundaries and order. Respecting rules is necessary in society, otherwise there is chaos. We must respect equality, but also difference. Each remains on his own land, 'One on a side'. So Frost's single event contains a complex issue: boundaries connect and divide. The two neighbours can also be seen as reflecting the two contrasting facets of Frost – the wall toppler who delights in wildness, breaking rules, being disruptive; and the builder who abides by strict rules, form, grammar and the traditional structure of poems. Such insights are what attracts me to Frost's work.

3 I also enjoyed the idea that there is a force in nature that does not like the way men construct boundaries. When I think of the Native Americans who did not believe in land ownership but rather guardianship and care of Mother Earth, I agree that 'Something there is that doesn't love a wall'. I think it was a particularly good poem to read to President Khrushchev, particularly at a time of the Cold War and the Iron Curtain: 'I'd ask to know what I was walling in or walling out'.

4 The Romantic influence can be seen in the subject matter of 'The Road Not Taken'. Nature is the stimulus for an insight. This poem deals with decisions taken when young. We are all facing tough decisions now regarding study, points and careers and will we be like Frost's friend who inspired this poem, and regret decisions we have made? Will we be thinking of things that might have been: 'I shall be telling this with a sigh'? When we look at our classmates and know that we will all take different roads and may not meet again for quite some time, don't the lines 'Yet knowing how way leads on to way, I doubted if I ever should come back' ring very true?

5 Nature provides a beautiful but passive background to the horrific event in 'Out, Out–'. Frost never read this poem at his readings as he regarded it as too cruel. It was inspired by a newspaper account about a young boy whose hand was amputated by a saw as he was doing a man's job and who subsequently died. This reminded me of how Bob Geldof created Live Aid from an item of TV news. Like the Victorians, Frost believed that there was no benevolent God compassionately caring for the world. Terrible things happen. For me, the most shocking thing in this poem was not the chainsaw as it became an animal and devoured the boy's hand; rather it was how the onlookers who 'since they were not the one dead, turned to their affairs'. This is chilling. But Frost believed one thing about life: 'It goes on'. When I consider the tragic life Frost lived, I can see how he understood the importance of endurance, however cold it may seem.

6 Frost's simple subject matter covers complex issues: 'There's always something else in my poetry.' His language allows us access to them. He did not follow the fashion of the time. Instead, he adopted the persona of the New England farmer inspired by natural events. But underpinning the colloquial language is a strict adherence to traditional forms and patterning. To him, free verse was like 'playing tennis without a net'. He used blank verse and iambic pentameter, which has rhythm but not rhyme: 'Something there is that doesn't love a wall'. There is a tension between the ordinary subject matter and the colloquial voice, as it is constrained by poetic patterning.

7 Frost believed in the sound of a poem; he said poems rather than read them, believing the sound carried the meaning. I see this clearly in 'The buzz saw snarled and rattled in the yard'. The sound of this line suggests a menacing element in the midst of beauty. The dust is beautifully described as 'sweet-scented stuff when the breeze blew across it'. The gentle 's' sound conveys the harmony in the timber yard, in contrast to the strident sound of the saw. I also enjoyed Frost's use of drama in his poetry, the moment of decision in 'The Road Not Taken' when he wrote: 'Two roads converged in a yellow wood' and the strange 'interrupted cry' in 'Acquainted with the Night' which left me wondering who had cried and why. No wonder I am just one of millions who enjoy Frost's poetic ideas and language.

(approx. 870 words)

GRADE: A1		
P	=	15/15
C	=	15/15
L	=	15/15
M	=	5/5
Total	=	50/50

EXAMINER'S COMMENT

A detailed exploration of the question and well-developed points on both subject matter and style supported by succinct quotations. The essay ranged widely and showed very good personal engagement with the poetry. Expression was varied and confidently managed throughout. A very assured response.

SAMPLE LEAVING CERT QUESTIONS ON FROST'S POETRY
(45–50 MINUTES)

1   'The appeal of Robert Frost's poetry for a young audience.'
Write an essay on this statement, focusing particular attention on his themes and how he expresses them. Support the points you make by reference to the poetry of Robert Frost on your course.

2   What impact did the poetry of Robert Frost make on you as a reader? In shaping your answer, you might like to consider the following:
   • Your overall sense or outlook of the poet.
   • The poet's use of language and imagery.
   • Your favourite poem or poems.

3   'Life by the throat' is a phrase often associated with the poetry of Robert Frost. How does the poetry catch life by the throat? Discuss, referring both to the content and style of the poems by Frost on your course.

SAMPLE ESSAY PLAN (Q2)

What impact did the poetry of Robert Frost make on you as a reader? In shaping your answer, you might like to consider the following:

• **Your overall sense or outlook of the poet.**
• **The poet's use of language and imagery.**
• **Your favourite poem or poems**.

Intro:	Interesting themes, individualistic style. His fascination with nature and human nature. Favourite poem – 'The Road Not Taken'.
Point 1:	Family – background tragic, yet it is the still, calm voice which sounds from the poem. He extends the invitation, 'you come too', as he explores man's relationship with nature.
Point 2:	'Sound of sense' – 'Writing with your ear to the voice'. Use of first person in 'Out, Out—'. Use of first person pronoun in 'The Road Not Taken'.
Point 3:	Formal patterning and rhyme – traditionalist, good craftsman, art deceptive, rhyme scheme in 'The Road Not Taken'. Terza rima in 'Acquainted with the Night'.

- *Point 4:* Metaphors – 'poetry is simply made up of metaphors'. Doesn't force, allows the metaphors to speak for themselves, e.g. road is a metaphor for a journey in 'The Road Not Taken'.
- *Point 5:* Other themes – natural world, endurance, ordinary life, etc.
- *Conclusion:* Wrote about ordinary people living ordinary lives. View of nature bleak. Aware of time and effect on human beings.

EXERCISE

Develop one of the above points into a paragraph.

POINT 5 – SAMPLE PARAGRAPH

The subject matter of Frost's poetry is rooted in the natural world. He believed that 'man has need of nature, but nature has no need of man'. But it was nature which was thought-provoking, a stimulus for the poet, leading to insight and revelation: 'A poem begins in delight and ends in wisdom.' This was in keeping with the Romantic poets, such as Wordsworth, and was in contrast to the Modernist movement that was in vogue at this time. They were urban poets who used classical references and were often obscure. Frost was and is accessible. He was influenced by current events – just like Geldof was inspired by a news item to create Live Aid, so Frost was inspired by a newspaper article to write the chilling poem of injured innocence, 'Out, Out—'. Frost believed in endurance: 'In three words I can sum up everything I've learned about life – it goes on.' He was influenced also by the Victorian poets like Hardy who did not believe in a world ruled by a benevolent God. Darkness erupts in a random manner with tragic consequences, as in 'Out, Out—'. He wrote about ordinary people living ordinary lives. But his view of the human condition was bleak and cold. He was aware of time and its effect on human beings.

EXAMINER'S COMMENT

As part of a full essay answer, the student has written a general exploration that shows a real understanding of Frost's aims. The paragraph focuses on the insight to be gained from a mature perception of nature. Grade A.

Robert Frost

Last Words

'Like a piece of ice on a hot stove, the poem must ride on its own melting.'

Robert Frost

'Robert Frost: the icon of the Yankee values, the smell of wood smoke, the sparkle of dew, the reality of farm-house dung, the jocular honesty of an uncle.'

Derek Walcott

'I'll say that again, in case you missed it first time round.'

Robert Frost

'Walk on air against your better judgement.'

Seamus Heaney (1939–)

Seamus Heaney was born in 1939 in Co. Derry and was the eldest of nine children. He was accepted into Queen's University, Belfast in 1957 to study English Language and Literature. Heaney's poetry first came to public attention in the 1960s, when he and a number of other poets, including Michael Longley and Derek Mahon, came to prominence. They all shared the same fate of being born into a society that was deeply divided along religious grounds and was to become immersed in violence, intimidation and sectarianism. In 1966, his first poetry collection, *Death of a Naturalist*, was published. Heaney spent many years lecturing in Belfast, Dublin and America. Throughout this time he was publishing prolifically and giving public readings. He has also written several volumes of criticism. Widely regarded as the finest poet of his generation, he was awarded the Nobel Prize for Literature in 1995 'for works of lyrical beauty and ethical depth, which exalt everyday miracles and the living past'. In accepting the award, Heaney stated that his life had been 'a journey into the wideness of language, a journey where each point of arrival ... turned out to be a stepping stone rather than a destination'.

PRESCRIBED POEMS (HIGHER LEVEL)

1 'The Forge' (p. 116)

At one level, the poem celebrates a traditional craft. However, its central focus is on the mystery and beauty of the creative process itself. The blacksmith's work is used as an extended metaphor for the shaping of any work of art.

2 'Bogland' (p. 120)

The poet contrasts the expansive North American grasslands with the narrowly bounded landscape of Ireland's boglands. For Heaney, the bogs are a precious museum of the island's past.

3 'The Tollund Man' (p. 125)

Photographs of the preserved body of an Iron Age man found in the bogs of Jutland, Denmark, prompted Heaney to trace parallels between the imagined circumstances of the Tollund Man's death and more recent violence in the North of Ireland.

4 'Mossbawn: Sunlight' (p. 131)

This wonderfully atmospheric poem is a nostalgic celebration of the poet's childhood on the family farm in Co. Derry and his close relationship with his aunt. The importance of place, family and the simple joys of ordinary life are central themes in Heaney's poetry.

5 'A Constable Calls' (p. 136)

Based on another memory from his boyhood, the poet describes an uneasy encounter when his father was questioned by a local policeman. At a deeper level, the poet explores the complex relationship between the two communities in Northern Ireland.

6 'The Skunk' (p. 142)

Sensuous language and an edgy, romantic atmosphere enhance this unusual and playful love poem. Seeing his wife, Heaney is reminded of a lonely time he once spent in California, where he eagerly awaited the nightly visit of a skunk.

7 'The Harvest Bow' (p. 147)

A tightly wrought personal poem based on the central image of a decorative 'throwaway love-knot'. The straw bow provides a physical link between Heaney and his father, the present and the past, nature and art.

8 'The Underground' (p. 152)

The poem explores the enduring love between Heaney and his wife. Based on a memory from their honeymoon, the newlyweds are compared to Orpheus and Eurydice as they hurry through a London Underground Tube station.

9 'Postscript' (p. 157)

In this short lyric, the poet succeeds in conveying the extraordinary by way of an everyday experience – the memory of a vivid journey westward to the Flaggy Shore of the Co. Clare coastline.

10 'A Call' (p. 161)

Another poem dealing with one of Heaney's favourite themes: the father–son relationship and the passing of time. The setting is a routine domestic scene of a father weeding, a son visiting and a mother talking.

11 'Tate's Avenue' (p. 166)

In this beautifully discreet and understated love poem, Heaney recalls three car rugs that mark important stages in the changing relationship between himself and his wife.

12 'The Pitchfork' (p. 170)

Another typical Heaney poem, celebrating traditional rural life. The poet makes 'a journey back into the heartland of the ordinary', where he is both observer and visionary.

13 'Lightenings viii' (p. 175)

In his short account of how a mysterious floating airship appeared above the monks' oratory at Clonmacnoise monastery, Heaney blurs the lines between reality and illusion, and challenges our ideas about life.

The Forge

Seamus Heaney

All I know is a door into the dark.
Outside, old axles and iron hoops rusting;
Inside, the hammered anvil's short-pitched ring,
The unpredictable fantail of sparks
Or hiss when a new shoe toughens in water.   5
The anvil must be somewhere in the centre,
Horned as a unicorn, at one end square,
Set there immoveable: an altar
Where he expends himself in shape and music.
Sometimes, leather-aproned, hairs in his nose,   10
He leans out on the jamb, recalls a clatter
Of hoofs where traffic is flashing in rows;
Then grunts and goes in, with a slam and a flick
To beat real iron out, to work the bellows.

'The unpredictable fantail of sparks'

GLOSSARY

The Forge: refers to a blacksmith's workshop, where iron implements are made and mended (in the poem, a smith is shaping horseshoes).

2 *axles*: bars or shafts on which wheels rotate.

3 *anvil*: iron block that the smith uses as a work surface.

7 *unicorn*: mythical animal (usually a white horse) with a spiralled horn growing from its forehead.

9 *expends*: burns up, expresses.

11 *jamb*: upright door support.

14 *bellows*: instrument for drawing air into a fire.

EXPLORATIONS

1 Describe the poet's attitude to the forge. Is he fascinated or fearful, or both? Support your answer with reference to the poem.

2 Based on your study of the poem, what is your impression of the blacksmith?

3 Comment on the effectiveness of the phrase 'The unpredictable fantail of sparks'.

STUDY NOTES

'The Forge' comes from Seamus Heaney's second collection, *Door into the Dark*, which was published in 1969. The sonnet form has a clear division of an octave (the first eight lines) and a sestet (the final six lines). While the octave, apart from its initial reference to the narrator, focuses on the inanimate objects and occurrences inside and outside the forge, the sestet describes the blacksmith and his work.

The poem's opening line ('All I know is a door into the dark') is both modest and assured. There is also a **mystical undertone** (a sense of otherworldliness) as Heaney revisits his childhood and his fascination with a local forge. The image, with its negative and mysterious connotations, incites our curiosity and invites us to find out what answers lie beyond. The poet recalls unwanted objects strewn outside, 'old axles and iron hoops rusting'. The irregular rhythm in line 2 suggests the disorder of what has been discarded. He **contrasts** the lifeless exterior scene with the vigorous atmosphere ('the hammered anvil's short-pitched ring') inside the forge. The world outside is decrepit and old, a wasteland, whereas the noisy forge is a place of brilliant sparks where iron is beaten out and renewed.

Heaney's visual and aural images are characteristically striking. His vivid metaphor of 'The unpredictable fantail of sparks' (line 4) lets us see the glorious flurry of erratic, flashing light and hear the twang of reverberating iron. **Onomatopoeic effects** add to our sense of the physical activity taking place as the blacksmith works on a new horseshoe. Suddenly, the incandescent metal begins to 'hiss when a new shoe toughens in water'. The **tone is sympathetic** and attentive as the poet reimagines the smells, sounds and tactile impressions of the blacksmith's workshop.

Lines 6–9 contain the sonnet's central image of the smith's anvil: 'an altar/Where he expends himself in shape and music'. Interestingly, the transition from the octave to the sestet is a run-on (or enjambment) based around this key metaphor. One effect of this is to enable us to experience the anvil as a **sacred or magical point of transition** between the material and immovable world of everyday life and the fluid, imaginative world of human consciousness. Heaney stresses the **mystery of the creative process**, associating it with the mythical creature of medieval fiction, 'Horned as a unicorn'. Although the simile seems somewhat strained, the comparison with a legendary beast still serves to highlight the mysterious qualities ('shape and music') of poetry.

The **final lines** focus on the blacksmith's physical characteristics. Heaney leaves us with a down-to-earth image of a gruff, hard working man, 'leather-aproned, hairs in his nose'. Is the poet suggesting that art – and poetry in particular – is independent of education and social class? Seemingly wary of the world at large, the smith remembers an earlier era of horse-drawn carriages, when his skills were fully appreciated. Contrasting images of 'a clatter/Of hoofs' and modern traffic 'flashing in rows' reflect the changes he has lived through. In the end, he grudgingly accepts that he must return 'into the dark' and resume doing what he does best: 'To beat real iron out, to work the bellows'.

Heaney's poem can immediately be read as an elegy to the past and a lament for the lost tradition of the blacksmith. Readers can also interpret the anvil as a metaphor of an unreachable heritage, a traditional craft made redundant by modernisation. Many critics have seen the blacksmith figure as a **symbol or construction of the role of the poet**, one who opens the 'door into the dark', the creative artist who ritually 'expends himself in shape and music' and who grunts and flicks words and language, forging his poems. As with so much of Heaney's work, the poem attests to his ability to subtly evoke resonance by making us wonder.

ANALYSIS

'Heaney's poetry is populated with a variety of characters who have inspired him.' To what extent is this true of 'The Forge'? Refer to the poem in your answer.

SAMPLE PARAGRAPH

'The Forge' is a good example of a poem where Heaney's central character, the old blacksmith, represents a disappearing way of life. As a child, the poet was drawn to the rural blacksmith's shop which to his innocent mind was a place of excitement. The images in the poem evoke the realistic sights and sounds of the blacksmith's work in 'the dark' – such as 'the fantail of sparks' coming from the hammering of red-hot metal when horseshoes were being made. Heaney uses the unnamed blacksmith as a symbolic representation of all creative people who work at their artistic gifts. Much of this poem deals with the hard physical work involved. I can certainly imagine Heaney as a child wondering about what the blacksmith was doing, even wishing to try for himself. The poet paints a picture of a simple man who doesn't speak – he 'grunts and goes in' to his work. He certainly seems to be a simple loner, dedicated to the 'shape and music' of his craft. The whole poem reflects Heaney's own sense of wonder about this dedicated rural blacksmith – and about the inspiration for poetry. He compares the blacksmith at his anvil to a priest saying mass – but not fully understanding the mystery of it. The ending of the poem suggests that neither the blacksmith nor Heaney himself can ever fully understand the true nature of art and craft.

EXAMINER'S COMMENT

This is a reasonably good attempt at addressing the question. There is some welcome personal engagement and apt references are included to convey Heaney's use of the blacksmith as an exemplary figure. The expression is slightly repetitive in places. A basic B grade standard overall.

CLASS/HOMEWORK EXERCISES

1   Comment on the poet's use of visual and aural images to create an overall picture of the blacksmith's forge.
2   Copy the table below into your own notes and fill in critical comments about the last two quotations.

Key Quotes

All I know is a door into the dark	The poem's opening line focuses on Heaney's fascination with the forge as an unknown and possibly frightening place of mystery.
the hammered anvil's short-pitched ring	Sound effects play an important part in recreating the reality of the forge and suggesting the deeper creative process. Note the sharp, shimmering effect of 'ring'.
he expends himself in shape and music	The artistry of the energetic work of the blacksmith – and of all creative people – is expressed in this memorable image. The verb 'expends' suggests the overwhelming effort involved in the smith's work.
recalls a clatter/ Of hoofs where traffic is flashing in rows	
beat real iron out	

Bogland

for T.P. Flanagan

We have no prairies
To slice a big sun at evening –
Everywhere the eye concedes to
Encroaching horizon,

Is wooed into the cyclops' eye   5
Of a tarn. Our unfenced country
Is bog that keeps crusting
Between the sights of the sun.

They've taken the skeleton
Of the Great Irish Elk   10
Out of the peat, set it up,
An astounding crate full of air.

Butter sunk under
More than a hundred years
Was recovered salty and white.   15
The ground itself is kind, black butter

Melting and opening underfoot,
Missing its last definition
By millions of years.
They'll never dig coal here,   20

Only the waterlogged trunks
Of great firs, soft as pulp.
Our pioneers keep striking
Inwards and downwards,

Every layer they strip   25
Seems camped on before.
The bogholes might be Atlantic seepage.
The wet centre is bottomless.

'Encroaching horizon, / Is wooed into the cyclops' eye / Of a tarn'

Seamus Heaney

EXPLORATIONS

1   In your opinion, what is Heaney's central theme or point? Briefly explain your response.
2   How does Heaney employ the senses to allow the reader to share in his experience of the bogland? Refer closely to the poem in your answer.
3   Trace the poet's tone throughout the poem. Comment on where, how and why, in your opinion, the tone changes. Support your views with reference to the text.

STUDY NOTES

'Bogland' (1969) is the result of a Halloween holiday Heaney spent with T.P. Flanagan (the artist to whom Heaney dedicated the poem). Flanagan recalls that 'the bogland was burnt the colour of marmalade'. Heaney felt it was 'one of the most important poems' he had written because 'it was something like a symbol. I felt the poem was a promise of something else ... it represented a free place for me.' He thought the bogland was a 'landscape that remembered everything that happened in and to it'. Heaney recalled when they were children that they were told 'not to go near the bog because there was no bottom to it'.

In the opening stanza, a **comparison** is drawn between the American prairies ('We have no prairies') and Ireland's bogs. Heaney said, 'At that time, I had ... been reading about the frontier and the west as an important myth in the American consciousness, so I set up – or rather, laid down – the bog as an answering Irish myth.' The prairie in America represents the vastness of the country, its unfenced expanse a metaphor for the freedom of its people to pursue their dreams and express their beliefs. At first, Ireland's bog represents opposite values. It seems narrow, constricting and inward looking: 'the eye concedes', 'Encroaching horizon', 'cyclops' eye'. In America, the pioneers moved across the country. In Ireland, the pioneers looked 'Inwards and downwards', remembering, almost wallowing in, the past. Is the poet suggesting that Ireland is defined by the layers of its difficult history? Or is each set of pioneers on an adventure, one set discovering new places, the other set rediscovering forgotten places?

Stanza two captures **the bog's fluidity** in the onomatopoeic phrase 'keeps crusting/Between the sights of the sun'. Heaney draws the changing face of the bog, its element of mystery and danger, as it did not always remain exactly the same, but subtly fluctuates. The poet's sense of awe at this place is expressed in stanza three as he recounts the discovery of the Great Irish Elk as 'An astounding crate full of air'. Here the poet is referring to another aspect of the bog – its **ability to preserve the past**.

In stanza four, the bog's capacity to hold and preserve is emphasised when 'Butter sunk under/More than a hundred years' was recovered fit for use, 'salty and white'. This place is 'kind'. Stanza four runs into stanza five in a parallel reference to the bog's fluidity. The bog never becomes hard; 'its last definition' is 'Missing', so it will never yield coal. The squidgy nature of the bog is conveyed in stanza six in the phrase 'soft as pulp'. The phrases of the poem are opening and melting into each other in imitation of the bog. Is this in stark contrast to the hardening prejudices of the two communities in the North of Ireland? This poem was written in 1969. **The Irish explore their past**; to them, history is important as they keep 'striking/Inwards and downwards'.

Heaney leaves us with an **open-ended conclusion** in stanza seven. He remembers that the bog 'seemed to have some kind of wind blowing through it that could carry on'. The boglands are feminine, nurturing, welcoming. 'The wet centre is bottomless'. The poet is aware of the depth and complexity of the national consciousness. Should we, like the bog, embrace all aspects of our national identity? Is this how we should carry on? Is there a final truth? Is it unreachable? The poem is written in seven spare, unrhymed stanzas and uses casual, almost colloquial language.

ANALYSIS

'There is a quality of vivid sensuousness in the poetry of Heaney.' Discuss this statement, supporting your opinion with references to the poem.

SAMPLE PARAGRAPH

Heaney, for me, captures the essence of the bog in words like 'soft as pulp', 'melting', 'Missing'. The gentle consonants and broad vowels create the oozing fluid quality of the bog. The thin surface of the bog is vividly caught in the phrase 'keeps crusting'. The sound of the hard 'k' and 'c' suggest, to me, the brittle surface of the bog as it barely forms a thin skin under the rays of the sun. The rich sibilance of 'sights of the sun' suggests the quiet passing days out in the peaceful bog. The musical alliteration of the explosive 'b' in 'black butter' further emphasises the gloopy, muddy bog. I particularly like the references to sight in this poem. The opening stanza, with its reference to 'We have no prairies/To slice a big sun at evening', reminds me of cowboy films like *The Big Country* with their endless panoramic views of prairie and a huge half disc of flaming red sun disappearing over the horizon at evening time. I imagine the sense of freedom and excitement of the Wild West pioneers as they strike out to provide a better life for themselves and their families. We, instead, are represented by another visual reference, in a completely different way. We are almost deformed, 'cyclops' eye'. The image at the end of the poem, however, moves from this negative thought, as the bog is represented as 'bottomless'. The vivid quality of this image entices us, like the tarn wooed the horizon, into the dark mystery of the bog.

EXAMINER'S COMMENT

A well-sustained response to the question. Good examination of Heaney's appeal to the senses. Emphasis on style was maintained throughout, with effective references to sound effects. Interesting and well-illustrated points are made about the rich musicality of Heaney's language. Grade A.

CLASS/HOMEWORK EXERCISES

1   'The importance of tradition and a sense of place are recurring features of Heaney's poetry.' Discuss this statement, supporting your answer with reference to 'Bogland'.

2   Copy the table below into your own notes and fill in critical comments about the last two quotations.

Key Quotes

We have no prairies/To slice a big sun at evening	Heaney evocatively draws a picture of an American sunset in the vast grasslands there. The verb 'slice' gives the line sharpness.
Encroaching horizon,/Is wooed into the cyclops' eye/Of a tarn	This phrase sums up the inward outlook of Irish people, as it seems as if the vast sky is swallowed up into a small bog pool. The reference to the one-eyed race of giants suggests that this outlook could be regarded as deformed.
Missing its last definition	The bog never becomes hard enough to form coal. Is there a suggestion that the bog's soft, all-embracing approach is one that Irish people could adopt?
Every layer they strip/Seems camped on before	
The wet centre is bottomless	

The Tollund Man

I

Some day I will go to Aarhus
To see his peat-brown head,
The mild pods of his eyelids,
His pointed skin cap.

In the flat country nearby   5
Where they dug him out,
His last gruel of winter seeds
Caked in his stomach,

Naked except for
The cap, noose and girdle,   10
I will stand a long time.
Bridegroom to the goddess,

She tightened her torc on him
And opened her fen,
Those dark juices working   15
Him to a saint's kept body,

Trove of the turfcutters'
Honeycombed workings.
Now his stained face
Reposes at Aarhus.   20

II

I could risk blasphemy,
Consecrate the cauldron bog
Our holy ground and pray
Him to make germinate

The scattered, ambushed   25
Flesh of labourers,
Stockinged corpses
Laid out in the farmyards,

Tell-tale skin and teeth
Flecking the sleepers   30
Of four young brothers, trailed
For miles along the lines.

III

Something of his sad freedom
As he rode the tumbril
Should come to me, driving,   35
Saying the names

Tollund, Grauballe, Nebelgard,
Watching the pointing hands
Of country people,
Not knowing their tongue.   40

Out there in Jutland
In the old man-killing parishes
I will feel lost,
Unhappy and at home.

*'Something of his
sad freedom'*

GLOSSARY

The Tollund Man: a reference to the well-preserved body found in 1950 by two turfcutters in Tollund, Denmark. The man had been hanged over 2,000 years earlier. One theory suggested that his death had been part of a ritualistic fertility sacrifice. The Tollund Man's head was put on display in a museum at Aarhus.

1   Aarhus: a city in Jutland, Denmark.
3   pods: dry seeds.
7   gruel: thin porridge.
10 girdle: belt.
13 torc: decorative metal collar.
14 fen: marsh or wet area.
16 kept: preserved.
17 Trove: valuable find.

18 Honeycombed workings: patterns made by the turfcutters on the peat.
21 blasphemy: irreverence.
22 Consecrate: declare sacred.
22 cauldron bog: basin-shaped bogland (some of which were associated with pagan rituals).
24 germinate: give new life to.
30 sleepers: wooden beams underneath railway lines.
31 four young brothers: refers to an infamous atrocity in the 1920s when four Catholic brothers were killed by the police.
34 tumbril: two-wheeled cart used to carry a condemned person to execution.
37 Tollund, Grauballe, Nebelgard: places in Jutland.

EXPLORATIONS

1   Comment on Heaney's tone in the first three stanzas of the poem.
2   Select one image from the poem that you find startling or disturbing and explain its effectiveness.
3   What is your understanding of the poem's final stanza? Refer closely to the text in your answer.

STUDY NOTES

Seamus Heaney was attracted to a book by P.V. Glob, *The Bog People*, that dealt with preserved Iron Age bodies of people who had been ritually killed. It offered him a particular frame of reference or set of symbols he could employ to engage with Ireland's historical conflict. The martyr image of the Tollund Man blended in the poet's mind with photographs of other atrocities, past and present, in the long rites of Irish political struggles. The poem comes from Heaney's third collection, *Wintering Out* (1972).

Part I opens quietly with **the promise of a pilgrimage**: 'Some day I will go to Aarhus'. The tone is expectant, determined. Yet there is also an element of detachment that is reinforced by the Danish place name, 'Aarhus'. Heaney's placid, almost reverential mood is matched by his economic use of language, dominated by simple monosyllables. The evocative description of the Tollund Man's 'peat-brown head' and 'The mild pods of his eyelids' conveys a sense of gentleness and passivity.

Lines 5–11 focus on the dead man's final hours in a much more realistic way. Heaney suggests that the Tollund Man's own journey begins when 'they dug him out', destroyed and elevated at the same time. The poet's meticulous observations ('His last gruel of winter seeds/Caked in his stomach') emphasise the dead man's **innocent vulnerability**. In the aftermath of a ritualistic hanging, we see him abandoned: 'Naked except for/The cap, noose and girdle'. While the poet identifies himself closely with the victim and makes a respectful promise to 'stand a long time', the action itself is passive.

Heaney imagines the natural boglands as the body of a fertility goddess. The revelation that the sacrificial victim was 'Bridegroom to the goddess' (line 12) conveys a more **ominous, forceful tone** as the bleak bog itself is also equated with Ireland, female and overwhelming: 'She tightened her torc on him'. Sensuous and energetic images in lines 13–16 suggest the physical intimacy of the couple's deadly embrace. The Tollund Man becomes 'a saint's kept body', almost a surrogate Christ, buried underground so that new life would spring up. He is left to chance, 'Trove of the turfcutters', and finally resurrected so that 'his stained face/Reposes at Aarhus'. The delicate blend of sibilance and broad vowel sounds suggest tranquillity and a final peace.

Part II suddenly becomes more emphatic and is filled with references to religion. Heaney addresses the spirit of the Tollund Man, invoking him to 'make germinate' (line 24) and give life back to the casualties of more recent violence in Northern Ireland. Heaney acknowledges his own discomfort ('I could risk blasphemy') for suggesting that we should search for an alternative deity or religious symbol to unite people. But although it appears to be in contrast with the earlier violence, the poet's restrained style actually accentuates the horror of one infamous sectarian slaughter ('Of four young brothers'). The callous nature of their deaths – 'trailed/For miles along the lines' – is associated with the repulsive rituals in ancient Jutland. Heaney's **nightmarish images** ('Stockinged corpses') are powerful and create a surreal effect. However, the paradoxical 'survival' and repose of the Tollund Man should, the poet implies, give him the power to raise others.

Part III returns to the mellow beginning, but instead of anticipation, there is sorrow and a sense of isolation. Heaney insists that the 'sad freedom' (line 33) of the Tollund Man 'Should come to me'. Along with religion and a sense of history and myth, evocative language is central to Heaney's poetry, and here the idea of isolation is brought sharply to the reader through the sense of being 'lost' in a foreign land. Yet ultimately the paradoxical nature of exile is realised: the poet feels at home in a state of homelessness, and welcomes the feeling of not belonging to society which he shares with the Tollund Man, who is no longer tied to religious forces. This estrangement from society is emphasised by the list of foreign names ('Tollund, Grauballe, Nebelgard'). **The poem ends on a note of pessimistic resignation** which describes both the familiar sense of isolation and hopelessness Heaney experiences: 'I will feel lost,/Unhappy and at home'.

Heaney's imaginary pilgrimage to Aarhus has led to **a kind of revelation**. By comparing modern Ulster to the 'old man-killing parishes' (line 42) of remote Jutland, the poet places the Northern Irish conflict in a timeless, mythological context. It is as though the only way Heaney can fully express the horrific scenes he has seen in Ireland is to associate them with the exhumed bodies of ancient bog corpses.

ANALYSIS

'Heaney's poetry manages to evoke passion and pain through language that is both simple and dignified.' In your opinion, is this true of 'The Tollund Man'? Refer to the poem in your response.

SAMPLE PARAGRAPH

Of all the Heaney poems I have studied, I find 'The Tollund Man' the most moving. Heaney imagines the short life and death of this sacrificial martyr who was executed sometime during the Iron Age and whose body was preserved in a Jutland bogland for over 2,000 years. The story is narrated in simple, colloquial language – 'I will go to Aarhus/To see his peat-brown head'. The poet is captivated by the man's gentle features – 'The mild pods of his eyelids' – as he reposes in death. While Heaney's tone of voice is always measured and respectful, there is also a passionate admiration for what the dead man has endured, only achieving a 'sad freedom' in being executed. He compares the Tollund Man to Irish people who have lost their lives here in sectarian violence. Again the language is direct but powerful – 'ambushed/Flesh of labourers'. For me, the poem sums up the lonely terror of innocent victims, past and present. What I really admire is Heaney's quiet strength of language – his realistic images and sincere tone in empathising with all those who are victims of conflict in our 'man-killing parishes'.

EXAMINER'S COMMENT

This is a clearly focused response which shows genuine interaction with the poem. Relevant points are supported with accurate illustrations, showing a very good knowledge of the text. Expression is fluent, varied and controlled throughout. An assured A grade.

CLASS/HOMEWORK EXERCISES

1 'Seamus Heaney presents us with a contradictory world that is both familiar and unnerving.' Discuss 'The Tollund Man' in light of this view, supporting your answer with reference to the poem.
2 Copy the table below into your own notes and fill in critical comments about the last two quotations.

Key Quotes

Some day I will go to Aarhus	Heaney's firm sense of a religious pilgrimage is central to the poem. The diction is simple and the tone is one of hushed reverence.
Bridegroom to the goddess	The bog itself is personified as an ancient fertility goddess and the killing is described as a ritual marriage.
Tell-tale skin and teeth/Flecking the sleepers	Typically well-crafted phrasing, graphic imagery, short lines and a fragmented rhythm emphasise the disturbing reality of violent death.
Something of his sad freedom	
I will feel lost,/Unhappy and at home	

Mossbawn: Sunlight

for Mary Heaney

Sunlight

There was a sunlit absence.
The helmeted pump in the yard
heated its iron,
water honeyed

in the slung bucket   5
and the sun stood
like a griddle cooling
against the wall

of each long afternoon.
So, her hands scuffled   10
over the bakeboard,
the reddening stove

sent its plaque of heat
against her where she stood
in a floury apron   15
by the window.

Now she dusts the board
with a goose's wing,
now sits, broad-lapped,
with whitened nails   20

and measling shins:
here is a space
again, the scone rising
to the tick of two clocks.

And here is love   25
like a tinsmith's scoop
sunk past its gleam
in the meal-bin.

Seamus Heaney

'to the tick of two clocks'

Mossbawn was Heaney's birthplace. 'Bawn' refers to the name the English planters gave to their fortified farmhouses. 'Ban' is Gaelic for 'white'. Heaney wonders if the name could be 'white moss' and has commented, 'In the syllables of my home, I see a metaphor of the split culture of Ulster.'
Dedication: The poem is dedicated to the poet's aunt, Mary Heaney, who lived with the family throughout Heaney's childhood. He shared a special relationship with her, 'a woman with a huge well of affection and a very experienced, dry-eyed sense of the world'.

7   *griddle*: circular iron plate used for cooking food.
10 *scuffled*: moving quickly, making a scraping noise.
13 *plaque*: area of intense heat, originally a hot plate.
21 *measling*: red spots on legs made by standing close to heat.
24 *the tick of two clocks*: the two time sequences in the poem, past and present.
26 *tinsmith*: person who made pots and pans from tin.
28 *meal-bin*: a container used to hold flour, etc.

EXPLORATIONS

1   Describe the atmosphere in the poem 'Mossbawn', with particular reference to Heaney's treatment of time.

2   What image of Mary Heaney, the aunt, is drawn? Do you find the picture appealing or unappealing? Quote from the poem in support of your views.

3   Choose one image or phrase from the poem that you found particularly effective, and say why you found it so.

STUDY NOTES

'Sunlight' appeared in the collection *North* (1975) and was the first of two poems under the title 'Mossbawn', the name of Heaney's family home. To the poet, this farm was 'the first place', an idyllic Garden of Eden, full of sunlight and feminine grace, a contrast to the brute reality of the outside world. At this time, terrible atrocities were being committed by both Catholics and Protestants in the sectarian struggle which was taking place in the North of Ireland.

This poem opens with a **vivid, atmospheric portrayal of the silent sunlit yard**, a beautiful, tranquil scene from Heaney's boyhood in the 1940s. The pump marked the centre of this private world, which was untroubled by the activities outside. American soldiers had bases in Northern Ireland during the Second World War. For the impressionable Heaney growing up, the water pump was a symbol of purity and life. This guardian of domestic life is described as 'helmeted', a sentry soldier on duty, ready to protect. The phrase 'water honeyed' (line 4) emphasises this slender iron idol as an image of deep and hidden goodness, the centre of another world. The poet creates a nostalgic picture of a timeless zone of slow, deep, domestic ritual and human warmth. Here are childhood days of golden innocence and security. The repetition of 'h' (in 'helmeted', 'heated' and 'honeyed') portrays the heating process as the reader exhales breath. The sun is described in the striking simile 'like a griddle cooling/against the wall'. This homely image of the iron dish of the home-baked flat cake evokes a view of a serene place.

Line 10 moves readers from the place to the person. 'So' introduces us to a **warm, tender portrait of Heaney's beloved Aunt Mary at work**. She is a symbol of the old secure way of life, when a sense of community was firm and traditional rural values were held in high esteem. We are shown the unspectacular routine of work; she 'dusts the board' for baking. We see her domestic skill, her hands 'scuffled' as she kneads the dough. Visual detail paints this picture as if it were a Dutch still life from the artist Vermeer: 'floury apron', 'whitened nails'. There is an almost religious simplicity on the essentials of life: bread, water, love (water 'honeyed', 'scone rising', 'here is love'). The people in this scene are not glamorous. Realistic details remind us of their ordinariness: 'broad-lapped', 'measling shins'.

The **closing simile** in lines 26–8, 'like a tinsmith's scoop/sunk past its gleam/in the meal-bin', **shows how the ordinary is transformed into the extraordinary** by the power of love. The hidden shine of love is present in the ordinary ritual of baking. Remembering the past, the poet makes it present, 'here is love'. The two time zones of passing time and a timeless moment are held in the alliterative phrase 'to the tick of two clocks'. We are invited to listen to the steady rhythm of the repetitive 't'. As the life-giving water lies unseen beneath the cold earth, the aunt's love is hidden, but constant, ready to be drawn on, like the water in the pump. The radiant glow of love is hidden like a buried light. The change of tenses at the word 'Now' brings the moment closer as the abstract becomes concrete, and the outside becomes inside. The short four-line stanzas run on, achieving their own momentum of contained energy in this still scene, which reaches its climax in the elevating last stanza.

ANALYSIS

Heaney explores local history, communicating the experience of his own place with customs, rituals, atmosphere and characters. Discuss this view of Heaney's poetry, with particular reference to the poem 'Mossbawn: Sunlight'.

SAMPLE PARAGRAPH

In Heaney's poem 'Sunlight', the pump stands squarely at the centre of this tranquil, magical place. Although American troops were on manoeuvres in the nearby fields, this place is untouched by outside forces. The pump seems to stand guard, 'helmeted' on this oasis of feminine grace. The custom of baking bread is referred to in the simile 'the sun stood/like a griddle cooling', and in the visual and aural details of the aunt, Mary Heaney, 'her hands scuffled/over the bakeboard'. I can almost hear the rasping of her nails as they hit the surface as she kneads the baking mixture. Even the last simile, 'like a tinsmith's scoop/sunk past its gleam/in the meal-bin', is a further reference to this custom of home baking, as it tells of the wonderful source of hidden love which exists between the aunt and the young boy. These rural references, 'the reddening stove', 'a goose's wing', reach back to a time which is pre-modern. It shows us a picture of an ideal way of living. The silence and peace of Mossbawn are portrayed in the phrases 'each long afternoon' and 'the tick of two clocks'. Time stands still in this idyllic place. Heaney makes the reader feel as if they have visited Mossbawn, seen the pump, tasted the 'honeyed water', saw and heard the aunt baking and savoured the peace and tranquillity of this traditional way of life.

EXAMINER'S COMMENT

A well-developed, focused answer displaying a clear appreciation of Heaney's poem. Quotations range widely over the entire text. Expression is varied and well controlled throughout. Grade A.

CLASS/HOMEWORK EXERCISES

1   The Royal Swedish Academy announced that Seamus Heaney's Nobel Prize for Literature was for 'lyrical beauty ... which brings out the miracles of the ordinary day and the living past'. Discuss this statement, referring closely to the text.

2   Copy the table below into your own notes and fill in critical comments about the last two quotations.

Key Quotes

There was a sunlit absence	This short line creates the still atmosphere of Heaney's home place. It also intrigues us – what exactly is absent?
her hands scuffled	Onomatopoeia suggests the repeated movement of his aunt's hands and lets the reader become part of the loving domestic scene.
and measling shins	The poet uses graphic, realistic details to show the ordinariness of this extraordinary person.
the scone rising/to the tick of two clocks	
like a tinsmith's scoop/sunk past its gleam/in the meal-bin	

A Constable Calls

His bicycle stood at the window-sill,
The rubber cowl of a mud-splasher
Skirting the front mudguard,
Its fat black handlegrips

Heating in sunlight, the 'spud'   5
Of the dynamo gleaming and cocked back,
The pedal treads hanging relieved
Of the boot of the law.

His cap was upside down
On the floor, next his chair.   10
The line of its pressure ran like a bevel
In his slightly sweating hair.

He had unstrapped
The heavy ledger, and my father
Was making tillage returns   15
In acres, roods, and perches.

Arithmetic and fear.
I sat staring at the polished holster
With its buttoned flap, the braid cord
Looped into the revolver butt.   20

'Any other root crops?
Mangolds? Marrowstems? Anything like that?'
'No.' But was there not a line
 Of turnips where the seed ran out

In the potato field? I assumed   25
Small guilts and sat
Imagining the black hole in the barracks.
He stood up, shifted the baton-case

Further round on his belt,
Closed the domesday book,   30
Fitted his cap back with two hands,
And looked at me as he said goodbye.

A shadow bobbed in the window.
He was snapping the carrier spring
Over the ledger. His boot pushed off   35
And the bicycle ticked, ticked, ticked.

*'The pedal treads hanging relieved/
Of the boot of the law'*

GLOSSARY

2 *cowl*: covering shaped like a hood.
5 *'spud'*: potato-like shape.
8 *the boot of the law*: heavy footwear of policeman; power and control of the law.
11 *bevel*: marked line on policeman's forehead made by his cap.
14 *ledger*: book containing records of farm accounts.
15 *tillage returns*: amount harvested from cultivated land.
19 *braid*: threads woven into a decorative band.

22 *Mangolds*: beets grown for animal feed.
22 *Marrowstems*: long green vegetables.
30 *domesday book*: William the Conqueror, the English king, had ordered a survey to be carried out of all the land and its value in England; also refers to Judgement Day, when all will be brought to account.
33 *bobbed*: moved up and down.
34 *carrier spring*: spiral metal coil on the back of a bike used to secure a bag, etc.

EXPLORATIONS

1 How does the poet create an atmosphere of tension in this poem? Support your response with reference to the text.

2 What type of relationship do you think the young boy has with his father? Refer closely to the text in your response.

3 Critics disagree about the ending of the poem. Some find it 'false', others 'stunning'. How would you describe the ending? Give reasons for your conclusions.

Seamus Heaney

STUDY NOTES

'A Constable Calls' was written in 1975 and forms the second part of the poem sequence 'Singing School'. The Heaneys were a Catholic family. The constable would have been a member of the Royal Ulster Constabulary and probably a Protestant. This poem was written when the tensions between the two communities in Northern Ireland were at their height. Heaney's 'country of community ... was a place of division'.

'A Constable Calls' is written from the **viewpoint of a young boy** caught in the epicentre of the Troubles, a time of recent sectarian violence in Northern Ireland. The poem explores fear and power from the perspective of the Nationalist community. The Catholics did not trust or like the RUC (Royal Ulster Constabulary). In the opening stanzas, crude strength, power and violence are all inherent in the cold, precise language used to describe the constable's bicycle. The 'handlegrips' suggest handcuffs, while the 'cocked back' dynamo hints at a gun ready to explode, its trigger ready for action. It also signifies confidence and cockiness. The oppression of the local authorities is contained in the phrase 'the boot of the law'. Heaney personifies the bicycle, which he describes as being 'relieved' of the pressure of the weight of the constable. This poem was written during the civil rights protest marches, when Nationalists were sometimes treated very severely by the RUC. This is evoked in the ugly sound of 'ow' in the word 'cowl', the assonance of the broad vowels in 'fat black' and the harsh-sounding repetition of 'ck' in the phrase 'cocked back'. Here are the observations of the child of a divided community. The character (and symbolic significance) of the constable is implicit in the description of his bicycle.

In stanzas three to five, Heaney gives us an explicit **description of the constable**. His uniform and equipment are all symbols of power, which the young boy notes in detail: 'the polished holster/With its buttoned flap, the braid cord/Looped into the revolver butt'. Here is no friendly community police officer. The repetition of 'his' tells us that the possession of power belongs to him and what he represents. He is not a welcome visitor. His hat lies on the ground. He is not offered refreshment, although he is presumably thirsty from his work. Even the one human detail ('slightly sweating hair') revolts us. Is he as tense as the Catholic family in this time of sectarian conflict? The print of his great authority is stamped on him like a 'bevel', but does his power weigh heavily on him?

The policeman's function was to oblige the boy's father to give an account of his farm crop returns. Their terse exchange underlines the **tension in this troubled community**. The interrogation by the constable consists of four questions: 'Any other root crops?/Mangolds? Marrowstems? Anything like that?' This is met by the father's short, clipped, monosyllabic reply: 'No'. The encounter is summed up succinctly in the line 'Arithmetic and fear'. In the seventh stanza, the young boy becomes alarmed as he realises that his father has omitted to account for 'a line/Of turnips'. He 'assumed/Small guilts'. His Catholic inferiority is graphically shown in the reference to the 'domesday book', or 'ledger', belonging to the constable. The child imagines a day of reckoning, almost like Judgement Day, when God calls every individual to account for past sins. He imagines the immediate punishment of 'the black hole in the barracks', the notorious police cell where offenders were held. This terror of being incarcerated by the law ran deep in the Catholic psyche throughout the Troubles.

In the end, the constable takes his leave (stanzas seven and eight), formally fitting 'his cap back with two hands'. We can empathise with the young boy as he 'looked at me'. In the final stanza, the oppressive presence of the visitor ('A shadow') is wryly described as 'bobbed', an ironic reference to the friendly English bobby – which this particular constable was not. The verbs in this stanza continue the underlying ominous mood: 'snapping', 'pushed off'. The **poem concludes** with an intimidating reference to the sound of the departing bicycle as a slowly ticking time bomb: 'And the bicycle ticked, ticked, ticked'. Does this suggest that the tension in this divided community was always on the verge of exploding? Do you consider this an effective image, or do you think the symbolism is too obvious?

ANALYSIS

Heaney has written a poem of childhood unease and fear. Do you agree or disagree with this statement? Support your opinion with references from the poem.

SAMPLE PARAGRAPH

Seamus Heaney was born in Derry and won a Nobel Prize for Literature in 1995. I think Heaney has written a good poem about a young childs unease and fear. I especially liked the last line with the ticking bomb. It was really good. I really think Heaneys poems are especially good. I think I will read lots of Heaneys poems in my lifetime. I could see the sweaty cap of the constable. I thought it was gross enough to scare any child. I thought the father stood up to the police man well, and in a convincing way. 'No' he said. I thought well done, the child must have been proud of him. I also thought the discription of the holster was good. 'Polished' means shining. The 'rubber cowl' of the 'mud-slasher' on the front mud-guard is fairly sinister, rather like hoodies on teenagers. The identity of the person cannot be seen. This threatens. This is a very good poem that really sums up childhood unease and fear.

SPELLCHECKER

child's
Heaney's
description

EXAMINER'S COMMENT

An under-developed answer, repetitive and lacking in depth of knowledge of the poem. Punctuation errors and repetition also mar the answer. The autobiographical detail is extraneous to the task required. Limited vocabulary. A basic grade D.

CLASS/HOMEWORK EXERCISES

1 Heaney has written a memory poem filled with lyrical beauty which brings out the miracles of the ordinary day. Having read 'A Constable Calls', would you agree or disagree with this view? Support your answer with reference to the text.

2 Copy the table below into your own notes and fill in critical comments about the last two quotations.

Key Qoutes

Its fat black handlegrips/Heating in sunlight	The run-on line and assonance in this phrase suggest the oppressive atmosphere experienced by the Nationalist minority in Northern Ireland at this time.
Arithmetic and fear	This succinct phrase sums up the tension. Many Catholics were being held to account and feared they would be subject to punishment if found guilty.
Closed the domesday book	In the young boy's imagination, the account book of tillage returns is associated with the Book of Accounts of the King of England, or the Book of Judgement used by God on the Last Day.
A shadow bobbed in the window	
And the bicycle ticked, ticked, ticked	

The Skunk

Up, black, striped and damasked like the chasuble
At a funeral Mass, the skunk's tail
Paraded the skunk. Night after night
I expected her like a visitor.

The refrigerator whinnied into silence.   5
My desk light softened beyond the verandah.
Small oranges loomed in the orange tree.
I began to be tense as a voyeur.

After eleven years I was composing
Love-letters again, broaching the word 'wife'   10
Like a stored cask, as if its slender vowel
Had mutated into the night earth and air

Of California. The beautiful, useless
Tang of eucalyptus spelt your absence.
The aftermath of a mouthful of wine   15
Was like inhaling you off a cold pillow.

And there she was, the intent and glamorous,
Ordinary, mysterious skunk,
Mythologized, demythologized,
Snuffing the boards five feet beyond me.   20

It all came back to me last night, stirred
By the sootfall of your things at bedtime,
Your head-down, tail-up hunt in a bottom drawer
For the black plunge-line nightdress.

'the skunk's tail / Paraded the skunk'

Skunks are small black and white striped American mammals, capable of spraying foul-smelling liquid on attackers.

1 *damasked*: patterned; rich, heavy damask fabric.

1 *chasuble*: garment worn by a priest saying Mass.

5 *whinnied*: sound a horse makes.

6 *verandah*: roofed platform along the outside of a house.

8 *voyeur*: a person who watches others when they are being intimate.

10 *broaching*: raising a subject for discussion.

12 *mutated*: changed shape or form.

14 *eucalyptus*: common tree with scented leaves found in California.

15 *aftermath*: consequences of an unpleasant event.

19 *Mythologized*: related to or found in myth.

22 *sootfall*: soft sound (like soot falling from a chimney).

24 *plunge-line*: low-cut.

EXPLORATIONS

1 In your opinion, how effective is Heaney in creating the particular sense of place in this poem? Refer closely to the text in your answer.

2 The poet compares his wife to a skunk. Does this image work, in your view? Quote from the poem in support of your response.

3 Comment on the poem's dramatic qualities. Refer to setting, characters, action and sense of tension/climax, particularly in the first and last stanzas.

STUDY NOTES

'The Skunk' comes from Heaney's 1979 collection, *Field Work*. The poet called it a 'marriage poem'. While spending an academic year (1971–2) teaching in America, he had been reading the work of Robert Lowell, an American poet. Lowell's poem, 'Skunk Hour', describes how isolation drives a man to become a voyeur of lovers in cars. Heaney's reaction to his own loneliness is very different; he rediscovers the art of writing love letters to his wife, who is living 6,000 miles away in Ireland. This separation culminated in an intimate, humorous, erotic love poem which speaks volumes for the deep love and trust between husband and wife.

In the opening stanza, the reader is presented with four words describing the skunk's tail, 'Up, black, striped and damasked'. The punctuation separates the different aspects of the animal's tail for the reader's observation. An unusual simile occurs in line 1. In a **playfully irreverent tone**, Heaney likens the skunk's tail to the black and white vestments worn by a priest at a funeral. He then gives us an almost cartoon-like visual image of the animal's tail leading the skunk. The self-importance of the little animal is effectively captured in the verb 'Paraded'. All the ceremony of marching is evoked. The poet eagerly awaits his nightly visitor: 'Night after night/I expected her like a visitor'.

In stanza two, the poet's senses are heightened. The verbs 'whinnied', 'softened' and 'loomed' vividly capture **the atmosphere of the soft, exotic California night.** The bright colours of orange and green are synonymous with the Sunshine State. The anticipation of stanza one now sharpens: 'I began to be tense'. He regards himself as a 'voyeur', but here there is no violation. He is staring into darkness, getting ready to communicate with his wife. In stanza three, the poet, after a break of 11 years, is penning love letters to his wife again. In this separation period, he realises how much he misses her. His wife's presence, although she is absent, fills his consciousness. He is totally preoccupied with her. He uses the simile 'Like a stored cask' to show how he values her as something precious. The word 'wife' is savoured like fine wine and his affection is shown in his appreciation of 'its slender vowel', which reminds him of her feminine grace. She is present to him in the air he breathes, 'mutated into the night earth and air/Of California'.

Heaney's depth of longing is captured in the **sensuous language** of stanza four. The smell of the eucalyptus 'spelt your absence'. The word 'Tang' precisely notes the penetrating sensation of loneliness. Even a drink of wine, 'a mouthful of wine', does not dull this ache. Instead it intensifies his longing, 'like inhaling you off a cold pillow'. Now, the skunk, long awaited, appears. It is full of contradictions: 'glamorous', 'Ordinary'. We hear in stanza five the sound the little animal makes in the onomatopoeic phrase 'Snuffing the boards'.

Only in stanza six is the comparison between the wife and the skunk finally drawn: 'It all came back to me last night'. Heaney is now back home. His wife is rummaging in the bottom drawer for a nightdress. She adopts a slightly comic pose, 'head-down, tail-up', reminding him of the skunk as she 'hunts'. The sibilance of the line 'stirred/By the sootfall of your things' suggests the tender intimacy between the married couple. The word 'sootfall' conveys the gentle rustle of clothes falling. The reader's reaction is also 'stirred' to amused surprise as the realisation dawns that the adjectives 'intent and glamorous,/ Ordinary, mysterious ... Mythologized, demythologized' also apply to his wife. A **mature, trusting relationship** exists between the couple.

Longer lines suggest ease. The poet is relaxed and playful, his language conversational and sensuous. All our senses are 'stirred'. The light is romantic ('softened') and the colour black is alluring. The touch of the 'cold pillow' will now be replaced by the warm, shared bed. The sounds of California and the couple's bedroom echo: 'Snuffing', 'sootfall'. The smell of the eucalyptus's

'Tang' hangs in the air. The 'aftermath of a mouthful of wine' lingers on the tongue. Here is a rarity, **a successful love poem about marriage**, tender but not cosy, personal but not embarrassingly self-revealing.

ANALYSIS

Heaney stated that 'poetry verifies our singularity'. How does this poem establish the unique relationship between husband and wife? Refer closely to the text in your answer.

SAMPLE PARAGRAPH

In the poem 'The Skunk', Seamus Heaney dares to compare his wife to a skunk. He must have known and trusted his wife's sense of humour and generosity of spirit to a great degree to chance such a risky comparison. But Heaney is writing about a long-established mature relationship which, unusually, recognises the 'ordinary' qualities of his wife, 'head-down, tail-up' and also her mysterious qualities, 'spelt your absence', 'glamorous', 'black plunge-line nightdress'. His year spent teaching in California sharpened his appreciation of his wife. He realised how valuable she was, 'Like a stored cask'. The phrase 'cold pillow' really made me realise how much Heaney wanted the shared intimacy of their relationship. I thought his wife must indeed be singular to inspire such feeling. In the last stanza, the onomatopoeia of 'the sootfall of your things', the soft whisper of silky garments slipping to the floor, showed me how the poet was still fascinated by this woman. The unique relationship between these two individuals is both ordinary and routine, 'demythologized', and also extraordinary and tender, 'Mythologized'. This poem's exploration of the relationship between the poet and his wife does indeed show the truth of human uniqueness.

EXAMINER'S COMMENT

A confident and focused treatment of the poem in relation to the task of this challenging question. A well-structured personal response and judicious use of quotation merits a grade A.

Seamus Heaney

1 'Relationships, personal or otherwise, lie at the heart of Seamus Heaney's poetry.' Discuss this statement and support your answer with reference to the text.

2 Copy the table below into your own notes and fill in critical comments about the last two quotations.

Key Quotes

damasked like the chasuble/ At a funeral Mass	In this cheeky simile, the skunk's appearance is compared to the rich patterned clothes worn by a priest officiating at a solemn occasion, a funeral.
The refrigerator whinnied into silence	The noise of the fridge is captured in the onomatopoeic verb 'whinnied' as Heaney personifies this object.
Mythologized, demythologized	As wonderful as an exotic myth or legend, as ordinary and familiar as everyday routine.
broaching the word 'wife'/Like a stored cask	
Your head-down, tail-up hunt in a bottom drawer	

The Harvest Bow

As you plaited the harvest bow
You implicated the mellowed silence in you
In wheat that does not rust
But brightens as it tightens twist by twist
Into a knowable corona,   5
A throwaway love-knot of straw.

Hands that aged round ashplants and cane sticks
And lapped the spurs on a lifetime of gamecocks
Harked to their gift and worked with fine intent
Until your fingers moved somnambulant: 10
I tell and finger it like braille,
Gleaning the unsaid off the palpable,

And if I spy into its golden loops
I see us walk between the railway slopes
Into an evening of long grass and midges,   15
Blue smoke straight up, old beds and ploughs in hedges,
An auction notice on an outhouse wall –
You with a harvest bow in your lapel,

Me with the fishing rod, already homesick
For the big lift of these evenings, as your stick   20
Whacking the tips off weeds and bushes
Beats out of time, and beats, but flushes
Nothing: that original townland
Still tongue-tied in the straw tied by your hand.

The end of art is peace   25
Could be the motto of this frail device
That I have pinned up on our deal dresser –
Like a drawn snare
Slipped lately by the spirit of the corn
Yet burnished by its passage, and still warm.   30

Seamus Heaney

'A throwaway love-knot of straw'

The harvest bow, an emblem of traditional rural crafts, was made from straw and often worn in the lapel to celebrate the end of harvesting. Sometimes it was given as a love-token or kept in the farmhouse until the next year's harvest.

2 *implicated*: intertwined; revealed indirectly.

2 *mellowed*: matured, placid.

5 *corona*: circle of light, halo.

8 *lapped the spurs*: tied the back claws of fighting birds.

8 *gamecocks*: male fowl reared to take part in cock-fighting.

9 *Harked*: listened, attuned.

10 *somnambulant*: automatically, as if sleepwalking.

11 *braille*: system of reading and writing by touching raised dots.

12 *Gleaning*: gathering, grasping; understanding.

12 *palpable*: what can be handled or understood.

15 *midges*: small biting insects that usually swarm near water.

22 *flushes*: rouses, reveals.

25 *The end of art is peace*: art brings contentment (a quotation from the English poet Coventry Patmore, 1823–96). It was also used by W.B. Yeats.

26 *device*: object, artefact.

27 *deal*: pine wood.

28 *snare*: trap.

30 *burnished*: shining.

EXPLPORATIONS

1 Based on your reading of the poem, what impression do you get of Heaney's father? Refer to the text in your answer.

2 In your view, is the harvest bow a symbol of love? Give reasons for your answer, using reference to the poem.

3 What do you understand by the line 'The end of art is peace'? Briefly explain your answer.

STUDY NOTES

'The Harvest Bow' (from the 1972 collection **Field Work**) is an elegiac poem in which Heaney pays tribute to his father and the work he did with his hands, weaving a traditional harvest emblem out of stalks of wheat. Remembering his boyhood, watching his father create the corn-dolly, he already knew that the moment could not last. The recognition of his father's artistic talents leads the poet to a consideration of his own creative work.

The poem begins with a measured description of Heaney's reticent father as he twists stalks of wheat into decorative love-knots. The delicate phrasing in stanza one ('You implicated the mellowed silence in you') reflects the poet's awareness of how **the harvest bow symbolised the intricate bond between father and son**. The poet conveys a subdued but satisfied mood as another farm year draws to a close. Autumnal images ('wheat that does not rust') add to the sense of accomplishment. Heaney highlights the practised techniques involved in creating this 'throwaway love-knot of straw'. The harvest bow 'brightens as it tightens twist by twist'. Emphatic alliteration and internal rhyme enliven the image, almost becoming a metaphor for the father's expertise. The bow is likened to 'a knowable corona', a reassuring light circle representing the year's natural cycle.

In stanza two, the intricate beauty of the straw knot prompts Heaney to recall some of the other manual skills his father once demonstrated 'round ashplants and cane sticks'. He acknowledges the older man's 'gift' of concentration and 'fine intent' as he fashioned the harvest bow ('your fingers moved somnambulant') **without conscious effort towards artistic achievement**. Is Heaney also suggesting that poets should work that way? Carefully handling the bow 'like braille', the poet clearly values it as an expression of undeclared love: 'Gleaning the unsaid off the palpable'.

The pleasurable sentiments of Heaney's childhood memories are realised by the strength of detailed imagery in stanza three: 'I see us walk between the railway slopes'. Such **ordinary scenes are enhanced by sensuous details** of 1940s rural life: 'Blue smoke straight up, old beds and ploughs in hedges'. Many of the sounds have a plaintive, musical quality ('loops', 'slopes', 'midges', 'hedges'). The poet seems haunted by his father's ghost, and the silence that once seemed to define their relationship is now recognised as a secret code of mutual understanding.

Stanza four focuses on the relentless passing of time. The **tone is particularly elegaic** as Heaney recalls his father 'Whacking the tips off weeds' with his stick.

In retrospect, he seems to interpret such pointless actions as evidence of how every individual 'Beats out of time' – but to no avail. The poet extends this notion of time's mystery by suggesting that it is through art alone ('the straw tied by your hand') that 'tongue-tied' communities can explore life's wonder.

At the start of stanza five, Heaney tries to make sense of the corn-dolly, now a treasured part of his own household 'on our deal dresser'. It mellows in its new setting and gives out heat. While 'the spirit of the corn' may have disappeared from the knot, the power of the poet's imagination can still recreate it there. So rather than being merely a nostalgic recollection of childhood, the poem takes on universal meaning in the intertwining of artistic forces. We are left with a deep sense of lost rural heritage, the unspoken joy of a shared relationship and the rich potential of the poet's art. For Heaney, **artistic achievements produce warm feelings of lasting contentment**. Whatever 'frail device' is created, be it a harvest bow or a formal elegy, *'The end of art is peace'*.

ANALYSIS

What is your personal response to Heaney's treatment of the relationship between himself and his father in 'The Harvest Bow'? Support the points you make with reference to the poem.

SAMPLE PARAGRAPH

'The Harvest Bow' is a good example of where Seamus Heaney shows his emotional side. He begins by describing his aged father at work. It is clear that he admires him very much even though the old man is totally immersed in weaving the stalks of wheat into a bow. There is a very moving 'mellow silence' between them, but the bow or 'love-knot' symbolises their feelings. For most of the poem Heaney treats his father with deep respect, admiring his artistic fingers which 'moved somnambulant' without effort. He even imitates his father as he fingers the love-knot – or 'frail device' – which he displays on his kitchen dresser. I liked the way Heaney was prepared to express his emotions for his father by including memories of times they shared together – 'I see us walking along the railway lines'. What was also interesting was the fact that Heaney did not glorify his father in a sentimental or false way. In some ways, the older man seems morose 'whacking the weeds', but this would be typical of Irish farmers. The relationship is presented in a realistic way, but I still get the feeling that Heaney really loved his father and models his own work as a poet – to 'work with fine intent' – on his mentor.

EXAMINER'S COMMENT

This is a reasonably well-focused response that addresses the given question in a sustained way. There is genuine personal engagement with the poem and the answer includes several interesting points. However, some of the quotations are imprecise. A basic B grade.

CLASS/HOMEWORK EXERCISES

1 'The Harvest Bow' is essentially a poem of celebration. To what extent do you agree? Give reasons for your response, using close reference to the text.

2 Copy the table below into your own notes and fill in critical comments about the last two quotations.

Key Quotes

A throwaway love-knot of straw	The colloquial description of the harvest bow is highly ironic, since Heaney greatly values the corn-dolly.
worked with fine intent	Just as his father used dedicated artistry to fashion the bow, the poet's self-acknowledged task is to knot his visions into language.
if I spy into its golden loops	The verb 'spy' has undertones of a secretive childhood game. The loops of the harvest bow open out into visions.
Gleaning the unsaid off the palpable	
The end of art is peace	

The Underground

Seamus Heaney

There we were in the vaulted tunnel running,
You in your going-away coat speeding ahead
And me, me then like a fleet god gaining
Upon you before you turned to a reed

Or some new white flower japped with crimson   5
As the coat flapped wild and button after button
Sprang off and fell in a trail
Between the Underground and the Albert Hall.

Honeymooning, mooning around, late for the Proms,
Our echoes die in that corridor and now   10
I come as Hansel came on the moonlit stones
Retracing the path back, lifting the buttons

To end up in a draughty lamplit station
After the trains have gone, the wet track
Bared and tensed as I am, all attention   15
For your step following and damned if I look back.

'Our echoes die in
that corridor'

GLOSSARY

In Greek mythology, Eurydice, the beloved wife of Orpheus, was killed by a venomous snake. Orpheus travelled to the Underworld (Hades) to retrieve her. It was granted that Eurydice could return to the world of the living, but on condition that Orpheus should walk in front of her and not look back until he had reached the upper world. In his anxiety, he broke his promise, and Eurydice vanished again – but this time forever.

1   *vaulted*: domed, arched.

2   *going-away coat*: new coat worn by the bride leaving on honeymoon.

3   *fleet*: fast; momentary.

4   *reed*: slender plant; part of a musical instrument.

5   *japped*: tinged, layered.

8   *the Albert Hall*: famous London landmark and concert venue.

9   *the Proms*: short for promenade concerts, a summer season of classical music.

11   *Hansel*: fairytale character who, along with his sister Gretel, retraced his way home using a trail of white pebbles.

EXPLORATIONS

1   Comment on the atmosphere created in the first two stanzas. Refer to the text in your answer.

2   From your reading of this poem, what do you learn about the relationship between the poet and his wife? Refer to the text in your answer.

3   Write a short personal response to 'The Underground', highlighting the impact it made on you.

STUDY NOTES

'The Underground' is the first poem in *Station Island* (1984). It recounts a memory from Heaney's honeymoon when he and his wife (like a modern Orpheus and Eurydice) were rushing through a London Underground Tube station on their way to a BBC Promenade Concert in the Albert Hall. In Dennis O'Driscoll's book, *Stepping Stones*, Heaney has said, 'In this version of the story, Eurydice and much else gets saved by the sheer cussedness of the poet up ahead just keeping going.'

The poem's title is infused with a piercing sense of threat. Underground journeys are shadowed with a certain menace. Not only is there a mythical association with crossing into the land of the dead, but there is also the actuality of accidents and terrorist outrages. The first stanza of Heaney's personal narrative uses everyday colloquial speech ('There we were in the vaulted tunnel running') to introduce his **dramatic account**. Broad vowel sounds ('vau', 'tun' and 'run') dominate the opening line with a guttural quality. The oppressively 'vaulted' setting and urgent verbs ('speeding', 'gaining') increase this sense of subterranean disquiet. For the poet, it is a psychic and mythic underground where he imagines his own heroic quest ('like a fleet god'). What he seems to dread most is the possibility of change and that, like a latter-day Orpheus, he might somehow lose his soulmate.

Cinematic images and run-on lines propel the second stanza forward. This **fast-paced rhythm is in keeping with the restless diction** – 'the coat flapped wild'. The poet's wife is wearing her going-away wedding outfit and in the course of her sprint, the buttons start popping off. Internal rhyme adds to the tension; 'japped' and 'flapped' play into each other, giving the impression that whatever is occurring is happening with great intensity.

The poem changes at the beginning of the **third stanza** and this is evident in the language, which is much more playful, reflecting Heaney's assessment of the occasion in hindsight. He now recognises the youthful insecurity of the time: 'Honeymooning, mooning around'. The wry reference to the fictional Hansel and Gretel hints at the immaturity of their relationship as newlyweds, and emphasises the couple's initial fretfulness. But recalling how he carefully gathered up the buttons, like Hansel returning from the wilderness, **Heaney appears to have now come to terms with his uneasy past**: 'Our echoes die in that corridor'.

This latent confidence underscores the poet's recollections in the **fourth stanza**. The action and speed have now ceased. After the uncertainty of the 'draughty lamplit station', he has learned to trust his wife and his own destiny. Unlike Orpheus, the tragic Greek hero, Heaney has emerged from his personal descent into Hades, 'Bared and tense'. Although **he can never forget the desolation of being threatened with loss**, the poet has been well served by the experience, having realised that it will always be him – and not his wife – who will be damned if he dares to look back.

The ending of the poem is characteristically compelling. Commenting on it in *Stepping Stones*, Heaney has said, 'But in the end, the "damned if I look back" line takes us well beyond the honeymoon.' Although some critics feel that the final outlook is more regretful, it is difficult to miss the sheer determination that is present in the poem's last line. The poet's stubborn tone leaves us with overwhelming evidence of his enduring devotion to love, an emotional commitment which seems to be even more precious with the passing of time.

ANALYSIS

'Heaney's poems are capable of capturing moments of insight in a strikingly memorable fashion.' Discuss this view, with particular reference to 'The Underground'.

SAMPLE PARAGRAPH

'The Underground' is really a love poem, written about the time Seamus Heaney and his wife were in London on honeymoon. They got delayed at a Tube station and Heaney had a panic attack. He imagined the legend of Orpheus rescuing Eurydice from the underworld, the next world. The comparison gave him a deeper insight into the love he felt for his new wife. Firstly, he was frightened that she would disappear among the crowd, but he eventually had faith in her (and himself) and refused to look back to find her in case he suffered the same bad luck as Orpheus. What I found of interest was the way Heaney suggested the nervousness he felt 'running' in the 'vaulted tunnel'. The uninterrupted rhythm of the young couple rushing through the station vividly captures their anxiety. His vivid imagery of the 'draughty lamplit station' brought home to me the loneliness he experienced. In the end, he learned from what happened to believe in the power of love and his final words reflect his strength of love – 'damned if I look back'. For me, Heaney really communicates the way true love grows stronger in this short dramatic poem. The insight came from his belief in the relationship with his wife. They made a promise to each other and had the courage to keep it.

EXAMINER'S COMMENT

This is a focused and sustained approach that addresses both aspects of the question. There is good personal interaction and evidence of close reading of the poem. Quotations are integrated effectively. Grade A standard.

CLASS/HOMEWORK EXERCISES

1   In Heaney's poem 'The Underground', the poet compares his wife and himself to the legend of Eurydice and Orpheus. In your opinion, how effective is this comparison? Refer to the text in your answer.
2   Copy the table below into your own notes and fill in critical comments about the last two quotations.

Seamus Heaney

Key Quotes

There we were in the vaulted tunnel running	This strong, visual image invites the reader into a fast-moving drama. The underground setting increases the uneasy atmosphere.
before you turned to a reed/ Or some new white flower	An underlying fear of change and loss of love is central to the early part of the poem.
Honeymooning, mooning around	Recalling the experience in the Underground station, Heaney's mood is more reflective and he acknowledges his earlier immaturity.
Our echoes die in that corridor	
and damned if I look back	

Postscript

And some time make the time to drive out west
Into County Clare, along the Flaggy Shore,
In September or October, when the wind
And the light are working off each other
So that the ocean on one side is wild   5
With foam and glitter, and inland among stones
The surface of a slate-grey lake is lit
By the earthed lightning of a flock of swans,
Their feathers roughed and ruffling, white on white,
Their fully grown headstrong-looking heads   10
Tucked or cresting or busy underwater.
Useless to think you'll park and capture it
More thoroughly. You are neither here nor there,
A hurry through which known and strange things pass
As big soft buffetings come at the car sideways   15
And catch the heart off guard and blow it open.

'along the Flaggy Shore'

EXPLORATIONS

1 Choose one image from the poem that you find particularly effective. Briefly explain your choice.

2 What is your understanding of the poem's final line?

3 In your opinion, is the advice given by Heaney in 'Postscript' relevant to our modern world? Give reasons to support your response.

STUDY NOTES

This beautiful pastoral lyric comes at the end of Seamus Heaney's 1996 collection, *The Spirit Level*. The title suggests an afterthought, something that was missed out earlier. As so often in his poetry, Heaney succeeds in conveying the extraordinary by way of an everyday experience – in this case, the vivid memory of a journey westwards. The poem resonates with readers, particularly those who have also shared moments when life caught them by surprise.

Line 1 is relaxed and conversational. The poet invites others (or promises himself, perhaps) to 'make the time to drive out west'. The phrase 'out west' has connotations both of adventurous opportunity and dismal failure. By placing 'And' at the start of the poem, Heaney indicates a link with something earlier, some unfinished business. **Keen to ensure that the journey will be worthwhile**, he recommends a definite destination ('the Flaggy Shore') and time ('September or October').

The untamed beauty of the Co. Clare coastline is described in some detail: 'when the wind/And the light are working off each other' (lines 3–4). The phrase 'working off' is especially striking in conveying the **tension and balance between two of nature's greatest complementary forces: wind and light**. Together, they create an effect that neither could produce singly.

Close awareness of place is a familiar feature of the poet's writing, but in this instance he includes another dimension – the notion of in-betweeness. The road Heaney describes runs between the ocean and an inland lake. Carefully chosen images **contrast** the unruly beauty of the open sea's 'foam and glitter' with the still 'slate-grey lake' (line 7). In both descriptions, the sounds of the words echo their sense precisely.

The introduction of the swans in line 8 brings unexpected drama. Heaney captures their seemingly effortless movement between air and water. The poet's **vigorous skill with language** can be seen in his appreciation of the swans' transforming presence, which he highlights in the extraordinary image of 'earthed lightning'. His expertly crafted sketches are both tactile ('feathers roughed and ruffling') and visual ('white on white'). Tossed by the wind, their neck feathers resemble ruffled collars. To Heaney, these exquisite birds signify an otherworldly force that is rarely earthed or restrained. In response, he is momentarily absorbed by the swans' purposeful gestures and powerful flight.

In line 12, the poet cautiously accepts that such elemental beauty can never be fully grasped: 'Useless to think you'll park and capture it'. Because we are 'neither here nor there', we can only occasionally glimpse 'known and strange things'. Despite this, the poem concludes on a redemptive note, acknowledging those special times when we edge close to the miraculous. **These experiences transcend our mundane lives** and we are shaken by revelation, just as unexpected gusts of winds ('soft buffetings') can rock a car.

Heaney's journey has been both **physical and mystical**. It is brought to a crescendo in line 16, where it ends in the articulation of an important truth. He has found meaning between the tangible and intangible. The startling possibility of discovering the ephemeral quality of spiritual awareness is unnerving enough to 'catch the heart off guard and blow it open'. The seemingly contradictory elements of comfort and danger add to the intensity of this final image. Heaney has spoken about the illumination he felt during his visit to the Flaggy Shore as a 'glorious exultation of air and sea and swans'. For him, the experience was obviously inspirational, and the poem that it produced might well provide a similar opportunity for readers to experience life beyond the material.

ANALYSIS

'Seamus Heaney involves himself in finding inspiration for the creation of poetry.' Using reference to his poem 'Postscript', give your opinion of this assessment of Heaney's work.

SAMPLE PARAGRAPH

'Postscript' is a typical Heaney poem in that it begins with a simple description of an unforgettable occasion which truly inspired him. Many of his poems entice readers to be open to marvellous moments of enlightenment in everyday life. His advice is to go to the windswept West of Ireland and experience the beauty and wonder of the coastline at the Flaggy Shore. It's clear that he has had something like a religious experience there as he felt 'the wind/And the light ... working off each other'. His simple description of the swans – 'white on white' – seems to have lifted his spirits and transported him to a world where 'strange things pass'. I have read some nature poems by Hopkins and Yeats, and the same fascination with nature can be seen. In his poem 'Lightenings', Heaney used the experience of the monks being taken to a higher level of consciousness through prayer and chanting. Much the same happened in 'Postscript', where the poet was at one with nature and his spiritual self for a moment – 'neither here nor there'. I liked the last line of this poem where Heaney is simply saying that if we stop rushing around and stop to admire nature's beauty once in a while, anybody can have their heart 'caught off guard' and blown open. Such inspiration will not make everyone write poetry – as Heaney did – but it will have a similar spiritual effect.

EXAMINER'S COMMENT

A good personal response to a challenging question, focusing well on the idea of inspiration – both for the poet and the reader. References and quotations are used effectively. Grade A.

CLASS/HOMEWORK EXERCISES

1 'The response to his experience of vivid scenery is a central feature of Seamus Heaney's poetry.' Discuss this view with reference to 'Postscript'.
2 Copy the table below into your own notes and fill in critical comments about the last two quotations.

Key Quotes

And some time make the time to drive out west	Heaney's advice is quietly insistent, emphasising the need to make good use of time. Later on in the poem, he is more critical of our hurried, modern lifestyle.
the wind/And the light are working off each other	In this subtle image, the phrase 'working off' captures the interplay between the natural elements.
the earthed lightning of a flock of swans	The shock of the swans' sudden appearance is conveyed in this sharp metaphor. For Heaney, it is an inspirational moment of magic.
A hurry through which known and strange things pass	
And catch the heart off guard and blow it open	

A Call

'Hold on,' she said, 'I'll just run out and get him.
The weather here's so good, he took the chance
To do a bit of weeding.'
                So I saw him
Down on his hands and knees beside the leek rig,   5
Touching, inspecting, separating one
Stalk from the other, gently pulling up
Everything not tapered, frail and leafless,
Pleased to feel each little weed-root break,
But rueful also...   10
             Then found myself listening to
The amplified grave ticking of hall clocks
Where the phone lay unattended in a calm
Of mirror glass and sunstruck pendulums...

And found myself then thinking: if it were nowadays, 15
This is how Death would summon Everyman.

Next thing he spoke and I nearly said I loved him.

'Pleased to feel each little weed-root break'

GLOSSARY

8 *tapered*: slender; reducing in thickness towards the end.
8 *frail*: weak.
10 *rueful*: expressing regret.
12 *amplified*: increased the strength of the sound.

14 *pendulums*: weights that hang from a fixed point and swing freely, used to regulate the mechanism of a clock.

EXPLORATIONS

1   How does Heaney dramatise this event? Refer to setting, mood, dialogue, action and climax in your response. Support your answer with reference to the text.

2   How would you describe the tone of this poem? Does it change? Quote to support the points you make.

3   One critic said that the 'celebration of people and relationships in Heaney's poetry is characterised by honesty and tenderness'. Do you agree or disagree? Refer to the text in your response.

STUDY NOTES

'A Call' comes from Heaney's collection *The Spirit Level* (1996) and deals with two of the poet's favourite themes: the father–son relationship and the passing of time. The setting is a routine domestic scene of a father weeding, a son visiting and a mother talking. *The Spirit Level* suggests balance, getting the level right, measuring. It also suggests poetry, which is on another plane, free-floating above the confines of the earth. In his Nobel Prize speech, Heaney said he was 'permitting myself the luxury of walking on air'.

This personal narrative opens with a conversational directness, as Heaney is told to 'Hold on' while his father is contacted. He is busy weeding the garden. 'The weather here's so good, he took the chance/To do a bit of weeding'. The rhythm of colloquial dialogue is realistically caught by the use of commonplace language. **The simple scene of domesticity is set.** In line 4, the poet now becomes the observer on the fringes of the scene, 'So I saw him'. The detail of 'Down on his hands and knees beside the leek rig' invites the reader to observe alongside the poet. The broken lines show the care and skill of the gardener's activity, 'Touching, inspecting, separating', as the father tends his vegetable patch. All farming tradition is associated with decay and growth, and for both animals and plants, the weakest is discarded, 'gently pulling up/Everything not tapered'. What is not a leek is removed. The onomatopoeia of the word 'break', with its sharp 'k' sound, suggests the snap of the root as it is pulled from the earth. The father takes pleasure ('Pleased to feel') in his work ('each little weed-root break') but he is, perhaps, regretful too ('rueful') that a form of life is ending, snapped from the nurturing earth. Or is he just sorry that he has not removed all of the weed's root and so it will grow again, giving him more work to do?

In line 11, the **visual imagery is replaced by aural imagery**. The focus changes from the father to the poet as he finds himself 'listening'. Time is passing in this little scene, not just for the weeds but also for man, measured by the 'grave ticking of hall clocks'. Here the poem begins to move between earthbound reality and airiness, as an almost surreal image of ticking clocks in a sea ('calm') of 'mirror glass and sunstruck pendulums' is presented. The broad vowel sounds create an air of serenity and otherworldliness. The echo of the clocks is vividly conveyed in the sound 'amplified'; we can imagine the loud ticking of the clocks as the sound increases in intensity, the 'ticking' filling this space. Is the sound increasing as time starts to end for man? Why is the phone unattended? Is a 'call' expected? From whom, to whom? Is communication no longer possible in this place?

In line 15, Heaney moves from observation to meditation, walking on air, 'And found myself then thinking'. He decides that Death would call ('summon') man to his final destination using this modern means, the telephone. The poet is pushing at the boundaries of what is real. The father, like the weeds, will be uprooted, spirited away to some afterlife. Here Heaney is 'seeing things'; he is mediating between states of awareness. **A sense of mortality informs the poem.** The last line stands apart, as he is jolted out of his reverie by: 'Next thing he spoke'. Family love is important to Heaney. Here it is the uncommunicated closeness of the father–son relationship. Here are the frustrating attempts at communication between father and son, 'and I nearly said I loved him'. Was it an awareness of his father's mortality, like the weeds, which prompts this reaction from the poet? The diction, relaxed and casual, holds the powerful love between these silent men, and the heartbreaking tension of the impossibility of articulating that love. In that final line – 'Next thing he spoke, and I nearly said I loved him' – father and son are both joined and separated.

The title of this poem is intriguing. It could signal the visit of the son to the family home, or the wife calling her husband to let him know his son has arrived. Or might it refer to a telephone call, or even the final summons 'Everyman' will receive from Death?

ANALYSIS

'Heaney habitually finds mystery and significance behind ordinary objects and events.' Discuss this statement in relation to the poem 'A Call' and support your response with reference to the text.

SAMPLE PARAGRAPH

I thought this poem was very deep, as Heaney describes a common event, his father weeding, and turns it into a reflection on mortality. The ordinary event is effectively set by the casual, conversational dialogue, as the wife tells the poet to 'Hold on'. The father's activity is vividly described in the verbs 'Touching, inspecting, separating'. For Heaney, creativity was held in the hands. But another layer of meaning suggests itself. Is Death, the final caller, checking us? I especially liked the word 'rueful'. The father is sorry that he is ending life, 'each little weed-root break'. Is this in contrast to the cold, dispassionate hand of death, who calls all men? This examination of the simple, ordinary growth in the garden gives way to an examination of death. A weird picture of loud ticking clocks in a fantastical hall of mirrors and sun is painted. The ominous ticking of passing time is given due respect, 'The amplified grave ticking'. I liked the pun on 'grave'. The glass mirrors suggest to me the different states of reality, of life and death, what is real, what is reflected. The broad vowel sounds of 'sunstruck pendulums' again emphasise the unstoppable passing of time, as the weights swing to and fro. Now from the physical detail of his father weeding, the poet moves to another level, Heaney said, 'One gains the air'. The 'unattended' phone makes him imagine that this is how Death would 'call' man to his inevitable fate. Here, Heaney is finding significance behind an ordinary object.

EXAMINER'S COMMENT

A sustained exploratory response, subtly addressing all aspects of the question in a personal way, and referring to both 'objects' and 'events'. Expression is varied throughout and points are aptly supported with integrated quotes. Grade A.

CLASS/HOMEWORK EXERCISES

1 'Heaney's poetry, whether explicit or implicit, is autobiographical in the main.' Would you agree or disagree with this view? Support your answer with reference to the poem 'A Call'.
2 Copy the table below into your own notes and fill in critical comments about the last two quotations.

Key Quotes

'Hold on'	The colloquial phrase communicates what is often said in telephone conversations. This dense use of language is a feature of Heaney's writing.
I'll just run out and get him	The conversational, colloquial tone sets the ordinariness of this little scene. It also reverberates at the end as a contrast to the difficulty the poet has in communicating with his father.
separating one/Stalk from the other	Sibilance suggests the endurance of the father as he carefully tends his garden. The line arrangement mirrors the organisation of his weeding.
Where the phone lay unattended	
and I nearly said I loved him	

Tate's Avenue

Not the brown and fawn car rug, that first one
Spread on sand by the sea but breathing land-breaths,
Its vestal folds unfolded, its comfort zone
Edged with a fringe of sepia-coloured wool tails.

Not the one scraggy with crusts and eggshells   5
And olive stones and cheese and salami rinds
Laid out by the torrents of the Guadalquivir
Where we got drunk before the corrida.

Instead, again, it's locked-park Sunday Belfast,
A walled back yard, the dust-bins high and silent   10
As a page is turned, a finger twirls warm hair
And nothing gives on the rug or the ground beneath it.

I lay at my length and felt the lumpy earth,
Keen-sensed more than ever through discomfort,
But never shifted off the plaid square once.   15
When we moved I had your measure and you had mine.

'And nothing gives on the rug'

STUDY NOTES

'Tate's Avenue' (from the 2006 collection *District and Circle*) is another celebration of Heaney's love for Marie Devlin. They married in 1965 and lived off Tate's Avenue in South Belfast during the late 1960s. Here, the poet reviews their relationship by linking three separate occasions involving a collection of car rugs spread on the ground by the couple over the years.

Stanza one invites us to eavesdrop on a seemingly mundane scene of everyday domesticity. It appears that the poet and his wife have been reminiscing – presumably about their love life over the years. Although the negative opening tone is emphatic ('Not the brown and fawn car rug'), we are left guessing about the exact nature of the couple's discussion. A few tantalising details are given about 'that first' rug, connecting it with an early seaside visit. Heaney can still recall the tension of a time when the couple were **caught between their own desire and strong social restrictions**. He describes the rug in terms of its texture and colours: 'Its vestal folds unfolded' (suggesting their youthful sexuality) contrasting with the 'sepia-coloured wool tails' (symbolising caution and old-fashioned inhibitions). As usual, Heaney's tone is edged with irony as he recalls the 'comfort zone' between himself and Marie.

The repetition of 'Not' at the start of **stanza two** clearly indicates that the second rug is also rejected, even though it can be traced back to a more exotic Spanish holiday location. Sharp onomatopoeic effects ('scraggy with crusts and eggshells') and the list of Mediterranean foods ('olive stones and cheese and salami rinds') convey **a sense of freedom and indulgence**. Although the couple's hedonistic life is communicated in obviously excessive terms ('Laid out by the torrents of the Guadalquivir'), Heaney's tone is somewhat dismissive. Is he suggesting that their relationship was mostly sensual back then?

'Instead' – the first word in **stanza three** – signals a turning point in the poet's thinking. Back in his familiar home surroundings, he recalls the rug that mattered most and should answer whatever doubts he had about the past. He has measured the development of their relationship in stages associated with special moments he and Marie shared. The line 'it's locked-park Sunday Belfast' conjures up memories of their early married life in the Tate's Avenue district. The sectarian 1960s are marked by dour Protestant domination, a time when weekend pleasures were frowned upon and even the public parks were closed.

Despite such routine repression and the unromantic setting ('A walled back yard, the dust-bins high and silent'), **the atmosphere is sexually charged**. Heaney is aware of the scene's underlying drama; the seconds tick by 'As a page is turned, a finger twirls warm hair'. The unfaltering nature of the couple's intimacy is evident in the resounding declaration: 'nothing gives on the rug or the ground beneath it'.

This notion of confidence in their relationship is carried through into stanza four and accentuated by the alliterative 'I lay at my length and felt the lumpy earth'. The resolute rhythm is strengthened by the robust adjectival phrase 'Keen-sensed' and the insistent statement: 'But never shifted off the plaid square once'. Heaney builds to a discreet and understated climax in the finely balanced last line: 'When we moved I had your measure and you had mine'. While there are erotic undertones throughout, the poet presents us with restrained realism in place of expansive sensuality. 'Tate's Avenue' is a **beautiful, unembarrassed poem of romantic and sexual love within a committed relationship**. Characteristically, when Heaney touches on personal relationships, he produces the most tender and passionate emotions.

ANALYSIS

How effective is Seamus Heaney's use of images in 'Tate's Avenue'? Refer to the poem in your answer.

SAMPLE PARAGRAPH

I was very impressed by Seamus Heaney's use of effective images in his poem 'Tate's Avenue'. He uses three separate settings to show how his lifetime love affair with his wife changed from their early courtship to a mature married relationship. The first image of them sharing a brown and fawn rug by the sea suggests the distant past – 'sepia-coloured'. The rug is personified – 'breathing' to symbolise their feelings for each other. But the memory of their first date is almost like a faded picture. The second scene Heaney remembers is vividly described – during a summer sun holiday as students going to a Spanish bullfight – 'we were drinking before the corrida'. The details also add to my understanding of the scene – 'eating our scraggy crusts and eggshells'. I thought the best images were used at the end of the poem when Heaney described his memories of lying with his wife on a blanket in their back garden in Belfast. The details of the mutual attraction were very true-to-life – 'a finger twirls warm hair'. I could sense their eye contact and body language in these images – 'We felt the lumpy earth'. Heaney has the ability to bring the reader into a scene and this is largely due to the precise images which he used to create a romantic mood between himself with his wife. Overall, I thought his use of clear images was very effective in 'Tate's Avenue'.

EXAMINER'S COMMENT

This is a reasonably successful personal response to the question, showing some familiarity with the images in the poem and how Heaney uses these to explore the theme of love. The point about the faded photograph was interesting. However, the incorrect quotes and slightly awkward expression reduce the standard to an average grade B.

CLASS/HOMEWORK EXERCISES

1   '"Tate's Avenue" has the drama and immediacy of feeling that is the hallmark of good love poetry.' Discuss this view, using reference to the poem.
2   Copy the table below into your own notes and fill in critical comments about the last two quotations.

Key Quotes

Spread on sand by the sea but breathing land-breaths	Sibilance and personification suggest the strong physical attraction between Heaney and his wife.
its comfort zone	As he remembers the importance of the rug in the couple's committed relationship, the poet's description is wry and sardonic.
it's locked-park Sunday Belfast	The image highlights an era of sectarian rule in Northern Ireland when Protestant-controlled councils insisted that parks and other amenities were closed on Sundays.
As a page is turned, a finger twirls warm hair	
When we moved I had your measure and you had mine	

The Pitchfork

Seamus Heaney

Of all implements, the pitchfork was the one
That came near to an imagined perfection:
When he tightened his raised hand and aimed with it,
It felt like a javelin, accurate and light.

So whether he played the warrior or the athlete   5
Or worked in earnest in the chaff and sweat,
He loved its grain of tapering, dark-flecked ash
Grown satiny from its own natural polish.

Riveted steel, turned timber, burnish, grain,
Smoothness, straightness, roundness, length and sheen.   10
Sweat-cured, sharpened, balanced, tested, fitted.
The springiness, the clip and dart of it.

And then when he thought of the probes that reached the farthest,
He would see the shaft of a pitchfork sailing past
Evenly, imperturbably through space,   15
Its prongs starlit and absolutely soundless –

But has learned at last to follow that simple lead
Past its own aim, out to an other side
Where perfection – or nearness to it – is imagined
Not in the aiming but the opening hand.   20

*'When he tightened his raised hand and
aimed with it'*

GLOSSARY

4 *javelin*: long spear thrown in a competitive sport as used as a weapon.
6 *chaff*: husks of grain separated from the seed.
7 *grain*: wheat.
7 *tapering*: reducing in thickness towards one end.
9 *Riveted*: fastened.
9 *burnish*: the shine on a polished surface.

12 *clip*: clasp; smack (colloquial).
12 *dart*: follow-on movement; small pointed missile thrown as a weapon.
13 *probes*: unmanned, exploratory spacecraft; a small measuring or testing device.
15 *imperturbably*: calmly, smoothly; unable to be upset.
16 *prongs*: two or more projecting points on a fork.

EXPLORATIONS

1   What is the tone of this poem? Does it change or not? Refer closely to the text in your response.

2   Select one image (or one line) that you find particularly interesting. Briefly explain your choice.

3   What do you think about the ending of this poem? Do you consider it visionary or far-fetched? Give reasons for your answer.

STUDY NOTES

'The Pitchfork' was published in Heaney's 1991 collection, *Seeing Things*. These poems turn to the earlier concerns of the poet. Craft and natural skill, the innate ability to make art out of work, is seen in many of his poems, such as 'The Forge'. Heaney is going back, making 'a journey back into the heartland of the ordinary'. The poet is now both observer and visionary.

In stanza one, Heaney describes a pitchfork, an ordinary farming 'implement'. Through looking at an ordinary object with intense concentration, the result is a fresh 'seeing', where the ordinary and mundane become marvellous, 'imagined perfection'. For Heaney, the creative impulse was held in the hand, in the skill of the labourer ('tightened his raised hand and aimed with it'). This skill was similar to the skill of the poet. They both practise and hone their particular ability. The pitchfork is now transformed into a sporting piece of equipment, 'a javelin'. The heaviness of physical work falls away as it becomes 'accurate and light' due to the practised capability of the worker. This is similar to the lightness of being and the freeing of the poet's spirit that Heaney allows himself to experience in this collection of poetry.

The worker is described as sometimes playing 'the warrior or the athlete' (stanza two). **Both professions command respect** and both occupations require courage and skill. But the worker's real work is also described realistically, 'worked in earnest in the chaff and sweat'. This is heavy manual labour, and Heaney does not shirk from its unpleasant side. However, the worker is not ground down by it because he 'loved' the beauty of the pitchfork. Here we see both the poet and the worker dazzled, as the intent observation of the humble pitchfork unleashes its beauty, its slender 'dark-flecked ash'. The shine of the handle is conveyed in the word 'satiny'. The tactile language allows the reader to feel the smooth, polished wooden handle. Now three pairs of eyes (the worker's, the poet's and our own) observe the pitchfork.

Close observation of the pitchfork in stanza three continues with a virtuoso display of description, as **each detail is lovingly depicted**, almost like a slow sequence of close-ups in a film. The meeting of the handle and fork is caught in the phrase 'Riveted steel'. The beauty of the wood is evoked in the alliteration of 'turned timber'. The marvellous qualities of the wood are itemised with growing wonder: its shine ('burnish'), its pattern ('grain'). It is as if the worker and the poet are twirling the pitchfork round as they exclaim over its 'Smoothness, straightness, roundness, length and sheen'. This is more like the description one would give to a work of art or a thoroughbred animal than to a farm implement. The skill that went into the making of the pitchfork is now explored in a list of verbs beginning with the compound word 'Sweat-cured'. This **graphically shows the sheer physical exertion that went into making this instrument**, as it was 'sharpened, balanced, tested, fitted'. The tactile quality of the pitchfork is praised: 'The springiness, the clip and dart of it'. The worker, just like the athlete or warrior, tests his equipment. The feel of the pitchfork in the hand is given to the reader, due to the 'Sweat-cured' poet's sensitive and accurate observation and description.

In stanza four, the labourer imagines space 'probes' searching the galaxy, 'reached the farthest'. The long line stretches out in imitation of space, which pushes out to infinity. The pitchfork now becomes transformed into a spaceship, 'sailing past/Evenly, imperturbably through space'. This ordinary pitchfork now shines like the metal casing of a spaceship, 'starlit', and moves, like the spaceship, through the vastness of outer space, 'absolutely soundless'. Stanza five shows the poet becoming a mediator between different states, actual and imagined, ordinary and fantastical. He stands on a threshold, exploring and philosophising about the nature of his observation as a familiar thing grows stranger. Together (poet, worker and reader), all follow the line of the pitchfork to 'an other side', a place where 'perfection' is 'imagined'. Perfection does not exist in our world. But it is not the 'tightened' hand, which was 'aiming' at the beginning of the poem, which will achieve this ideal state, but the 'opening hand' of the last stanza. Is the poet suggesting we must be open and ready to receive in order to achieve 'perfection'? Heaney states: 'look at the familiar things you know. **Look at them with … a quality of concentration … you will be rewarded with insights and visions.**' The poet has become a seer.

ANALYSIS

'Heaney's poetry celebrates traditional crafts. Heaney himself is also a master craftsman of poetry.' Discuss this view of the poet using close reference to the poems of Heaney on your course.

SAMPLE PARAGRAPH

I read the description of the humble pitchfork, which became like some other strange item, as the poet Heaney lovingly described this farm implement in close detail: 'Riveted steel, turned timber'. The hard 't' sound emphasised the fact that this was no pretty ornament, but a man's working instrument which did serious manual work in the 'chaff and sweat'. I was impressed at how the poet gave due respect to the skill not only of the farm labourer who played 'the warrior or the athlete' with his pitchfork as a 'javelin', but also to the craftsman who made this pitchfork. He was the man whose skill 'sharpened, balanced, tested, fitted' it. It seems to me that Heaney is suggesting that the craftsman is producing wonderful items honed by his skill. This is similar to the poet who is producing a wonderful poem which reaches beyond to another plane, 'imagined perfection'. The poet, it seems to me, is achieving this through the vision of the pitchfork as a spaceship probing the huge sky, as it moves 'starlit and absolutely soundless'. Here indeed poetry is translating the ordinary into mystery, as the poet moves from detailed observation and description into the visionary state. The skilled craft of the poet transforms the pitchfork into the spacecraft. We experience its appearance ('Its prongs starlit') and its silence ('absolutely soundless'). The poet makes us see and hear this vision. The master craftsman is at work as both he and we soar 'imperturbably through space'.

EXAMINER'S COMMENT

The student shows a real personal engagement in this sustained response. There is a clear focus on the task and a succinct conclusion to the paragraph. Good use of well-integrated quotations. Grade A.

CLASS/HOMEWORK EXERCISES

1 'Heaney's language is both realistic and mystical.' Discuss this view of the poet's work, referring particularly to 'The Pitchfork'.
2 Copy the table below into your own notes and fill in critical comments about the last two quotations.

Key Quotes

It felt like a javelin, accurate and light	This simile effectively transforms the pitchfork into a powerful piece of sporting or fighting equipment.
tapering, dark-flecked ash	The vivid description of the pitchfork's slim handle appeals to our sense of sight. The compound word 'dark-flecked' is particularly evocative, as the repetition of 'k' suggests the small, intricate pattern of the wood.
The springiness, the clip and dart of it	In this tactile description, the poet enables the reader to feel the sensation of holding the pitchfork in his or her hand.
when he thought of probes	
Not in the aiming but the opening hand	

Lightenings viii

The annals say: when the monks of Clonmacnoise
Were all at prayers inside the oratory
A ship appeared above them in the air.

The anchor dragged along behind so deep
It hooked itself into the altar rails   5
And then, as the big hull rocked to a standstill,

A crewman shinned and grappled down the rope
And struggled to release it. But in vain.
'This man can't bear our life here and will drown,'

The abbot said, 'unless we help him.' So   10
They did, the freed ship sailed, and the man climbed back
Out of the marvellous as he had known it.

'out of the marvellous'

1 *annals*: monastic records.	2 *oratory*: place of prayer, small chapel.
1 *Clonmacnoise*: established in the sixth century, the monastery at Clonmacnoise was renowned as a centre of scholarship and spirituality.	7 *shinned*: climbed down, clambered.
	10 *abbot*: head of the monastery.

GLOSSARY

EXPLORATIONS

1 How is the surreal atmosphere conveyed in this poem? Quote in support of your response.

2 Choose one striking image from the poem and comment on its effectiveness.

3 In your view, what does the air-ship symbolise? Refer to the text in your answer.

STUDY NOTES

Written in four tercets (three-line stanzas), 'Lightenings viii' (from Seamus Heaney's 1991 collection, *Seeing Things*), tells a legendary story of a miraculous air-ship which once appeared to the monks at Clonmacnoise, Co. Offaly. Heaney has said: 'I was devoted to this poem because the crewman who appears is situated where every poet should be situated: between the ground of everyday experience and the airier realm of an imagined world.'

Heaney's matter-of-fact approach at the start of stanza one leads readers to expect a straightforward retelling of an incident recorded in the 'annals' of the monastery. The story's apparently scholarly source seems highly reliable. While they were at prayers, the monks looked up: 'A ship appeared above them in the air'. We assume that the oratory is open to the sky. The simplicity of the colloquial language, restrained tone and run-through lines all ease us into a **dreamlike world** where anything can happen. But as with all good narratives, the magic ship's sudden appearance raises many questions: Why is it there? Where has it come from? Is this strange story all a dream?

Then out of the air-ship came a massive anchor, which 'dragged along behind so deep' (stanza two) before lodging itself in the altar rails. The poet makes **effective choices in syntax (word order) and punctuation**, e.g. placing 'so deep' at the end of the line helps to emphasise the meaning. The moment when the ship shudders to a halt is skilfully caught in a carefully wrought image: 'as the big hull rocked to a standstill'.

A crewman clambered down the rope to try to release the anchor, but he is unsuccessful. Heaney chooses his words carefully: 'shinned', 'grappled', 'struggled' (stanza three) are all powerful verbs, helping to create a clear picture of the sailor's physical effort. The phrase 'But in vain' is separated from the rest of the line to emphasise the man's hopelessness. The contrasting worlds of magic and reality seem incompatible. Ironically, the story's turning point is the abbot's instant recognition that **the human, earthly atmosphere will be fatal to the visitor**: 'This man can't bear our life here and will drown'.

But a solution is at hand: 'unless we help him' (stanza four). The unconditional generosity of the monks comes naturally to them: 'So/They did'. The word 'So' creates a pause and uncertainty before the prompt, brief opening of the next line: 'They did'. When the anchor is eventually disentangled and 'the freed ship sailed', **the crewman will surely tell his travel companions about the strange beings he encountered** after he 'climbed back out of the marvellous as he had known it'. This last line is somewhat surprising and leaves the reader wondering – marvelling, even.

Heaney's poem certainly raises interesting questions, blurring the lines between reality and illusion, and challenging our ideas about human consciousness. **The story itself can be widely interpreted.** Is the ship a symbol of inspiration while the monks represent commitment and dedication? Presumably, as chroniclers of the annals (preserving texts on paper for posterity), they were not aware of the miracle of their own labours – crossing the barrier from the oral tradition to written records – which was to astonish the world in the forthcoming centuries and help spread human knowledge.

'Lightenings viii' is a beautiful poem that highlights the fact that **the ordinary and the miraculous are categories defined only by human perception.** For many readers, the boat serves as an abstract mirror image, reversing our usual way of seeing things. In Heaney's rich text, we discover that from the outsider's perspective, the truly marvellous consists not of the visionary or mystical experience, but of the seemingly ordinary experience.

ANALYSIS

What aspects of 'Lightenings viii' are typical of Heaney's distinctive poetry? Refer closely to the text in your answer.

SAMPLE PARAGRAPH

I found many parallels between 'Lightenings' and some of the other Heaney poems we studied. His writing style is direct and colloquial – and this is typical of him. His poetry is dramatic – populated with memorable characters – and this is also true of 'Lightenings'. He used simple images to describe the surreal scene where the monks imagine a vision of a flying ship hovering over their altar – 'the big hull rocked to a standstill'. 'The Forge' also deals with an imaginary vision – 'the dark' interior of the blacksmith's workshed. The religious references are present here as well in the image of the 'altar' where the blacksmith 'expends himself in shape and music'. I have also noticed how Heaney contrasts completely different moods in his poetry. In both 'A Constable Calls' and 'The Harvest Bow', he is inspired by moments of unspoken tension. Firstly, the poet is aware through 'small guilts' that his father might be arrested for breaking the law. In the second poem, the nervous silence between himself as a boy and his non-communicative father becomes the basis of poetry later on in his adult life. In 'Lightenings', the theme also centres around two distinct worlds – the mundane monks and the magical sailors. By contrasting the two, Heaney made me think about the way ordinary life, which we take for granted, could be seen from a very different point of view. In my opinion, 'Lightenings' is an unmistakable Heaney poem.

EXAMINER'S COMMENT

This is a fresh and focused response that addresses the question directly. A range of interesting comparisons is made with several other Heaney poems. References show good knowledge and personal engagement. Ideas are handled very effectively throughout. Grade A.

CLASS/HOMEWORK EXERCISES

1   In much of his poetry, Heaney quietly disturbs our complacent distinction between the visionary and the real. Discuss this view based on your study of 'Lightenings viii'. Support the points you make with reference to the text.
2   Copy the table below into your own notes and fill in critical comments about the last two quotations.

Key Quotes

The annals say	The poem begins on a scholarly note, establishing a serious, authoritative tone in advance of the fanciful story that follows. Is Heaney being playful?
A ship appeared above them in the air	Detached in prayer from the ordinary world, the monks live curious, visionary lives and would not be strangers to miracles.
the big hull rocked to a standstill	Broad assonant sounds suggest the enormous bulk of the ship, while the verb 'rocked' reflects its laden movement as it settles 'in the air'.
A crewman shinned and grappled down the rope	
the man climbed back/ Out of the marvellous	

Seamus Heaney

LEAVING CERT SAMPLE ESSAY

> **Q** **'Dear Seamus Heaney …'**
>
> **Write a letter to Seamus Heaney telling him how you responded to some of his poems on your course. Support the points you make by detailed reference to the poems you choose to write about.**

MARKING SCHEME GUIDELINES

Reward responses that show clear evidence of engagement with the poems and/or the poet. While a conversational approach is suggested by the question, expect and allow for a wide variety of approaches in candidates' answering. Candidates are obviously free to challenge and 'confront' the poet. Accept treatment of positive and negative aspects of Heaney's poetry.

Some of the following areas might be addressed:
- Powerful use of everyday language.
- Vividly detailed imagery.
- Poet's focus on memory, especially memories of childhood.
- Personal character of the writing.
- Political and social perspectives of the poems.
- Striking love poetry, etc.

SAMPLE ESSAY
(Letter to Seamus Heaney)

1 *Dear Seamus Heaney,*

I have been studying a selection of your poems for my Leaving Certificate, and I wanted to write to tell you what impact your poems had on a 17-year-old teenager.

2 *I was particularly struck by 'The Tollund Man'. It made me think about humanity and the stupid things we do. Using the man found in the bogland, you showed that humankind is still committing acts of needless violence. The graphic imagery and fragmented rhythm of the lines 'Tell-tale skin and teeth/Flecking the sleepers/Of four young brothers, trailed/For miles along the rails' contribute* to the shocking deed. You show how the innocent are affected by violence. You made the Tollund Man look like a martyr by creating a holy atmosphere: 'risk blasphemy', 'consecrate', 'pray'. I thought it was interesting how you told us that the bog (the Mother Goddess of the ground who needed bridegrooms) preserved him, 'Those dark juices working', as if he were a saint, 'a saint's kept body'.

3 I could really relate to this man's experience as a foreigner in a strange country. I was on an exchange to Germany, and I couldn't speak the language and so the phrase 'Watching the pointing hands/Of country people,/Not knowing their tongue' summed up the ordeal of 'them' and 'us'. I can imagine you driving along ('Saying the names'), as the Tollund Man was driven, calling out all the foreign names of places you both pass, almost like a litany of holy names, 'Tollund, Grabaulle, Nebelgard'. I can also understand how you, a Northern Irishman, would feel 'at home' in the 'man-killing parishes'. Both in Jutland and in Ireland, you remind us that man was sacrificed for a cause, a need of the community, whether it was the search for fertility or freedom.

4 Another poem that deals with the tensions in the North is 'A Constable Calls'. I found it interesting how you gave us the sketch of the character of the policeman from the details of his bicycle. The perception of an almost sinister hidden force of the Royal Ulster Constabulary is contained in the word 'cowl', a hood. It reminds me of the hoods of the Ku Klux Klan, or the hood worn by a hangman, or even some young teenagers, up to no good, in their 'hoodies'. The image of the 'boot of the law' reinforces this. The dynamo light 'cocked back' was the most threatening image of all for me. This was a tense society, as at any moment sectarian violence could erupt. The hard 'c' sounds reflect this.

5 I could see the awkwardness of his visit. He is not made welcome, as his cap was 'upside down/On the floor'. No one offered to take it. His 'slightly sweating hair' suggests the effort he is making, but there is no mention of anything to drink. You show the tense interrogation very effectively, in my opinion, as he snaps out four questions and what was the terse response? A curt, monosyllabic 'No' is the response from the father. You convey the full majesty of the law through the details of the policeman's equipment; 'the polished holster/With its buttoned flap' shows that the law was enforced, if need be, with violence.

6 The love poems are original and fresh. In 'The Skunk', I liked your descriptions of sounds ('Snuffing', 'whinnied'), smells ('Tang of eucalyptus'), and colour

('Small oranges loomed in the orange tree') of an exotic California. But in this paradise there is a flaw, the pain of loneliness, the elements of California merely pointing out what the poet is missing, 'spelt your absence'. Your powerful longing cannot even be dulled by drink, 'The aftermath of a mouthful of wine/Was like inhaling you off a cold pillow'. But love is rewarded, as you recall the 'sootfall' of your wife's things at bedtime. Usually love poetry is associated with young lovers, but you dared to talk about mature love's attractions, 'the black plunge-line nightdress'. The soft 's' and long vowel sound in 'sootfall' make me hear the whisper of silky garments sliding to the floor. I must say I think your wife has some sense of humour, and you are a very lucky man that she is not offended by the comparison of herself to a skunk, 'head-down, tail-up'. She is indeed a 'stored cask', as I think a sense of humour helps a person through the darkest times.

7 I found your poems honest, thought provoking, original and direct. Your choices of unusual associations made me look at some things in a new light. Thank you for the experience.

Yours sincerely,
Paul

(approx. 770 words)

GRADE: A1		
P	=	15/15
C	=	15/15
L	=	15/15
M	=	5/5
Total	=	50/50

EXAMINER'S COMMENT

A personal response that is focused and well supported. The candidate displays a clear knowledge of Heaney's work. In-depth discussion on a single poem is rewarded, as it fulfils the task set in the question. There is a good sense of appreciation of sound. Quotations are accurate and successfully integrated into the general commentary. Grade A.

SAMPLE LEAVING CERT QUESTIONS ON HEANEY'S POETRY (45–50 MINUTES)

1   'The subjects of Heaney's poems are treated with great love and sympathy together with a keen eye for significant detail.'
How true is this statement of the poems by Seamus Heaney that you have studied? Support your discussion with relevant references from the poems on your course.

2   'Sensuously evocative and rich in imagery' is a phrase used to describe the language of Seamus Heaney's poetry. Would you agree or disagree? Quote in support of your views from the prescribed poetry on your course.

3   'Heaney's poetry appeals to the modern reader for many reasons.' Write an essay in which you outline the reasons why the poems by Seamus Heaney you have studied have this wide appeal. Support your reasons with detailed references from your prescribed poems.

SAMPLE ESSAY PLAN (Q3)

'Heaney's poetry appeals to the modern reader for many reasons.' Write an essay in which you outline the reasons why the poems by Seamus Heaney you have studied have this wide appeal. Support your reasons with detailed references from your prescribed poems.

• *Intro*:	Heaney's use of vivid imagery, realistic detail, use of memory, universality of theme all appeal to the modern reader.
• *Point 1*:	'The Forge' – magical quality of blacksmith's work contained in appealing imagery; 'fantail of sparks', 'unicorn'. Today's reader enjoys the 'otherworld' quality.
• *Point 2*:	'Sunlight' – realistic detail conveys beloved Aunt Mary to the reader; 'measling shins', 'broad-lapped', etc. Homely image of scoop shows the depth of love, which is appealing.
• *Point 3*:	'A Constable Calls' – imagery conveys power and tension in this divided community. Interesting perspective given of recent Troubles in Northern Ireland.

- *Point 4*: 'The Harvest Bow' – Heaney's silent father is remembered in this intricately structured poem, which mirrors the skill used by his father in making the harvest bow. All readers are intrigued by family relationships.

- *Point 5*: 'Bogland' – Heaney shows us through his treatment of the bog the limitations and possibilities of dealing with our fractured past. History has never been so important as in the modern world. We run the risk that those who cannot remember the past are doomed to repeat it.

- *Conclusion*: Heaney is a great observer of ordinary lives/places, but he also forces his reader to consider wider issues that impact on their lives. This is the appeal of Heaney's poetry.

EXERCISE

Develop one of the above points into a paragraph.

CONCLUSION – SAMPLE PARAGRAPGH

I feel that Seamus Heaney speaks eloquently to the modern reader when he is drawing a picture of the wonderful serenity of the Mossbawn farmyard in the poem 'Sunlight', with its two ticking clocks of past and present time, his realistic imagery conveying the wonderful, modest love warming this place as the oven warms and bakes the bread. He clearly shows us the magic in homely skills such as those of the blacksmith ('The Forge'), or indeed of his father ('The Harvest Bow'), as he uses memory to get us to consider the present and the future. He bravely confronts the unpleasant in 'A Constable Calls'. The tension of the Catholic community is palpable in the description of the policeman's bicycle, appearance and behaviour. In 'Bogland' he uncovers the essence of the fluid bog, which holds and embraces the past. Here is a lesson for all of us, both from Heaney and the bog. How could Heaney, therefore, not appeal to the modern reader, as he conveys, remembers, reminds and teaches us with such skill?

EXAMINER'S COMMENT

As part of a full essay answer, the student has written a B grade paragraph and gives a summary of what has been dealt with in the main body of the essay. The concluding paragraph could have been improved with a quotation from either Heaney or a critic which makes a statement about poetry in general or Heaney's poetry in particular.

Last Words

'Heaney has an uncanny capacity to transform basic intuitions into universal insights'.
John McGurk

'He [Heaney] is proposing an idea of poetry which combines psychic investigation with historical inquiry.'
Elmer Andrews

'The best moments are those when your mind seems to implode and words and images rush of their own accord into the vortex.'
Seamus Heaney

'Poetry has to do with the reality of spirit.'

Patrick Kavanagh (1904–67)

Born in 1904 near Inniskeen, Co. Monaghan, in the shadow of Ulster's 'hungry hills', **Patrick Kavanagh** left school at the age of 13, apparently destined to plough the 'stony-grey soil' rather than write about it. But his interest in literature won out – 'I dabbled in verse,' he said, 'and it became my life.' Many of his poems celebrate the simple beauty and mystery of nature. In 1936, his first book of verse, *Ploughman and Other Poems*, was published, and in 1938 he followed this up with the autobiographical *The Green Fool*. For over 20 years, Kavanagh worked on the small family farm before moving to Dublin in 1939 to try and establish himself as a writer. However, Dublin's literary community saw him as a country farmer and cynics referred to him as 'That Monaghan Boy'. His epic poem, 'The Great Hunger', was published in 1942. Sombre, intense and emotive, it presented a disturbing view of rural poverty and repression. Kavanagh's reputation as a poet is based largely on the lyrical quality of his work, his mastery of language and form and his ability to transform the ordinary into something of significance. He is regarded by many as one of the most influential Irish poets, whose main achievement was to give an authentic voice to the peasant culture of rural Ireland during the insular de Valera era.

PRESCRIBED POEMS (HIGHER LEVEL)

1 'Inniskeen Road: July Evening' (p. 190)

This well-known sonnet focuses on Kavanagh's role as a poet and his relationship with the local rural community in Co. Monaghan.

2 'Shancoduff' (p. 194)

One of Kavanagh's favourite poems, it illustrates his poetic appreciation of the ordinary life of the Monaghan countryside.

3 *from* 'The Great Hunger' (p. 199)

This long, powerful piece traces the life and times of Patrick Maguire, an elderly bachelor farmer. Kavanagh's critical view of Irish rural society is grim and disturbing.

4 'Advent' (p. 207)

Originally titled 'Renewal', the poem uses a two-sonnet structure to explore Kavanagh's religious experience of the Advent season.

5 'A Christmas Childhood' (p. 212)

Kavanagh describes a memorable Christmas when he was six years old and recalls how his 'child poet' associated the occasion with the birth of Christ in Bethlehem.

6 'Epic' (p. 218)

Based on an actual dispute over a small area of land in Co. Monaghan, the poem addresses wider aspects of conflict and the theme of poetic inspiration.

7 'Canal Bank Walk' (p. 222)

Written after a lengthy stay in hospital, the poet is keen to enjoy the wonderful gifts of nature, poetry and the overwhelming experience of being alive.

8 'Lines Written on a Seat on the Grand Canal, Dublin' (p. 226)

Another sonnet expressing Kavanagh's wish to be commemorated in one of his favourite places. Characteristically, he celebrates the wonder and greatness of ordinary things.

9 'The Hospital' (p. 230)

After recovering from a serious illness, the poet considers his newfound appreciation of natural beauty and the mystery of life itself while time allows.

10 'On Raglan Road' (p. 234)

Set on the streets of Dublin, this bittersweet ballad of unrequited love reveals much that is of interest about Kavanagh's own personality.

Inniskeen Road: July Evening

Patrick Kavanagh

The bicycles go by in twos and threes –
There's a dance in Billy Brennan's barn tonight,
And there's the half-talk code of mysteries
And the wink-and-elbow language of delight.
Half-past eight and there is not a spot   5
Upon a mile of road, no shadow thrown
That might turn out a man or woman, not
A footfall tapping secrecies of stone.

I have what every poet hates in spite
Of all the solemn talk of contemplation.   10
Oh, Alexander Selkirk knew the plight
Of being king and government and nation.
A road, a mile of kingdom, I am king
Of banks and stones and every blooming thing.

'a mile of kingdom'

The townland of Mucker near
Inniskeen, Co. Monaghan was
Kavanagh's birthplace. He lived
there on the small family farm until
the late 1930s.

2 *Billy Brennan's barn*: a local
   farmhouse where country dances
   took place.

10 *solemn talk of contemplation*: poets
    regard themselves as deep thinkers.

11 *Alexander Selkirk*: famous Scottish
    sailor (1676–1721) marooned on
    an uninhabited Pacific island for
    five years. His experience was the
    model for Daniel Defoe's novel,
    Robinson Crusoe.

14 *blooming*: flowering; also a
    colloquial expletive for impatience.

EXPLORATIONS

1   There is a lively mood of excitement in the poem's opening lines. How does Kavanagh's use of language achieve this effect?

2   Comment on the effectiveness of the comparison with Alexander Selkirk.

3   In your opinion, what are the feelings expressed by Kavanagh in the last two lines of the poem?

STUDY NOTES

Taken from Kavanagh's first collection, *Ploughman and Other Poems*, this sonnet provides an interesting presentation of the poet's relationship with nature and the local community as well as providing a glimpse of Irish rural life in the 1930s. Kavanagh's dual role – as both a member of and a commentator on society – is succinctly dramatised. The octave (first eight lines) focuses on the local environment, while the sestet (final six lines) sums up Kavanagh's own reflections on his life as a poet.

Lines 1–2 set the scene as young people from Kavanagh's parish make their way to the local dance. **Colloquial language and energetic rhythms echo everyday speech**: 'There's a dance in Billy Brennan's barn tonight'. The alliterative 'b' sound and use of the present tense add to the mood of lively anticipation. Kavanagh's diction becomes more poetic in lines 3–4 as he makes a sceptical observation about 'the half-talk code of mysteries/And the wink-and-elbow language of delight'. In distancing himself from the groups cycling to the dance, the poet emphasises his own sense of exclusion. Examine the tone Kavanagh uses – is it ironic, cynical, superior, self-pitying? It's difficult to know if he is enjoying the excited gestures of the carefree passers-by or if he is envious of them – or both.

The social atmosphere and relaxed camaraderie of the opening quatrain is followed by a more **reflective commentary** in lines 5–8. Left alone on the roadside, Kavanagh is drawn by the intense solitude ('no shadow thrown') of his surroundings. There is a certain poignancy to his loneliness, especially since he seems all too aware of the nature of his isolation. But although the poet is detached from human company ('man or woman'), he has the comfort of being close to nature – the 'secrecies of stone'. Of course, the secrets are never disclosed. Is Kavanagh thinking about the wonders of the natural world or the secret lives of the young dance-goers? Or even of his own poetic imagination? We can only guess. At any rate, the slower pace of this second quatrain, combined with the broad vowel assonance, contribute much to the pensive tone and mood of bittersweet alienation.

The sestet offers the poet's own explanation for most of the questions raised in the opening eight lines. Addressing the reader directly, Kavanagh outlines the reality of what it means to be a poet – and for him it is a **double-edged sword**. He 'hates' the popular perception that poets are introspective philosophers constantly immersed in serious 'contemplation'. In **line 11**, he compares himself to the marooned sailor, Alexander Selkirk. While the reference seems to be only half-serious, it serves to highlight the artist's role and relationship with society. Writing is a solitary occupation (a 'plight'), but it also guarantees the freedom and independence 'Of being king and government and nation'.

The ironic tone of **lines 13–14** reminds readers of the **contradictions of the poet's life**. As the self-styled 'king' of 'every blooming thing', Kavanagh illustrates the contradictory aspects of a literary life. The pun on 'blooming' underlines both the positive and negative sides of being a writer. Kavanagh may be somewhat removed from his own community, but he is gifted with a creative imagination which allows him to appreciate the wonders of nature.

ANALYSIS

From your reading of 'Inniskeen Road: July Evening', what do you learn about Kavanagh himself? Refer to the text in your answer.

SAMPLE PARAGRAPH

Kavanagh strikes me as a highly intelligent person and a shrewd judge. He understands his own life as a working writer and that he is different to his peer group, the other young men in his area. At the beginning, he sees himself as a loner, an outsider. His friends pass him by 'in twos and threes'. I think Kavanagh knows well that he is different and he admits that he is outside the circle, cut off from what he calls 'the wink-and-elbow language of delight'. But he acknowledges that this is the price a poet must pay. He is an observer and he seems to almost enjoy being unlike the others. He has special status. At the same time, he is honest enough to admit that it is a lonely life. He is like the great explorer Alexander Selkirk who was abandoned on a desert island. The ending of the poem tells me most about Kavanagh. He seems resigned to his 'plight' because he is at one with nature. In fact he jokes that he is 'king/Of banks and stones and every blooming thing'. I find the tone of this to be good-humoured and proof that he was happy enough with the simple joys of Inniskeen. He has come to terms with his loneliness and is really making the most of his life even though it isn't perfect.

EXAMINER'S COMMENT

This is a clear, well-sustained response that ranges over the text in search of appropriate evidence about the poet's personality. There is some good personal engagement and a lively style throughout. A little more thorough analysis would have raised the standard above a basic B grade.

CLASS/HOMEWORK EXERCISES

1 One literary critic described 'Inniskeen Road: July Evening' as 'a love poem to a place, written towards the end of the affair'. Write your response to this comment, using close reference to the text of the poem.
2 Copy the table below into your own notes and fill in critical comments about the last two quotations.

Key Quotes

The bicycles go by in twos and threes	Kavanagh conveys a sense of excitement through the use of colloquial language and alliteration.
A footfall tapping secrecies of stone	While the phrase suggests Kavanagh's isolation, it also highlights his poetic imagination.
Of all the solemn talk of contemplation	Kavanagh's self-deprecating tone reflects his mock-serious attitude to the myth that poets are moody intellectuals who enjoy their own company.
the half-talk code of mysteries	
A road, a mile of kingdom	

Shancoduff

My black hills have never seen the sun rising,
Eternally they look north towards Armagh.
Lot's wife would not be salt if she had been
Incurious as my black hills that are happy
When dawn whitens Glassdrummond chapel.   5

My hills hoard the bright shillings of March
While the sun searches in every pocket.
They are my Alps and I have climbed the Matterhorn
With a sheaf of hay for three perishing calves
In the field under the Big Forth of Rocksavage.   10

The sleety winds fondle the rushy beards of Shancoduff
While the cattle-drovers sheltering in the Featherna Bush
Look up and say: 'Who owns them hungry hills
That the water-hen and snipe must have forsaken?
A poet? Then by heavens he must be poor'.   15
I hear and is my heart not badly shaken?

'My black hills have never seen the sun rising'

Shancoduff: Old Black Hollow, from the Irish words '*sean*' (old) and '*dubh*' (black).

3 *Lot's wife*: reference to the Bible story where the wife of Lot was turned into a pillar of salt for disobeying God.

6 *shillings*: small silver coins from old Irish currency.

8 *Matterhorn*: the highest peak of the Alps, a mountain range in Switzerland.

11 *sleety*: icy rain.

14 *snipe*: marshland bird.

EXPLORATIONS

1 There are two distinct views of Shancoduff. Who holds these opposing views and why do you think they are different? Refer to the poem in your answer.

2 What effect does the naming of local places have on the poem? What does it tell you about Kavanagh and his relationship with Shancoduff?

3 What evidence is there of Kavanagh's self-deprecating humour in this poem? Why do you think he uses this?

STUDY NOTES

Kavanagh had a love–hate relationship with the place he grew up in, Inniskeen. Shancoduff, a north-facing hill, is shown in winter. Kavanagh's family had bought a small farm there, not far from his home. His brother, Peter, said Kavanagh regarded it as 'wonderland'. The view stretched 15 miles to the Mourne Mountains.

Like an indulgent lover, Kavanagh turns the negatives of this hostile place into positives, just as a lover refuses to see bad in his loved one. The hills may be drab and 'Incurious' and mean (they 'hoard'), but they are his. The ownership is stressed in the protective, possessive adjective 'My': 'My black hills', 'My hills', 'my Alps'. He recognises that the land will remain 'Eternally' while the people come and go.

He personifies this land with verbs and adjectives: 'look', 'Incurious', 'happy', 'hoard'. Kavanagh loves the local. He sees magic here as he describes dawn breaking over the little country church in line 5: 'dawn whitens Glassdrummond chapel'. The place becomes luminous and radiant. These hills can't be bothered to look at the sun; 'they look north'. The poet turns their lack of curiosity into a positive, saying look at what happened to Lot's wife for her curiosity – she looked at a forbidden sight, the destruction of the sinning cities Sodom and Gomorrah, and was turned into a pillar of salt. Kavanagh, like his hills, also turned his face, refusing to accept the literary scene in Dublin.

The **litany of place names**, rather like the proud parent naming the names of her children or the naming of saints in a religious ceremony, is a feature of Kavanagh's poetry, and points to the pride he had in Shancoduff. To him, these hills were as important and as impressive as the Alps, the famous mountain range in Switzerland. The polysyllabic sounds of these place names are masculine, tough, threatening, full of the fierce pride of a border place as they stand like heroes in an old film, surveying all before them. An ordinary act of feeding the calves becomes a heroic feat in this place in **line 8**: 'I have climbed the Matterhorn'. This is an example of Kavanagh's use of **hyperbole**. These hills are rebellious; they won't follow the rhythm of nature, they don't change in tune with the seasons. Like misers, they 'hoard' the bright pockets of ice and snow while the sun desperately tries to thaw the land, as it is springtime. The exasperation of the sun's effort is vividly caught in the description of the sun searching the pockets of the hills. These miserly hills won't give up their 'shillings', yet Kavanagh praises their thriftiness.

The tenderness of the lover is caught in the verb 'fondle', as Kavanagh again personifies this bleak place in **line 11**: the 'rushy beards of Shancoduff'. But **a negative note is struck as the drovers and farmers sneer** at 'them hungry hills'. They look dispassionately at this place, as the hills won't produce. The use of direct speech brings the conflict flickering into life, as they criticise not only the land but the profession of the owner, 'a poet'. To these men, he must be mad. **The rhetorical question at the end shows the poet's devastation at this criticism**, rather like a lover being made to face the reality that his loved one is ugly. Reality, like the biting winds, is piercing the poet's illusions: 'I hear and is my heart not badly shaken?' Is it the lack of potential for farming or the fear that these hills will not provide sufficient creative stimulus that leaves the poet 'badly shaken'? Whatever the answer, these places pushed Irish poetry into a new direction, showing that an emphasis on the ordinary (and even banal) is a worthwhile subject for poetry.

ANALYSIS

'The relationship between place and person is central to the poetry of Patrick Kavanagh.' Discuss this statement in relation to the poem 'Shancoduff'.

SAMPLE PARAGRAPH

Although Kavanagh has a love–hate relationship with his birthplace, Inniskeen, it is this very conflict that inspired Kavanagh to write. At this time, in the 1930s and 1940s in rural Ireland, the poet was looked at as someone strange and odd. He didn't quite fit into the rural scene. We hear this in the direct speech, in this poem, of the cattle-drovers, as they looked disparagingly at the bleak hill of Shancoduff and its owner. 'Who owns them hungry hills ... A poet?' They speak as if he wouldn't know what to do with the land. This criticism stung Kavanagh: 'I hear and is my heart not badly shaken?' To him, Shancoduff was a magical place, a 'wonderland', his brother tells us. This protective attitude of a caring lover, the poet, is evident in the repetition of the possessive adjective 'my'. He excuses all faults of the loved one; he thinks it is good that the hills are 'Incurious'. He feels they are happy once they see the chapel of Glassdrummond shining incandescently in the dawn light. They don't have to see the sun. He even delights in the miserliness of the hills that won't give up the last patches of ice that the sun is frantically trying to thaw: 'the sun searches in every pocket'. The love he has for the place is evident as we see the importance he places on the poor little hill, 'my Alps'. A common event is transformed into something heroic because it takes place there. Feeding the 'shivering' calves is now 'I have climbed the Matterhorn', the most dangerous peak in the Alps. Shancoduff is not beautiful, with its 'rushy beards', but to the poet, it is. So he imagines the sleety winds 'fondle' the small hill. This poem is firmly rooted in the harsh countryside of Monaghan, and this place is firmly rooted in Kavanagh's heart. Under the poet's loving gaze, this ordinary hill has become extraordinary.

EXAMINER'S COMMENT

A sensitive reading of the poem. A grade standard, strongly supported throughout with relevant quotations. The candidate has discussed the importance of this place to the poet, and has therefore fulfilled the required task.

CLASS/HOMEWORK EXERCISES

1   Would you consider the poetry of Kavanagh to be the poetry of 'rediscovery and celebration'? Discuss this statement in relation to the poem 'Shancoduff'.
2   Copy the table below into your own notes and fill in critical comments about the last two quotations.

Patrick Kavanagh

Key Quotes

My black hills have never seen the sun rising	Shancoduff faces north and the sun rises in the east, so the hills only see the reflection of the dawn.
My hills hoard the bright shillings of March	Ironically, Kavanagh uses the metaphor of miserliness to show his delight in the beauty of the season.
They are my Alps	These hills are as important to Kavanagh as the great mountain ranges of Europe.
The sleety winds fondle the rushy beards of Shancoduff	
I hear and is my heart not badly shaken?	

from **The Great Hunger**

Clay is the word and clay is the flesh
Where the potato-gatherers like mechanized scare-crows move
Along the side-fall of the hill – Maguire and his men.
If we watch them an hour is there anything we can prove
Of life as it is broken-backed over the Book   5
Of Death? Here crows gabble over worms and frogs
And the gulls like old newspapers are blown clear of the hedges,
    luckily.
Is there some light of imagination in these wet clods?
Or why do we stand here shivering?
                                    Which of these men   10
Loved the light and the queen
Too long Virgin? Yesterday was summer. Who was it promised
    marriage to himself
Before apples were hung from the ceilings for Hallowe'en?
We will wait and watch the tragedy to the last curtain,
Till the last soul passively like a bag of wet clay   15
Rolls down the side of the hill, diverted by the angles
Where the plough missed or a spade stands, straitening the way.

A dog lying on a torn jacket under a heeled-up cart,
A horse nosing along the posied headland, trailing
A rusty plough. Three heads hanging between wide-apart   20
Legs. October playing a symphony on a slack wire paling.
Maguire watches the drills flattened out
And the flints that lit a candle for him on a June altar
Flameless. The drills slipped by and the days slipped by
And he trembled his head away and ran free from the world's
    halter,   25
And thought himself wiser than any man in the townland
When he laughed over pints of porter
Of how he came free from every net spread
In the gaps of experience. He shook a knowing head
And pretended to his soul   30
That children are tedious in hurrying fields of April
Where men are spanging across wide furrows,
Lost in the passion that never needs a wife –
The pricks that pricked were the pointed pins of harrows.

Children scream so loud that the crows could bring   35
The seed of an acre away with crow-rude jeers.
Patrick Maguire, he called his dog and he flung a stone in the air
And hallooed the birds away that were the birds of the years.
Turn over the weedy clods and tease out the tangled skeins.
What is he looking for there?   40
He thinks it is a potato, but we know better
Than his mud-gloved fingers probe in this insensitive hair.

'Move forward the basket and balance it steady
In this hollow. Pull down the shafts of that cart, Joe,
And straddle the horse,' Maguire calls.   45
'The wind's over Brannagan's, now that means rain.
Graip up some withered stalks and see that no potato falls
Over the tail-board going down the ruckety pass –
And *that's* a job we'll have to do in December,
Gravel it and build a kerb on the bog-side. Is that Cassidy's ass   50
Out in my clover? Curse o' God –
Where is that dog?
Never where he's wanted.' Maguire grunts and spits
Through a clay-wattled moustache and stares about him from the
    height.
His dream changes like the cloud-swung wind   55
And he is not so sure now if his mother was right
When she praised the man who made a field his bride.

Watch him, watch him, that man on a hill whose spirit
Is a wet sack flapping about the knees of time.
He lives that his little fields may stay fertile when his own body 60
Is spread in the bottom of a ditch under two coulters crossed in
    Christ's Name.

He was suspicious in his youth as a rat near strange bread
When girls laughed; when they screamed he knew that meant
The cry of fillies in season. He could not walk
The easy road to his destiny. He dreamt   65
The innocence of young brambles to hooked treachery.
O the grip. O the grip of irregular fields! No man escapes.
It could not be that back of the hills love was free
And ditches straight.

No monster hand lifted up children and put down apes   70
As here.
                              'O God if I had been wiser!'
That was his sigh like the brown breeze in the thistles.
He looks towards his house and haggard. 'O God if I had been
    wiser!'
But now a crumpled leaf from the whitethorn bushes   75
Darts like a frightened robin, and the fence
Shows the green of after-grass through a little window,
And he knows that his own heart is calling his mother a liar.
God's truth is life – even the grotesque shapes of its foulest fire.

The horse lifts its head and cranes   80
Through the whins and stones
To lip late passion in the crawling clover.
In the gap there's a bush weighted with boulders like morality,
The fools of life bleed if they climb over.

The wind leans from Brady's, and the coltsfoot leaves are holed
    with rust,   85
Rain fills the cart-tracks and the sole-plate grooves;
A yellow sun reflects in Donaghmoyne
The poignant light in puddles shaped by hooves.

Come with me, Imagination, into this iron house
And we will watch from the doorway the years run back,   90
And we will know what a peasant's left hand wrote on the page.
Be easy, October. No cackle hen, horse neigh, tree sough, duck
    quack.

'The drills slipped by and the days
                slipped by'

Patrick Kavanagh

The 'Great Hunger' was a common name for the 1840s famine. Kavanagh used the term symbolically to refer to the hunger for fulfilment and satisfactory relationships.

1 *Clay is the word*: the phrase echoes the biblical account of creation: 'In the beginning was the Word'.

6 *gabble*: cry, squabble noisily.

11–12 *the queen ... Virgin*: the poet personifies the barren farmland.

18 *heeled-up*: upended.

22 *drills*: ploughed potato rows.

25 *halter*: restraint for controlling a horse.

32 *spanging*: jumping; striding.

34 *harrows*: ploughing implements.

39 *skeins*: root strands.

47 *Graip*: dig with a small fork.

48 *ruckety*: uneven.

54 *clay-wattled*: soiled; unclean.

59 *a wet sack*: used by farmers to keep their clothes dry.

61 *coulters*: plough blades.

73 *haggard*: storage area for fodder.

85 *coltsfoot*: creeping yellow weed.

86 *sole-plate*: horseshoe; underside of farm implement.

87 *Donaghmoyne*: parish near Inniskeen.

91 *what a peasant's left hand wrote*: probably refers to Kavanagh himself as the authentic voice of rural Ireland.

92 *sough*: sigh.

EXPLORATIONS

1 What impression of Maguire and his men do you get from lines 1–9 of the poem? Refer to the text in your answer.

2 Describe the mood in the last eight lines of the poem. How does Kavanagh create this mood?

3 In your view, how effective is Kavanagh's description of rural Ireland? Refer closely to the poem in your answer.

STUDY NOTES

'The Great Hunger' was written in 1942 when Kavanagh was living in Dublin. This epic narrative reveals the harsh realities of rural Irish life and focuses primarily on one character's relationship with the land. The poem also explores the effects of grinding poverty and sexual inhibition. Kavanagh challenges the romantic notion of the happy-go-lucky peasant that had been promoted elsewhere in Ireland's literary tradition. Throughout the poem, Kavanagh uses a narrator to present Patrick Maguire and to link key scenes in the character's unfulfilled life.

The extract's opening section (lines 1–17) portrays Patrick Maguire and his farm labourers in their natural element – 'Along the side-fall of the hill'. The sluggish rhythm and mock-serious biblical tone ('Clay is the word and clay is the flesh') reflect the helplessness of these men who are, in every sense, stuck in the mud. They are depicted as less than human, 'like mechanized scare-crows', in a **relentlessly desolate setting**. This hostile environment of 'wet clods' has left them 'broken-backed'. Kavanagh's imagery suggests a primitive world where 'crows gabble over worms and frogs'. The narrative voice informs us of the emptiness of life here and invites us to observe Maguire's 'tragedy to the last curtain'. Particular emphasis is placed on loneliness and sexual longing ('Who was it promised marriage to himself'). Forlorn rhetorical questions echo the men's deep feelings of regret. Their despair is succinctly expressed in the evocative sentence 'Yesterday was summer', a devastatingly bleak acceptance of lost opportunity.

Immediately following this prologue to Maguire's story, lines 18–38 include several **images of failure**: 'a torn jacket', a 'rusty plough', a 'Flameless' candle. Although the sexual allusions are somewhat overstated, Maguire's frustration is still as pitiful as it is easy to mock. Kavanagh's extended lines, delivered largely at a plodding pace, suggest a monotonous existence: 'The drills slipped by and the days slipped by'. Yet despite being tied down like a tethered horse, Maguire deludes himself that he is happy and considers himself 'wiser than any man in the townland'. He even sneers at family life ('children are tedious'), but it is all pretence, as much of an empty act of bravado as his vain gesture when he 'flung a stone in the air' to scare away 'the birds of the years'.

The narrator's attitude to Maguire is somewhat ambivalent: it is seemingly sympathetic and yet highly critical at times. Consider, for instance, the tone of line 41: 'He thinks it is a potato, but we know better'. Is the voice superior and patronising, or sincere and understanding? Maguire speaks for himself in lines 43–57 and confirms our initial impressions of a boorish man whose entire life revolves around farming. His curt utterances reflect the realistic rhythms of country life: 'Pull down the shafts of that cart'. This picture of a rough, hard-working farmer who 'grunts and spits' is convincingly constructed. But **Kavanagh also explores Maguire's secret life**. Deep down, the ageing bachelor is plagued by doubts about the sacrifices he has made for the sake of the land and 'is not so sure now if his mother was right/When she praised the man who made a field his bride'. While the brooding introspection is not completely unexpected, it is nonetheless a compelling expression of the human tragedy that affected an entire generation of men like Patrick Maguire.

The softer tone of narrative comment in lines 58–61 is in keeping with Kavanagh's essential sympathy for **people whose emotional, sexual and spiritual needs were being stifled**. Maguire's depressed spirit is compared to 'a wet sack flapping about the knees of time'. The metaphor conveys a disconcerting sense of the ageing farmer's futile struggle. Ironically, he will give up his own happiness so that 'his little fields may stay fertile'. Such a sacrifice is hardly glorious. The image of Maguire's corpse buried 'under two coulters crossed in Christ's Name' provides a final symbol of depression. Throughout much of this section, Kavanagh controls the rhythm carefully, maintaining a funereal pace in line with the poem's sombre atmosphere.

Lines 62–79 take us back to Maguire's youthful years, a time of embarrassment and confusion which he has come to regret: 'O God if I had been wiser!' The poet's negative language ('suspicious', 'treachery', 'irregular', 'frightened') underlines a scathing **tone of bitter recrimination**. Repetition and the use of exclamations add to the feeling of resentment towards an earlier culture of ignorance and insensitivity: 'O the grip. O the grip of irregular fields!' Images of 'a crumpled leaf' and 'a frightened robin' symbolise the powerlessness of young people growing up in a narrow-minded era of deprivation.

Maguire again singles out one person for particular attention: 'And he knows that his own heart is calling his mother a liar'. **Kavanagh is probably using the figure of the Irish mother to represent powerful institutions of official Ireland that he was critical of,** such as the Catholic Church, the family and the country's education system. The poet's message could not be more lucid. For Kavanagh, Irish society's traditional repression of human sexuality was a denial that 'God's truth is life – even the grotesque shapes of its foulest fire'.

Lines 80–87 include a number of natural images from the familiar Irish landscape. **The poet's cinematic technique is atmospheric,** creating a mood of yearning and endurance, evoked by glimpses of the 'poignant light' of a 'yellow sun'. Despite the pervading sense of despondency, there is a recognition of the timeless beauty that typifies Kavanagh's sense of place. In lines 89–92, readers are asked to use their imaginations to watch 'the years run back' on Patrick Maguire's sullen life. The final hushed tone is reassuringly lyrical, echoing the voice of an elderly man at work on his farm: 'Be easy, October. No cackle hen, horse neigh'. The scene is set for the rest of Maguire's tragic story.

ANALYSIS

How effective is Kavanagh's portrayal of Irish rural society in Part I of 'The Great Hunger'? Refer to the text of the poem in your answer.

SAMPLE PARAGRAPH

Of the Kavanagh poems I have studied, the extract from 'The Great Hunger' gave me the best insight into what Irish rural life was like during the early decades of the twentieth century. The first word in the poem is 'Clay'. It sets the downbeat tone simply and directly. 'Clay is the word and clay is the flesh' told me that Kavanagh saw farm work almost as a type of religion. His central character is Patrick Maguire, a mature farmer who has never married. Maguire was typical of tens of thousands of lonely bachelors who gave their lives to the land in the 'hungry' 1930s and 1940s. The poet really brought Maguire to life for me and I imagined him as a grumpy workaholic who lived and breathed farming. He 'grunts and spits' and puts on an act in public that he is content with his lonely life. I disliked him as a character, but also felt sorry for him. The very fact that I took Maguire seriously at all is proof of how convincing a portrait Kavanagh created. The poet's detailed description is dramatic and very effective. Maguire and his men work like 'mechanized scare-crows'. Maguire laughs 'over pints of porter'. But it's all false. Kavanagh lets us hear Maguire's own sad voice, saying, 'O God if I had been wiser'. By the end of the poem, it's clear that he really is desperately lonely, filled with regret and anger because of his wasted life. He calls his mother 'a liar' and resents the waste of his youth. Kavanagh fills the poem with powerful images of decay: 'weedy clods', 'whins and stone', a 'rusty plough'. To me these create an atmosphere of a rural Ireland that was failing and depressed. It is a negative picture, but a very compelling one.

EXAMINER'S COMMENT

This is a successful individual response that shows clear engagement with the poem. The answer remains focused on the question throughout. Discussion points are well supported with references and short quotations. Grade A.

CLASS/HOMEWORK EXERCISES

1 In your view, does the poet feel sympathy for Maguire? Refer closely to the text of the poem in your answer.
2 Copy the table below into your own notes and fill in critical comments about the last two quotations.

Patrick Kavanagh

Key Quotes

life as it is broken-backed	Kavanagh's vivid physical image describes the bent-over potato-gatherers at work while also symbolising their oppressed lives.
'O God if I had been wiser!'	Maguire's mantra is poignant and pathetic, a searing indictment of a heartbreaking waste of human life.
we will know what a peasant's left hand wrote	The poet's individual account of Maguire's brutalised life will expose the truth about the effects of frustration and lack of fulfilment.
He was suspicious in his youth as a rat near strange bread/When girls laughed	
And he knows that his own heart is calling his mother a liar	

Advent

We have tested and tasted too much, lover—
Through a chink too wide there comes in no wonder.
But here in this Advent-darkened room
Where the dry black bread and the sugarless tea
Of penance will charm back the luxury   5
Of a child's soul, we'll return to Doom
The knowledge we stole but could not use.

And the newness that was in every stale thing
When we looked at it as children: the spirit-shocking
Wonder in a black slanting Ulster hill   10
Or the prophetic astonishment in the tedious talking
Of an old fool will awake for us and bring
You and me to the yard gate to watch the whins
And the bog-holes, cart-tracks, old stables where Time begins.

O after Christmas we'll have no need to go searching   15
For the difference that sets an old phrase burning—
We'll hear it in the whispered argument of a churning
Or in the streets where the village boys are lurching.
And we'll hear it among simple decent men too
Who barrow dung in gardens under trees,   20
Wherever life pours ordinary plenty.
Won't we be rich, my love and I, and please
God we shall not ask for reason's payment,
The why of heart-breaking strangeness in dreeping hedges
Nor analyse God's breath in common statement.   25
We have thrown into the dust-bin the clay-minted wages
Of pleasure, knowledge and the conscious hour—
And Christ comes with a January flower.

'The why of heart-breaking strangeness in dreeping hedges'

Patrick Kavanagh

Advent: the four weeks before Christmas, which in Kavanagh's time was a period of penance and fasting in preparation for the coming of Christ.

1 *lover*: soul; spiritual self.

4 *dry black bread*: eaten during Advent penance.

6 *we'll return to Doom*: we will discard as useless.

13 *whins*: furze/gorse bushes.

14 *Time begins*: after the birth of Christ, the calendar was changed and BC became AD.

16 *difference ... burning*: allows us to see wisdom in an old saying.

17 *churning*: cream is stirred and turned until butter is made.

23 *reason's payment*: rational explanation.

24 *dreeping*: dripping.

26 *clay-minted wages*: useless payment.

28 *January flower*: symbol of the return of innocence.

EXPLORATIONS

1 In the first stanza, the poet wishes to leave the world of adult experience and return to a world of childhood innocence. How do you interpret the phrase 'the luxury/Of a child's soul'?

2 Why does Kavanagh consider 'wonder' and 'astonishment' to be so important? What is the opposite of these? Why does he dislike the opposite?

3 Which vivid detail strikes you most in the second sonnet, lines 15–28? Why does this detail appeal to you?

STUDY NOTES

This poem was first published on Christmas Eve 1942 in *The Irish Times* and was originally called 'Renewal'. It concerns Kavanagh's early years in Dublin. He was a man of little formal education, as he had left school at 13 to work the land, and here he is remaking his soul and announcing, in these two sonnets, that he is a poet of wonder. He finds that in order to go on, he must go back.

The sound of **world-weary, jaded senses** are vividly caught in the first sonnet's opening: 'We have tested and tasted too much'. The hard repetitive 't' sound and the use of the past tense capture the empty round of excess partying and too much drink. The reference to 'lover' suggests an intimate presence in the poet's life, whether a friend or his spiritual self. He has done too much, seen too much. He longs for the simple life. The poem is set in Advent, the four weeks prior to Christmas. This was a time of self-denial when people fasted and did penance to purify themselves in readiness for the coming of Christ at Christmas. They denied themselves sugar and butter as a penance ('dry black bread and the sugarless tea'). The short, gloomy evenings of winter are shown in the phrase 'Advent-darkened room'.

Kavanagh has written that 'revelations come as an aside'. Here, the 'chink' offers a tantalising glimpse into another mysterious world. He is saying that when everything is laid out in front of you, there is no desire for it. **This is what he doesn't want**. What he does want is the 'luxury/Of a child's soul'. The ability to look at things with breathless curiosity and awestruck wonder is what he desires now. He has experienced much, but like Adam and Eve in the Garden of Eden, he has knowledge that he cannot use. He wants to return it 'to Doom'. Innocence has gone and knowing is worthless.

In the next seven lines, **the poet tells us what he wants**, using a striking paradox: 'the newness that was in every stale thing'. **He wants to look again at the world through the eyes of a child** so that his soul can be shocked by an experience: 'the spirit-shocking/Wonder in a black slanting Ulster hill'. As a child, he could see the menacing threat in the dark hill silhouetted against the dying light of the sky. Paradoxes graphically show this poetic rebirth so that listening to a repetitive old man becomes a source of childish surprise, rather than the cynical reaction of an adult that this talking is boring. The sonnet concludes with a wonderful image of 'You and me' leaning over a gate, waiting, observing and realising that in the most ordinary things lies the extraordinary. An old stable was where Christ was born and time was refigured.

In the second sonnet, the tense now moves to the future as he imagines with the expressive, heartfelt 'O' what will happen if he opens himself up to experiencing the **'ordinary plenty'**. He will understand the wisdom in an old saying, 'the difference that sets an old phrase burning'. The onomatopoeia allows us to hear it, along with the poet, in the line 'We'll hear it in the whispered argument of a churning'. The simple sights of corner boys and men tending their gardens are all shown to be where life is pouring out its riches. The intimate tone of the poet continues in the phrase 'Won't we be rich, my love and I' as he asks us **not to over-analyse, but rather experience**.

The beauty of a damp December evening on a remote Irish road is shown vividly in the 'heart-breaking strangeness of dreeping hedges'. Kavanagh coins a new word, 'dreeping', to convey the saturated weight of water on the hedgerow. But we are not to ask 'The why'. Our language ('common statement') is not adequate enough to comprehend 'God's breath'. Instead, we will discard what is useless, 'the clay-minted wages' of the senses, 'pleasure, knowledge'. We will leave aside knowingness, 'the conscious hour'. The second sonnet concludes in the present tense with the birth of Christ: 'And Christ comes with a January flower'. The innocence of childhood and purity has been regained and the creative impulse is in full bloom.

ANALYSIS

The original title of this poem was 'Renewal'. What type of renewal was Kavanagh seeking and why? Support your response with quotation from the poem.

SAMPLE PARAGRAPH

Kavanagh moved to Dublin, after 30 years spent in Monaghan, and he described it as the 'worst mistake of my life'. He was uneducated and was called, disparagingly, 'The Monaghan Boy' by the literati of the day in Dublin. He overindulged and felt empty and as if he had betrayed what was good and special about himself. This is why the poem begins with its tired, jaded phrase, recognising, almost as if at an AA meeting, the real truth, 'We have tested too much, lover'. He needed to go back to go forward. He needed to recapture the innocent eye of childhood, 'the luxury/Of a child's soul', so that he could experience the world without asking for 'reason's payment'. He wants to be moved, 'spirit-shocking', 'astonished'. He doesn't want to know things and be aware, 'knowledge and the knowing hour'. He looks forward to a rebirth, just as the people of his time purified themselves so that they were worthy to receive the sacraments on Christmas Day. The enjambment adds to the air of excitement in this process of renewal. The shining simplicity of the last line, 'And Christ comes with a January flower', with its use of the present tense, suggests that Kavanagh has realised this rebirth, from the cynical excesses of the pleasures of the flesh and the intellect, to the more mysterious gifts of the imagination and creative impulse. The use of the first person plural 'We' and the phrase 'You and I' include the reader in this journey towards rebirth, and the genius of Kavanagh allows us to see what he saw, the 'dreeping' hedges, and hear what he heard, 'whispered arguments of churning'. This enables us to share in this rebirth and renewal.

EXAMINER'S COMMENT

This answer has responded in a clear way to the task of exploring what renewal meant for the poet. The answer focused less on why this was important to Kavanagh. There were also some misquotes. Overall, a solid B grade performance.

CLASS/HOMEWORK EXERCISES

1   What connection exists in Kavanagh's mind between penance, innocence, wonder and happiness? Refer to the text in your answer.
2   Copy the table below into your own notes and fill in critical comments about the last two quotations.

Key Quotes

Through a chink too wide there comes in no wonder	Kavanagh's metaphor suggests that when everything is displayed, there is no mystery and thus no interest.
and the newness that was in every stale thing/When we looked at it as children	The poet wishes to capture the experience of looking at the world with the innocent eyes of a child who appreciates the world's wonders.
Wherever life pours ordinary plenty	This is Kavanagh's poetic manifesto.
and please/God we shall not ask for reason's payment	
And Christ comes with a January flower	

A Christmas Childhood

I

One side of the potato-pits was white with frost—
How wonderful that was, how wonderful!
And when we put our ears to the paling-post
The music that came out was magical.

The light between the ricks of hay and straw   5
Was a hole in Heaven's gable. An apple tree
With its December-glinting fruit we saw—
O you, Eve, were the world that tempted me

To eat the knowledge that grew in clay
And death the germ within it! Now and then   10
I can remember something of the gay
Garden that was childhood's. Again

The tracks of cattle to a drinking-place,
A green stone lying sideways in a ditch
Or any common sight the transfigured face   15
Of a beauty that the world did not touch.

II

My father played the melodeon
Outside at our gate;
There were stars in the morning east
And they danced to his music.   20

Across the wild bogs his melodeon called
To Lennons and Callans.
As I pulled on my trousers in a hurry
I knew some strange thing had happened.

Outside in the cow-house my mother   25
Made the music of milking;
The light of her stable-lamp was a star
And the frost of Bethlehem made it twinkle.

A water-hen screeched in the bog,
Mass-going feet   30
Crunched the wafer-ice on the pot-holes,
Somebody wistfully twisted the bellows wheel.

My child poet picked out the letters
On the grey stone,
In silver the wonder of a Christmas townland,   35
The winking glitter of a frosty dawn.

Cassiopeia was over
Cassidy's hanging hill,
I looked and three whin bushes rode across
The horizon—the Three Wise Kings.   40

An old man passing said:
'Can't he make it talk'—
The melodeon. I hid in the doorway
And tightened the belt of my box-pleated coat.

I nicked six nicks on the door-post   45
With my penknife's big blade—
There was a little one for cutting tobacco.
And I was six Christmases of age.

My father played the melodeon,
My mother milked the cows,   50
And I had a prayer like a white rose pinned
On the Virgin Mary's blouse.

'the wonder of a Christmas townland'

Patrick Kavanagh

3 *paling-post*: wooden support for wire fence.

5 *ricks*: large stacks of hay or straw.

6 *Heaven's gable*: a gable is the side wall of a house. As a child, Kavanagh imagined a bright part of the sky as a lit window in heaven's gable.

8–9 *O you ... knowledge*: in the Bible account of the Garden of Eden, Eve tasted the forbidden fruit and then gave it to Adam. For disobeying God, they lost their innocence and were banished from paradise.

15 *transfigured*: glorified; spellbound.

17 *melodeon*: small accordion.

30 *Mass-going feet*: the sound of the poet's Catholic neighbours on their way to mass.

32 *wistfully*: quietly and sadly.

32 *bellows wheel*: used to keep traditional turf and coal fires alight.

37 *Cassiopeia*: 'W'-shaped group of stars.

EXPLORATIONS

1 To what extent is 'A Christmas Childhood' a religious poem? Refer to the text in your answer.

2 Select any two images from the poem that you find particularly interesting. Briefly explain your choice in each case.

3 From your reading of the poem, what evidence can you find in Kavanagh's childhood that suggests he would become a poet in later life?

STUDY NOTES

Originally published as two separate poems, 'A Christmas Childhood' recreates Kavanagh's memories of a magical occasion when he was six years old. While he celebrates the intense feelings he had as a child for his parents, nature and his Christian faith, the poet is also aware of the passing of time and the loss of innocence.

Part I opens with a vivid image from Kavanagh's childhood: 'One side of the potato-pits was white with frost'. This enduring memory is followed immediately by the adult poet's **nostalgic reflection**: 'How wonderful that was, how wonderful!' This pattern of commenting on early experiences continues throughout the poem. The mysterious beauty of nature is central to Kavanagh's time as a child on the family farm and his most enduring memories are of colours, light and music.

For the innocent six-year-old boy, reverberating sounds from the wires between paling-posts created 'magical' music. A gap of sky between the high hay ricks became 'a hole in Heaven's gable'. He imagined an ordinary apple tree as the Tree of Knowledge which led to Adam and Eve's original sin and their expulsion from the Garden of Eden. The adult voice that dominates **lines 9–16** is filled with **regret at the loss of innocence**. He seems to resent adulthood, contrasting it with the 'Garden that was childhood's'. Part I ends with two 'common' recollections – the 'tracks of cattle' and a 'green stone lying sideways in a ditch' – both fixed in his memory as timeless images of 'a beauty that the world did not touch'.

Kavanagh's adult voice is almost entirely absent from Part II of the poem. Instead, we experience the excitement of Christmas through the child's eyes: 'I knew some strange thing had happened'. In particular, **he recalls people and music**, often together: 'My father played the melodeon', 'my mother/Made the music of milking'. Simple language and vivid images convey a clear sense of eager anticipation. Kavanagh remembers that even the stars in the sky 'danced'. The special atmosphere of the festive occasion affected every family ('Lennons and Callans') in the close-knit parish.

Religious imagery becomes increasingly prominent as the young narrator makes connections between his own Christmas in Co. Monaghan and Christ's nativity. The lamp in the farm outhouse becomes 'a star/And the frost of Bethlehem made it twinkle'. The **rich onomatopoeia** in lines 29–32 is characteristic of Kavanagh's musical effects. Carefully chosen verbs, such as 'screeched' and 'Crunched', are especially evocative. The gentle sibilance of 'Somebody wistfully twisted the bellows wheel' gives us a quiet sense of Irish country life a century ago.

The final stanzas continue to dramatise 'the wonder of a Christmas townland'. In retrospect, the poet recognises the first indications of his poetic imagination, his 'child poet', picking out the shapes of letters on frosted stones. **The mystery of creation always absorbed Kavanagh** and he can never forget the fascination of the night sky in winter: 'Cassiopeia was over/Cassidy's hanging hill'.

The poem concludes with a remarkable self-portrait of a wide-eyed child, 'six Christmases of age', a young boy who is intensely aware of the sensation of each moment of being alive. We see him gazing out at the great big world ('I hid in the doorway') as he tests his new penknife: 'I nicked six nicks on the door-post'. The colloquial language and flowing rhythm of lines 45–48 echo the child's newfound sense of his place in life. The last stanza provides an impressive overview of **the poet's closeness to his family**, especially his mother: 'And I had a prayer like a white rose pinned/On the Virgin Mary's blouse'. The clarity and simplicity of the image (white roses are rare and very beautiful), together with the poet's reverential tone, leave us with a memorable sense of Kavanagh's tender feelings.

ANALYSIS

It has been said that Kavanagh's poetry has been primarily concerned with a sense of loss. To what extent is this true of 'A Christmas Childhood'?

SAMPLE PARAGRAPH

I would agree that feelings of loss and regret are central to many of the Kavanagh poems I have studied. The title of 'A Christmas Childhood' is itself nostalgic. The life of the grown-up poet has been shaped by his vivid youthful experiences in Inniskeen. He always seems to be yearning for a return to those happy times, the innocent experiences of what he calls 'the gay garden of childhood'. Growing up in the remote countryside in 1910, Kavanagh's life was very simple, dominated by his Catholic religion. It is clear from the poem that he was an inquisitive child, lively and full of wonder. This is what he misses most – the innocence he experienced. The poem is filled with ordinary memories which were once great mysteries to him – the strange look of frosty potato-pits, the unexplained 'music' from the paling-posts and images of the first Christmas story which he imagined around the farm, such as the three whin bushes (the 'Wise Kings'). The whole poem is written in a nostalgic and wistful tone, suggesting deep loss. His parents play a key role in the flashbacks. He has fond memories of his father and mother, and he associates them both with music – 'My father was playing the melodeon', 'my mother made the music of milking'. He compares his mother to Christ's mother at the end of the poem in a moving metaphor which shows his love and loss – 'I had a prayer like a white rose on the Virgin Mary's blouse'. This poignant conclusion suggests yearning for an earlier innocent time.

EXAMINER'S COMMENT

Reveals a reasonably good understanding of the poem. Quotations are slightly inaccurate, but help to support key points well. A little more analysis of the poet's tone would have improved the answer. Grade B.

CLASS/HOMEWORK EXERCISES

1 What similarities and/or differences can you find between the two sections of the poem? Refer to both theme and style of writing in your answer.

2 Copy the table below into your own notes and fill in critical comments about the last two quotations.

Key Quotes

And death the germ within it	The poet compares his adulthood to Adam and Eve's fall from grace. For him, it is the death of innocence.
I looked and three whin bushes rode across / The horizon—the Three Wise Kings	Kavanagh associates sights and sounds from childhood with the story of Christ's birth, as seen in the vivid personification.
An old man passing said:/'Can't he make it talk'	The poem celebrates traditional rural culture and colloquial language.
My child poet picked out the letters/On the grey stone	
And I had a prayer like a white rose pinned/ On the Virgin Mary's blouse	

Epic

I have lived in important places, times
When great events were decided who owned
That half a rood of rock, a no-man's land
Surrounded by our pitchfork-armed claims.
I heard the Duffys shouting 'Damn your soul'   5
And old McCabe stripped to the waist, seen
Step the plot defying blue cast-steel—
'Here is the march along these iron stones'
That was the year of the Munich bother. Which
Was more important? I inclined   10
To lose my faith in Ballyrush and Gortin
Till Homer's ghost came whispering to my mind
He said: I made the *Iliad* from such
A local row. Gods make their own importance.

'I made the Iliad from such / A local row.'

Epic: (noun) long poem about heroic events; (adj) ambitious; impressive.

3 *half a rood*: small portion of land – a rood is a quarter of an acre.

7 *Step the plot*: traditional method of measuring the land by walking it.

8 *march*: boundary.

9 *Munich bother*: the poet's wry description of a crisis just before the outbreak of World War Two.

10 *most important*: Kavanagh is hesitating between the importance of the local or international row.

11 *Ballyrush and Gortin*: townlands near Inniskeen, Co. Monaghan.

12 *Homer*: Greek epic poet who wrote the *Iliad* about a dispute between the Greeks and the Trojans which led to the long, bloody Trojan Wars.

EXPLORATIONS

1   At first the reader is not sure whether the poet is making a sarcastic joke
    about the local row. What phrases indicate that he is serious?
2   Do you think the title of the poem is misleading or mischievous? What
    leads you to that opinion?
3   How effective do you think the reference to Homer at the end of the poem
    is? What importance did Homer have for the poet? Refer to the text in your
    answer.

STUDY NOTES

> This poem was written about a local row. Kavanagh's brother, Peter,
> recalls 'the row over half-a-rood of rock in 1938'. This poem was set before
> the poet made the decision to move to Dublin, and just before the
> outbreak of the Second World War. Kavanagh believed in the
> importance of the local.

Epic poetry is usually very long, telling of great heroic exploits over a vast area
and involving thousands of people. This small sonnet opens on a grand,
authoritative scale, declaring that the poet had 'lived in important places'
(line 1) and had been witness to great decisions. **Wryly humorous**, the poet
then describes a local row between two Irish farmers over an eighth of an acre
of stony ground. Yet all the fire and passion of a real conflict is there, as
McCabe defiantly steps out the land, shouting, 'Here is the march'.

The use of real names for the people and the places adds **a sense of immediacy
and authenticity** to this event. They almost take on a magical significance. The
quoted outbursts, such as 'Damn your soul' (line 5), add drama and excitement
as we feel that we are really hearing the bitterness and passion overflow in this
parochial quarrel. However, the use of the phrases 'no-man's land' and 'armed
claims' broaden the scope of the poem, showing it to be a microcosm of what
is being played out on an international scale ('the Munich bother'). This
careless, casual remark referring to the row over international boundaries which
led to the Second World War also leads to the central question of the sonnet:
'Which/Was more important?' The poet begins to hesitate, and the assured
tone of the opening starts to waver ('I inclined/To lose my faith') in the
importance of the local row at a time of international crisis.

Suddenly, the ghost of Homer appears to reassure the poet that great works
such as the *Iliad* were made from 'such/A local row'. The onomatopoeia of the

word 'whispering' suggests a hidden secret being passed between two poets. The poet regains his former confidence and realises that **it is the poet who decides on the significance of the event**: 'Gods make their own importance' (line 14). The use of the run-on lines in this poem shows the literal spilling over of boundaries and also cleverly hides the normal rhyme of the sonnet form. In times of war, all boundaries fluctuate.

ANALYSIS

The poet Michael Longley has declared that Patrick Kavanagh is a 'mythologist of the ordinary'. How does Kavanagh bind together the ordinary and myth in this poem? How effective is it? Support your discussion with reference to and quotation from the poem.

SAMPLE PARAGRAPH

Kavanagh takes an ordinary local row and explores it in such a way that the parochial becomes universal. The use of the title 'Epic', which normally refers to a very long poem, often a thousand lines, to a short 14-line sonnet is evidence of this. The poem begins in a self-important way as the speaker announces that he has 'lived in important places' and also at times when 'great events were decided'. So the reader assumes that the speaker is someone who has travelled widely and knows about world affairs at close hand. The immediacy of the scene is captured by the use of real names of people, 'Duffys' and 'McCabe', and places, 'Ballyrush and Gortin'. The dialogue also adds to this real feeling. However, we are then brought into an international context with the carelessly tossed phrase 'the Munich bother', referring to events which led to the outbreak of war. He wonders is the local or the international row more important? Both were about boundaries. He hesitates about the local issue: 'I inclined/To lose my faith' until he receives assurances from Homer, the Greek poet, who whispers that he had composed his great epic work, the *Iliad*, from 'such/A local row'. Kavanagh's confidence is restored in the right of the poet to determine the great value of an event. 'Gods make their own importance.' In this way, the ordinary and the mythic are interwoven to state the justification Kavanagh had in his own ability to mythologise the parochial, to see the extraordinary in the ordinary.

EXAMINER'S COMMENT

The weaving together of the ordinary and the mythic are ably examined in this response. A little more attention might have been given to the 'effective' element of the question. Overall, a very good, solid performance underpinned by succinct quotations and impressive expression. Grade A.

CLASS/HOMEWORK EXERCISES

1   In your opinion, is the mood of this poem confident and assertive, or hesitant and diffident? Refer closely to the text in your response.
2   Copy the table below into your own notes and fill in critical comments about the last two quotations.

Key Quotes

a no-man's land/Surrounded by our pitchfork-armed claims	A reference to a contested area of land between two opposing forces.
That was the year of the Munich bother	Kavanagh casually refers to one of the leading events of the outbreak of the Second World War in a throwaway line, rather like the use of the term 'the Troubles' to refer to the conflict in Northern Ireland.
Which/Was more important?	The poet hesitates about deciding which event was of greatest significance. The rhetorical question involves the reader.
Homer's ghost came whispering to my mind	
Gods make their own importance	

Canal Bank Walk

Patrick Kavanagh

Leafy-with-love banks and the green waters of the canal
Pouring redemption for me, that I do
The will of God, wallow in the habitual, the banal,
Grow with nature again as before I grew.
The bright stick trapped, the breeze adding a third   5
Party to the couple kissing on an old seat,
And a bird gathering materials for the nest for the Word,
Eloquently new and abandoned to its delirious beat.
O unworn world enrapture me, encapture me in a web
Of fabulous grass and eternal voices by a beech,   10
Feed the gaping need of my senses, give me ad lib
To pray unselfconsciously with overflowing speech
For this soul needs to be honoured with a new dress woven
From green and blue things and arguments that cannot be proven.

*'Leafy-with-love banks and
the green waters'*

EXPLORATIONS

1 In your own words, explain what you understand by the 'redemption' Kavanagh mentions in line 2.
2 Select one image from the poem that you found particularly interesting and effective. Justify your choice.
3 Comment on the effectiveness of the poet's use of verbs in the sestet.

STUDY NOTES

This sonnet was written in the mid-1950s after Kavanagh had been seriously ill. He spent much of his time convalescing by the banks of Dublin's Grand Canal. It was a time of spiritual and poetic renewal for the poet and he began to celebrate all the wonders of creation. As he wrote in his *Self-Portrait* (1964), 'as a poet, I was born in or about 1955, the place of my birth being the banks of the Grand Canal'. He added that this period of time marked a return to the simplicity of his earliest poems.

The poem begins on an enthusiastic note: 'Leafy-with-love'. This innovative phrase has a vivid, childlike quality that sets the upbeat mood of the sonnet. Throughout the **first quatrain**, **Kavanagh finds a sense of redemption** in 'the green waters of the canal' and feels inspired to do the 'will of God'. Water is used in both a literal and metaphorical way. It is free and fast-flowing, but it also purifies the poet's soul and restores his spirit, like the sacramental water of baptism. Along with the present tense, the energetic pace and run-through lines (enjambment) work to produce an exuberant atmosphere. The poet is eager to share his desire to 'wallow' in the canal's miraculous surroundings so that he can 'Grow with nature again'. Sensing that he has been given a second chance at life, he is determined to appreciate every moment.

The **second quatrain** focuses even more closely on Kavanagh's immediate environment and illustrates **the poet's observational skill**. Everything around him takes on an astonishing freshness, almost as though he is conscious of the world for the first time: 'Eloquently new and abandoned to its delirious beat'. He seems spellbound by the most common sights in nature (the 'bright stick') and in human nature ('the couple kissing'). His avid mood is explained by the crucial reference to divine creation: 'the Word'. Like other 'nature poets', Kavanagh intuitively recognises God's presence in the natural world. This is adroitly expressed in the invigorating image of the small bird in its element, 'gathering materials for the nest'.

The **sestet** is more obviously reverential in tone: 'O unworn world enrapture me, encapture me'. The emphasis comes from a combination of the exclamatory 'O', internal rhyme and repetition. Urgent verbs add further intensity to the **sincerity of feeling** in lines 9–14. The poet is anxious to retain his heightened awareness of nature, with its 'fabulous grass and eternal voices by a beech'. But he has another hope – that he can 'pray unselfconsciously', using language in the same simple way as the overflowing canal water.

The sonnet ends confidently. Lines 13–14 are extended, the rhythm relaxed and leisurely. In imagining his own rebirth, Kavanagh returns to the earlier baptism image: 'this soul needs to be honoured with a new dress'. In his case, the baptismal clothes will be made 'From green and blue things and arguments that cannot be proven'. The language has a refreshing quality that echoes his rediscovered passion for life. He is finally conte**nt to accept the mysteries of nature and God's will** without question. From now on, Kavanagh's poetry will celebrate the beauty and wonder of creation through innocent eyes.

ANALYSIS

To what extent do you agree that 'Canal Bank Walk' celebrates ordinary life through the use of everyday language? Refer to the poem in your response.

SAMPLE PARAGRAPH

To some extent this is a very true statement. Patrick Kavanagh had just come out of hospital after a very serious operation. He then started to see life as extremely precious, something to live one day at a time. To him, it was really like a religious experience. The language he uses is very simple especially when he is talking about the colours and sounds of the canal water. Colour images are very important in his description e.g. 'green waters of the canal'. He also uses ordinary childish expressions e.g. 'leafy-with-love' and 'green and blue things'. The kind of simple language a young child would come out with. I think his language is like Wordsworth's. He also becomes very aware of God as the Creator of all the world. Kavanagh describes everyday objects and then finds the ordinary to be extraordinary e.g. the 'bright stick'. An old stick lying along the canal bank is not exactly a thing of beauty, but it is to Kavanagh. Everything in the universe is mystical, part of God's work. Not all of his language is colloquial e.g. 'enrapture me' but many of his descriptions e.g. the 'couple kissing' are very ordinary and add realism to the poem.

EXAMINER'S COMMENT

Some reasonable attempts at examining the poet's use of language are made. The expression was flawed in places – both 'very' and 'e.g.' are overused. Some analysis of rhythm or sound would have improved the answer. An average C grade.

CLASS/HOMEWORK EXERCISES

1   Comment on Kavanagh's use of imagery, rhythm and sound in 'Canal Bank Walk'. Refer closely to the text in your answer.
2   Copy the table below into your own notes and fill in critical comments about the last two quotations.

Key Quotes

Pouring redemption for me	The phrase suggests the movement of the canal water, but also refers to Kavanagh's own spiritual renewal, similar to baptism.
abandoned to its delirious beat	The poet felt liberated and at one with nature, and sensed that his own soul became part of the universal spirit.
enrapture me, encapture me	Kavanagh uses hyperbole (exaggerated statements) to express his feelings. Rhyme and repetition also add intensity.
wallow in the habitual, the banal	
arguments that cannot be proven	

Lines Written on a Seat on the Grand Canal, Dublin

'Erected to the Memory of Mrs Dermot O'Brien'

O commemorate me where there is water,
Canal water preferably, so stilly
Greeny at the heart of summer. Brother
Commemorate me thus beautifully
Where by a lock niagarously roars   5
The falls for those who sit in the tremendous silence
Of mid-July. No one will speak in prose
Who finds his way to these Parnassian islands.
A swan goes by head low with many apologies,
Fantastic light looks through the eyes of bridges –   10
And look! a barge comes bringing from Athy
And other far-flung towns mythologies.
O commemorate me with no hero-courageous
Tomb – just a canal-bank seat for the passer-by.

*'just a canal bank seat for
the passer-by'*

EXPLORATIONS

1   Look at the new words in the poem that Kavanagh coined, such as 'stilly', 'Greeny', 'niagorously', 'hero-courageous'. How do they help to communicate the central message of the poem?

2   In your view, how effective is Kavanagh's image of the swan? How is it relevant to the central theme of the poem?

3   Would you consider the tone of this poem to be solemn or celebratory? Support your answer with relevant quotation.

STUDY NOTES

This poem was written while Kavanagh was convalescing from lung cancer, contracted in 1955. The poet, in a new mood of serenity and calm, admired the idea of having a seat as a symbol of remembrance. This poem is the conclusion of his poetic journey.

Kavanagh **wishes that his memory should be honoured beside the canal**. The Grand Canal in Dublin was a place of contentment and acceptance of life for the poet. He believed water purified, just as it does in the sacrament of baptism, causing a rebirth so that the child may come to a state of grace. The colour green recalls the natural world. The phrase 'stilly/Greeny' seems childish and almost silly at first, but the poet wanted to **view things as he had as a child**, with wonder and amazement. He also wanted us to share this view with him. The poem is set in the 'heart of summer' (line 3). The canal bank occupies a special place in the heart of the poet. He addresses humanity as 'Brother'. The old bitterness of the early poems has gone; now he is filled with love towards his fellow man. He humorously imagines the roar of the lock on the canal in Dublin as having the force of Niagara Falls. This is typical of Kavanagh's wry use of hyperbole. The onomatopoeia of 'roars' coupled with the newly coined polysyllabic word 'niagorously' effectively communicates the powerful *whoosh* of the water through the lock gate. All this movement and noise is contrasted with the great stillness of mid-summer: 'the tremendous silence'.

This wish to be commemorated is not an act of pride, but one of generosity. He wants others to share this positive experience of rebirth, which he had the privilege of undergoing beside the canal. He feels that they, too, will be inspired: 'No one will speak in prose' (line 7). He likens the stretch of canal to Mr Parnassus, the famous Greek mountain, a source of inspiration to all those involved in the arts. This hyperbole is similar to that used in the poem 'Shancoduff', when he refers to 'my Alps'. There are wonderful simple pleasures to be experienced on the canal, such as the 'bridges', the 'swan' and the 'barge', but these simple sights are transformed by the power of the poet's creativity. 'Fantastic light' is seen spilling from the personified bridges: 'through the eyes of bridges'. We, too, can see the sharp, shooting light searing through the bridge arches. The graceful curve of the swan's neck is highlighted by the phrase 'head low with many apologies'. The simple barge incorporates the heroic deeds and strange tales of the past: 'far-flung towns mythologies' (line 12).

Yeats wrote an epitaph for himself: 'Horseman, pass by'. Kavanagh wished to distance himself from what he regarded as the self-importance of Yeats. He did not want the viewer to look at the memorial, the seat, but rather at the view from the seat. Then **the viewer could see the same stretch of water** which had 'Pour[ed] redemption' for Kavanagh. He hoped others would benefit from this, as he had done. The opening and ending of the sonnet forms what seems like the black edge of the memorial card for the dead, 'O commemorate me' (line 13). This sense of place is very important to Gaelic poets. Kavanagh is paying tribute not to a place in the past, but to one in the present on the Grand Canal of Dublin.

ANALYSIS

Kavanagh wrote of how he had come 'back to where I started'. His poetic journey ends on the canal bank. Discuss this view with reference to the poem 'Lines Written on a Seat', using references and quotations to back up your opinion.

SAMPLE PARAGRAPH

Kavanagh sat quietly in the 'tremendous silence' of 'mid-July' and let the sounds and sights of the canal bank make him feel born again. He learns to look with a wondering, child's eye at the great elements of nature. His childish phrase, 'stilly/Greeny' water, masks a deeper meaning. We must learn to look with the innocent eye of a child if we wish to be saved. He makes us hear the lock 'roar' as he uses his new word, 'niagorously'. All the power and flow of the great Niagara Falls is likened to the water gushing through the lock gate in Dublin. Here, he has regained his poetic inspiration: 'No one will speak in prose'. Why? He is able to appreciate the beauty and grace in ordinary things, such as the swan with its 'head low with many apologies'. The serenity of the swan is deftly captured with a few well-chosen words. He makes us look, as children, with wonder at the 'Fantastic light'. We are coming back to where we started off, seeing stories, 'far-flung towns mythologies', everywhere. The poetic journey for Kavanagh ends here as he invites us to study the scene before us from the vantage point of a seat commemorating his memory.

EXAMINER'S COMMENT

A very well-expressed response which focuses clearly on the assigned task to discuss the poetic journey of Kavanagh. Short quotations are used effectively. Clear and to the point throughout. Grade A.

CLASS/HOMEWORK EXERCISES

1   Kavanagh felt one should not take oneself too 'sickly seriously', so he uses 'outrageous rhyming' such as 'bridges' and 'courageous'. Comment on Kavanagh's use of unusual words elsewhere in this sonnet, considering whether they contribute to or detract from the poem.

2   Copy the table below into your own notes and fill in critical comments about the last two quotations.

Key Quotes

O commemorate me where there is water	Kavanagh's simple wish for remembrance.
Where by a lock niagorously roars/The falls	The poet uses hyperbole to suggest the importance of the locks to him.
No one will speak in prose	He is enthusiastic about nature. After these wonderful experiences, everyone will be inspired.
Fantastic light looks through the eyes of bridges	
just a canal-bank seat for the passer-by	

The Hospital

Patrick Kavanagh

A year ago I fell in love with the functional ward
Of a chest hospital: square cubicles in a row,
Plain concrete, wash basins – an art lover's woe,
Not counting how the fellow in the next bed snored.
But nothing whatever is by love debarred, 5
The common and banal her heat can know.
The corridor led to a stairway and below
Was the inexhaustible adventure of a gravelled yard.

This is what love does to things: the Rialto Bridge,
The main gate that was bent by a heavy lorry, 10
The seat at the back of a shed that was a suntrap.
Naming these things is the love-act and its pledge;
For we must record love's mystery without claptrap,
Snatch out of time the passionate transitory.

'I fell in love with the functional ward'

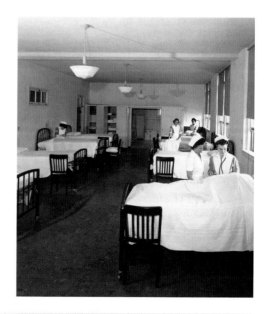

EXPLORATIONS

1 From your reading of the poem, what is your impression of the hospital ward that Kavanagh describes?
2 Comment on the main tone (or tones) that you can identify in the octave (lines 1–8).
3 In your opinion, what is the central message of the poem?

STUDY NOTES

'The Hospital' is an unusual love poem. Nondescript wards are unlikely objects of affection. Kavanagh wrote the sonnet in 1956 while recovering from a lengthy stay in Dublin's Rialto Hospital. His experience as a patient had a profound effect on him. He became much more positive about life and regained some of the innocent wonder of his childhood. To a large extent, the poem is about himself and his attitude to writing poetry.

Kavanagh's opening lines are clearly meant to surprise. He casually announces his latest romance: 'A year ago I fell in love with the functional ward/Of a chest hospital'. The picture he paints, however, could hardly be less passionate: 'Plain concrete, wash basins – an art lover's woe'. This **mock-serious posture** is also evident in his disclosure that 'the fellow in the next bed snored'.

In lines 5–8, the poet's true voice emerges and his earlier flippancy is replaced with a more focused tone: 'But nothing whatever is by love debarred'. Kavanagh wants us to know that love transcends all expectations and has no limits. He personifies the emotion – 'The common and banal her heat can know' – to highlight the intensity of love. What is important to Kavanagh is the experience of love as an expression of **appreciating the world in a fresh and positive way**. The seemingly unremarkable hospital itself is just one of countless wonders around him, such as 'the inexhaustible adventure of a gravelled yard'.

In the sestet, Kavanagh considers the far-reaching effects of love. As in the Canal Bank sonnets, he lists some of the ordinary things that would not be immediately seen as suitable subjects for love poetry – the Rialto Bridge, a damaged gate, a secluded garden seat. The poet's own beliefs are summed up in line 12: 'Naming these things is the love-act and its pledge'. By creating poems out of ordinary life, **Kavanagh can express his own appreciation of the world's simple wonders**. Poetry even gives them a certain immortality.

The tone of lines 13–14, in which Kavanagh speaks on behalf of other writers, is more forceful and didactic: 'we must record love's mystery without claptrap'. For the poet, **love is a sense of natural integration with all of creation**. In turn, love poems should be realistic and sincere, written in direct, unpretentious language ('without claptrap'). He illustrates this in the final line, where he recognises that because love is subject to time, love poetry (which registers such intense feelings) is all the more important. The poet's primary role, therefore, is to 'Snatch out of time the passionate transitory'.

ANALYSIS

In your view, is 'The Hospital' a love poem? Refer closely to the text of the poem in your answer.

SAMPLE PARAGRAPH

Patrick Kavanagh includes the word 'love' at least five times in 'The Hospital'. He starts off by shocking us slightly with his claim that he has fallen 'in love with the functional ward/Of a chest hospital'. We know he is just being funny in a sardonic sort of way, but it is enough to get our attention. He then makes fun of the place, with its concrete walls and ugly washrooms. What soon becomes clear, though, is that it isn't the actual building he's in love with at all. He is actually in love with life itself. I know of a few people who have had life-threatening illnesses and they are transformed by it. That is why I see the poem as a love poem. Kavanagh really is aware that precious time is slipping away. So even the most ordinary and ugly things – what he calls 'common and banal' – are suddenly worthy of love. I find his tone to be sincere when he says that 'nothing whatever is by love debarred'. He now fully understands the magic of ordinary, everyday things – buildings, bridges, an old gravel yard. He talks about the 'inexhaustible adventure' of such things. As a poet, his duty is to write about commonplace subjects without any 'claptrap'. For him, this is a true 'love-act'. Kavanagh has written an interesting love poem, but his tone is passionate – especially at the end where he advises poets like himself to follow their hearts and celebrate 'love's mystery'.

EXAMINER'S COMMENT

This is a well-written, clear response that handles quotations effectively. There is some good personal engagement with the poem and the final sentence offers a succinct overview. Grade A.

CLASS/HOMEWORK EXERCISES

1   Nature and human nature are central to much of Kavanagh's poetry. To what extent is this true of 'The Hospital'? Support the points you make by close reference to the poem.

2   Copy the table below into your own notes and fill in critical comments about the last two quotations.

Key Quotes

square cubicles in a row	The image of a functional ward reflects Kavanagh's ironic attitude that, depending on one's mood, it is possible to love anything.
the inexhaustible adventure of a gravelled yard	The poet develops his theme of how love can bring people into touch with the magical and the mystical.
we must record love's mystery without claptrap	By the end of the poem, Kavanagh is certain about the function of poetry. His use of the colloquial 'claptrap' emphasises his point that poetry should be unpretentious.
But nothing whatever is by love debarred	
Naming these things is the love-act and its pledge	

On Raglan Road

Patrick Kavanagh

(Air: 'The Dawning of the Day')

On Raglan Road on an autumn day I met her first and knew
That her dark hair would weave a snare that I might one day rue;
I saw the danger, yet I walked along the enchanted way,
And I said, let grief be a fallen leaf at the dawning of the day.

On Grafton Street in November we tripped lightly along the ledge   5
Of the deep ravine where can be seen the worth of passion's
    pledge,
The Queen of Hearts still making tarts and I not making hay –
O I loved too much and by such, by such, is happiness thrown
    away.

I gave her gifts of the mind, I gave her the secret sign that's known
To the artists who have known the true gods of sound and stone   10
And word and tint. I did not stint for I gave her poems to say
With her own name there and her own dark hair like clouds over
    fields of May.

On a quiet street where old ghosts meet I see her walking now
Away from me so hurriedly my reason must allow
That I had wooed not as I should a creature made of clay –   15
When the angel woos the clay he'd lose his wings at the dawn of
    day.

'On a quiet street
where old ghosts
meet'

GLOSSARY

Raglan Road is a tree-lined street off Pembroke Road where Kavanagh lived for a time.

2 *snare*: trap with a noose.

2 *rue*: feel regret for.

6 *ravine*: narrow, steep-sided valley gouged out by a stream.

6 *pledge*: solemn promise.

7 *Queen of Hearts*: reference to a nursery rhyme character; also the name of a card.

10–11 *sound and stone/And word and tint*: art forms; music, sculpture, literature, painting.

11 *not stint*: was not miserly with.

14 *my reason must allow*: thinking logically.

EXPLORATIONS

1 What do you think Kavanagh's opinion of love is in the opening of 'On Raglan Road'? Support your answer with references from the poem.

2 Would you regard the poet as a proud man? Give evidence from the poem to support your view.

3 In your opinion, what is the poet's mood at the end of the poem: resigned, distraught, bitter, angry, nostalgic, etc.? Give reasons for your response, based on close reference to the text.

STUDY NOTES

This rare love poem of Kavanagh's, with its bittersweet lament for lost love, was first published on 3 October 1946 in **The Irish Press**. It was inspired by a beautiful young medical student, Hilda Moriarty. It has been recorded as a sung ballad by many artists to the tune of 'The Dawning of the Day'.

The poet's **disappointment in love** leads him to warn against placing trust in love and against loving too much. One of the strengths of this poem is its firm rooting of time and place, which adds to the authenticity of the experience. The action takes place on an autumn day in Dublin on Raglan Road. This is where he first saw and fell in love with a dark-haired beauty. Throughout the **first** stanza, he presents himself as naïve; he knew it was dangerous, but he continued and was willing to accept 'grief'. He seems helpless, lured by beauty and the possibility of love: 'the enchanted way'. He is resigned to the possibility of sorrow, representing it as a natural outcome, as real as a 'fallen leaf' in autumn at dawn: 'let grief be a fallen leaf at the dawning of the day'.

The second stanza moves to winter. The couple seem oblivious to the dangers ('tripped lightly') as they walk along Grafton Street. The assonance of the slender vowel sound 'i' and the repetition of the 'l' in 'lightly along the ledge' capture the carefree spirit of early love. However, this is a dangerous balancing act – someone could get hurt and go hurtling into 'the deep ravine' if 'passion's pledge' proves to be worthless. Is there a suggestion that this is an obsessive love, unrealistic, as it places the loved one on a pedestal? 'The Queen of Hearts' refers to the nursery rhyme and also to the card from a deck of cards. This is a successful woman who is in control of her destiny, whereas the poet, blinded by love, is not attending to his business: 'not making hay'. Kavanagh has gambled heavily on love ('O I loved too much') and lost ('and by such, by such, is happiness thrown away'). The **ballad form of four-line stanzas** with its regular rhyme, in this case *aabb*, is admirably suited to this simple yet universal tale of lost love. The rhythm is taken from the song 'The Dawning of the Day'. The long, winding lines captivate the reader/listener as effectively as Kavanagh was ensnared all those years before. The use of internal rhyme ('hair'/'snare', 'grief'/'leaf') comes from the old bardic tradition of Gaelic poetry.

This poem is written entirely from the poet's perspective, and in stanza three, Kavanagh proudly declares all the gifts he gave her: 'I gave her gifts of the mind'. He gave her something very precious, 'the secret sign', which is known only to artists, those who have been in communication with the gods of music, sculpture, literature and painting: 'the artists who have known the true gods of sound and stone'. She was allowed into this special community. The poet also says he was not mean, as he gave her poems with her name in them. The reader becomes a little uneasy as he asks what more she could possibly want. Notice the frequent use of the first-person singular pronoun 'I'. What is this suggesting about Kavanagh's attitude? However, **the sweet longing for love is beautifully captured in the image of her hair** as billowing dark clouds sailing over the bright fields in early summer: 'and her own dark hair like clouds over fields in May'. The broad vowels of this line suggest the volume and cascading beauty of his beloved's hair. Suddenly, our sympathy returns to the awkward countryman hopelessly in love.

The closing stanza returns to the present. The relationship has ended and now Kavanagh sees her walking quickly away from him. Ruefully, he has to conclude that he did not love her as an ordinary human being, but as someone to be worshipped. He decides that she did not deserve this. He dismissively calls her 'a creature made of clay'. He adopts a much grander persona for himself, regarding himself as an angel, someone not entirely of this world. **Kavanagh had a great sense of the importance of the poet's place in society.** He concludes the poem by saying that the poet loses his special gifts ('lose his wings') if he courts the woman in this way. Are we still sympathetic to the poet's plight at the end of the poem?

ANALYSIS

'Kavanagh takes the local and ordinary and makes it of universal significance.' Discuss this statement in relation to the poems on your course and quote in support of your opinions.

SAMPLE PARAGRAPH

Countless singers have performed this ballad, with its universal theme of lost love. The four four-line stanzas tell of a particular day and place, the 'local and the ordinary'. Here on an autumn day in 1940s Dublin on Raglan Road an awkward 40-year-old Monaghan man who had left school at 13 saw the beautiful 22-year-old medical student, Hilda Moriarty, and fell head over heels in love. The spell of female beauty is evocatively captured in the phrase 'her dark hair would weave a snare'. Yet the love-struck poet walks willingly to his destiny: 'I saw the danger, yet I walked along the enchanted way'. What person has not fallen for someone totally out of their reach, yet with the blindness of love, foolishly continued the pursuit? The carefree joy of early love is suggested by the assonance of the slender vowels 'tripped lightly' as the pair went along Grafton Street. But the danger is always there, the 'deep ravine'. It is possible to fall in love and end up being very hurt. The gamble of love is shown in the naming of the girl as 'The Queen of Hearts'. All lovers give their beloveds beautiful gifts, and Kavanagh is no exception: 'I gave her gifts of the mind'. The last line of this third stanza is, to my mind, one of the most beautiful as he recalls that he 'gave her poems to say/With her own name there and her own dark hair like clouds over fields of May'. The internal rhyme 'there'/'hair', reminiscent of old Gaelic poetry, makes the line soar, as his heart must have soared as he became entangled in Hilda's clouds of dark black hair. Sadly, they drifted apart, and who has not met a former love who is only too anxious to hurry away, 'walking now/Away from me'? The nostalgic tone of lost love echoes from 'On a quiet street where old ghosts meet'. I think this ballad is timeless. Its content with its warning against loving too much, 'O I loved too much', reminds me of Yeats's poem 'The Sally Gardens' as 'she bid me take love easy'. The imagery makes us nod ruefully as we recognise the universal experience of lost love, which is unfortunately as natural a process as 'a fallen leaf' on an autumn morning.

Patrick Kavanagh

EXAMINER'S COMMENT

This detailed response shows a real engagement with the poem as the answer traces how the local is made universal by the poet's skill. The style and control of the answer merits an A grade.

CLASS/HOMEWORK EXERCISES

1 'Kavanagh's poetry is pervaded by a deep sense of loss.' Do you agree or disagree with this statement? Support the points you make with reference to the text.

2 Copy the table below into your own notes and fill in critical comments about the last two quotations.

Key Quotes

That her dark hair would weave a snare that I might one day rue	The poet is aware that this relationship could end in tears for him.
And I said, let grief be a fallen leaf at the dawning of the day	Kavanagh is resigned to the possibility that this relationship may not work out, but he is willing to risk it.
the deep ravine where can be seen the worth of passion's pledge	A promise made when in love becomes worthless when the relationship is ended. The alliterative 'p' emphasises the passion.
I gave her the secret sign	
When the angel woos the clay he'd lose his wings at the dawn of day	

LEAVING CERT SAMPLE ESSAY

> **Q** **Imagine you were asked to select one or more of Patrick Kavanagh's poems from your course for inclusion in a short anthology entitled *The Essential Kavanagh*. Give reasons for your choice, quoting from or referring to the poem or poems you have chosen.**

MARKING SCHEME GUIDELINES

Expect the focus of the answer to be on the reason(s) given for including the poem(s) in the anthology. Evidence of genuine engagement with the poetry should be rewarded.

The range of reasons offered might include the following:
- Early poems provide an insight into rural Irish life.
- Poems celebrate the ordinary, familiar world.
- They reveal an ironic affection for the local surroundings.
- Engaging mood/atmosphere of the poems.
- Distinctive patterns of language and imagery, etc.

SAMPLE ESSAY
(The Essential Kavanagh)

1 *Kavanagh protrays Irish rural life in 'Inniskeen Road', and the feelings of both belonging and isolation resonate from this sonnet. We all know the tremendous pleasure of a shared joke among friends, so vividly captured by the poet in the phrase 'the wink-and-elbow language of delight', which describes the young people as they go to the local dance. For someone who is not a part of this scene, it is 'the half-talk code of mysteries' as he, like Kavanagh, is not part of the group. When a person is alone, the world seems made up of couples and groups, 'The bicycles go by in twos and threes'. The poet is the outsider, the observer, he is left alone at half-past eight 'Upon a mile of road, no shadow thrown'. A silent stone is transformed by the onomatopoeia in the line 'A footfall tapping out secrecies of stone'. He is in splendid isolation, because he has chosen to be a poet, regarded then by the locals as something strange. He rules over 'banks and stones', alone. In the sestet, he lets us know the price he has paid for his proffesion, 'hates', 'plight'.*

2 In 'Advent', the modern reader is brought back to the weeks before Christmas, the season of Advent, when it was customary for Catholics to fast. Now people sometimes abstain from drink, before they overindulge at Christmas. This sense of excess is captured by Kavanagh as he uses the alliteration of 't' in 'We have tasted too much'. He wrote this poem about his experiances in Dublin. He suggests the atmosphere of a dull, November evening, 'Advent darkened room', as the shorter days pass. Two details suggest a time of penance, 'dry black bread and sugarless tea'. He wants to return to innocence, 'the luxury of a child's soul', so that he could experiance 'the newness that was in every stale thing'. Kavanagh then recreates for us what it is like to look at the world through the unspoiled eyes of a child, 'spirit-shocking, black slanting Ulster hill'. I can relate to Kavanagh contemplating 'bog-holes, cart-tracks,' suddenly realising that Time as we measure it (AD) began with the birth of Christ in an old stable. Again we are shown the extraordinary in the ordinary.

3 In the last section of the poem he shows, through the use of onomatopoeia, how to look at life, 'the whispered arguement of a churning'. The soft slapping sound the milk makes as it is being made into butter is there for us to hear. Just experiance it, Kavanagh is telling us, don't 'analyse God's breath'. Leave aside knowledge, he tells us, 'the conscious hour', and then you won't have to go 'searching', as 'Christ comes with a January flower'. Nowadays we read of people finding themselves, and they explore lots of different ways of living. Kavanagh is telling us to be still and look around us. It is all there. 'Won't we be rich'? We miss it because we are too busy with our 'clay-minted wage'. Kavanagh places it in front of us as he shows us the 'heart-breaking strangeness in dreeping hedges'.

4 In 1955 Kavanagh contracted cancer. He beat the illness and emerged with a new outlook on life. The poem 'Canal Bank Walk' reflects this new serenity. The word 'Leafy-with-love' captures the goodness of nature. He feels saved as he sits on the canal bank, recuperating. He feels the joy of nature, and the green water of the canal 'pouring redemption'. He has got what he wished for in the previous poem, he is enjoying the simple things, 'a bright stick trapped'. He prays eloquently, 'enrapture me'. We are given stunning visions of ordinary things, 'fabulous grass'. I can imagine lying in the long grass as it stretches, green against the blue sky. He longs for spontaineity 'give me ad lib', not to be reasoning. Instead he will honour his soul with 'green and blue things'. His spiritual side will be fed from the abundance of nature.

5 *Kavanagh makes up words, if he feels there is not one to fit what he wishes to describe. 'Niagorously' in 'Lines Written' refers to the water which spills from the lock of the Grand Canal, as if it were the great waterfall, Niagora Falls. The word gives us a hint of the dry humour of the poet, that this little lock gate is thundering, 'roars', like the famous waterfall. This is similar to 'Epic', where he likens a dispute between two farmers to Homer's poem, the Iliad, 'I made the Iliad from such a local row', he has Homer's ghost telling him. I think he wants us to realise that we have the wonders of the whole world spread out in front of us if we just sit and observe. 'A barge comes bringing from Athy'. Kavanagh is not as he described himself, 'a proud one', but one who understood the importance of idleness, the things that really matter are insignificant little things. Today he has got his wish, 'O commemorate me where there is water', and a canal seat adorns the side of the Grand Canal in Dublin, with a seated figure of Kavanagh, inviting us to leave the busy, weary world a while, and sit and be still, so that we can 'Feed the gaping need' of our senses. This to me is the 'Essential Kavanagh'.*

(approx. 900 words)

SPELLCHECKER
portrays
profession
experience
argument
spontaneity

GRADE: A2	
P	= 15/15
C	= 13/15
L	= 11/15
M	= 4/5
Total	= 43/50

EXAMINER'S COMMENT

This is a very personal and well-sustained response to the exploration of the essential Kavanagh. References are used succinctly, and a genuine awareness of the poet and his work is communicated throughout. Some spelling errors and inaccurate quotations were penalised.

SAMPLE LEAVING CERT QUESTIONS ON KAVANAGH'S POETRY (45–50 MINUTES)

1. 'Kavanagh's poetry celebrates the local and the ordinary.' To what extent do you agree with this view? Support the points you make by quotation from or reference to the poems by Kavanagh on your course.

2. 'An autobiography in poetry form.'
Write a response to the view that the poetry of Patrick Kavanagh reflects the highs and lows of his life. Support the points you make with the aid of suitable reference to the poems you have studied.

3. 'Kavanagh's poetry has continuing relevance for the modern reader.' Discuss this statement, supporting your points with reference to the poems by Kavanagh on your course.

SAMPLE ESSAY PLAN (Q2)

2 **'An autobiography in poetry form.'**

Write a response to the view that the poetry of Patrick Kavanagh reflects the highs and lows of his life. Support the points you make with the aid of suitable reference to the poems you have studied.

- *Intro:* Kavanagh's poetry is a journey from Monaghan to the banks of the Grand Canal, a journey of discovery and exploration, filled with highs and lows.
- *Point 1:* 'Inniskeen Road' and 'Shancoduff' – early years in Inniskeen, rural setting and farming, love–hate relationship with the land.
- *Point 2:* 'Advent' – early Dublin years, 'the worst mistake of my life', loss of childlike wonder, realisation of the need for a spiritual dimension to his life.
- *Point 3:* 'Canal Bank Walk' – love poem to a place, rebirth after illness.
- *Point 4:* 'On Raglan Road' – bittersweet love poem of unrequited love, poet's belief in himself.
- *Point 5:* 'Lines Written' – gratitude to God, lack of ego.
- *Point 6:* Style – lyrical, rhythmic use of language, word fusion, imagery, sonnet, ballad 'the lines that speak the passionate heart'.
- *Conclusion:* Reader accompanies Kavanagh, 'that Monaghan boy', on his journey from love–hate to ecstatic appreciation of the beauty of nature, and finally to calm serenity.

EXERCISE

Develop one of the above points into a paragraph.

POINT 4 – SAMPLE PARAGRAPH

Kavanagh wrote this rare love poem, which has been made famous by the singer Luke Kelly of The Dubliners. It is a love poem tinged with regret. He describes himself as an innocent who has been unable to resist 'a snare' of 'her dark hair'. He loved not wisely, but too well. The image of the Queen of Hearts suggests a gamble, in this case an unsuccessful one. Kavanagh comes across as quite arrogant as he declared he gave her 'gifts of the mind'. He even named her in some of his poems. He decides she did not deserve his love, 'a creature made of clay'. He, on the other hand, was an 'angel' who 'lost his wings'. But although we may take this view of the poem, nevertheless it is the music in the mid-line rhyme, from Gaelic poetry, which remains echoing in our hearts: 'hair'/'snare', 'grief'/'leaf', 'woos'/'lose'. This is what leaves the lament, sung to the tune 'The Dawning of the Day', hanging in the air, while the long lines flow dreamily and sweetly as 'On Grafton Street in November we tripped lightly along the ledge/Of the deep ravine where can be seen the worth of passion's pledge'. Here, indeed, is a low point in Kavanagh's life.

EXAMINER'S COMMENT

A successful examination of a low in Kavanagh's life, when love is lost. Good use is made of quotations. One or two of the ideas could have been developed more effectively. However, there is a sensitive awareness of the musical effects used in this poem, while acknowledging the questionable attitude of the poet himself. B grade.

Last Words

'Kavanagh gave you permission to dwell without cultural anxiety among the usual landmarks of your life. He brought us back to where we came from.'
Seamus Heaney

'At his memorial seat on the Grand Canal, visitors are asked to sit with their backs to the memorial description, reading instead the scene before them.'
Antoinette Quinn

'I've often wondered if I'd be different if I had been brought up to love better things.'
Patrick Kavanagh

'The Ideal exists not in
our achievement of it
but in our aspiration
toward it.'

Thomas Kinsella   (1928–)

Thomas Kinsella was born in Inchicore, Co. Dublin in 1928, and educated through the medium of Irish at the local Model School and the O'Connells Christian Brothers School. He attended University College Dublin in 1946, initially to study science. After a few terms in college, he went to work in the Irish Civil Service and continued his studies at night, having switched to Humanities. His earliest poems were printed in university magazines and in *Poetry Ireland*. He began publishing short collections in 1952. Influenced by W.H. Auden and dealing with a primarily urban landscape and with questions of identity and relationships, Kinsella's early work marked him out as distinct from the mainstream Irish poets of the 1950s. While his earlier poems tended to be introspective and soul searching, he was increasingly drawn to mythology and tradition. During the 1970s, his work was influenced by contemporary American writers, such as Robert Lowell and Ezra Pound. In later years, his themes included political and historical trends. This developed into a sometimes darkly satirical focus throughout the late 1980s and 1990s, when he was Professor of English at Philadelphia's Temple University. Kinsella has said that his poetry is largely concerned with love and death. An acclaimed translator and editor, he received the Honorary Freedom of the City of Dublin in May 2007. Thomas Kinsella has been credited with bringing modernism to Irish poetry and is regarded by many as one of the leading Irish poets of his generation.

PRESCRIBED POEMS (HIGHER LEVEL)

1

'Thinking of Mr D.' (p. 248)

In this early poem, Kinsella recalls a memorable Dublin character from his past. But Mr D.'s animated personality masks a darker, more troubled self as he struggles to turn 'aside from pain'.

2 'Dick King' (p. 252)

The poet considers the significance of an elderly neighbour who was an important presence in his childhood. Love, loss and memory are central to Kinsella's assessment of Dick King's life and its essential goodness.

3 'Mirror in February' (p. 258)

Ageing and lost youth are key themes in the poem. While casually shaving on a damp February morning, the sudden realisation of time's erosive impact has a dramatic effect on Kinsella.

4 'Chrysalides' (p. 263)

The poet tells the story of a youthful summer cycling trip through the countryside, a memory that he has come to understand as marking the end of youth. Familiar themes include the effects of time as well as life's beauty and horror.

5 *from* 'Glenmacnass': 'VI Littlebody' (p. 268)

Kinsella's imagined encounter with a demonic music-making leprechaun provides the basis for expressing his own belief that creativity should never be sacrificed for notoriety or financial gain.

6 'Tear' (p. 274)

This detailed memory of visiting his grandmother as she lay dying allows Kinsella to examine people's attitudes to suffering and death. The poem also contrasts fearful innocence with the wisdom that comes with old age.

7 'Hen Woman' (p. 281)

The poem's opening description of a hen laying an egg becomes a symbol for all of life's mystery and possibilities. In the dreamlike scenes that follow, Kinsella addresses the processes of poetry and memory, prominent themes throughout his work.

8 'His Father's Hands' (p. 289)

A moment of conflict between father and son moves to memories of the poet's grandfather at his work and playing the fiddle. Family history, community and the creative tradition are recurring themes in the poem.

9 *from* 'Settings': 'Model School, Inchicore' (p. 298)

Kinsella's nostalgic look at his early schooldays evokes the innocence and enthusiasm of young minds. However, time changes everything, as the poet reflects on how he became more introspective and alienated in adult life.

10 *from* 'The Familiar': 'VII' (p. 304)

The poem examines the complex nature of one couple's relationship and how it changes over the years. Kinsella uses sensual details and draws on religious images to suggest love's subtle dimensions.

11 *from* 'Belief and Unbelief': 'Echo' (p. 309)

This short poem also explores the themes of love, transience and death. Characteristically realistic, Kinsella acknowledges that honesty is an essential requirement of a successful relationship.

Thinking of Mr D.

Thomas Kinsella

A man still light of foot, but ageing, took
An hour to drink his glass, his quiet tongue
Danced to such cheerful slander.

He sipped and swallowed with a scathing smile,
Tapping a polished toe.   5
His sober nod withheld assent.

When he died I saw him twice.
Once as he used retire
On one last murmured stabbing little tale
From the right company, tucking in his scarf.   10

And once down by the river, under wharf-
Lamps that plunged him in and out of light,
A priestlike figure turning, wolfish-slim,
Quickly aside from pain, in a bodily plight,
To note the oiled reflections chime and swim.   15

'still light of foot, but ageing'

GLOSSARY

3 *slander*: insult, slur.
4 *scathing*: mocking, derisive.
6 *assent*: agreement.

11 *wharf*: riverside, quayside.
15 *chime*: ring.

EXPLORATIONS

1 Based on your reading of the first two stanzas, what do you learn of Mr
   D.'s character?

2 Choose one interesting image from the poem and comment on its
   effectiveness.

3 In your opinion, what is the central theme or message of this poem? Refer
   to the text in support of your answer.

STUDY NOTES

Through much of his poetic career, Thomas Kinsella has been concerned
with human disappointment and people's engagement with the presence
of uncertainty in their lives. 'Thinking of Mr D.' (published in 1958)
focuses on Dublin's nocturnal pub society. While the poem typifies
Kinsella's bleak suspicion of a distasteful world, his dry, compassionate
irony is also present.

The poet introduces Mr D. as a well-groomed man of contradictions, 'still light
of foot, but ageing'. In his local public house, he gives the appearance of being
happy enough, drinking slowly, delighting in ridicule and malicious gossip.
The **tone is circumspect** and guarded from the start. What seems to interest
Kinsella is Mr D.'s contrasting 'cheerful slander'. Beneath the genial
appearance lies a more calculating nature, emphasised by the sharp reference
to his 'scathing smile' (line 4). The underlying image conveyed is of a cynical
character with a deeply resentful side to his personality.

Pent-up frustration adds to Mr D.'s inscrutability. Is he finding it hard to accept
that he cannot escape the inevitability of ageing? Or is he struggling with the
reality of an unfulfilled existence? The poet goes on to review Mr D.'s **seemingly
dissatisfied life** ('When he died I saw him twice') and locates him in two telling
moments. The first memory focuses on his habit of leaving a social gathering
after 'one last murmured stabbing little tale' (line 9). This revealing gesture,
with its hint of petty violence, is further evidence of Mr D.'s small-minded
disaffection. Is Kinsella suggesting that he is typical of those who lack the
courage of their convictions and who will only express their views where it is
safe to do so in 'the right company'?

The poet's second recollection is darker still. In the shadowy riverside setting
'that plunged him in and out of light', Mr D. is depicted as a 'priestlike figure',

becoming increasingly predatory ('wolfish-slim'). Surrounded by **desolate urban images**, Kinsella imagines him 'turning' away from reality ('pain') as though 'in a bodily plight' **(line 14)**. The poem's final image is of this silhouetted character staring at the river (presumably the Liffey), seeking some meaning – or escape – in its 'oiled reflections'. We are left wondering about the poet's attitude to this man. Does he have any sympathy for him? Does he identify with him? It is characteristic of Kinsella to combine compassion and criticism at the same time.

But **Mr D. seems incapable of action**, as indecisive as a latter-day Hamlet. We do not know exactly what he is running away from – an unhappy life, old age, death? Is he on the verge of ending his misery? Although he is severely troubled, he can still find some respite in the river's enticing beauty. But while the phrase 'chime and swim' indicates hope, it is inconclusive. It's hardly surprising that critics have seen Mr D. as an ageing Stephen Dedalus, the cynical hero of James Joyce's novel, *A Portrait of the Artist as a Young Man*. Stephen struggled to find fulfilment and took perverse pleasure in his increasing alienation. Mr D. has also been associated with the embittered Italian writer Dante Alighieri and with the sceptical Irish poet Austin Clarke.

ANALYSIS

'Kinsella uses effective contrasts to unveil his portrait of Mr D.' Discuss this view, referring to the poem in your answer.

SAMPLE PARAGRAPH

Kinsella describes Mr D in a series of contradictions – 'cheerful slander' suggests that he ridiculed other people, but did so in a quite good-natured way. I thought this added mystery to the old man's paradoxical charachter. It was never clear whether he was simply malicious or not. His 'scathing smile' added to his puzzling charachter. The most intresting use of contrast comes at the end of the poem where Kinsella protrays Mr D as a man 'in and out of light'. This brightness and darkness suggests the good and evil balance in his charachter, the tension inside him. He describes him as 'priestlike' but also as 'wolfish'. These are disturbing images to me which make Mr D seem unpredactable. I got the distinct impression that Kinsella wanted us to see Mr D as a typical flawed human being – a mixture of good and evil, happiness and depression. I didn't think it was a very positive picture in the end, as if Kinsella himself believed that Mr D's life was a bitter disappointment – 'bodily plight'. The contrasts helped to show his inner struggle very well.

SPELLCHECKER

character
interesting
portrays
unpredictable

EXAMINER'S COMMENT

This average C grade response includes one or two good points that address the poet's use of contrast to reveal a complex character. References are reasonably effective and there is some personal interaction with the poem. Language is poorly controlled in places and there are a number of spelling errors.

CLASS/HOMEWORK EXERCISES

1 In your opinion, what is the dominant mood in 'Thinking of Mr D.'? Refer closely to the text of the poem in your answer.
2 Copy the table below into your own notes and fill in critical comments about the last two quotations.

Key Quotes

still light of foot, but ageing	Contrasts play an important part in uncovering Mr D.'s complex and somewhat regretful personality.
one last murmured stabbing little tale	The character's deeply rooted anger and frustration are revealed in this slightly violent and cowardly gesture.
A priestlike figure turning	Mr D.'s behaviour beside the river, whether actual or imagined, suggests someone who is intensely uneasy within himself.
wolfish-slim	
the oiled reflections chime and swim	

Dick King

Thomas Kinsella

In your ghost, Dick King, in your phantom vowels I read
That death roves our memories igniting
Love. Kind plague, low voice in a stubbled throat,
You haunt with the taint of age and of vanished good,
Fouling my thought with losses.   5

Clearly now I remember rain on the cobbles,
Ripples in the iron trough, and the horses' dipped
Faces under the Fountain in James's Street,
When I sheltered my nine years against your buttons
And your own dread years were to come: 10

And your voice, in a pause of softness, named the dead,
Hushed as though the city had died by fire,
Bemused, discovering ... discovering
A gate to enter temperate ghosthood by;
And I squeezed your fingers till you found again   15
My hand hidden in yours.

                    I squeeze your fingers:

          Dick King was an upright man.
          Sixty years he trod
          The dull stations underfoot.   20
          Fifteen he lies with God.

          By the salt seaboard he grew up
          But left its rock and rain
          To bring a dying language east
          And dwell in Basin Lane.   25

          By the Southern Railway he increased:
          His second soul was born
          In the clangour of the iron sheds,
          The hush of the late horn.

          An invalid he took to wife.   30
          She prayed her life away;

Her whisper filled the whitewashed yard
Until her dying day.

And season in, season out,
He made his wintry bed.   35
He took the path to the turnstile
Morning and night till he was dead.

He clasped his hands in a Union ward
To hear St James's bell.
I searched his eyes though I was young,   40
The last to wish him well.

*'Clearly now I remember rain on
the cobbles'*

1   *phantom*: slight, ghostly.
2   *roves*: wanders through.
3   *plague*: bother, trouble.
3   *stubbled*: unshaven, spiky.
5   *Fouling*: upsetting, tainting.
6   *cobbles*: cobblestones (used for
    paving streets).
13 *Bemused*: puzzled, preoccupied.
14 *temperate*: gentle, mild.
20 *stations*: railway stations.

22 *salt seaboard*: west coast of Ireland.
28 *clangour*: noise, ringing.
29 *late horn*: sound of the factory horn
    in the evening.
36 *turnstile*: entrance gate; mechanical
    barrier.
38 *clasped*: joined hands (in prayer).
38 *Union ward*: trade union retirement
    home.
39 *St James's*: local church.

EXPLORATIONS

1   Based on the evidence of the poem's opening stanza, what are Kinsella's feelings towards Dick King?

2   In your opinion, what does this poem tell you about Thomas Kinsella's own attitude to life? Refer to the text in your answer.

3   Write a short personal response to the poem, supporting the points you make with reference to the text.

STUDY NOTES

Thomas Kinsella has emphasised the importance of 'personal places' in his writing. Many of his early poems are set in the small courtyard at Dublin's Basin Lane. It was here that he spent his childhood near the canal and the brewery. For Kinsella, it was a 'separate world', a place of 'selfless kindness'. Dick King had come from the west coast of Ireland to live there. He worked on the Great Southern Railway and became a close friend of the Kinsella family. The poem is another example of Kinsella's fondness for the meditative sequence.

Lines 1–5 have the plaintive quality of a conventional elegy. Dick King's name ('your phantom vowels') has revived **conflicting memories of love and loss** in the poet. Kinsella addresses his former neighbour directly, recalling his 'low voice in a stubbled throat'. The poet's sentiments are couched in resentful terms: 'You haunt with the taint of age and of vanished good'. Prominent assonant sounds add to the underlying sense of aggrieved sorrow as Kinsella accuses the old man's restless spirit of 'Fouling my thought with losses'.

Lines 6–10 take the poet back to a time when he felt especially close to the old man: 'When I sheltered my nine years against your buttons'. A series of **nostalgic images** ('rain on the cobbles', 'the horses' dipped/Faces under the Fountain in James's Street') are particularly evocative, reflecting Kinsella's fondness for this former life. But the reflection is abruptly checked from lapsing into sentimentality as the poet acknowledges the destructive effects of time and the inevitability of death ('your own dread years').

The flashback is extended into lines 11–16, where effective sibilance ('your voice, in a pause of softness') echoes the poet's own poignant feelings. The past was clearly important to the old man, who – like many elderly people – must have frequently 'named the dead'. It seems evident that Dick King's death has made an astonishing impact on Kinsella, leaving him 'Bemused, discovering ... discovering'. **This early bereavement marks a critical stage in his self-awareness**, encompassing both personal grief and a much wider understanding of human mortality. However, the repeated references to death ('named the dead', 'the city had died', 'temperate ghosthood') are balanced by a more positive view, celebrating the powerful friendship between Dick King and the young Kinsella: 'I squeezed your fingers till you found again/My hand hidden in yours'. The natural spontaneity of the gesture defines the warmth of a companionship that has never been forgotten. This enduring connection – based on the sensation of physical contact – has transcended time, allowing the poet to continue experiencing love at will.

Line 17 ('I squeeze your fingers') represents a turning point in the poem. Isolated and out of time, the poet's imaginary act, described in the present tense, allows him to use the lively rhymes and jaunty rhythms of childhood street games to suggest Dick King's austere life. The second half of the poem is distinctive for its **portrayal of Dublin's working class** in the 1930s. The ironic quality of line 18 ('Dick King was an upright man') combines both respect and pity for this virtuous man who struggled ('trod') through a long lifetime of hardship. Details from King's relentless routine emphasise the tragic history of this dependable rail worker (the reference to 'stations' even has associations with Christ's Way of Sorrows towards Calvary).

It is ironic that images of sacrifice and death define Dick King's solitary life. The 'dying language' (line 24) he had brought from his West of Ireland birthplace was of little use in Dublin's Basin Lane, where daily life was measured by 'the clangour of the iron sheds' and factory sirens. But at least 'he increased' and found **some self-worth in honest labour**: 'His second soul was born'. At times, Kinsella's depiction edges close to droll bleakness, particularly in his description of King's dependent wife, who 'prayed her life away'. An equally sardonic voice sums up the old man's entire existence as working 'Morning and night till he was dead'.

The poem's **final lines** focus on Dick King's initial impact on the poet: 'I searched his eyes though I was young'. **We can only wonder about the child's questions**, but they may well have touched on the fragile mystery of existence itself. Although Kinsella later described life as 'a given ordeal', there is no doubt about his enduring affection for his elderly neighbour. But while the poet seems heartened that he was the 'last to wish him well', readers will not be unaware of the tragic reality that Dick King's lonely life was neither happy nor fulfilled. Nevertheless, this unusual elegy has immortalised an ordinary person from this ordinary community. In his own way, King was at one with the world, and his simple acceptance of life seems to characterise an entire generation's resilience.

ANALAYSIS

'Thomas Kinsella's poems reveal a great deal about the poet himself.' Discuss this view, using reference to Kinsella's poem 'Dick King'.

SAMPLE PARAGRAPH

In my opinion, 'Dick King' tells us much about the man who wrote the poem. Kinsella is a highly introspective poet, always trying to come to terms with the past and to make sense of things. He is very clearly obsessed with death – and images of ghosts and dying are found throughout the poem. Many of his poems are based on and around his youthful experiences around St James's Street. Names of people, such as 'Dick King', and places, e.g. 'Basin Lane', give his poetry a strong sense of realism. I thought Kinsella revealed himself as someone with a genuine sense of belonging for the buildings and local community in Dublin. His childhood seems to have been a happy one – 'I squeezed your fingers' and his genuine friendship with Mr King is something which is central to the poem. Kinsella seems to have been a great observer and the poem is filled with detailed images – 'Ripples in the iron trough' as he describes the horses dipping their heads to drink in the street fountain. He also has a dry sense of humour, describing Dick almost killing himself with work on the railway – 'He took the path to the turnstile'. The second half of the poem recalls Kinsella's own childhood games and the happy times he had growing up. Overall, I thought that Kinsella's poem showed him as proud of his past and the hard-working community he grew up in, so 'Dick King' is revealing.

EXAMINER'S COMMENT

This is a reasonably good personal response to the poem and includes a number of well-supported points. There is a sustained attempt to remain focused throughout and references are supportive. However, the expression is awkward in places. Grade B.

CLASS/HOMEWORK EXERCISES

1 'Love, death and the artistic process are Kinsella's most prominent themes.' To what extent is this true of 'Dick King'? Refer to the text of the poem in your answer.

2 Copy the table below into your own notes and fill in critical comments about the last two quotations.

Key Quotes

death roves our memories	Kinsella's memories of Dick King are constantly diverted into meditations about the passing of time and the inevitability of death. The verb 'roves' even suggests a ghost haunting him.
Kind plague	This apparent contradiction reminds us that the poet's tender love for his childhood friend is inseparable from the grief and sense of loss he feels.
My hand hidden in yours	The simplicity of the image conveys the trust and naturalness of the friendship between the elderly neighbour and the young child.
I squeeze your fingers	
The last to wish him well	

Mirror in February

The day dawns with scent of must and rain,
Of opened soil, dark trees, dry bedroom air.
Under the fading lamp, half dressed – my brain
Idling on some compulsive fantasy –
I towel my shaven jaw and stop, and stare,   5
Riveted by a dark exhausted eye,
A dry downturning mouth.

It seems again that it is time to learn,
In this untiring, crumbling place of growth
To which, for the time being, I return.   10
Now plainly in the mirror of my soul
I read that I have looked my last on youth
And little more; for they are not made whole
That reach the age of Christ.

Below my window the awakening trees,   15
Hacked clean for better bearing, stand defaced
Suffering their brute necessities,
And how should the flesh not quail that span for span
Is mutilated more? In slow distaste
I fold my towel with what grace I can,   20
Not young and not renewable, but man.

'Hacked clean for
better bearing'

1 *must*: staleness.
2 *opened soil*: ploughed ground.
4 *compulsive*: compelling, obsessive.
6 *Riveted*: fixed, fascinated.
14 *age of Christ*: 33 years (the age Christ lived to).

16 *Hacked*: cut down, pruned.
18 *quail*: recoil, flinch.
18 *span*: stage, phase.
19 *mutilated*: disfigured, maimed.

EXPLORATIONS

1 Based on your reading of the poem, comment on the effectiveness of the title 'Mirror in February'.

2 In your view, does the poet find nature uplifting or depressing, or both? Give reasons for your answer.

3 Select one line (or image) from the poem to show the poet's keen eye for rich description. Comment briefly on the effectiveness of Kinsella's language.

STUDY NOTES

The sudden awareness of lost youth is a recurring theme for many poets. 'Mirror in February' was written when Kinsella was in his early thirties. It is a haunting, disturbing yet beautiful reflection on the experience of growing older and on the dawning realisation that perfection evades everyone. Nature provides a background for the development of his soul-searching and his examination of life's great mysteries. Thomas Kinsella used mirrors in his poetry as a means of exploring inner and outward reflections of self.

The poem opens dramatically as Kinsella locates himself in a particular time and place. From the start of **stanza one**, his **elegantly sonorous tone defines the physical setting**: 'opened soil, dark trees, dry bedroom air'. A deep feeling of dejection is suggested by such **sensuous detail** and clashing vowels. Readers can clearly imagine the mouldy 'scent of must and rain'. In the mechanical routine of an early morning shave, the poet suddenly catches sight of his 'dark exhausted eye', the carefully chosen adjectives defining Kinsella's unflattering imagery. The poet's return to the familiar surroundings of an awakening orchard prompts him to consider the cycle of growth and decay. He seems caught between the world of dreams and reality ('Under the fading lamp, half dressed'), his world-weary voice emphasised by a laboured rhythm: 'I towel my shaven jaw and stop, and stare'. However, Kinsella is soon wrenched from his 'compulsive fantasy' to face the reality of ageing. His mood of **startled sullenness** is heightened by the repetition of 'dark' and 'dry', and more particularly by the alliterative sound of the deadening letter 'd'.

In **stanza two**, the poet's mood becomes more reflective as he contrasts himself with the natural world outside his window. Unlike the ploughed garden in springtime, he must accept that 'I have looked my last on youth'. While nature is paradoxically a 'crumbling place of growth', **his own decaying life will not be renewed**. Imagining a spiritual mirror in his soul, he is immediately disheartened by an inherent sense of failure. In contrast to Christ (who fulfilled his destiny on earth at the age of 33), Kinsella feels that he has achieved nothing. Instead, he recognises his own mortality and insignificance: 'I have looked my last on youth/And little more'. The **dismissive tone of this central image reveals an acute awareness of loss**. As in the first stanza, the final unrhymed line is strikingly abrupt, enhancing our understanding of his inner disorder.

Stanza three introduces another paradox, reminding the poet of his inescapable decline: 'the awakening trees,/Hacked clean for better bearing'. This vivid image illustrates the irony of natural regeneration and reflects Kinsella's own deep-rooted frustration. His **graphic diction** has underlying associations with Christ's suffering ('brute necessities', 'mutilated') and reflects a distasteful view of human existence. The rhetorical question 'And how should the flesh not quail that span for span/Is mutilated more?' is intensely dramatic and emphasises his revulsion.

There is a definite air of finality in the grudging gesture as Kinsella folds his towel 'with what grace I can'. The pun on 'grace' (referring to both God's blessing and his own unconvincing attempt to retain some dignity) is a reminder of the poet's droll humour. The poem concludes on a realistic note of stoical acceptance, with a dignified acknowledgement that he is 'Not young and not renewable, but man'. Kinsella's response to the realisation that he has looked his 'last on youth' is **open to several interpretations**, ranging from bitterness and self-mockery to courage and resignation. Whether we see the ending as triumph or defeat, there seems to be some hint of purpose as the poet comes to terms with the challenge of getting on with life.

ANALYSIS

'Mirror in February' provides a good example of Kinsella's sense of the dramatic. Discuss this view of the poem, supporting the points you make with reference to the text.

Thomas Kinsella

SAMPLE PARAGRAPH

There are many dramatic features in 'Mirror in February'. The poem has a distinctive setting – dawn in the bedroom of a country retreat where Kinsella has returned 'for the time being'. He himself is the central figure in the drama as he stares into the mirror and tries to make sense of his life. The present tense adds to the dramatic effect – 'The day dawns with scent of must and rain'. To me, Kinsella is experiencing a mid-life crisis, comparing himself with the orchard outside which is ironically coming to life again in springtime. The opening reminds me of a movie scene where a character confronts himself – 'I towel my shaven jaw and stop, and stare'. Kinsella's language is also highly compelling – especially his use of specific adjectives, such as 'dark', 'compulsive' and 'brute'. He is forced to accept that life is slipping by and he can do nothing about it. In a final dramatic action, he slowly folds the towel he is using and concludes that he has little choice but to make the most of his remaining years because like everyone else, he is 'not renewable, but man'. I thought that the mood and atmosphere were edgy throughout the poem – and a striking example of psychological drama.

EXAMINER'S COMMENT

A well-illustrated personal response that is firmly focused on the poem's dramatic qualities. Points about setting and style are made effectively and are nicely rounded off by the confident final sentence. Expression throughout the paragraph is clear and controlled. Grade A standard.

CLASS/HOMEWORK EXERCISES

1   Contrasts play an important part in the poetry of Thomas Kinsella. To what extent is this true of 'Mirror in February'? Refer to the poem in your answer.
2   Copy the table below into your own notes and fill in critical comments about the last two quotations.

Thomas Kinsella

Key Quotes

The day dawns with scent of must and rain	The early morning setting marks a blurred transition from sleep to waking in which Kinsella is poised dramatically between dreams and reality.
for they are not made whole/That reach the age of Christ	Unlike Christ, the poet is mortal and imperfect and feels like a failure. Does this also mean that Kinsella feels Christianity has let him down?
the awakening trees	The personification of nature suggests spring's renewal and contrasts sharply with Kinsella's own sense of physical and spiritual decay.
this untiring, crumbling place of growth	
Not young and not renewable, but man	

Chrysalides

Thomas Kinsella

Our last free summer we mooned about at odd hours
Pedalling slowly through country towns, stopping to eat
Chocolate and fruit, tracing our vagaries on the map.

At night we watched in the barn, to the lurch of melodeon music,
The crunching boots of countrymen – huge and weightless   5
As their shadows – twirling and leaping over the yellow concrete.

Sleeping too little or too much, we awoke at noon
And were received with womanly mockery into the kitchen,
Like calves poking our faces in with enormous hunger.

Daily we strapped our saddlebags and went to experience   10
A tolerance we shall never know again, confusing
For the last time, for example, the licit and the familiar.

Our instincts blurred with change; a strange wakefulness
Sapped our energies and dulled our slow-beating hearts
To the extremes of feeling – insensitive alike   15

To the unique succession of our youthful midnights,
When by a window ablaze softly with the virgin moon
Dry scones and jugs of milk awaited us in the dark,

Or to lasting horror: a wedding flight of ants
Spawning to its death: a mute perspiration   20
Glistening like drops of copper, agonised, in our path.

'flight of ants/Spawning to its death'

GLOSSARY		
Chrysalides (plural of chrysalis): insect pupae, especially of moths or butterflies; the hard case enclosing this.	3	*vagaries*: unexpected and mysterious changes.
	20	*Spawning*: releasing or depositing eggs.

EXPLORATIONS

1   The title of this poem is intriguing. What is unusual or interesting about the word 'chrysalides'? Does the word have any links with the rest of the poem? Support your response with reference to the text.

2   Which image in this poem appeals to you most? Give reasons for your choice.

3   In your opinion, where does the tone of the poem change? Why does this change take place? Refer closely to the text in your answer.

STUDY NOTES

'Chrysalides' first appeared in *Downstream*, published in 1962. In this collection, Kinsella developed ways of feeling and seeing that coped with his constrained universe. The book begins with an idealised portrait of domestic happiness, but then examines the destructive aspects of this world. The poet finds his own words and imagery for exploring the aggressive elements of his inner and outer world. Neither his struggles with himself nor his struggles with his poetry have been much affected by the examples of other writers.

The poem opens with a **celebration of young love**, tinged with melancholy, precisely because love itself and the lovers are subject to change ('Our last free summer'). The long vowel sounds in the phrase 'mooned about at odd hours' suggest the seemingly never-ending time of youthful love. Kinsella often associates love with eating, a satisfying of the senses, 'stopping to eat/Chocolate and fruit'. The lovers' early journeys were on a whim; there was no pre-planning or purpose; the world and time were theirs ('vagaries on the map')'. Lines 1–3 vividly illustrate this idyllic time. Lines 4–6 show the couple as observers, somewhat isolated as they watched the countrymen dancing. The lilting music is conveyed in the onomatopoeic verb 'lurch' and the soft alliterative 'm' sound in 'melodeon music'. The hard rasping of the big farmers' footsteps on cement is heard in the onomatopoeic phrase, 'The crunching boots'. An almost grotesque tableau now unfolds as the shadows of these men are described as 'twirling and leaping over yellow concrete'. There is no mention of the young couple joining in this strange dance.

Lines 7–9 also add to the **dreamy mood of the young couple**, 'Sleeping too little or too much'. They are greeted with 'womanly mockery' as they come looking for food. The simile 'Like calves poking our faces in with enormous hunger' reinforces the innocence and simplicity of the passionate young couple in contrast with the knowing women ('womanly mockery'). The couple are joined with the fundamental rhythms of the natural world as they strapped saddlebags on and 'went to experience/A tolerance we shall never know again'. Everything seemed right then, 'licit and familiar' (**line 12**), but that period of unthinking existence was coming swiftly to a close.

Lines 13–15 speak of a world when **humanity is placed within the perspective of time and space** and this calls attention to human littleness and impermanence. The verbs 'blurred', 'Sapped' and 'dulled' all show the destructive passage of time. The run-on line from **stanza five** to **six** shows how heedless the young were of their special time, 'insensitive alike/To the unique succession of our youthful midnights'. **Lines 16–18** give a magical picture of a romantic night, 'ablaze softly with the virgin moon'. The reference to 'virgin' further suggests the innocence of the young couple. The Irish scene of 'Dry scones and jugs of milk' awaiting the couple shows a world far removed from present-day Irish society. Does the adjective 'dry' point to more than the scones? Is it implying decay or death?

Lines 19–21 bring the poem to a **chilling state** as a flight of ants appear, 'Spawning to its death'. This is a favourite theme of Kinsella's, the recognition that there is life in death and death in life. Again, a detailed simile, 'Glistening like drops of copper', describes the hard shells of the ants as they journey on. They, too, like us, are agonised by the ordeal of life. The poem is open ended, as it does not reach a definite conclusion. Kinsella has examined an unendurable reality. Out of waste, he has tried to create beauty. By shaping experience into lyric form, he achieves a victory over mutability. The poet sees the world as flawed because his perception never allows him to forget the forces that take away innocence. The title of the poem refers to the little egg of an insect before it hatches, so the egg itself contains life, as does the young couple and even the ants. In the midst of life, there is death. Kinsella has remarked: 'I believe now, with a certain nervousness, that you simply go back from where you came from – which is nowhere.'

ANALYSIS

'Kinsella's work dramatises one man's varied relationship with a desolate universe in which there are great, if precarious, consolations.' Discuss this statement in relation to the poem 'Chrysalides'. Support your view with quotation and reference.

SAMPLE PARAGRAPH

This poem certainly contains the elements of a mini-drama. The scene is set firmly in the countryside in summer. The main characters are established as a young couple head-over-heels in love, 'Our last free summer we mooned about at odd hours'. Time nor place have touched this pair. The slow action is caught in the verbs 'mooned', 'Pedalling slowly' and 'tracing'. A leisurely pace is described. The desolation comes in the fifth stanza, although there have been warnings earlier, 'last', 'confusing ... the licit and the familiar'. The reality of the transient nature of man is forensically described: 'blurred', 'Sapped'. They are unaware of the 'succession', time is passing. They are unaware also of the horror of this human existence which contains death in every breath we take. However, love is the consolation for Kinsella in this cold, unwelcoming world. But this consolation does not last. He uses the symbol of the ants breeding and dying on their wedding march as an effective illustration of the precarious nature of the consolation of love. It does not last.

EXAMINER'S COMMENT

This is a competent answer to a challenging question that focuses on the dramatic tension between the poet and his loved one, as well as the relationship between the poet and the world. Although the lack of length does not allow for much development, expression is very good throughout. Grade B.

CLASS/HOMEWORK EXERCISES

1 'To be able to write exploratory narratives that absorb particular surroundings is to clarify Kinsella's relationship with the outside world.' Discuss this statement in relation to 'Chrysalides'. Support your answer with reference to the text.

2 Copy the table below into your own notes and fill in critical comments about the last two quotations.

Key Quotes

tracing our vagaries on the map	The young lovers are leisurely exploring the countryside in a haphazard fashion.
Like calves poking our faces in with enormous hunger	This simile suggests youthful innocence and a natural desire to enjoy life to the full.
Our instincts blurred with change	The couple no longer live by their senses. Time has passed and they have changed.
insensitive alike/ To the unique succession of our youthful midnights	
a wedding flight of ants/Spawning to its death	

Thomas Kinsella

from Glenmacnass: VI Littlebody

Thomas Kinsella

Up on the high road, as far as the sheepfold
into the wind, and back. The sides of the black bog channels
dug down in the water. The white cottonheads
on the old cuttings nodding everywhere.
Around one more bend, toward the car shining in the distance.   5

From a stony slope half way, behind a rock prow
with the stones on top for an old mark,
the music of pipes, distant and clear.

*

I was climbing up, making no noise
and getting close, when the music stopped,   10
leaving a pagan shape in the air.

There was a hard inhale,
a base growl,
and it started again, in a guttural dance.

I looked around the edge   15
– and it was Littlebody. Hugging his bag
under his left arm, with his eyes closed.

I slipped. Our eyes met.
He started scuttling up the slope with his gear
and his hump, elbows out and neck back.   20

But I shouted:
                'Stop, Littlebody!
I found you fair and I want my due.'

He stopped and dropped his pipes,
and spread his arms out, waiting for the next move.   25
I heard myself reciting:

'Demon dwarf
with the German jaw,
surrender your purse
with the ghostly gold.'   30

He took out a fat purse,
put it down on a stone
and recited in reply, in a voice too big for his body:

'You found me fair,
and I grant your wishes.   35
But we'll meet again,
when I dance in your ashes.'

He settled himself down once more
and bent over the bag,
                    looking off to one side.   40

'I thought I was safe up here.
You have to give the music a while to itself sometimes,
up out of the huckstering

– jumping around in your green top hat
and showing your skills   45
with your eye on your income.'

He ran his fingers up and down the stops,
then gave the bag a last squeeze.
His face went solemn,

his fingertips fondled all the right places,   50
and he started a slow air
                    out across the valley.

                    *

I left him to himself.
And left the purse where it was.
I have all I need for the while I have left   55

without taking unnecessary risks.
And made my way down to the main road
with my mind on our next meeting.

Thomas Kinsella

'You have to give the music a while to itself sometimes'

STUDY NOTES

Published in 2000, 'Littlebody' makes up one part of a longer sequence, 'Glenmacnass' (a scenic valley in Co. Wicklow). Kinsella is keen to celebrate both the beauty of the natural Irish landscape and to argue the importance of art for its own sake. The poem has a vibrant, dreamlike quality and is driven by what the poet Gerald Dawe called 'the complex accidental moment of the here and now'.

Kinsella's narrative opening – itself a tribute to Ireland's storytelling tradition – is set amid the remote windswept hillsides, 'Up on the high road'. The poet is drawn to this remote Irish landscape, a setting often associated with Celtic mythology, with its distinctive 'black bog channels' and 'white cottonheads' (lines 2 and 3). **He is attracted by the ruggedness of the terrain and the natural freedom it offers.** This is suggested by the broad vowel assonance ('rock prow', 'stones on top') and the many references to the barren terrain. Increasingly aware of the haunting atmosphere around him, Kinsella encounters another sound: 'the music of pipes, distant and clear' (line 8).

In his visionary experience, he is confronted with 'a pagan shape', a dancing leprechaun – 'it was Littlebody'. The roguish sprite ('eyes closed') is caught up in his own merry-making and seems intent on 'scuttling up the slope'. But Kinsella is tempted by the leprechaun's purse of gold and immediately tries to claim it: 'Stop, Littlebody!/I found you fair and I want my due' (lines 22–3). **The mood is both playful and antagonistic.** The music stops dramatically as the poet challenges the 'Demon dwarf' to hand over his 'ghostly gold'. The leprechaun surrenders the 'fat purse', but issues a sobering warning of the inevitable consequences: 'we'll meet again/when I dance in your ashes'.

Littlebody goes on to explain himself further, criticising the poet for intruding on his music-making: 'I thought I was safe up here'. At this point, Kinsella's didactic voice takes over and he uses the exchange to illustrate an age-old conflict about art for art's sake. Music does not need an audience. **The leprechaun articulates the voice of the purist – 'You have to give the music a while to itself sometimes'** (line 42) – and takes Kinsella to task for his money-grabbing 'huckstering'. The tone here is particularly contemptuous. Littlebody also reprimands the poet for seeking affirmation among his own people and showing off in public: 'jumping around in your green top hat'. Clearly disgusted by such egotism and greed, the 'solemn' leprechaun takes refuge in his own music and plays a 'slow air' that reaches 'out across the valley' (lines 51 and 52).

While self-deprecation marks Kinsella's sardonic tone throughout this whimsical tale, he ends on a serious note, leaving Littlebody 'to himself' and 'the purse where it was'. Clearly recognising that **genuine art should not be compromised,** neither for fame nor fortune, he comes to an important conclusion: 'I have all I need for the while I have left' (line 55). This realisation brings a deep feeling of contentment, allowing the poet to return to his ordinary life 'without taking unnecessary risks', but wondering about the 'next meeting' – after death – when he is likely to come face to face with Littlebody again.

Having committed most of his adult life to his own art as poet and translator, Kinsella's views are as clear as they are predictable. For him, the pursuit of 'income' and publicity are false rewards that are untrue to himself. The poem's final lines are heartfelt, a gentle reminder that death is always closer than we think – and that **the artist should therefore make the most of the creative impulse,** just as Littlebody's 'fingertips fondled all the right places'.

ANALYSIS

'Kinsella's poetry is primarily concerned with the artistic experience.' Discuss this view with particular reference to 'Littlebody'.

SAMPLE PARAGRAPH

I enjoyed reading Kinsella's fairytale poem, 'Littlebody'. The poem was really a moral story, making the point that music is a reward in itself. Kinsella is often said to be obscure and difficult to understand, but in this poem, the meaning is clear enough. To my mind, Littlebody represents the real artist, totally into his music – 'the music of pipes, distant and clear'. The gold under his arm is of no interest to him, except to warn him of false musicians who are only interested in payment or cheap notoriety – 'huckstering'. To my mind, the main theme is that such an interest in 'ghostly gold' will be the end of any true artist. Luckily, the speaker who is almost fooled by the attraction of the fairy's 'fat purse' gets sense in the end and realises that he will have wasted his creative and imaginative talent. Fortunately, he reconsiders his situation and saves himself just in time – 'And left the purse where it was'. This is Kinsella's key point – the real artist must put his or her work first – this is the process that is most important. Littlebody himself is a good example of this – he works hard playing the pipes – 'eyes closed'. To my mind, this concentration and commitment represent Kinsella's own philosophy and his fairy story demonstrates this very well for the ordinary reader.

EXAMINER'S COMMENT

A good attempt at addressing the question directly. Apt references and quotations are used effectively in supporting the poet's central point about the importance of the artistic process. The language lacks control in places and there is some repetition. Grade B.

CLASS/HOMEWORK EXERCISES

1 'Conflict between opposing forces is central to much of Kinsella's writing.' To what extent is this true of 'Littlebody'? Support the points you make with reference to the poem.
2 Copy the table below into your own notes and fill in critical comments about the last two quotations.

Key Quotes

the music of pipes, distant and clear	Slender vowels and soft sibilance give a special musical quality, creating a pleasant mood.
There was a hard inhale,/a base growl	Playing the pipes takes great effort and Littlebody works hard to make music. The harsh onomatopoeic effects suggest the labour involved in the artistic process.
I have all I need for the while I have left	The speaker in the poem (presumably Kinsella himself) resists the temptation to 'sell' his artistic soul.
You have to give the music a while to itself sometimes	
my mind on our next meeting	

Thomas Kinsella

Tear

I was sent in to see her.
A fringe of jet drops
chattered at my ear
as I went in through the hangings.

I was swallowed in chambery dusk.   5
My heart shrank
at the smell of disused
organs and sour kidney.

The black aprons I used to
bury my face in   10
were folded at the foot of the bed
in the last watery light from the window

(Go in and say goodbye to her)
and I was carried off
to unfathomable depths.   15
I turned to look at her.

She stared at the ceiling
and puffed her cheek, distracted,
propped high in the bed
resting for the next attack.   20

The covers were gathered close
up to her mouth,
that the lines of ill-temper still
marked. Her grey hair

was loosened out like a young woman's   25
all over the pillow,
mixed with the shadows
criss-crossing her forehead

and at her mouth and eyes,
like a web of strands tying down her head   30
and tangling down toward the shadow
eating away the floor at my feet.

I couldn't stir at first, nor wished to,
for fear she might turn and tempt me
(my own father's mother)   35
with open mouth

– with some fierce wheedling whisper –
to hide myself one last time
against her, and bury my
self in her drying mud.   40

Was I to kiss her? As soon
kiss the damp that crept
in the flowered walls
of this pit.

Yet I had to kiss.   45
I knelt by the bulk of the death bed
and sank my face in the chill
and smell of her black aprons.

Snuff and musk, the folds against my eyelids,
carried me into a derelict place   50
smelling of ash: unseen walls and roofs
rustled like breathing.

I found myself disturbing
dead ashes for any trace
of warmth, when far off   55
in the vaults a single drop

splashed. And I found
what I was looking for
– not heat nor fire,
not any comfort,   60

but her voice, soft, talking to someone
about my father: 'God help him, he cried
big tears over there by the machine
for the poor little thing.' Bright
drops on the wooden lid   65
for my infant sister.

Thomas Kinsella

My own wail of child-animal grief
was soon done, with any early guess

at sad dullness and tedious pain
and lives bitter with hard bondage.   70
How I tasted it now –
her heart beating in my mouth!

She drew an uncertain breath
and pushed at the clothes
and shuddered tiredly.   75
I broke free

and left the room
promising myself
when she was really dead
I would really kiss.   80

My grandfather half looked up
from the fireplace as I came out,
and shrugged and turned back
with a deaf stare to the heat.

I fidgeted beside him for a minute   85
and went out to the shop.
It was still bright there
and I felt better able to breathe.

Old age can digest
anything: the commotion   90
at Heaven's gate – the struggle
in store for you all your life.

How long and hard it is
before you get to Heaven,
unless like little Agnes   95
you vanish with early tears.

Thomas Kinsella

'She drew an uncertain breath'

GLOSSARY

5 *chambery*: closeted, enclosed.
15 *unfathomable*: immeasurable, unknowable.
19 *propped*: raised, supported.
20 *attack*: sickness, coughing fit.
30 *strands*: stray hair, tresses.

37 *wheedling*: coaxing, demanding.
49 *Snuff*: powdered tobacco.
49 *musk*: greasy odour.
50 *derelict*: neglected, dilapidated.
70 *bondage*: suffering, hardship.
90 *commotion*: fuss, turmoil.

EXPLORATIONS

1   Select one image from the poem that evokes the boy's sense of discomfort in the presence of his dying grandmother. Comment on its effectiveness.

2   From your reading of the poem, what do you understand by the phrase 'her heart beating in my mouth' (line 72)?

3   Comment on the ending of the poem. In your opinion, what is Kinsella's attitude to the cycle of life and death? Refer to the text in your answer.

STUDY NOTES

Kinsella has written that his grandparents 'seemed very dark in themselves'. He described his grandmother as a 'formidable' woman who managed a small shop in Dublin. 'Tear' is taken from his 1973 collection, *New Poems*, in which he explored some of his earliest 'awarenesses' and absorbed 'the textures of life'. For a very young observer, some random details were hard to grasp fully, but were equally hard to forget. This collection marked a striking change in the poet's style, especially a preference for writing in free verse.

The poet begins his childhood memory of visiting his grandmother as she lay dying in the 'chambery dusk' (line 5). From the outset, we are plunged into a suffocating household environment, **a world of urgent unease**: 'My heart shrank'. The scene is recalled with intense clarity, with Kinsella's detailed recollection of fearful reluctance bordering on revulsion. Time is subtly and sensitively suspended. Feeling out of place and powerless ('I was sent', 'I was swallowed', 'I was carried off'), he recalls being overwhelmed by the experience and focuses on such 'unfathomable' sensations as 'the smell of disused/organs'.

Already confused by the order to 'say goodbye to her' (line 13), he is shocked by the appearance of the 'distracted' old lady who seems strangely unfamiliar. The young boy narrator is particularly **startled by her age and decrepitude**. He notices her 'puffed' cheek and her grey hair 'loosened out like a young woman's'. The onset of death is suggested by images of wrinkled skin, wayward strands of hair 'tying down her head' and 'shadows/criss-crossing her forehead'. Kinsella dramatises the scene: 'I couldn't stir at first'. The grandmother figure lies on her deathbed in the half-light that threatens to engulf the young boy. He is horrified at the prospect of having to draw close to the dying woman, who has suddenly become 'fierce', her skin resembling 'drying mud' (line 40).

The poet exaggerates the eerie atmosphere. His childish dilemma over what he should do ('Was I to kiss her?') is eventually resolved when the boy finds strength ('any trace/of warmth') in another memory ('a derelict place/smelling of ash'), where he can again relate to the grandmother he once loved. For the first time, we hear the old lady's voice commenting on an earlier tragedy – the death of the poet's infant sister. For the poet, **the traumatic occasion is marked by the tears of three generations**, unified in helpless sorrow. Kinsella is deeply moved by the grandmother's compassion for his distraught father: 'God help him, he cried/big tears' (lines 62–3). In retrospect, the poet is able to understand how this life-shaping occurrence made sense of his own 'wail of child-animal grief' and strengthened his awareness of family history, identified by 'lives bitter with hard bondage' (line 70).

The experience is a turning point for Kinsella, propelling him into the past and offering him a clearer grasp of his own identity. It is no longer the grandmother who is the centre of attention, but the child poet's awed perception of her: 'How I tasted it now –/her heart beating in my mouth'. This is a **coming of age episode** that he recollects as a moment of liberation: 'I broke free' (line 76). Characteristically, for a poet associated with self-preoccupation,

Kinsella's writing style is often fragmentary, with multiple voices jostling for attention.

The closing section of the poem records his exit from the bedroom in a precise series of friezes. Although there is no direct communication with his grandfather ('I fidgeted beside him for a minute'), the earlier sense of terror has disappeared. Retreating to the small family shop, Kinsella remembers feeling 'better able to breathe' (line 88). But **he now acknowledges the resilience and wisdom of his grandparents**: 'Old age can digest/anything'. The poet concludes by paying tribute to all the previous generations who were never far removed from death ('the commotion/at Heaven's gate'). Kinsella's final thoughts are a poignant reminder of his personal heartache at the loss of his young sister. Ironically, unlike her grandmother, who endured a long life of hardship, 'little Agnes' was destined to 'vanish with early tears'.

ANALYSIS

'Although Thomas Kinsella is associated with obscure introspection, his poetry has a universal significance.' Discuss this statement with particular reference to 'Tear'. Refer to the text of the poem in your answer.

SAMPLE PARAGRAPH

I thought 'Tear' was obscure and hard to understand in places, but the main narrative of the poem was very moving and did have some significance for me. Kinsella describes two deaths in his family, his grandmother and his infant sister. As a boy, he was terrified by the dying figure of his sick grandmother. The images he recalls fill him with fear and revulsion – 'the smell of disused/organs', 'black aprons'. Young children are still terrified of the unknown. Kinsella was totally unaware of how changed his grandmother had become as she drew close to death. Yet by remembering a time when the old woman had been sympathetic to his father during the funeral of 'little Agnes', the poet's sister, Kinsella is able to see a more human side to his grandmother. The whole experience helped him to develop and learn about the reality of death. I found the poem interesting because it was really a sequence of dramatic moments. These reflected the intensity of what the poet had experienced and it felt almost timeless. I think we all store memories in this way – almost like dramatic fragments, and that is why the poem does have a wider relevance. All of us are faced with time passing and the reality of death.

EXAMINER'S COMMENT

This is a competent response to a challenging question. The answer takes a personal approach and attempts to remain focused, although more discussion of Kinsella's soul-searching would have been useful. The expression is reasonably well controlled overall. Grade B standard.

CLASS/HOMEWORK EXERCISES

1 Kinsella has said that his three themes are love, death and the poetic process. To what extent is this true of 'Tear'? Support your answer with reference to the poem.

2 Copy the table below into your own notes and fill in critical comments about the last two quotations.

Key Quotes

I was swallowed in chambery dusk	The metaphor highlights the young boy's traumatic sense of foreboding and dread as he entered his dying grandmother's darkened room.
the shadows/criss-crossing her forehead fear	Symbols of darkness are used throughout the poem to suggest and menace.
'God help him, he cried/big tears over there by the machine/for the poor little thing.'	Complex personal relationships are at the heart of the poem. The grandmother's sensitivity towards his grieving father humanises her again in Kinsella's eyes.
I broke free	
Old age can digest/anything: the commotion/at Heaven's gate	

Hen Woman

The noon heat in the yard
smelled of stillness and coming thunder.
A hen scratched and picked at the shore.
It stopped, its body crouched and puffed out.
The brooding silence seemed to say 'Hush...'   5

The cottage door opened,
a black hole
in a whitewashed wall so bright
the eyes narrowed.
Inside, a clock murmured 'Gong...'   10

(I had felt all this before.)

She hurried out in her slippers
muttering, her face dark with anger,
and gathered the hen up jerking
languidly. Her hand fumbled.   15
Too late. Too late.

It fixed me with its pebble eyes
(seeing what mad blur).
A white egg showed in the sphincter;
mouth and beak opened together;   20
and time stood still.

Nothing moved: bird or woman,
fumbled or fumbling – locked there
(as I must have been) gaping.

                    *

There was a tiny movement at my feet,   25
tiny and mechanical; I looked down.
A beetle like a bronze leaf
was inching across the cement,
clasping with small tarsi
a ball of dung bigger than its body.   30

The serrated brow pressed the ground humbly,
lifted in a short stare, bowed again;
the dung-ball advanced minutely,
losing a few fragments,
specks of staleness and freshness.   35

                    *

A mutter of thunder far off
– time not quite stopped.
I saw the egg had moved a fraction:
a tender blank brain
under torsion, a clean new world.   40

As I watched, the mystery completed.
The black zero of the orifice
closed to a point
and the white zero of the egg hung free,
flecked with greenish brown oils.   45

It fell and turned over slowly.
Dreamlike, fussed by her splayed fingers,
it floated outward, moon-white,
leaving no trace in the air,
and began its drop to the shore.   50

                    *

I feed upon it still, as you see;
there is no end to that which, not understood,
may yet be hoarded in the imagination,
in the yolk of one's being, so to speak,
there to undergo its (quite animal) growth,   55

dividing blindly, twitching, packed with will,
searching in its own tissue
for the structure in which it may wake.
Something that had – clenched in its cave –
not been now as was: an egg of being.   60

Through what seemed a whole year it fell
– as it still falls, for me, solid and light,
the red gold beating in its silvery womb,
alive as the yolk and white of my eye.
As it will continue to fall, probably, until I die,   65
through the vast indifferent spaces
with which I am empty.

*

It smashed against the grating
and slipped down quickly out of sight.
It was over in a comical flash.   70
The soft mucous shell clung a little longer,
then drained down.

She stood staring, in blank anger.
Then her eyes came to life, and she laughed
and let the bird flap away.   75

          'It's all the one.
There's plenty more where that came from!'

'fussed by her splayed fingers'

	GLOSSARY
19	*sphincter*: a ring of muscle that surrounds an opening.
29	*tarsi*: groups of small bones in the ankle or foot.
31	*serrated*: having a jagged edge like the tooth of a saw.
40	*torsion*: the action of twisting or being twisted.
42	*orifice*: an opening in a body.
47	*splayed*: spread out.
71	*mucous*: slimy substance used for lubrication or protection.

EXPLORATIONS

1   The opening of this poem is a mini-drama. Comment on the poet's use of setting, atmosphere, characters and action. Support your response with reference from the poem.

2   The poet reflects on the motion of the falling egg. What, in your opinion, does this symbolise for Kinsella? Quote from the poem to support your views.

3   Two lines of dialogue end the poem. Is this an effective conclusion to this open-ended work? Refer closely to the text in your answer.

STUDY NOTES

'Hen Woman' comes from Thomas Kinsella's collection *New Poems*, published in 1973. He is among the most innovative poets in modern Ireland. He regularly touches on one of the most difficult aspects of contemporary life, isolation, which is very much part of the human condition. This, together with the theme of disappointment, pervades much of Kinsella's writing. He is experimental, bringing touches of international modernism to Irish verse.

In his short memoir, *A Dublin Documentary*, Thomas Kinsella spoke of a 'world dominated' by people, some of whom were 'formidable women', both family and neighbours: 'I remember many things of importance happening to me for the first time. And it is in their world that I came to terms with these things as best I could, and later set my attempts at understanding.' He speaks of 'taking in the textures of life in their random detail'. Kinsella is a poet of place, 'the yard outside, a silent square courtyard at the back, off Basin Lane, with a couple of white-washed cottages in the corners, with half-doors. A separate world, with a few other people. And cats and hens and a feel of the country. A whole place that has long disappeared.' **This place becomes a mindscape as well as a real place,** with the poet using it as a vehicle for understanding his own identity, separate from yet part of a whole community.

Readers are presented with an extraordinarily **detailed recollection of Kinsella's childhood** 'with a deliberate troubled intensity of focus that slows time down and creates a series of friezes'. Immediately, urgently, we are part of this world without introduction or preamble. The scene is set in a hot backyard, with the threat of thunder in the background. A hen scratches the ground. A woman appears in a doorway. A clock strikes. Kinsella himself comments on the poem as a 'scene ridiculous in its content, but of early awareness of self and process: of details insisting on their survival, regardless of any immediate significance'. One approach to this poem would be to divide it into four sections: lines 1–24, the opening drama; lines 25–50, the moment of birth/being; lines 51–67, furious rumination in an urge to know; and lines 68–77, the open-ended conclusion. This fragmentary poem falls within a defined structural design.

In this poem, the 'I', **a watchful attender**, tells the story as a witness. The tone is serious, brooding, alert and perceptive. The small event of the falling egg is noted, and the trivial scene is packed with significance. In lines 1–24, the narrative freezes the moment: the woman hurries out, the egg falls and breaks in slow motion ('time stood still'). All three characters (poet, woman and hen) are caught: 'locked there ... gaping'. The **dramatic tension** is caught in the brooding atmosphere, conveyed vividly by the sensuous sibilant 's' ('stillness', 'silence'). This is the calm before the storm. The setting is shown as a series of contrasts between the blinding white of the walls and the mysterious darkness of the 'black hole' shown when the cottage door opens. Time present and past is referenced: 'a clock murmured' and 'I had felt all this before'. Suddenly a storm erupts in the form of an irate woman, 'her face dark with anger'. The theme of disappointment is emphasised: 'Too late. Too late'. The **dynamic detail** is described when the hen 'fixed me with its pebble eyes'. The effort of creation, 'mouth and beak opened together', is conveyed as the hen tried to lay the egg. The white spaces between the solitary and conclusive asterisks seem to be as much a part of the drama as the written text is. Readers are being invited to remain within that silence before proceeding to the next moment that has grown out of it.

In lines 25–50, **the tiny movement suggests life**. The poet's mind is arrested by the detail of 'A beetle like a bronze leaf'. The verbs 'inching' and 'clasping' show that even the smallest creature contains the impulse of life. The minute observation of the poet, 'clasping with small tarsi/a ball of dung bigger than its body', draws the reader to look closely at the little insect. Even its brow is noted: 'serrated'. Kinsella's child/poet is fascinated by the dignity of the insect as it goes about its business ('pressed the ground humbly'). The **sharply focused attention on detail contrasts with the blurred narrative**. The back-stories are not told. Another asterisk leads us gently into the next section.

The **tension grows** as the silence of the first section gives way to the 'mutter of thunder', an effective personification of the grumbling sky. Time is passing, 'not quite stopped'. The child/poet sees that the egg is moving, ready to be released. Forceful onomatopoeia in the word 'torsion' conveys the twisting movement as the egg struggles to escape. Now the egg hangs free, a 'white zero'. Is Kinsella describing its shape? Or saying that it is nothing, as it has not yet experienced the world? Is it 'a tender blank'? The **movement of the falling egg is dreamlike**, as it floats through space, making its bid for a separate identity. Do you think this detail references Kinsella's own bid for separate identity?

Lines 51–67 show **detail becoming a single impulse to find 'structure'** for the poet's 'mess of angers'. 'I feed upon it still, as you see'. Kinsella's poems are experienced rather than understood. This relentless urge to know, the 'yolk of one's being', is the poet's inward journey and its impetus is graphically caught in the description 'twitching, packed with will,/searching in its own tissue/for the structure in which it may wake'. This searching into the substance is presented as part of the way in which the imagination seizes experience and takes it in. The egg, before release, was 'clenched in its cave'. Then it was not – but now it is – 'an egg of being'. Kinsella felt that after each new beginning we are 'penetrating our context to know ourselves'. But this is doomed to disappointment. Is it the fate of the watchful to be disappointed? Is this poem **a progress towards exhaustion and disillusionment**? Does the process continue until we fail? Echoes of T.S. Eliot's 'The Waste Land' resonate in the final lines of this section: 'through the vast indifferent spaces/with which I am empty'. The terror of modern alienation is exposed.

The final section, lines 68–77, deals with the **inevitability of destruction** in this existence: 'It smashed against the grating'. Life's brief experience is depicted as being almost funny: 'over in a comical flash'. Now the woman's anger evaporates as the poem concludes with her comment that nothing matters, 'It's all the one'. She comforts herself with the thought that there will be more eggs: 'There's plenty more where that came from'. Is Kinsella also consoling himself that life continues despite its endings? Is there anything more to come? Is there no end to discovering oneself?

The vibrant and dynamic **use of colourful imagery** shimmers through this fragmented narrative. Stark black and white (the mystery of 'a black hole', the blinding brightness of 'a whitewashed wall') moves to the dull glow of bronze, 'A beetle like a bronze leaf'. The black and white contrast emerges again in the description of the laying of the egg: a 'white zero' from the 'black zero'. It attains an almost surreal existence of opposites as the egg floats 'moon-white'. The mucous slime of nature clinging to the egg is evoked in the phrase 'greenish brown oils'. The life within the egg, 'the red gold beating', glows warmly in contrast to the cool paleness of the egg's 'silvery womb'. Kinsella's adept use of colour to clearly etch detail resonates in our consciousness long after the poem is read. So where is the end? Does Kinsella's poem confound the usual expectation of resolution?

ANALYSIS

'The energy of Kinsella's poetry comes from the mind arrested by detail.' Discuss this statement in relation to the poem 'Hen Woman'. Support your views with reference and quotation.

SAMPLE PARAGRAPH

I totally agree with this statement, because I think that Kinsella, through his minute observation and cinematic detail, draws the eye of the reader down to observe the minutiae of life almost as if looking through a powerful magnifying glass. One detail which captured my attention was his energetic description of the 'tiny and mechanical' beetle carrying the ball of dung. To me it represents the potential of life as well as the waste of death. I liked the simile 'A beetle like a bronze leaf'. The hard 'b' sound reminded me of the hard scaly outer casing of the little beetle, and the adjective 'bronze' suggested the flat shimmer of its little body. Kinsella carefully describes the delicate movement of the insect, 'inching across the cement' as it goes methodically and carefully about its business, 'clasping with small tarsi'. There seems to be a note of admiration for the hard-working insect as we are told it carried a ball of dung 'bigger than its body'. The strange beauty of the beetle is captured in the adjective 'serrated', which is used to describe the jagged appearance of its brow. The dignity of the insect is shown by its polite actions, 'pressed the ground humbly', 'bowed again'. The child/poet is fascinated by its efforts, 'the dung-ball advanced minutely'. In this hushed moment, time slows down, as reader, poet and beetle are 'locked' into the effort of this activity. The energy of Kinsella's poetry comes from the clarity of its detail.

EXAMINER'S COMMENT

This paragraph shows a sensitive reading of Kinsella's poetry. A clear focus on the task is maintained throughout in this fluent response, which comments well on the effectiveness of style features such as similes and adjectives. Grade A.

CLASS/HOMEWORK EXERCISES

1   'For poets, place is always as much a mindscape as it is a landscape.' Discuss this statement in relation to 'Hen Woman' by Thomas Kinsella. Support your answer with close reference to the poem.

2   Copy the table below into your own notes and fill in critical comments about the last two quotations.

Key Quotes

A hen scratched and picked at the shore	The onomatopoeic verbs 'scratched' and 'picked' allow the reader to hear the minute scraping sound of the action of the hen in this tense little drama.
(I had felt all this before.)	Time fades out from its chronological line as the poet experiences the same thoughts and sensations again.
clasping with small tarsi	The unusual word 'tarsi', describing the little feet of the insect, emphasises the strangeness of familiar objects when examined in detail.
an egg of being	
'It's all the one. / There's plenty more where that came from!'	

His Father's Hands

I drank firmly
and set the glass down between us firmly.
You were saying.

My father
Was saying.   5

His finger prodded and prodded,
marring his point. Emphas·
emphasemphasis.

I have watched
his father's hands before him   10

          cupped, and tightening the black Plug
between knife and thumb,
carving off little curlicues
to rub them in the dark of his palms,

or cutting into new leather at his bench,   15
levering a groove open with his thumb,
insinuating wet sprigs for the hammer.

He kept the sprigs in mouthfuls
and brought them out in silvery
units between his lips.   20

I took a pinch out of their hole
and knocked them one by one into the wood,
bright points among hundreds gone black,
other children's – cousins and others, grown up.

          Or his bow hand scarcely moving,   25
scraping in the dark corner near the fire,
his plump fingers shifting on the strings.

To his deaf, inclined head
he hugged the fiddle's body

whispering with the tune   30
with breaking heart
whene'er I hear
in privacy, across a blocked void,

the wind that shakes the barley.
The wind...   35
round her grave...

on my breast in blood she died...
But blood for blood without remorse
I've ta'en...

Beyond that.   40

*

Your family, Thomas, met with and helped
many of the Croppies in hiding from the Yeos
or on their way home after the defeat
in south Wexford. They sheltered the Laceys
who were later hanged on the Bridge in Ballinglen   45
between Tinahely and Anacorra.

From hearsay, as far as I can tell
the Men Folk were either Stone Cutters
or masons or probably both.
                          In the 18   50
and late 1700s even the farmers
had some other trade to make a living.

They lived in Farnese among a Colony
of North of Ireland or Scotch settlers left there
in some of the dispersions or migrations   55
which occurred in this Area of Wicklow and Wexford
and Carlow. And some years before that time
the Family came from somewhere around Tullow.

Beyond that.

*

Littered uplands. Dense grass. Rocks everywhere,   60
wet underneath, retaining memory of the long cold.
First, a prow of land
chosen, and wedged with tracks;
then boulders chosen
and sloped together, stabilized in menace.   65

I do not like this place.
I do not think the people who lived here
were ever happy. It feels evil.
Terrible things happened.
I feel afraid here when I am on my own.   70

                              *

Dispersals or migrations.
Through what evolutions or accidents
toward that peace and patience
by the fireside, that blocked gentleness...

That serene pause, with the slashing knife,   75
in kindly mockery,
as I busy myself with my little nails
at the rude block, his bench.

The blood advancing
– gorging vessel after vessel –   80
and altering in them
one by one.

Behold, that gentleness already
modulated twice, in others:
to earnestness and iteration;   85
to an offhandedness, repressing various impulses.

                              *

Extraordinary... The big block – I found it
years afterward in a corner of the yard
in sunlight after rain

Thomas Kinsella

and stood it up, wet and black: 90
it turned under my hands, an axis
of light flashing down its length,
and the wood's soft flesh broke open,
countless little nails
squirming and dropping out of it.   95

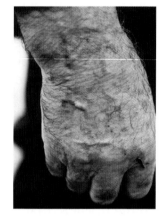

'his father's hands'

GLOSSARY

11 *Plug*: piece of solid tobacco.
13 *curlicues*: decorative curls or twists.
17 *sprigs*: wedge-shaped nails often
    used for mending shoes.
21 *pinch*: a number of nails that can be
    held between finger and thumb.
42 *Croppies*: name of Irish rebels in
    1798 Rebellion.

42 *Yeos*: yeomen, a volunteer force in
    the British army, composed mainly
    of wealthy farmers.
62 *prow*: pointed front part of land or a
    ship.
85 *iteration*: to do or say repeatedly.

EXPLORATIONS

1   The repetition in lines 1–8 contribute to a mood of confrontation and masculine posturing. How does Kinsella's language convey this? Support your response with reference to the poem.

2   How many generations of the Kinsella family are mentioned in the poem? How does this illustrate the poet's theme of continuity? Pay particular attention to the action of the hands, which helps to illustrate this. Refer closely to the text in your answer.

3   Write a personal response to this poem, using reference and quotation to illustrate your views.

STUDY NOTES

'His Father's Hands' comes from Thomas Kinsella's collection *New Poems*, published in 1973. Kinsella contextualised the poem in his memoir, *A Dublin Documentary*: 'The details absorb their own order. It was later in life, when I was on equal terms with my father, that something else important out of that early time became clear: the dignity and quiet of his own father, remembered as we talked about him. With an awareness of the generations as they succeed each other. That process, with the accompanying awareness, recorded and understood, is a vital element in life as I see it now.'

Kinsella **remembers an occasion he shared with his father**. The atmosphere in lines 1–24 is tense. This is emphasised by the repetition of the adverb 'firmly' to describe the action of the poet as he drank and set down his glass. Father and son mirror each other's obstinacy. 'You were saying' is a common phrase used between men socialising in pubs. The poet shows the forceful presence of his father by the repetition of 'saying'; there is also a sense of family pride in 'My father'. Repetition is used to describe the earnest conversation as his father seeks to drive home his point, 'His fingers prodded and prodded'. A new compound word adds to the very serious conversation: 'Emphas-/emphasemphasis'. The scene changes in line 9; the poet is now watching his grandfather. Has the conversation ignited this picture? The grandfather is cutting slivers off a hard piece of solid tobacco, 'the black Plug'.

Then the poet remembers another action, of his grandfather cutting 'new leather' (line 15). Again, tiny pieces are shaved off. Although this refers to mending shoes, which many people used to do at home in this period in Dublin, the poet's grandfather was a barge-pilot on the tugs that ran between Guinness's brewery and the sea-going vessels in Dublin Port. This was regarded in the community as a steady job. Kinsella is coaxing the reader to follow him in search of understanding, as he has said, 'back to the dark/and the depth that I came from'. He is arrested by detail as he tells stories, each of which is minutely particularised. The timeline becomes blurred, as the poet recalls his action that repeats his grandfather's action as he mended the family shoes: 'I took a pinch'. Kinsella also knocked in the nails ('sprigs'), as others in his family had done before him.

This **is a poem of 'blood and family'** with sharply focused attention on details of damp places and people, and yet at the same time it is slightly blurred, like old sepia photographs. Kinsella has said, 'I always remembered/who and what I am'. In lines 25–40, the poet recalls another action of his grandfather, playing the violin, 'his plump fingers shifting on the strings'. The onomatopoeic 'scraping' allows the reader to hear the shrill tone of the old fiddle as the grandfather gives a rendition of a traditional Irish tune, 'the wind that shakes the barley'. This song is written from the perspective of a young Wexford rebel who is about to sacrifice his relationship with his loved one and plunge into the cauldron of violence associated with the 1798 rebellion in Ireland. The reference to barley in the song also alludes to the fact that barley often marked the 'croppy-holes', mass unmarked graves into which the slain rebels were thrown. This symbolised the regenerative nature of Irish resistance to British rule. Kinsella adopts **the lyrics of the song as a metaphor for Ireland's tragic past**. In contrast to the sharp tone of the fiddle, the grandfather is 'whispering', almost like the soft surge of the wind through the crops. Both poet and grandfather are brought back 'with breaking heart' by the words of the song to another time, 'Beyond that'.

An asterisk leads us into the family's past. Kinsella places asterisks in this poem almost like pinpricks of light to lead the way into his past. The poet is keen to share his thinking process through the different, strongly defined subsections. An uncle of Kinsella's, Jack Brophy, **recorded part of the family's history** as follows: 'The Men Folk were either Stone Cutters or Masons, or probably both. In the 17 and late 1800s, even the Farmers had some other trade to make a living. The Kinsellas lived in Farnese ... among a colony of North of Ireland or Scotch, settlers left there in some of the dispersals, or migrations which occurred in this Area of Wicklow, Wexford and Carlow, even after the '98 Rebellion of which this part was a centre, between two big Battles, Hacketstown and Ballyrahan ... The Kinsellas met with and helped many of the Croppies in hiding from the Yeos or on their way home after the defeat in south Wexford. And some years before that time the Family came from somewhere round Tullow.'

Most of this passage (lines 41–59) is an almost verbatim account of the family history written by Kinsella's uncle. The horror of the sacrifice of these people is couched in **simple, unadorned language**: 'They sheltered the Laceys/who were later hanged on the Bridge in Ballinglen/between Tinahely and Anacorra'. This reinforces the terror of these times, but the lines have their own music due to the lilting polysyllables of the Irish place names: 'Ballinglen', 'Tinahely', 'Anacorra'. Is Kinsella asking us to consider whether the land was worth this sacrifice? Again, we are invited to travel back, 'Beyond that', as the second asterisk beckons us to closely observe the actuality of this place.

Lines 60–70 describe **a landscape that is 'Littered'.** Does it contain more than the rocks strewn 'everywhere'? Is it holding the stories of the past and its people as it retains the 'memory of the long cold'? Does this refer to the cold of the 'wet' ground, or the cold dead bodies of those 'hanged' and defeated? The verbs 'wedged' and 'stabilized' suggest persistence. Who was persisting, the Yeos or the Croppies, or both? There is a sense of threat ('menace') and the poet admits, 'I do not like this place'. Kinsella felt that an individual must engage with evil, absorb it and transmute it. He believes the people were never happy here. 'It feels evil'. He is scared: 'I feel afraid here when I am on my own'.

Lines 71–86 echo an earlier part of the poem, 'Dispersals or migrations'. This ground from where Kinsella's family emerged was **a place of flux and change,** as people moved here and there. But the 'blocked void' of the earlier section of the poem changes to 'blocked gentleness', and calm returns, 'That serene pause'. This is a welcome respite from the savagery of the past contained in the detail of 'the slashing knife'. In the present day, this knife does not murder as it did in the past; now the poet's hands re-enact his grandfather's actions, 'as I busy myself with my little nails/at the rude block, his bench'. The scene melts at the edges as the stagger and recovery of the spirit is described in the metaphor of 'The blood advancing/– gorging vessel after vessel –/and altering in them/one by one'. Evil is being transmuted to gentleness as the blood passes through the generations, 'modulated twice'. Successively, they perform the same action, 'iteration'. Blood, a link with primal sources, is part of both an impersonal biological and a personal social inheritance. These **disturbing images lift the transitory into the never-ending.** They transform our individual destiny into the destiny of mankind.

The final asterisk introduces us to **lines 87–95** and a wonderfully **clear moment of insight.** A last metaphor concludes the poem. The abandoned **block of wood,** surviving through the years, gives birth, beautifully, to its legacy, 'an axis/of light flashing down its length'. The disintegration of the rotting block reveals the energy and effort of Kinsella's ancestors. Does the insight reveal the possibilities of source, the availability of redemption? Growth and renewal or continuity are shown in the interaction of past and present, in the heritage of time, in the very nature of things: 'the wood's soft flesh broke open,/countless little nails/squirming and dropping out of it', almost like woodlice. The language of change and movement ('squirming', 'dropping', 'flashing') enacts the dynamic of possibility. Ghostly presences and ancestors emerging from the wood permeate barriers of time, space and matter. Hoarded cumulative images, represented by the 'countless little nails', are now released in a burst of imaginative vitality. Kinsella undergoes, yet again, **the mythical experience of death and rebirth**. Here is a sense of death in the midst of life, which resonates in the wet, black Irish landscape.

The block of wood is a visible symbol of the poem itself, tracing the line of the Kinsella family from son to father to grandfather, and back to the previous generations who lived at a time of great strife. This poem does indeed capture an awareness of the generations as they succeed one another and it becomes part of their record.

ANALYSIS

Kinsella stated that 'there are established personal places that receive our lives' heat and adapt in their mass, like stone'. Discuss this statement in relation to the poem 'His Father's Hands'. Support your response with illustrations from the text.

SAMPLE PARAGRAPH

Kinsella's poem 'His Father's Hands' echoes through time and place, and in my opinion, this area around Farnese in Co. Wicklow particularly resonates with Kinsella's 'blood and family'. I liked the section in the sequence lines 41–59, when he quotes his uncle's writings about the family: 'They lived in Farnese among a Colony/of North of Ireland or Scotch settlers'. In the third sequence, he describes this land where bitter battles between the Croppies and the Yeos raged, this 'prow of land' certainly received 'lives' heat'. He shows, through strong verbs, the physical effort expended, as things were 'wedged', 'sloped together' and 'stabilized in menace'. We wonder who had done this, the Yeos or the Croppies? Or both in their effort to lay claim to this ground? This was a frightful place, as he says, 'It feels evil'. Even the use of the present tense brings home to the reader how this human evil transformed the physical shape of the land, 'Terrible things happened'. The land was shaped by the mass graves of the rebels, as well as by the barriers erected by both sides. This evil reverberates to this day, 'I feel afraid here when I am on my own'. The 'dispersals or migrations' had shaped these 'Littered uplands'. I wonder are they strewn just with rocks, or also with the suffering of those who lived there? I feel the dreadful events which occurred in this place did indeed make the land adapt in its mass, like stone.

EXAMINER'S COMMENT

This paragraph shows a close reading of Kinsella's poem. A well-controlled response to a challenging question, developing relevant points and confidently using pertinent quotation from the poem. Grade A.

CLASS/HOMEWORK EXERCISES

1   'The beginning must be inward. Turn inward.' How does Kinsella's poem 'His Father's Hands' illustrate this statement? Support your answer with reference to the text.
2   Copy the table below into your own notes and fill in critical comments about the last two quotations.

Key Quotes

carving off little curlicues/to rub memory them in the dark of his palms	Kinsella's private, microscopic details the action of his grandfather's hands. The hard 'c' alliteration clearly conveys the graceful action of the hands as they form the small curling shavings of the tobacco.
the wind that shakes the barley	A reference to the Irish ballad by Robert Dwyer Joyce (1836–83), which refers to the rebellion of 1798. It also alludes to a force of nature, as time passes through the generations.
stabilized in menace	The very land was shaped into a threat. The issues for the reader to consider are by whom and for whom was this landscape changed.
The blood advancing	
the wood's soft flesh broke open,/ countless little nails/squirming and dropping out of it	

from Settings: Model School, Inchicore

Miss Carney handed us out blank paper and marla,
old plasticine with the colours
all rolled together into brown.

You started with a ball of it
and rolled it into a snake curling   5
around your hand, and kept rolling it
in one place until it wore down into two
with a stain on the paper.

We always tittered at each other
when we said the adding-up table in Irish   10
and came to her name.

*

In the second school we had Mr Browne.
He had white teeth in his brown man's face.

He stood in front of the blackboard
and chalked a white dot.   15

'We are going to start
decimals.'

I am going to know
everything.

*

One day he said: 20
'Out into the sun!'
We settled his chair under a tree
and sat ourselves down delighted
in two rows in the greeny gold shade.

A fat bee floated around   25
shining amongst us

Thomas Kinsella

and the flickering sun
warmed our folded coats
and he said: 'History...!'

*

When the Autumn came   30
and the big chestnut leaves
fell all over the playground
we piled them in heaps
between the wall and the tree trunks
and the boys ran races   35
jumping over the heaps
and tumbled into them shouting.

*

I sat by myself in the shed
and watched the draught
blowing the papers   40
around the wheels of the bicycles.

Will God judge
        our most secret thoughts and actions?
God will judge
        our most secret thoughts and actions 45
and every idle word that man shall speak
he shall render an account of it
on the Day of Judgment.

*

The taste
of ink off   50
the nib shrank your
mouth.

GLOSSARY

1 *marla*: plasticine (soft modelling
   material).
48 *Day of Judgment*: Catholic schools
   taught that every person's soul

would eventually be judged by God.
Depending on the state of the soul,
it would go to heaven or hell.

Thomas Kinsella

'I am going to know/everything'

EXPLORATIONS

1   How does the poet convey a sense of childhood innocence in lines 1–19? Refer to the text in your answer.

2   Select one image from the poem that demonstrates the young Kinsella's feeling of closeness to nature. Comment on its effectiveness.

3   How would you describe the tone of lines 38–48? In your opinion, is it confused? Dismissive? Frightened?

STUDY NOTES

Kinsella received his primary education through the medium of Irish at The Model School in Inchicore from 1932 until 1940. This poem is taken from the 1985 pamphlet *Songs of the Psyche*, published by his own Peppercanister Press. It is a mixture of memory and stream of consciousness, exploring the roots of his inspiration as a poet.

Unlike so many of his poems, which begin on a note of weariness or mental exhaustion, 'Model School, Inchicore' opens with a series of **precise and powerful details evoking the intense wonder of Kinsella's schooldays**: 'Miss Carney handed us out blank paper and marla'. The poet addresses his youthful sense of being immersed in an early classroom activity, modelling plasticine: 'You started with a ball of it/and rolled it into a snake' (lines 4–5). Tactile imagery ('curling', 'rolling it') emphasises the concentration involved in the exercise. Kinsella's interest in identifying people and places is evident throughout. Miss Carney's name provided innocent amusement in class when the children chanted their arithmetic tables in Irish (the word for four, *ceathair*, is not unlike the Irish for Carney, *Cathnirnigh*).

This childish delight in words and associations is also evident in the playful description of another of the poet's primary teachers, Mr Browne: 'He had white teeth in his brown man's face' (line 13). Although the language used in the poem has an accessible prose sense that largely avoids metaphors and symbolism, there is **an implicit impression of 'blank' young minds about to discover new worlds**. Kinsella draws on voices from the past to dramatise the excitement of learning as he mimics the teacher's introduction to studying decimals with his self-assured response: 'I am going to know/everything.' The child's statement is both touching and ironic, particularly as this initial confidence seems to have been so disappointed by the adult poet's retrospective awareness of how much he does not know.

Lines 20–37 continue to explore the poet's formative years through vividly realised images and incidents. Presumably his teachers are remembered because they made sense of things for him. Kinsella's recollection of Mr Browne's enthusiasm and spontaneity are particularly nostalgic: 'One day he said:/"Out into the sun!"' The delights of shared pleasures having lessons in the open air are expressed through **vigorous run-on rhythms and colourful descriptions** of nature's 'greeny gold shade'. The natural world has always provided a background against which Kinsella carries out his examination of life. But references to the 'flickering sun' and 'big chestnut leaves' are a stark reminder of life's transience.

The contrast between the carefree childhood games ('boys ran races') and the lonely image of Kinsella's introspective development ('I sat by myself in the shed') illustrates the **origins of his poetic imagination**. At the end of the poem, he considers the deep fears raised by early religion lessons from the Catholic School Catechism: 'God will judge/our most secret thoughts and actions' (lines 44–5). As the lines grow shorter, they become sharper. Kinsella concludes by returning to an unforgettable sensuous detail: 'The taste/of ink off/the nib shrank your/mouth'. The sensation marked his youth in several ways, allowing him to experience everyday self-awareness while suggesting a growing consciousness of the decaying process. This engagement with inner self is present in much of Kinsella's poetry and is characterised by a bittersweet preoccupation with earthly decay and human mortality.

ANALYSIS

'Kinsella's poetry is primarily concerned with tensions of one kind or another.' Discuss this statement with reference to 'Model School, Inchicore'.

SAMPLE PARAGRAPH

Thomas Kinsella's poems are usually edgy and dramatic. To some extent, he is a brooding pessimist whose ideas are difficult to understand, but this is not so in his poem 'Model School, Inchicore', where he looks back on his national schooling in a sentimental way. The first section of the poem is filled with pleasant memories of using play-dough in the classroom with his friends – 'We always tittered at each other'. The poet uses positive images of nature and its 'greeny gold shade'. One teacher took the children outside to study History, and Kinsella remembers that the class 'sat ourselves down delighted'. However, by contrast, there are personal tensions in the second half of the poem where he recalls being alone and frightened of the religious teaching he had learned – especially about the Last Judgment – 'Will God judge/our most secret thoughts and actions?' Feelings of guilt gripped him at that stage, taking away his childish delights and making him terrified of hell. The language in this part of the poem is condensed and repetitive, suggesting his troubled thoughts. I thought that the tensions related mainly to fear of death and the fact that as a child, he was very impressionable.

EXAMINER'S COMMENT

A good personal response, demonstrating solid engagement with the poem in the second half of the poem. Quotations are well used here to highlight Kinsella's ability to create contrasting atmospheres. The reference to the poet's use of language is interesting, but might have been developed more. Grade B standard.

CLASS/HOMEWORK EXERCISES

1 'What distinguishes Thomas Kinsella's writing is a tragic sense of lost youth and lost innocence.' Write a response to this view of Kinsella's poetry, with particular reference to 'Model School, Inchicore'.
2 Copy the table below into your own notes and fill in critical comments about the last two quotations.

Key Quotes

old plasticine with the colours/ all rolled together into brown	Kinsella's precise description and intense tone reflect his childhood fascination with everyday experiences.
A fat bee floated around/shining amongst us	The poet's sense of self-awareness is expressed through his early acknowledgement of nature's wonder.
When the Autumn came	The sobering effect of time (bringing change and decay) is an important feature of the poem.
I am going to know/everything	
The taste/of ink off/the nib shrank your/mouth	

from The Familiar: VII

Thomas Kinsella

I was downstairs at first light,
looking out through the frost on the window
at the hill opposite and the sheets of frost
scattered down among the rocks.

The cat back in the kitchen.   5
Folded on herself. Torn and watchful.

*

A chilled grapefruit
– thin-skinned, with that little gloss.
I took a mouthful, looking up along the edge of the wood

at the two hooded crows high in the cold   10
talking to each other,
flying up toward the tundra, beyond the waterfall.

*

I sliced the tomatoes in thin discs
in damp sequence into their dish;
scalded the kettle; made the tea,   15

and rang the little brazen bell.
And saved the toast.
                    Arranged the pieces

in slight disorder around the basket.
Fixed our places, one with the fruit   20
and one with the plate of sharp cheese.

*

And stood in my dressing gown
with arms extended
over the sweetness of the sacrifice.

Her shade showed in the door.   25
Her voice responded:
'You are very good. You always made it nice.'

'I sliced the tomatoes in thin discs / in damp sequence into their dish'

GLOSSARY

12 *tundra*: vast, flat, treeless Arctic region, whose subsoil is permanently frozen.
14 *sequence*: particular order in which related things follow each other.

16 *brazen*: made of brass; bold, shameless, defiant.
21 *sharp*: tapering to a point; strong and slightly bitter.

EXPLORATIONS

1   Comment on the title of the poem, 'The Familiar'. Do you think it suggests being bored with routine, or drawing comfort from the well-known? Refer closely to the poem in your response.

2   In your opinion, which aspects of the woman are evoked in the poem? Is she lover, judge, goddess, companion, friend? Illustrate your response with references to the text.

3   The poem concludes with two spoken sentences from the woman beloved. Are they positive and affirming comments? Or are they patronising and almost belittling? Support your views with close reference to the poem.

STUDY NOTES

Thomas Kinsella wrote this seven-part narrative poem, 'The Familiar', in 1999. The poet believes in the importance and enabling power of love. Here he is examining his relationship with his lover. Love is seen as a countermeasure to human isolation. The full poem sequence explores his lonely condition before they met, the intricate feelings experienced as they began their shared life together, and finally their intimacy. The seventh section details an ordinary daily ritual: the poet has risen early and is preparing their breakfast.

The **cinematic opening of the first sequence** of the poem (lines 1–6) shows the poet 'downstairs at first light'. Kinsella believes that these transitional moments between night and day are important times when real insightful truth can be glimpsed. The scene outside is cold and forbidding: 'frost on the window', 'sheets of frost/scattered'. Is this a metaphor for the coldness and isolation of modern relationships? Inside the kitchen; the atmosphere seems warm and cosily domestic: 'The cat ... Folded on herself'. However, a note of tension creeps in as the cat is described as 'Torn'. Has it been fighting? The cat also scrutinises the poet's movements, 'watchful'.

In the second section (lines 7–12), a close-up of the citric 'chilled grapefruit' is visually striking, 'thin-skinned, with that little gloss'. The slight bitterness of the fruit and the adjective 'chilled' both hint at **a certain discomfort being experienced**. Kinsella often uses the metaphor of eating when speaking of relationships. The phrase 'I took a mouthful' could relate to Kinsella's whole-hearted engagement with this attachment. He now looks out again and notices two crows flying 'high in the cold/talking to each other'. They symbolise the coming together of the poet and his loved one as they go through this forbidding life in companionship and close communication. The crow is a symbol from Celtic mythology of Morrigan, the Goddess of War. The turbulent nature of love is hinted at again.

In the third section (lines 13–21), the poet carefully and methodically prepares their breakfast with great solemnity. He 'sliced the tomatoes in thin discs'. Assonance of the slender vowel 'i' suggests the wafer thinness of the slices. Again, Kinsella's eye for detail draws the reader firmly into the narrative, as the feel of the tomatoes is shown in the adjective 'damp'. The **imposition of order**, another Kinsella preoccupation, is stressed through the word 'sequence'. This ritual continues as he 'scalded the kettle; made the tea'. A careful preparation now takes on the overtones of a religious ceremony, the Mass. The breaking of bread is mirrored in saving 'the toast'. The disorder of the toast slices is cleverly imitated by the slight disorder in lines 18–19. The tang of the 'sharp cheese' also hints that the relationship could at times hurt.

In the final section (lines 22–7), the poet now assumes the gesture of the priest at the moment of consecration, 'And stood in my dressing gown/with arms extended'. The preparation of the breakfast that is about to be shared is seen as the 'sweetness of the sacrifice'. Do people in a relationship have to surrender their individuality and personal preferences in compromise for the good of the relationship? The breakfast has been offered to his beloved. Now she appears, 'Her shade showed in the door'. **The soft alliterative 'sh' evokes a hushed, almost spiritual dimension to the woman**, as if she were a goddess who will accept or reject the poet's 'sacrifice', the carefully prepared breakfast. She affirms his effort in measured tones: 'You are very good. You always made it nice.' Does this response show an equal relationship, or does it suggest that the poet is 'always' trying to please/appease this woman, and waits slightly in fear of her judgment? Through his sensitive use of imagery, the poet has involved the reader in the intricate entanglement of human emotions.

The poem resonates with uneasiness and a veiled tension. This is conveyed in the **detailed imagery** through words like 'Torn', 'watchful', 'thin-skinned', 'disorder', 'sharp', 'sacrifice'. The hesitant rhythm ('scalded the kettle; made the tea') adds to the fraught atmosphere. At the conclusion of the poem, the woman's comment underlines why the poet is on edge. Does the familiar inspire dread?

ANALYSIS

'The enduring strength of love is a recurring theme in the poetry of Thomas Kinsella.' Discuss this statement, referring to the poem 'The Familiar: VII'. Quote from the text in support of your views.

SAMPLE PARAGRAPH

I found this poem of Kinsella's slightly unnerving. I thought the contrast between the frozen scene outside, 'sheets of frost/scattered', and the cosy scene inside, 'The cat ... Folded on herself', very comforting at first. But soon, it appeared to me that cracks began to show in the relationship. The cat was 'Torn and watchful', as it lay scrutinising the poet. There had obviously been a fight the night before. All the fruit is acidic and slightly bitter, 'chilled grapefruit', 'tomatoes', 'sharp cheese'. I thought the poet was making a tremendous effort in getting the breakfast prepared 'just right'; he even had got up 'at first light'. There is a suggestion of previous criticism in the phrase 'And saved the toast'. He called the breakfast a 'sacrifice'. Was this a making-up gesture after a row? The strength in this relationship, seems to me, to belong to the woman, as she appeared when all was ready, and delivered her judgment, 'You are good. You always made it nice.' I feel this man spends a lot of time trying to please this woman. I found a slight hint of condescension in her comment, 'You are good'. I

Thomas Kinsella

think Kinsella is very honest in his portrayal of 'enduring love'. Love is an effort, it is something to be suffered and endured if it is to exist in the long term. Kinsella portrays this idea very effectively in the poem, although I do think the relationship is rather one-sided.

EXAMINER'S COMMENT

The second half of the paragraph shows some good engagement with the question. However, the first section is off task. The emphasis should be on Kinsella's attitude to love. While the expression is very good, the lack of focus reduces the standard to a grade C.

CLASS/HOMEWORK EXERCISES

1 'A troubled intensity of focus is the hallmark of much of Thomas Kinsella's poetry.' Discuss this view, with particular reference to 'The Familiar: VII'. Support your answer with reference to the text.
2 Copy the table below into your own notes and fill in critical comments about the last two quotations.

Key Quotes

Torn and watchful	The adjectives suggest that the cat has been in a scrap and is carefully following the poet's movements. Is this also relating to the woman in his life?
thin-skinned, with that little gloss	The description of the sour grapefruit is evocative of more than just the fruit; it can also refer to the poet's bittersweet relationship.
with arms extended	This gesture is the traditional pose adopted by the priest at the moment of Consecration in the Catholic Mass. Is Kinsella being slightly ironic?
the sweetness of the sacrifice	
'You are very good. You always made it nice.'	

from **Belief and Unbelief: Echo**

He cleared the thorns
from the broken gate,
and held her hand
through the heart of the wood
to the holy well.   5

They revealed their names
and told their tales
as they said that they would
on that distant day
when their love began.   10

And hand in hand
they turned to leave.
When she stopped and whispered
a final secret
down to the water.   15

'He cleared the thorns/from the broken gate'

GLOSSARY

In Greek mythology, Echo was a nymph who loved her own voice. She was punished for telling tales and had her voice taken away, except to repeat another's words. She fell in love with Narcissus, a vain young man who rejected her. Echo fled to lonely places where she mourned her lost love and wasted away until only her voice remained.

EXPLORATIONS

1   This poem has the feel of a fairytale. What details in the text support this view? Use quotation from the poem to illustrate your response.

2   Having read the glossary concerning the myth of Echo, why do you think Kinsella chose this as his title for the poem? Support your answer with references from the text.

3   This poem reveals and conceals. Paying particular attention to the final stanza, what, in your view, is being hidden and what is being shared?

STUDY NOTES

'Echo' is part of the collection *Belief and Unbelief*, published in 2007 by Thomas Kinsella. Kinsella returns, again, to one of his particular themes, the examination of love, relationships and death. He is examining process, how we discover and how we understand.

In the first stanza, **the lovers embark on a pilgrimage**, a journey with a religious purpose. They travel as a result of a promise they made when they fell in love. The man is strong as he 'cleared the thorns', pushing away obstacles and problems. The thorns suggest suffering, reminiscent of Christ on the cross. The man assumes a protective role in relation to the woman ('held her hand'). He acts as a guide. The 'holy well' is a place sanctified by a blessing from the Irish saints, where people went to be healed and comforted and to receive reassurance in times of sickness or trouble. The Celts thought these places were access points to another world. Woods ('the heart of the wood') and magic wells are the stuff of legend and fairytale. The mood in this stanza is similar to the hushed atmosphere of the children's story of Sleeping Beauty. The stanza flows smoothly in a single sentence as the couple enter by the 'broken gate'. This is an interesting image. A gate, if locked, bars access, but if broken, it permits entrance, as it is no longer a barrier. It becomes useless.

Stanza two is full of **self-revelation**, as the couple declare 'their names'. They told their stories ('tales') to fulfil a promise made at the beginning of their relationship. The simple language reinforces this impression of an ancient legend or fairytale, 'as they said that they would'. They have been together a long time, 'on that distant day when their love began'. A sense of union and harmony has been created in this second fluid sentence. The pledge has been honoured.

The **third stanza** begins with a clear picture of the lovers as equals, who leave 'hand in hand'. But now the punctuation (a full stop) halts the flowing movement of the poem. The reader is made to pause in synchronisation with the couple. The woman 'stopped and whispered'. **Relationships require openness and honesty** if they are to succeed, yet most relationships have some secrets. There is always something withheld. But this is the 'final secret' to be disclosed. Is everything now open between the couple? The steady rhythm of the two-beat line would suggest this. The relationship seems to go on. Yet the longer third line, with its sibilant 's' ('stopped', 'whispered'), seems to suggest that all is not as it might appear. Is she mimicking the action of Narcissus, the beloved of Echo, as he lay speaking to his own reflection in the water? Is she still self-absorbed? Is she sharing the 'final secret' with the man or her reflection in the water? Is this action an image of openness or concealment?

This poem reveals and hides. It ends, yet it is not concluded – what will happen next? Are the couple more united now that they have fulfilled their promise and come to this place, or is there still some distance between them, private thoughts which they have not shared with each other? Is this the true nature of relationships, that someone always holds something back? Does anyone ever really know everything about another person?

ANALYSIS

'Happiness is qualified in this life.' Discuss how this statement could refer to the poem 'Echo' by Thomas Kinsella. Refer closely to the poem in your response.

SAMPLE PARAGRAPH

This poem has a fairytale feel to it with the details of the 'broken gate' and the 'heart of the wood' and the 'holy well'. So I thought that this poem would be describing a happy-ever-after scene. I was therefore rather surprised in the third stanza when I realised that Kinsella was exploring a great truth about all human relationships, that none of them are perfect, there is always something hidden, the 'final secret'. It is not clear to me that the man in the poem hears what the 'final secret' is. The woman 'whispered/a final secret/down to the water', not to him. I thought she was like the character in the story of Echo, Narcissus. He had fallen in love with his own reflection and so ignored the loving Echo who pined away until only the sound of her voice remained. I think this woman is mostly concerned with herself, as all people are. So now the fairytale element of the story, the happy ending, goes, and we are given a portrait of happiness in life which is not the picture perfect image in stories, as it says, 'And hand in hand'. Nobody tells another person everything. Secrets are always there between people, total honesty is not possible. The punctuation in this third stanza, the full stop after the word 'leave' mirrors this insight. The smooth flow of the poem is interrupted by the action of the woman. I think that the verb 'whispered' suggests that the poet has not heard the 'final secret' between them and so a distance still remains in their relationship. 'Happiness is qualified in this life.'

EXAMINER'S COMMENT

This paragraph shows a personal engagement with the theme of Kinsella's poem. A competent answer, though at times the syntax is awkward and the expression can be repetitive. Some points, e.g. about the punctuation in the third stanza, are not developed. Grade B.

CLASS/HOMEWORK EXERCISES

1   'The expression of love is central to Kinsella's work.' How does the poem 'Echo' illustrate this statement? Support your answer with reference to the text.
2   Copy the table below into your own notes and fill in critical comments about the last two quotations.

Key Quotes

He cleared the thorns	This simple, tender image suggests that the man is sweeping aside problems to allow clear access. Is a metaphorical sense also intended?
the holy well	A reference to the Irish tradition of visiting holy springs to seek favours or cures. People often leave a token, a coin or a piece of cloth tied on a branch nearby.
And hand in hand	The phrase suggests an idyllic relationship between the couple, one of perfect unity and equality.
told their tales	
When she stopped and whispered/ a final secret	

LEAVING CERT SAMPLE ESSAY

> **Q** 'Kinsella is a poet drowning in a sea of disappointment.'
>
> **Using the above statement as your title, write an essay on the poetry of Thomas Kinsella. Support the points you make by reference to the poetry of Kinsella on your course.**

MARKING SCHEME GUIDELINES

Expect candidates to agree and/or disagree with the given statement. The poet's treatment of themes, subjects, attitudes and issues should be discussed, as well as his individual style, manner, phraseology, appropriate vocabulary, imagery, etc.

The candidate should show a clear sense of personal engagement with the poetry.

Some of the following areas might provide material for candidates:
- Poet's disillusioned views on life/relationships.
- Recurring despondent themes: transience, death.
- Fragmented rhythm, disjointed detail.
- Patterns of bleak and disturbing imagery/language.
- Melancholy, morose tone in the texts.
- Kinsella celebrates the past.
- A realistic approach to themes.
- Energetic, varied, innovative style, etc.

SAMPLE ESSAY
(Kinsella Is a Poet Drowning in a Sea of Disappointment)

1 *One criticism that has been hurtled at Kinsella's work is that it is 'good in parts' as he seems to have an 'uncertainty where to stop'. Kinsella responded to this by stating that 'others read what I do ... disappointment is the invariable outcome of that'. But while others may be 'disappointed', because his poems, as he remarked, didn't come to 'an end with the last line', he is not disappointed and neither am I.*

He, in my opinion, intended his poetry to reflect the sifting process through details of memory stored in the depths of his mind. He persistently self-analyses, and as he recognises imperfections he is dissatisfied, and yet, he gives us an insight into the very processes of life itself. He gives the ordinary 'profound significance'.

2 *In the poem 'His Father's Hands', Kinsella remembers a moment he shared with his father. Both son and father share the same obstinacy, emphasised by the repetition of the adverb 'firmly' and the verbs 'saying' and 'prodded'. Here were two strong men squaring up to each other. But this remembered detail becomes transformed into a meditation on family connections, as he recalls in cinematic detail his grandfather paring 'curlicues' from a piece of solid tobacco, 'the black Plug'. The scene is drawn in such concrete terms that the reader shares the memory as intensely as the poet remembered it. Kinsella and the reader travel 'back to the dark/and the depth' that he came from. This is not 'drowning in a sea of disappointment', rather it is a tender recall of a cherished memory, as his grandfather plays the violin. The onomatopoeic 'scraping' allows the reader to hear the rasping noise of the violin as the 'wind that shakes the barley' is played 'with breaking heart'.*

3 *The ending of the poem is a similar moment of clear and positive insight, as the block of 'wood's soft flesh broke open', and 'countless little nails' came 'squirming and dropping out of it'. It is as if Kinsella's ancestors were pushing through the barriers of time and space. The dynamic image of continuing life is captured in the active verbs 'squirming and dropping'. The block of wood is a symbol that stands for Kinsella's family, from son to father, to grandfather and beyond. It remains firmly rooted in the real world of the dark, Irish landscape.*

4 *This realism permeates the poem 'The Familiar: VII', which deals with a taut relationship between a man and a woman. Although the details here, 'Torn' cat, the 'chilled grapefruit', the acidic 'thin discs' of tomatoes and the 'sharp cheese', suggest a brittle, tense relationship, nevertheless the energy and devotion of the man is what we remember and uplifts us. He 'scalded the kettle; made the tea', ordinary actions which are transformed into the 'sweetness of the sacrifice' as the action takes on the resonance of the sacrifice of the Mass, as he stood 'with arms extended'. The poem concludes with two sentences of dialogue from the woman. She speaks in measured terms, accepting the gift offered, 'You always made it very nice'. This brittle type of relationship is also examined in the poem 'Echo'.*

5 In 'Echo', a fairytale poem of a couple renewing a pledge, the man, again, is shown working hard at the relationship, 'cleared the thorns', 'held her hand'. They both 'revealed their names/and told their tales'. But this poem pauses with the woman who 'stopped and whispered'. The soft sibilant 's' lets us hear the quiet confession of 'a final secret'. Yet it is not to the man the woman confesses, but 'down to the water'. Is this disappointment? I do not think so, as the couple are described as 'hand in hand'. I believe it is Kinsella stating the truth of human relationships, that none are perfect, always something is held back and that a couple have to take time to nurture their relationship, 'as they said they would/on that distant day/when their love began'. The simple language used in this poem conceals the depth and profundity of insight hidden in this dreamlike poem.

6 The poem 'Chrysalides' also examines through remembered details the truth of a relationship, beginning with a celebration of young love, as they moon 'about at odd hours'. The disregard for time is emphasised by the long vowel sounds used. The lovers felt that they were at the centre of the universe, all revolved around them. They satisfied their senses, 'stopping to eat/Chocolate and fruit'. The magical mood of young love is conveyed in the picture of the moonlit night as 'ablaze softly with the virgin moon'. This is also another poem that concludes open-ended with an image that is very similar to the block of wood at the conclusion of 'His Father's Hands'. In 'Chrysalides', a flock of ants, 'Spawning to its death', appears. Kinsella may see the world as flawed, but he is not disenchanted or upset. The title of the poem refers to the egg that contains the insect before it hatches, the egg contains life, as do the young couple and the ants. I believe Kinsella saw love as a consolation in this cold, bitter world. He may recognise the reality of transience, but it is the sweet image of young love that remains with the reader. Out of waste the poet has fashioned beauty as we are invited to share the 'unique succession' of 'youthful midnights'. The lyric transcends mutability.

7 So, Kinsella's poetry, although lacking a clear narrative, instead allows us to experience the 'complex, accidental moment of the here and now'. Instead of story, the poet presents us with detail. Instead of conclusion, we are asked to experience the pursuit of the real. Kinsella sails, but does not drown, in the sea of disappointment of life guided unerringly by his almost forensic attention to detail.

(approx. 1,000 words)

GRADE: A1
P = 15/15
C = 13/15
L = 14/15
M = 5/5
Total = 47/50

EXAMINER'S COMMENT

This well-prepared, focused response takes a positive view of Kinsella. It shows real personal engagement with the poetry. There is a slight drift away from the question in paragraph 3. The expression is formal and mature, and well-interwoven quotations are evident.

SAMPLE LEAVING CERT QUESTIONS ON KINSELLA'S POETRY (45–50 MINUTES)

1   Thomas Kinsella has said, 'We simply go back from where you came from – which is nowhere.' Discuss this statement, focusing particular attention on Kinsella's themes and how he expresses them. Support the points you make by reference to the poetry of Thomas Kinsella on your course.

2   What impact did the poetry of Thomas Kinsella make on you as a reader? In shaping your answer, you might like to consider the following:
    *   Your overall sense or outlook of the poet.
    *   The poet's use of language and/or imagery.
    *   Your favourite poem or poems.

3   'Kinsella is the quintessential Dublin poet' (Andrew Fitzsimons). Discuss this view, referring both to the subject matter, themes and style of the poetry of Thomas Kinsella on your course.

SAMPLE ESSAY PLAN (Q3)

'Kinsella is the quintessential Dublin poet' (Andrew Fitzsimons). Discuss this view, referring both to the subject matter, themes and style of the poetry of Thomas Kinsella on your course.

• *Intro:*	'His Dublin will sell few beers.' Kinsella is battered and baffled by the actual. Dublin provides a background to his poetry, which is cumulative and fragmented.
• *Point 1:*	City of his childhood – narrow streets, dark yards. 'Thinking of Mr D.' – 'lamps that plunged him in and out of light'. 'Hen Woman' – 'The noon heat in the yard'.
• *Point 2:*	Family history is a central feature. 'His Father's Hands' – traces Kinsella's family back to his father, grandfather and his ancestors. 'I have watched his father's hands before him/cupped, and tightening the black Plug', 'Beyond that'. Detailed memories that are the essence of old Dublin.
• *Point 3:*	Community history details the ghostly failures that stagger and recover. 'Dick King' – 'You haunt with the taint of age and vanished good/Fouling my thoughts with losses'. 'Thinking of Mr D.' – 'under wharf-/Lamps that plunged him in and out of light,/A priestlike figure turning'.
• *Point 4:*	A record of established personal places that mark our lives. 'Model School, Inchicore' – 'I sat by myself in the shed/and watched the draught/blowing the papers/around the wheels of the bicycles'.
• *Point 5:*	Captures the authentic sound of Dublin speech. 'You were saying', 'We are going to start/decimals, 'Out into the sun', 'scalding the kettle'.
• *Conclusion:*	A difficult, provocative, stubborn poet in the tradition of Yeats and Joyce, capturing the essence of 'old, dirty Dublin'. A unique voice in contrast to the traditional rural Irish poets, Kavanagh and Heaney.

EXERCISE

Develop one of the above points into a paragraph.

CONCLUSION – SAMPLE PARAGRAPH

In his book *The Poetry of Thomas Kinsella*, the critic Maurice Harmon states, 'There are no final conclusions' in the poetry of Kinsella. This difficult, provocative poet gives us a dry view of 'dirty Dublin' in the 1930s and 1940s in the tradition of Joyce and Yeats. The old city is brought to a dim glow as railway, brewery, backyard and old schoolrooms are brought to life from the microscopic precision of Kinsella's memory. Ghostly figures emerge from the city background as the universal processes of growth, maturing and extinction take their inevitable course. The stultifying atmosphere of this time in the city, a place of silent pints and hushed backyards, emerges from Kinsella's poetry in black and white, just like old grainy photographs. A unique Irish city voice is now heard in marked contrast to the traditional rural voice of Kavanagh and Heaney. As Kinsella says, 'I have devoted my life to the avoidance of affectation.' So Kinsella continues writing his poetry in the manner of 'A beetle like a bronze leaf ... inching across the cement,/clasping with small tarsi'. This is the dull glow of a marginalised poet sifting through his quintessential Dublin, 'noted and hoarded in the imagination'.

EXAMINER'S COMMENT

As the conclusion of a full essay answer, this is a thoughtful summary that shows a real understanding of the aims of Kinsella. The paragraph focuses successfully on the essence of the poet. The response also benefits greatly from well-integrated quotations. Grade A.

Last Words

'Writing for most of my life has been a solitary matter – trying to respond as precisely as I could to mostly private impulses.'

> Thomas Kinsella *(on being honoured as a Freeman of Dublin)*

'The interruption of the immediate by the mediative and meditative is a constant in Kinsella's work.'

> Peter Sirr

'All of these poems, whatever their differences, have a feature in common: a tendency to look inward for material – into family or self.'

> Thomas Kinsella

*'An event provides a
lead into a poem.'*

Philip Larkin   (1922–85)

Philip Larkin was born in 1922 in Coventry, England. He did not enjoy his childhood:
'Get out as early as you can/And don't have any kids yourself'. Nor did he like school.
He had a stammer and was short-sighted, although he read widely and contributed to
the school magazine. After graduating from Oxford, he went on to become a librarian.
Larkin became a great admirer of Thomas Hardy's poetry, learning from Hardy how to
make the commonplace and often dreary details of his life the basis for extremely
tough, unsparing and memorable poems. He published several collections of poetry,
much of which reflected ordinary English life. His searing, often mocking wit rarely
concealed the poet's dark vision and underlying obsession with universal themes of
mortality, love and human solitude. Yet Larkin's poems face the trials of living and dying
with an orderly elegance that always moves the reader. Philip Larkin believed poetry
should come from personal experience: 'I write about experiences ... simple everyday
experiences ... I hope other people will come upon this ... pickled in verse ... and it will
mean something to them.'

PRESCRIBER POEMS (HIGHER LEVEL)

1 'Wedding-Wind' (p. 324)

A celebration of the healing power of love and marriage. The speaker is a young bride who is looking forward to a life of happiness.

2 'At Grass' (p. 329)

A nostalgic narrative poem describing retired racehorses, in which the poet reflects on the changes brought about by time and the contentment of old age.

3 'Church Going' (p. 334)

Conversational and self-mocking, Larkin meditates on the role and significance of churches and religious practice in people's lives.

4 'An Arundel Tomb' (p. 341)

This bittersweet exploration of the power of love to transcend time was written after the poet visited the tomb of the medieval Earl and Countess of Arundel.

5 'The Whitsun Weddings' (p. 347)

The central theme is marriage in all its complexity and its importance within an increasingly urbanised society.

6 'MCMXIV' (p. 354)

The Roman numeral title stands for 1914, the start of World War I. For Larkin, the date marked the end of innocence for the young soldiers and their families.

7 'Ambulances' (p. 359)

This poem uses the symbol of an ambulance to outline Larkin's views on the futility of life and the inevitable reality of death.

8 'The Trees' (p. 364)

This short poem, contrasting nature (the trees) and the lives of human beings, is another review of the theme of transience.

9 'The Explosion' (p. 368)

An affirmative poem based on a tragic coalmine accident. There were reports that at the time of the explosion, some of the miners' wives saw visions of their husbands.

10 'Cut Grass' (p. 373)

Another short lyric about the cycle of life and death. The poem's title image suggests how life and natural growth can be abruptly ended.

Wedding-Wind

Philip Larkin

The wind blew all my wedding-day,
And my wedding-night was the night of the high wind;
And a stable door was banging, again and again,
That he must go and shut it, leaving me
Stupid in candlelight, hearing rain,   5
Seeing my face in the twisted candlestick,
Yet seeing nothing. When he came back
He said the horses were restless, and I was sad
That any man or beast that night should lack
The happiness I had.   10

                    Now in the day
All's ravelled under the sun by the wind's blowing.
He has gone to look at the floods, and I
Carry a chipped pail to the chicken-run,
Set it down, and stare. All is the wind   15
Hunting through clouds and forests, thrashing
My apron and the hanging cloths on the line.
Can it be borne, this bodying-forth by wind
Of joy my actions turn on, like a thread
Carrying beads? Shall I be let to sleep   20
Now this perpetual morning shares my bed?
Can even death dry up
These new delighted lakes, conclude
Our kneeling as cattle by all-generous waters?

'and the hanging
cloths on the line'

GLOSSARY

12 *ravelled*: pulled apart and untangled.

16 *thrashing*: moving; beating violently.

18 *borne*: carried by, endured.

EXPLORATIONS

1   How realistic do you think Larkin's portrayal of marriage is? Support your views with reference to the text.

2   Trace the tone in this poem. Does it change? What is different in the attitude of the speaker in the second section?

3   In your opinion, why does the poem end with three questions?

STUDY NOTES

'Wedding-Wind' was published in 1946. This narrative poem (Larkin was also a novelist) records details of a wedding day, night and the morning after. Larkin adopts the persona of a young bride to tell the story. He said, 'I can imagine ... the emotions of a bride ... without ever having been a woman or married.' This poem is a celebration of the joy of passionate love.

This direct, personal poem's opening section begins with the young bride stating that 'The wind blew all my wedding-day'. This 'high wind' blew throughout her day and the wedding night. Is it a **symbol for passion and change**? Is the poem linking the energy of the natural world with the force of human love? The adjective 'high' for Larkin meant elevated and elevating experiences. People rise above the ordinary to experience a spiritual feeling. The restless atmosphere of the day and night is caught in the description of the stable door 'banging, again and again'. This mundane detail shows Larkin's ear for the ordinary. The young woman relates how her husband has to 'go and shut' the banging door. Larkin believed that life as it was lived by ordinary people should and could provide the subject for poetry. The young bride feels inadequate, 'Stupid in candlelight', 'seeing nothing'. Her new husband returns, saying 'the horses were restless'. She feels compassion for all living things that are not experiencing the happiness 'I had'.

The second section of the poem is an interior monologue by the bride as she observes the destruction caused by the 'wind's blowing'. 'All's ravelled under the sun': the debris of the storm is clear for everyone to see. Both the world and the bride have been changed by some huge elemental force. She is now a **woman of responsibilities**. She recognises the practicalities of farming. There is no honeymoon. 'He has gone to look at the floods' and she has gone to feed the chickens. The detail of her 'chipped pail' lends a human, imperfect note to the scene. She sets the pail down and begins to reflect ('stare').

Now, unlike last night, **she is seeing**. The wind, this powerful force of nature, was a predator, 'Hunting through clouds and forests' (line 16). The violent force of the wind is contained in the verb 'thrashing'. Does this have connotations of the violent passion of love? Again, an ordinary sight, clothes hanging on a washing line ('My apron and the hanging cloths on the line'), makes the poem accessible to all, academic and non-academic. There is no exclusive reference to classical mythology, but the common stuff of life. The poem concludes with three questions. The young woman wonders if she will survive the 'joy my actions turn on'. The compound word 'bodying-forth' and the verb 'borne' suggest pregnancy. The simile 'like a thread/Carrying beads' implies praying and the sacredness of the holy state of matrimony. Or this thread could refer to a necklace, a gift or symbol of love given between the young couple.

The second question poses the problem of sleep: 'Shall I be let to sleep' (line 20). The bride now feels that every day is 'perpetual morning', as life seems full of exciting possibilities, so it is impossible to rest. She feels so blessed by love that she has almost been made immortal: 'Can even death dry up' her joy? She believes that these 'new delighted lakes' can never be 'dry', even though the wind dries water from the land. She is compelled to make a sign, 'conclude/Our kneeling as cattle'. The biblical tones of the compound word 'all-generous' show **an optimistic view that joy can outlive death**.

Larkin wanted his readers to experience his poetry and say, 'I've never thought of it that way before, but that's how it is.' **He believed poetry should come from personal experience**. Larkin disliked the idea that poetry should come from other poems. He was opposed to Modernism, a poetry movement that is allusory and inaccessible to the ordinary person. It is interesting to note that this poem takes a private, human experience and links it with nature. Does this lend a note of danger to the experience of young, passionate love? Parallel to the poem, dramatic changes were taking place in English society. The Second World War had just ended, followed by the depression of the 1950s, the affluence and student unrest of the 1960s and the emergence of socialism and multiculturalism. This rural English experience of young love is preserved by Larkin, 'pickled as it were in verse', despite all the changes taking place.

ANALYSIS

Larkin believed that poetry should help us 'enjoy and endure'. Do you agree or disagree with this statement? Support your view with references from the poem.

SAMPLE PARAGRAPH

I believe that this poem helps us enjoy life, thanks to the beautiful, passionate narrative of this young bride. The wind represents change and dynamism in the natural world, as well as in the world of the young woman. It is 'sacred', a 'high wind', which both scatters and cleans, 'All's ravelled under the sun by the wind's blowing'. The human details of ordinary life shine under the craftsmanship of Larkin, 'chipped pail', 'stable door ... banging, again and again', 'hanging cloths on the line'. The ordinary, somewhat irksome chores which we all must endure become the basis of passionate poetry as the young bride wonders whether all this 'joy of action' can be 'borne'. We are elevated, as the woman is, by the optimistic, mystical vision that love cannot be dimmed by death. We kneel at the 'all-generous waters'. Larkin has helped us to enjoy and endure.

EXAMINER'S COMMENT

This short paragraph addresses both aspects of the question (enjoy and endure). The response shows a real appreciation of Larkin's poetic beliefs. More detailed analysis and comment on the key quotations would have resulted in a higher grade. However, the style throughout is assured and vocabulary and expression are very good. Grade B.

CLASS/HOMEWORK EXERCISES

1 Write a paragraph on how effectively Larkin uses metaphors to communicate his message in this poem. Support your answer with reference to the text.
2 Copy the table below into your own notes and fill in critical comments about the last two quotations.

Key Quotes

And my wedding-night was the night of the high wind	The reflective tone and adjective 'high' suggest that the wind is a sacred force for change.
All is the wind/Hunting through clouds and forests	The entire scene is pervaded by the personification of the wind as a hunter, on its lookout for prey.
this bodying-forth by wind/ Of joy my actions turn on	This terse line conveys the swelling motion of the wind enmeshed in the happiness experienced by the young bride.
Now this perpetual morning shares my bed	
Our kneeling as cattle by all-generous waters	

At Grass

The eye can hardly pick them out
From the cold shade they shelter in,
Till wind distresses tail and mane;
Then one crops grass, and moves about
– The other seeming to look on –   5
And stands anonymous again.

Yet fifteen years ago, perhaps
Two dozen distances sufficed
To fable them: faint afternoons
Of Cups and Stakes and Handicaps,   10
Whereby their names were artificed
To inlay faded, classic Junes –

Silks at the start: against the sky
Numbers and parasols: outside,
Squadrons of empty cars, and heat,   15
And littered grass: then the long cry
Hanging unhushed till it subside
To stop-press columns on the street.

Do memories plague their ears like flies?
They shake their heads. Dusk brims the shadows.   20
Summer by summer all stole away,
The starting-gates, the crowds and cries –
All but the unmolesting meadows.
Almanacked, their names live; they

Have slipped their names, and stand at ease,   25
Or gallop for what must be joy,
And not a fieldglass sees them home,
Or curious stop-watch prophesies:
Only the groom, and the groom's boy,
With bridles in the evening come.   30

Philip Larkin

'The starting-gates, the crowds and cries'

GLOSSARY

At Grass: a reference to the retirement of old racehorses.

3 *mane*: the hair on the back of a horse's neck.

4 *crops*: eats, chews.

8 *Two dozen distances sufficed*: 24 races were enough.

9 *To fable*: to make famous.

10 *Cups and Stakes and Handicaps*: various types of horse races.

11 *artificed*: displayed (on trophies, etc.).

12 *inlay*: ornamental fabric.

12 *classic*: traditional, important June races.

13 *Silks*: shirts ('colours') worn by jockeys.

14 *Numbers*: betting numbers displayed by bookies.

14 *parasols*: ladies' umbrellas.

15 *Squadrons*: long lines (of parked cars).

18 *stop-press*: news update (latest racing results).

19 *plague*: irritate.

23 *unmolesting*: harmless, gentle.

24 *Almanacked*: listed in the racing records.

29 *groom*: worker who looks after the horses.

30 *bridles*: restraints placed on the heads of horses.

EXPLORATIONS

1 Using close reference to the text, describe the atmosphere/mood in the opening stanza.

2 How does Larkin convey the excitement of the racecourse in stanza three? Refer to the text in your answer.

3 Choose two memorable images from the poem and briefly explain their effectiveness.

STUDY NOTES

'At Grass' was written in 1950 after the poet had seen a documentary film about a retired racehorse. Larkin, himself a lover of horses, saw them as exploited during their racing careers. This strikingly reflective poem, exploring the changes brought about by the passage of time, has been interpreted as a criticism of the passing fashion of celebrity, and as a requiem for a bygone age.

Stanza one begins with a short description of two horses sheltering in the distance. Larkin remarks that 'The eye can hardly pick them out' before he has even explained what there is to pick out. It is only when a slight breeze 'distresses tail and mane' that the horses come to life. Even then, the 'cold shade' setting has a vague suggestion that these forgotten ('anonymous') animals are close to death. There is an **evocative visual quality** within these early lines and a **mood of wistful sadness** dominates.

In contrast to this feeling of stillness, Larkin begins to imagine the racehorses in their prime 'fifteen years ago'. The **nostalgic flashback** in the second and third stanzas recalls their triumphs in 'Cups and Stakes and Handicaps', enough 'To fable them' and ensure their reputation in racing history. The thrill and glamour of 'classic Junes' is recreated through vibrant images of the jockeys' colours ('Silks') and the 'Numbers and parasols'. Cinematic details ('empty cars', 'littered grass') and the excited cheering ('the long cry') of the crowds all convey the joy of unforgettable race meetings.

Stanza four returns to the present as Larkin considers the conscious experiences of the horses themselves. The line 'They shake their heads' is playfully ambiguous, both a negative response to the earlier question ('Do memories plague their ears like flies?') and an actual movement which horses carry out naturally. Larkin's elegant imagery communicates the subtle advance of time: 'Summer by summer' as 'Dusk brims the shadows'. There is a strong sense that at the end of their lives, these once-famous horses deserve to take their ease in 'unmolesting meadows'. Interestingly, the most remarkable verbs in the poem – 'fabled', 'artificed', 'inlay', 'Almanacked' – are all concerned with the way people have seen and recorded these horses. They have become racecourse stories, names engraved into trophies and recorded in official histories.

The **dignified language and slow rhythm** of stanza five suggest both the tranquil freedom of these retired horses and the reality that they are nearing the end of their long lives. For the moment, though, they 'gallop for what must be joy' – a typical Larkin comment which throws doubt onto an assertion even while in the process of making it. The poem ends on a consolatory note. Now that the horses have 'slipped their names' and are no longer chasing fame or glory, they can 'stand at ease', enjoying the peace and quiet. Broad assonant effects emphasise their sense of quiet fulfilment: 'Only the groom, and the groom's boy,/With bridles in the evening come'. The inverted syntax and mellow tone add to the sense of finality. In completing the natural cycle of their lives, Larkin's racehorses offer a model for the human condition of youth, achievement and old age. Characteristically, the development of thought in the poem moves from observation to reflection, leaving us to appreciate the blend of celebration and sadness that mark this beautiful poem.

ANALYSIS

Using close reference to the text, comment on the poet's use of contrast in 'At Grass'.

SAMPLE PARAGRAPH

Philip Larkin uses two distinct settings in 'At Grass'. This is a very effective device to highlight the past and present lives of the racehorses. At the start of the poem, he describes two horses grazing – but they are 'anonymous'. There is a dreamy, timeless feeling to the picture Larkin paints. I thought that even the title of the poem was similar to the title used of a painting of racehorses. There is very little movement involved in the description of the retired horses – in complete contrast with the middle section of the poem, where Larkin brings us back to their glory days, winning 'Cups, Stakes and Handicaps'. The hustle and bustle of the busy racetracks is seen in the colourful images and lively rhythms – 'Silks at the start against the blue sky'. The scene is noisy, with race goers shouting and reporters rushing to write their 'stop-press columns' after the winners are announced. The two contrasting atmospheres are very different. At the end of the poem, we see the two old horses 'stand at ease' – even the gentle sibilant sounds are in contrast with the hectic description of 'littered grass' at the race meetings. The tone in the last lines of the poem as the grooms 'in the late evening come' is gentle and subdued, highlighting the final days of these champion horses. Overall, Larkin uses contrasts very effectively to show the dramatic changes in the lives of these great horses, who have swapped their past glory for a well-earned rest.

EXAMINER'S COMMENT

This is a well-sustained and focused response that examines the poet's use of contrasting settings, moods and sound effects in some detail. The commentary is informed and interesting. However, the answer is less successful due to the inaccurate quotations. A basic grade B.

CLASS/HOMEWORK EXERCISES

1 Describe the tone of the poem. Is it celebratory, sorrowful, resigned or realistic, or a combination of these? Refer to the text in your answer.

2 Copy the table below into your own notes and fill in critical comments about the last two quotations.

Key Quotes

From the cold shade they shelter in	The description of sheltering horses in the shadows suggests the inevitability of impending death.
Two dozen distances sufficed/ To fable them	Alliteration echoes the energy and triumph of these great horses in their prime.
Summer by summer all stole away	The passing of time is a central theme in the poem, evoked in the bittersweet sibilance and fluent rhythm of this memorable image.
Almanacked, their names live	
Only the groom, and the groom's boy,/ With bridles in the evening come	

Philip Larkin

Church Going

Once I am sure there's nothing going on
I step inside, letting the door thud shut.
Another church: matting, seats, and stone,
And little books; sprawlings of flowers, cut
For Sunday, brownish now; some brass and stuff 5
Up at the holy end; the small neat organ;
And a tense, musty, unignorable silence,
Brewed God knows how long. Hatless, I take off
My cycle-clips in awkward reverence,

Move forward, run my hand around the font. 10
From where I stand, the roof looks almost new –
Cleaned, or restored? Someone would know: I don't.
Mounting the lectern, I peruse a few
Hectoring large-scale verses, and pronounce
'Here endeth' much more loudly than I'd meant. 15
The echoes snigger briefly. Back at the door
I sign the book, donate an Irish sixpence,
Reflect the place was not worth stopping for.

Yet stop I did: in fact I often do,
And always end much at a loss like this, 20
Wondering what to look for; wondering, too,
When churches fall completely out of use
What we shall turn them into, if we shall keep
A few cathedrals chronically on show,
Their parchment, plate and pyx in locked cases, 25
And let the rest rent-free to rain and sheep.
Shall we avoid them as unlucky places?

Or, after dark, will dubious women come
To make their children touch a particular stone;
Pick simples for a cancer; or on some 30
Advised night see walking a dead one?
Power of some sort or other will go on
In games, in riddles, seemingly at random;
But superstition, like belief, must die,
And what remains when disbelief has gone? 35

Grass, weedy pavement, brambles, buttress, sky,
A shape less recognisable each week,
A purpose more obscure. I wonder who
Will be the last, the very last, to seek
This place for what it was; one of the crew   40
That tap and jot and know what rood-lofts were?
Some ruin-bibber, randy for antique,
Or Christmas-addict, counting on a whiff
Of gowns-and-bands and organ-pipes and myrrh?
Or will he be my representative,   45

Bored, uninformed, knowing the ghostly silt
Dispersed, yet tending to this cross of ground
Through suburb scrub because it held unspilt
So long and equably what since is found
Only in separation – marriage, and birth,   50
And death, and thoughts of these – for which was built
This special shell? For, though I've no idea
What this accoutred frowsty barn is worth,
It pleases me to stand in silence here;

A serious house on serious earth it is,   55
In whose blent air all our compulsions meet,
Are recognised, and robed as destinies.
And that much never can be obsolete,
Since someone will forever be surprising
A hunger in himself to be more serious,   60
And gravitating with it to this ground,
Which, he once heard, was proper to grow wise in,
If only that so many dead lie round.

*'Which, he once heard, was proper to
grow wise in, / If only that so many dead
lie round'*

GLOSSARY

9 *cycle-clips*: old-fashioned clips that fasten a cyclist's trouser leg.

10 *font*: stone bowl in a church used to store holy water.

13 *lectern*: a tall stand from which a speaker can read.

13 *peruse*: read carefully.

14 *Hectoring*: bullying, blustering.

15 *'Here endeth'*: Church of England services end each reading with the phrase 'Here endeth the lesson'.

24 *chronically*: lasting a long time; very badly.

25 *parchment*: animal skin formerly used for writing on.

25 *plate*: bowls, cups, etc. made of gold or silver and used for religious ceremonies.

25 *pyx*: container in which the blessed bread of the Eucharist is kept.

28 *dubious*: doubtful.

30 *simples*: medicinal herbs.

30 *cancer*: malignant growth.

31 *Advised*: recommended.

36 *buttress*: support for a wall.

41 *rood-lofts*: galleries in the shape of a cross.

42 *ruin-bibber*: someone fond of old buildings.

42 *randy*: excited.

44 *gowns-and-bands*: clerical dress.

44 *myrrh*: sweet-smelling resin used in incense at a religious ceremony.

46 *silt*: deposit left behind.

49 *equably*: calm and even-tempered.

53 *accoutred*: dressed; equipped.

53 *frowsty*: stale smelling; musty.

56 *blent*: blended, mixed.

56 *compulsions*: irresistible urges to do something.

58 *obsolete*: out of date.

61 *gravitating*: attracted towards.

EXPLORATIONS

1 What impression do you have of the speaker in the first two stanzas of this poem? Support your answer with reference to the text.

2 List two images that you consider to be spiritual in 'Church Going'. Comment on their effectiveness.

3 How does this poem change after the first two stanzas? What are the main considerations of the poet? Refer closely to the poem in your response.

STUDY NOTES

'Church Going' was written in 1954 as part of Larkin's poetry collection *The Less Deceived*. He adopts his famous persona of the self-deprecating, observant, conversational outsider. Larkin said he felt the need to be on 'the periphery of things'. The title is a pun, suggesting both the attendance of religious ceremonies (church-going) and also suggesting that religious practice/religion itself was on the way out, passé. The inspiration for the poem came from an actual event experienced by Larkin when he stopped to look at a church while on a cycling trip.

In the first stanza, Larkin is an interloper/intruder who only enters the church when he's sure it's empty ('nothing going on'). The run-on line movement mirrors the poet popping inside ('I step inside'). The onomatopoeic closing of the door echoes in 'thud shut'. We hear what is happening. A jaded tone of one who has seen and done it all before sounds from the phrase 'Another church'. He now gives us a general view of the church from floor to wall: matting, wooden seats, stone walls. He then closes in for a detailed view: 'little books', flowers that are 'brownish now'. This telling detail suggests something is not fresh; it's dying. Is this similar to church-going? Larkin felt strongly that when you go into church, you get **a feeling that something is over, derelict**.

He now becomes dismissive as he describes the sacred objects as 'some brass and stuff'. He says it is 'Up at the holy end'. **He is indifferent rather than ignorant**: 'I don't bother about that kind of thing,' he once declared. The atmosphere is 'tense', not serene; the church is 'musty', stale-smelling. The silence is all-pervasive, 'unignorable'. The atmosphere has been stewing or fermenting a long time, like tea or beer – only 'God knows how long'. This fact makes him anxious to show respect. He had already removed his hat, but now he cuts a slightly ridiculous figure as he removes his cycle-clips in 'awkward reverence'.

He moves around in the second stanza, like an **uninformed tourist**, randomly touching things ('run my hand around the font'). The use of the present tense in the first two stanzas gives an immediacy to the description. A telling question 'Cleaned, or restored?' shows the poet's mind at work. It also shows that there is a community at work, and therefore continuity. The roof is being preserved, just as Larkin is preserving the church in his poem. Yet the dismissive, casual, conversational tone returns when he says that he thinks 'the place was not worth stopping for'.

A more **formal, serious voice now is heard** as the poet's inner self comes into focus. He begins to meditate in stanza three on the importance of churches ('wondering, too,/When churches fall completely out of use/What we shall turn them into'). This knowledgeable voice knows the ecclesiastical vocabulary: 'parchment', 'pyx'. In the future, these will no longer be used for ceremonies, but stored 'in locked cases'. Larkin was fond of the traditions of the Anglican Church, but now the old world is fading. He imagines the future of these churches as 'rent-free', worth nothing, housing only 'rain and sheep'. Here is a desolate outlook. The use of the plural first person pronoun 'we' suggests that Larkin thinks we will all be confronted with what to do with these large empty buildings. The negative view continues as the churches are described as 'unlucky places'.

In **stanza four, superstition is overtaking belief**. This is 'dark', 'dubious'; Larkin doesn't approve. However, he feels the power will remain ('Power of some sort'), and eventually, as always happens, nature will reclaim it: 'Grass ... brambles ... sky'. This landscape recalls the opening view of the interior of the church. Now, in Larkin's imaginings, it lies open to the elements. The long sentence shows the ruminative mood of the poet, as he wonders, in **stanza five**, who will be the last to seek out this place for what it once was, a dynamic church. He dismisses the learned academics ('ruin-bibber'), someone mad for old buildings.

In **stanza six**, Larkin wonders if his 'representative', 'Bored', will be one who understood the church's role in marking the great human landmarks of a life: birth, marriage and death. The poet is happy to be part of this space: 'It pleases me to stand in silence here'. In the **seventh stanza**, the contemplative voice states, 'A serious house on serious earth it is'. He realises he will be someone who is drawn to this place, as it is a place 'to grow wise in' as he experiences the **essence of life, being alone** ('dead lie around').

Larkin uses a **traditional form of English poetry**, a formal stanza pattern of seven nine-line stanzas. The rhythm is iambic pentameter, the traditional rhythm of English verse. The large, spacious form of the poem echoes the cavernous space of the church. The regular rhyme scheme punctuates this ordered but disappearing world. This poem is reminiscent of Shakespeare's sonnet recording the ruins of England's monasteries: 'Bare ruined choirs, where late the sweet birds sang'. Both poems are shot through with melancholy for a disappeared world.

ANALYSIS

After reading 'Church Going', do you feel a sense of disappointment and depression, or a feeling of optimism? Support your view with references from the poem.

SAMPLE PARAGRAPH

I feel I have gained insight from this poem, as the poet, although he is dismissive in the first stanzas, when he flippantly remarks that the place was 'not worth stopping for', and that he donated an 'Irish sixpence' (inferior coinage?). Nevertheless, he feels that this place merits reverence, however 'awkward'. This place has a 'Power of some sort'. When his more serious side emerges, at the end of the poem, he acknowledges, rather like the Communists, that people need religion/belief, 'A hunger in himself'. We cannot exist totally on the level of animals, or in the shallow state of the cynical, critical sneer. He uses the word, 'gravitating', as if he/we are pulled by an irresistible force 'to this ground'. He has been told, 'he once heard', that there is a 'proper' place 'to grow wise in'. 'If only that so many dead lie round' shows us that this place marks the reality and finality of life-death. We live our lives in the shadow of our death, our loved ones' deaths, and the death of all living things. The poem has given me a real insight into the pessimistic reality of human affairs.

EXAMINER'S COMMENT

This general response does not focus directly on the question. While expression and vocabulary are good, a treatment of stylistic effects, such as tone, would have improved the answer. Grade C.

CLASS/HOMEWORK EXERCISES

1 Larkin stated that the 'impulse to preserve lies at the bottom of all art'. What is Larkin trying to preserve in the poem 'Church Going'? In your opinion, does he succeed or fail? Support your answer with reference to the text.

2 Copy the table below into your own notes and fill in critical comments about the last two quotations.

Philip Larkin

Key Quotes

Brewed God knows how long	The metaphor of brewing emphatically underlines the length of time the church has been here.
Yet stop I did: in fact I often do	The casual tone of this line shows the first voice of the poem, that of the disinterested tourist.
Pick simples for a cancer	Superstition will replace belief as the churches die. People are looking for miracle cures for their ailments.
knowing the ghostly silt/Dispersed	
In whose blent air all our compulsions meet	

An Arundel Tomb

Side by side, their faces blurred,
The earl and countess lie in stone,
Their proper habits vaguely shown
As jointed armour, stiffened pleat,
And that faint hint of the absurd –   5
The little dogs under their feet.

Such plainness of the pre-baroque
Hardly involves the eye, until
It meets his left-hand gauntlet, still
Clasped empty in the other; and   10
One sees, with a sharp tender shock,
His hand withdrawn, holding her hand.

They would not think to lie so long.
Such faithfulness in effigy
Was just a detail friends would see: 15
A sculptor's sweet commissioned grace
Thrown off in helping to prolong
The Latin names around the base.

They would not guess how early in
Their supine stationary voyage   20
The air would change to soundless damage,
Turn the old tenantry away;
How soon succeeding eyes begin
To look, not read. Rigidly they

Persisted, linked, through lengths and breadths   25
Of time. Snow fell, undated. Light
Each summer thronged the glass. A bright
Litter of birdcalls strewed the same
Bone-riddled ground. And up the paths
The endless altered people came,   30

Washing at their identity.
Now, helpless in the hollow of
An unarmorial age, a trough

Philip Larkin

Of smoke in slow suspended skeins
Above their scrap of history,   35
Only an attitude remains:

Time has transfigured them into
Untruth. The stone fidelity
They hardly meant has come to be
Their final blazon, and to prove   40
Our almost-instinct almost true:
What will survive of us is love.

*'What will survive
of us is love'*

EXPLORATIONS

1   How would you describe the tone in the first stanza? Reverential? Intrigued? Superior?

2 Select two illustrations from the poem to show Larkin's keen eye for detail. Comment briefly on the effectiveness of each example.

3 Write a short personal response to this poem, highlighting the impact it made on you.

STUDY NOTES

'An Arundel Tomb' was written in 1956 after Larkin had visited Chichester Cathedral. He said that the effigies were unlike any he had ever seen before and that he found them 'extremely affecting'. The poem can be viewed in many ways – as a meditation on love and death, a tribute to the power of art, or even as a celebration of English history. Despite differences of interpretation, 'An Arundel Tomb' has always been a favourite of Larkin readers. It was read aloud at his memorial service held in London's Westminster Abbey in 1986.

In stanza one, we are immediately located before the stone statue of the Earl and Countess of Arundel. Larkin's description of the couple seems detached, the **tone one of ironic hesitation**. The couple's 'blurred' faces (eroded by time) are indistinct. Indeed, the earl's outdated armour and the 'little dogs under their feet' add a ludicrous dimension (a 'faint hint of the absurd') to the commemorative monument.

The poet continues to criticise the 'plainness' of the lifeless sculpture in stanza two. It is etched in an unappealingly dull 'pre-baroque' style. But he is suddenly taken by one particular detail. The earl's left hand has been withdrawn from its 'gauntlet' and is 'holding her hand'. This affectionate gesture between husband and wife has an immediate **impact on Larkin – 'a sharp tender shock'**. The image of 'His hand withdrawn, holding her hand' stops the poet in his tracks. We can sense Larkin's concentration in the slow rhythm and emphatic 'h' alliteration of line 12. Do the joined hands represent the triumph of love over time, or is that just wishful thinking?

In stanza three, Larkin reflects on the relationship between the earl and countess. Line 13 is puzzling: 'They would not think to lie so long'. Is this an obvious reference to the couple's long rest in the tomb? Or have they failed to find a heavenly afterlife? Might there be a pun on the word 'lie'? Perhaps the loving hand-holding is an untrue representation? Larkin wonders if the sculptor invented this demonstrative touch to make the statue more interesting to the general public and to 'prolong' the earl's family name long after the Latin inscription would be understood.

Stanzas four and five focus particularly on the **passing of time**, a central theme in the poem. The earl and countess could not have imagined the effects of the damp cathedral air ('soundless damage') eroding their tomb. Great social change has also happened over the centuries; 'the old tenantry' and the use of Latin – and the importance of Christianity, presumably – have disappeared. Larkin's strikingly sensory images evoke the changing seasons: 'Snow fell, undated. Light/Each summer thronged the glass'. The signs of natural vitality and rejuvenation are in stark contrast to the 'Bone-riddled ground' over which modern-day visitors to the cathedral ('endless altered people') arrive to view the monument.

The countless tourists to the medieval couple's tomb have long been 'Washing at their identity' (stanza six). There is a suggestion of erosion (the earl and countess are no longer understood as they once were) and purification (the couple are idealised as romantic and artistic symbols). Larkin asserts that the effigies are 'helpless' in this 'unarmorial age'. The **poet's cynical tone** reflects his distaste for the vulgarity and ignorance around him. Today's generation has a shallow appreciation of love – 'Only an attitude remains'.

This idea is developed in stanza seven, where **Larkin questions the public's misguided response to the statue**. For him, the sentimental yearning to see the couple's 'fidelity' as a triumph of love over death is an 'Untruth', and something the earl and countess probably never intended. Nonetheless, the instinctual desire for enduring love may well be another admirable aspect of human behaviour. Many commentators view the final lines ('Our almost-instinct almost true:/What will survive of us is love') as a positive affirmation by Larkin. Others see in it a typically despondent statement of the opposite (namely, self-deluding hope in the face of reality). Like the rest of the poem, the ending is typically paradoxical and thought provoking, allowing us to decide for ourselves about Larkin's attitude concerning the power of love to transcend time.

ANALYSIS

Comment on Larkin's use of ambiguous language in 'An Arundel Tomb'.

SAMPLE PARAGRAPH

Philip Larkin's poem 'An Arundel Tomb' is noted for its ambiguity. The opening description of the rigid figures carved in stone is both sympathetic and satirical at the same time. Their expressions are described as 'blurred', suggesting that they are faceless and unreal. Larkin adds that there are 'little dogs under their feet'. He finds this ridiculous and might be hinting that this privileged earl and countess were used to being spoiled and pampered. On the other hand, the image makes the elderly pair seem human. The word 'lie' is used a number of times. The couple 'lie in stone'. This might simply refer to the position of the bodies, but it could also mean that they are sending out a false message that they are a loving couple whose love has conquered death. Yet the earl and his wife 'would not think to lie so long', suggesting that they never planned to give this false impression. Although Larkin's ambivalent approach engaged my interest in the poem, I am still not exactly sure about his own point of view as to the true relationship between the earl and countess. However, the effect of his wordplay is to produce a poem which is very rich and suggestive in meaning, encouraging us to think twice before judging by appearances.

EXAMINER'S COMMENT

A well-illustrated personal response that examines Larkin's subtle use of language at various points in the poem. The expression throughout the paragraph is clear and varied. Grade A standard.

CLASS/HOMEWORK EXERCISES

1   Outline the main theme presented in 'An Arundel Tomb'. In your answer, trace the way the poet develops his ideas during the course of the poem.

2   Copy the table below into your own notes and fill in critical comments about the last two quotations.

Philip Larkin

Key Quotes

The earl and countess lie in stone	The image conveys a sense of looking directly at the monument. Is the word 'lie' used ambiguously to suggest the illusion of the couple's love?
Their supine stationary voyage	Contrasting references to inactivity and action (death and life) are a distinctive feature of the poem.
A bright/Litter of birdcalls	Slender vowels and alliteration add to the vitality of this memorable image.
Washing at their identity	
What will survive of us is love	

The Whitsun Weddings

That Whitsun, I was late getting away:
  Not till about
One-twenty on the sunlit Saturday
Did my three-quarters-empty train pull out,
All windows down, all cushions hot, all sense   5
Of being in a hurry gone. We ran
Behind the backs of houses, crossed a street
Of blinding windscreens, smelt the fish-dock; thence
The river's level drifting breadth began,
Where sky and Lincolnshire and water meet.   10

All afternoon, through the tall heat that slept
  For miles inland,
A slow and stopping curve southwards we kept.
Wide farms went by, short-shadowed cattle, and
Canals with floatings of industrial froth;   15
A hothouse flashed uniquely: hedges dipped
And rose: and now and then a smell of grass
Displaced the reek of buttoned carriage-cloth
Until the next town, new and nondescript,
Approached with acres of dismantled cars.   20

At first, I didn't notice what a noise
  The weddings made
Each station that we stopped at: sun destroys
The interest of what's happening in the shade,
And down the long cool platforms whoops and skirls   25
I took for porters larking with the mails,
And went on reading. Once we started, though,
We passed them, grinning and pomaded, girls
In parodies of fashion, heels and veils,
All posed irresolutely, watching us go,   30

As if out on the end of an event
  Waving goodbye
To something that survived it. Struck, I leant
More promptly out next time, more curiously,
And saw it all again in different terms: 35

The fathers with broad belts under their suits
And seamy foreheads; mothers loud and fat;
An uncle shouting smut; and then the perms,
The nylon gloves and jewellery-substitutes,
The lemons, mauves, and olive-ochres that   40

Marked off the girls unreally from the rest.
   Yes, from cafés
And banquet-halls up yards, and bunting-dressed
Coach-party annexes, the wedding-days
Were coming to an end. All down the line   45
Fresh couples climbed aboard: the rest stood round;
The last confetti and advice were thrown,
And, as we moved, each face seemed to define
Just what it saw departing: children frowned
At something dull; fathers had never known   50

Success so huge and wholly farcical;
   The women shared
The secret like a happy funeral;
While girls, gripping their handbags tighter, stared
At a religious wounding. Free at last,   55
And loaded with the sum of all they saw,
We hurried towards London, shuffling gouts of steam.
Now fields were building-plots, and poplars cast
Long shadows over major roads, and for
Some fifty minutes, that in time would seem   60

Just long enough to settle hats and say
   I nearly died,
A dozen marriages got under way.
They watched the landscape, sitting side by side
– An Odeon went past, a cooling tower,   65
And someone running up to bowl – and none
Thought of the others they would never meet
Or how their lives would all contain this hour.
I thought of London spread out in the sun,
Its postal districts packed like squares of wheat: 70

There we were aimed. And as we raced across
   Bright knots of rail

Past standing Pullmans, walls of blackened moss
Came close, and it was nearly done, this frail
Travelling coincidence; and what it held   75
Stood ready to be loosed with all the power
That being changed can give. We slowed again,
And as the tightened brakes took hold, there swelled
A sense of falling, like an arrow-shower
Sent out of sight, somewhere becoming rain.   80

Philip Larkin

*'now and then a smell
of grass'*

Whit (Pentecost) Sunday, the seventh after Easter, was a popular time for weddings.
19 *nondescript*: ordinary.
25 *skirls*: high-pitched cries.
26 *larking*: joking, carrying on.
28 *pomaded*: perfumed.
29 *parodies*: imitations.
30 *irresolutely*: hesitantly.
37 *seamy*: lined.
38 *smut*: rude or suggestive comments.
38 *perms*: waved hairstyles popular at the time.
40 *olive-ochres*: green and gold colours.
41 *unreally*: falsely.
44 *annexes*: reserved areas.
57 *gouts*: great spurts.
65 *Odeon*: popular cinema name.
73 *Pullmans*: luxury rail carriages (sleeping cars).
79 *arrow-shower*: short outburst of rain.

EXPLORATIONS

1   What is Larkin's attitude to the wedding parties that he describes in stanzas three and four? Refer to the text in your answer.

2   Select two visual images from the poem to show Larkin's eye for observational detail. Comment briefly on the effectiveness of each example.

3   Write a short personal response to 'The Whitsun Weddings', highlighting the impact it made on you.

STUDY NOTES

> Larkin began writing 'The Whitsun Weddings' in 1957, and spent over a year drafting it. He said, 'You couldn't be on that train without feeling the young lives all starting off, and that just for a moment you were touching them. Doncaster, Retford, Grantham, Newark, Peterborough, and at every station more wedding parties. It was wonderful, a marvellous afternoon.' While the poem is lengthy by Larkin's standards, it moves typically from specific observation to an insightful reflection of love and marriage.

The poem's positive title immediately suggests celebration. Larkin's personal narrative makes use of everyday colloquial speech ('I was late getting away') to introduce this seemingly ordinary account of his afternoon journey from Hull to London. The opening lines of stanza one build to a steady rhythm, like a train leaving a railway station. At first, the poet's senses are engaged but not fully absorbed in his surroundings. However, his language ('The river's level drifting breadth') conveys the numbing drowsiness of a warm summer day. Larkin's **characteristic eye for detail** evokes the claustrophobic atmosphere inside the carriage: 'All windows down, all cushions hot'. The panoramic picture of the outside view 'Where sky and Lincolnshire and water meet' reveals his appreciation of nature and an enthusiasm for the English landscape.

Although the poet seems somewhat removed from the rest of society, his sense of place and expressive description continue into stanza two: 'Wide farms went by, short-shadowed cattle'. The June weather is personified ('the tall heat that slept'), adding to an already oppressive mood. Occasional run-through phrasing ('hedges dipped/And rose') echoes the movement of the train on its 'curve southwards'. Always a realist, Larkin includes a number of **unappealing images** associated with the industrial age: 'floatings of industrial froth' and 'acres of dismantled cars'. This convincing sense of the familiar is characteristic of a poet who is known for vividly recording life in post-war England.

Stanza three focuses on the various wedding groups arriving on the station platforms. Larkin gradually realises that the 'whoops and skirls' he hears on the platforms are the animated voices of 'grinning and pomaded' girls who are seeing off the honeymooners. **The poet's tone wavers** between derision of the guests' style ('parodies of fashion') and admiration of their glamorous 'heels and veils'.

Despite his ironic detachment, Larkin cannot help but be increasingly attracted ('more curiously') to the small dramas taking place around him. He observes the various groups – 'fathers with broad belts under their suits', 'mothers loud and fat'. For much of stanza four, **his attitude is condescending**, referring to one vulgar uncle 'shouting smut'. He is equally disdainful of the clothes on show ('lemons, mauves and olive-ochres') and the cheap 'jewellery-substitutes'.

The **poet's apparent class superiority** is also evident in stanza five as he begins to wonder about the tawdry wedding receptions that have been taking place in 'cafés' and 'banquet-halls up yards'. Despite all this derision, Larkin detects a more important undertone beneath the brash celebrations. All the newlywed couples are about to leave their familiar lives behind. The inherent sadness and inevitability of the moment are summed up as 'The last confetti and advice were thrown'. Meanwhile, real life resumes for the children after the enjoyment of the day, while proud fathers feel relieved that all the fuss is over. For Larkin himself, however, the occasion has brought him closer to the people he has been observing and criticising.

Stanza six marks a change in the poet's outlook. More sensitive than before, he imagines how the **older, more realistic wives view married life pragmatically** as 'a happy funeral', likely to bring both joy and sorrow. This 'secret' is not yet understood by the impressionable younger girls carefully 'gripping their handbags tighter' and who presumably have more romantic notions about marriage. Larkin sees them as facing 'a religious wounding', a typically ambiguous comment, suggesting both the wedding ritual and the likely hurt that lies ahead. From this moment, the poet associates himself more closely with the newlywed couples aboard the train ('Free at last'). He is no longer merely a detached observer as 'We hurried towards London'. The poem's rhythm gathers pace, perhaps reflecting his growing mood of optimism.

The lines maintain their momentum in stanza seven as Larkin's fellow-passengers relive the excitement of the day ('*I nearly died*'). The train journey has let the poet realise that **the people he has seen are all interconnected** ('their lives would all contain this hour'). This is coupled with the poignant understanding that it is only Larkin himself who is conscious of this fact ('none/Thought of the others they would never meet'). This overview of how the random lives of individuals form a greater pattern is teased out further as he uses an inventive rural simile to describe London's numerous 'postal districts packed like squares of wheat'.

At the start of stanza eight, there is little doubt that Larkin is aware of the full significance of this weekend outing. The 'dozen marriages' have made a lasting impact on the poet. As the train arrives at its destination, he reflects on 'this frail/Travelling coincidence'. **Is he simply saying that all of life can be viewed as a journey** where we meet people by chance, and that some of these encounters have the power to change us? The last lines reach a high point 'as the tightened brakes took hold' and the poem ends on a dramatic note ('A sense of falling'), suggesting both danger and adventure. The final image of the distant 'arrow-shower ... becoming rain' is an exciting one, hinting at romance, beauty and even sadness. Elusive to the end, Larkin's poem invites us to consider the wonderful experience of life in all its richness.

ANALYSIS

It has been said that Philip Larkin's poetry is gloomy and pessimistic. In your opinion, is this true of 'The Whitsun Weddings'? Refer to the poem in your answer.

SAMPLE PARAGRAPH

Larkin is more of a realistic poet than a pessimistic one. In my opinion, he celebrated traditional English life in 'The Whitsun Weddings'. He has a love for the English landscape. Even the fish-dock in Hull get his attention. His description of the horizon 'where the sky over Lincolnshire and the water meet' is evidence of his love of his native land. He seems obsessed by the young wedding couples and their families when he sees them at the rail stations. He might be poking fun at them here and there, but it is all good-natured, never mean. Larkin laughs at the 'nylon gloves and the jewellery substitutes' and at the 'uncle shouting out smut' at the honeymooners. This is all very good-natured. And certainly not gloomy. I think the speaking tone he uses shows that he admires these happy wedding guests. He's almost envious of their enjoyment. Philip hears the 'whoops' of the 'mothers loud and very fat', but he seems to be just smiling at their sense of fun. Not that Larkin is a complete bundle of laughs. There are some serious bits, of course. However, he is just being real when he describes the secret comments of the experienced wives who see married life as 'a happy funeral'. Overall, I think Larkin is upbeat and celebrates working-class life.

EXAMINER'S COMMENT

While this lively paragraph makes a reasonable attempt to address the question in a focused way, some points lack development and the expression isn't always controlled. Some of the quotations are also incorrect. Grade C standard.

CLASS/HOMEWORK EXERCISES

1   It has been said of Larkin that he observes 'ordinary people doing ordinary things'. To what extent do you agree with this statement in light of your reading of 'The Whitsun Weddings'?

2   Copy the table below into your own notes and fill in critical comments about the last two quotations.

Key Quotes

That Whitsun, I was late getting away	From the outset, Larkin's colloquial style and personal narrative approach draw in the reader.
I leant/ More promptly out next time	The image illustrates the poet's increasing fascination with the lives of the wedding parties.
The women shared/ The secret like a happy funeral	Larkin contrasts different reactions to the newlyweds. Does the realism of the older women reflect his own sceptical attitude towards marriage?
and none/ Thought of the others they would never meet	
like an arrow-shower/ Sent out of sight, somewhere becoming rain	

MCMXIV

Those long uneven lines
Standing as patiently
As if they were stretched outside
The Oval or Villa Park,
The crowns of hats, the sun   5
On moustached archaic faces
Grinning as if it were all
An August Bank Holiday lark;

And the shut shops, the bleached
Established names on the sunblinds,   10
The farthings and sovereigns,
And dark-clothed children at play
Called after kings and queens,
The tin advertisements
For cocoa and twist, and the pubs   15
Wide open all day;

And the countryside not caring:
The place names all hazed over
With flowering grasses, and fields
Shadowing Domesday lines   20
Under wheat's restless silence;
The differently-dressed servants
With tiny rooms in huge houses,
The dust behind limousines;

Never such innocence,   25
Never before or since,
As changed itself to past
Without a word – the men
Leaving the gardens tidy,
The thousands of marriages   30
Lasting a little while longer:
Never such innocence again.

'Those long uneven lines'

GLOSSARY

The title refers to the Roman numerals for 1914, the year that World War I began. It became known as the Great War, a landmark event in the twentieth century.

4 *The Oval*: famous cricket ground near London.

4 *Villa Park*: Birmingham home ground of Aston Villa football club.

6 *archaic*: dated, old-fashioned.

8 *lark*: celebration, spree.

11 *farthings and sovereigns*: currency used at the time. The copper farthing was just a quarter of a penny, while the gold sovereign coin was worth £1.

15 *twist*: probably refers to a small piece of tobacco.

20 *Domesday*: medieval spelling of Doomsday (or Judgment Day); in 1086, William the Conqueror compiled a record of English land ownership in the Domesday Book.

24 *limousines*: luxury cars.

EXPLORATIONS

1 Suggest a reason to explain why the poet chose to write the title in Roman numerals. (Where else might the letters MCMXIV be seen?)

2 In your opinion, is Larkin's view of the past accurate and realistic, or is it sentimental and idealised? Refer to the text in your answer.

3 What do you think is meant by the final line, 'Never such innocence again'? Briefly explain your answer.

STUDY NOTES

This elegiac poem, written in 1960, has often been read as a nostalgic account of a vanished English way of life. The Roman numerals of the title evoke war memorials and the detailed descriptions seem to suggest old photographs. The whole poem consists of one long sentence, giving a sense of timelessness and connecting readers with the men lining up for army service.

Larkin's meditation begins with a description of an old photograph of 'uneven lines' of British volunteers outside an army recruiting office at the start of World War I. In stanza one, the poet observes that the men are queuing happily, as if for a game of cricket or football. The **tragic irony of their fate** is suggested by the image of the sun shining on their 'moustached archaic faces' and their carefree expressions, 'Grinning' as if it was all just a 'lark'. Larkin's tone seems unclear. Does he admire the men's idealism and courage, or is there a sense that these raw recruits are naïvely seeking adventure?

The holiday atmosphere continues in stanza two with a **wistful celebration of pre-war English life**. Larkin lists some of the hallmarks of a bygone era: 'farthings and sovereigns', 'children at play', 'cocoa and twist'. Trusted shops ('Established names') and public houses ('Wide open all day') add to this relaxed feeling of security. Overall, this idealised image of a long-lost England is one of innocence, freedom and stability.

The poet swaps the familiar town setting for the open countryside in stanza three. At first, the mood seems untroubled ('not caring'). The alliterative effect and soft sibilant sounds of 'flowering grasses, and fields' evoke England's green and pleasant land. But the positive mood is suddenly overshadowed by the reference to 'Domesday lines' – a chilling echo of the earlier 'uneven lines' of men whose lives are likely to end on the battlefield. The reality of mass war graves is further stressed by the unsettling image of the 'wheat's restless silence'. **Larkin's tone becomes increasingly critical** as he focuses on the class divisions ('differently-dressed servants') prevalent within English society. Images of 'tiny rooms in huge houses' and 'dust behind limousines' suggest that social inequality was hidden away hypocritically.

The powerfully emotive force of stanza four emphasises **the passing of an innocent age**: 'Never before or since'. Purposeful rhythm and repetition ('never' is used three times) reflect Larkin's shocking realisation that the war would mark a turning point in our understanding of man's inhumanity to man. The compelling image of countless naïve volunteers leaving their homes, unaware that their marriages would only last 'a little while longer', is undeniably poignant. Rather than being a hymn of sentimental nostalgia, the poem is dark with the shadow of unexpected death, and we are left with an enduring sense of the human tragedy involved.

ANALYSIS

In your view, how well does Larkin's poem 'MCMXIV' convey the innocence of pre-war England?

SAMPLE PARAGRAPH

Many of Philip Larkin's poems on our course, e.g. 'Ambulances' and 'The Whitsun Weddings', give me a good insight into the past and ordinary English life. This is certainly true of his war poem 'MCMXIV'. The poem begins with a series of images showing long lines of young men signing up to enlist in the war. They are 'Grinning' and have no notion of the horrors before them. Their innocence is very well seen in the way Larkin shows them standing 'patiently' as though they were waiting to enter a football stadium. There is a photographic quality to his descriptions. Life seems simple, carefree. The poet suggests this with images of bank holidays, familiar shop advertisements, young children playing and the pubs 'Wide open all day'. But there is another, darker side to pre-war society – social division. Larkin reminds us of the 'differently-dressed servants' who are slaving away in 'tiny rooms' for the upper classes. By the end of the poem, he suggests that the innocent pre-war years were about to be replaced with a horrifying time of conflict, mass destruction and death. I found the final verse very effective, repeating the awful truth – 'Never such innocence again'. The peace and harmony of the past would be shattered for all time.

EXAMINER'S COMMENT

An assured personal response, focused throughout and well illustrated. Quotations are integrated effectively and the answer ranges widely over the positive and negative aspects of English life presented in the poem. Grade A.

CLASS/HOMEWORK EXERCISES

1   How does Larkin establish the underlying sense of death that pervades the poem? Refer closely to the text in your answer.
2   Copy the table below into your own notes and fill in critical comments about the last two quotations.

Key Quotes

Those long uneven lines	The description of the enlisting men, as yet undisciplined, is in contrast to the grim reality of what lies ahead.
An August Bank Holiday lark	The archaic word 'lark' (meaning fun) exposes the innocence of the volunteers. How much sympathy does Larkin have for them?
Under wheat's restless silence	This subtle image foreshadows the mass war graves of Europe. Sibilance adds to the poignant mood.
tiny rooms in huge houses	
Never such innocence again	

Ambulances

Closed like confessionals, they thread
Loud noons of cities, giving back
None of the glances they absorb.
Light glossy grey, arms on a plaque,
They come to rest at any kerb: 5
All streets in time are visited.

Then children strewn on steps or road,
Or women coming from the shops
Past smells of different dinners, see
A wild white face that overtops   10
Red stretcher-blankets momently
As it is carried in and stowed,

And sense the solving emptiness
That lies just under all we do,
And for a second get it whole,   15
So permanent and blank and true.
The fastened doors recede. *Poor soul,*
They whisper at their own distress;

For borne away in deadened air
May go the sudden shut of loss   20
Round something nearly at an end,
And what cohered in it across
The years, the unique random blend
Of families and fashions, there

At last begin to loosen. Far   25
From the exchange of love to lie
Unreachable inside a room
The traffic parts to let go by
Brings closer what is left to come,
And dulls to distance all we are.   30

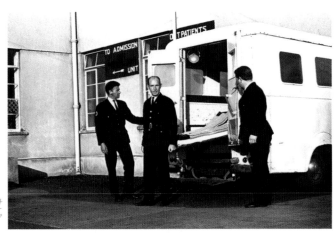

'They come to rest at any kerb'

1 *confessionals*: small, box-like rooms used by Catholic priests to hear confessions.	7 *strewn*: scattered around.
	12 *stowed*: stored.
	17 *recede*: move away.
4 *plaque*: shiny metal sign on the side of the ambulance.	22 *cohered*: brought together.

EXPLORATIONS

1 How does Larkin present the ambulances in stanza one? Are they mysterious? Comforting? Disturbing? Refer to the text in your answer.

2 From your reading of the second stanza, what evidence can you find of the poet's superb eye for interesting detail?

3 Critics have said that Philip Larkin's poems are more realistic than pessimistic. In your opinion, is this the case in 'Ambulances'? Give reasons for your answer.

STUDY NOTES

'Ambulances' is a reflection on life and mortality, written in the early 1960s when an ambulance was usually associated with bad news. Larkin once remarked that everything he wrote had 'the consciousness of approaching death in the background'.

What do you think of when you see an ambulance? A serious road accident or some other emergency? Do you feel a sense of fear, or of hope? People usually become apprehensive when they hear an ambulance siren. Are they genuinely concerned, or are they just being inquisitive and voyeuristic?

From the outset of 'Ambulances', the tone is uneasy. There is an immediate sense of threat from these anonymous 'grey' vans which prowl around 'loud noons of cities'. Even in the hustle and bustle of urban life, nobody escapes. Larkin sees these vehicles as **symbols of death**. An ambulance can take anyone away at any time. The patient is confined and vulnerable in much the same way as everyone is unable to escape dying: 'All streets in times are visited'. The dramatic opening line of the **first stanza** compares the ambulance van to a confessional – a place where people experience spiritual rebirth and make their peace with God. This religious image forces readers to face up to the inevitability of death. The poet personifies the vehicles, but they are as unresponsive as a corpse, 'giving back none of the glances they absorb'. Bystanders glance nervously at passing ambulances, perhaps hoping deep down that their time has not yet come. However, the randomness of death is starkly emphasised by the line 'They come to rest at any kerb'. We are all powerless against the **stark reality of our mortality**.

Stanza two demonstrates Larkin's keen eye for vivid detail as he describes the **reaction of onlookers** when an ambulance arrives and disturbs a quiet neighbourhood. The street is suddenly transformed. Normal life stops for a moment as people consider the significance of what is happening. Simple, colloquial language illustrates the sharp contrast between everyday life ('children strewn on steps or road') and the hidden terror of death as the patient (now an unknown body described as 'it') is carried out to the ambulance. The **colour images** highlight the anguish of life-threatening illness ('A wild white face') and danger ('Red stretcher-blankets').

Larkin's tone is much more reflective in **stanza three**. This is typical of his writing. The crowd of spectators watching the small drama taking place 'sense the solving emptiness/That lies just under all we do'. They have been forced to confront the one underlying truth that all life ends with the mystery of dying. The poet himself was an atheist who could only believe in the 'emptiness' of oblivion after death. Unlike the earlier third-person description in the opening stanzas, the introduction of the pronoun 'we' gives the poem a **universal significance**. Death is our common fate and, in Larkin's belief, makes life meaningless. This seems to be the central **moment of truth**, or epiphany, in the poem – the morbid discovery that human existence is futile. Modern secular society avoids death. It is a taboo subject that we only think about when we are forced to.

For Larkin, all of our daily concerns – cooking, playing, etc. – are merely ways of filling time until death transports us to a state of 'permanent and blank' nothingness. As the ambulance pulls away, the poet suggests that people's whispered sympathy ('*Poor soul*') for the patient is really a selfish expression of 'their own distress'. Such **irony is a common feature** of Larkin's cynical observations of everyday life.

In the **final two stanzas**, **the mood of depression deepens** as Larkin considers the dying patient experiencing 'the sudden shut of loss'. Stark imagery and a deliberate rhythm combine to suggest the great change that death will bring, separating the individual from family and identity. The sensation of being isolated inside the ambulance ('Unreachable inside a room') echoes the earlier alienation of the confessional and adds to the growing sense of panic. Death will eventually alter ('loosen') everything.

Although the syntax (order of words) is complex at the end, Larkin manages to give a clear impression of his own **sombre philosophy**. As with much of his work, he is able to take a particular circumstance and find a general truth in it. The poem ends on a sweetly serene note of disillusion. Although ambulances try to save lives, they are actually the messengers of unavoidable death. The final disarming image leaves a lingering sense of bleakness. As the traffic parts and the ambulance siren quickly fades away, death also 'dulls to distance all we are'. For Larkin, there is no higher purpose to human existence, no comforting afterlife.

ANALYSIS

Write a paragraph on Larkin's use of vivid and realistic images in 'Ambulances'.

SAMPLE PARAGRAPH

The opening lines of 'Ambulances' contain many authentic images of the vans weaving in and out of traffic as they 'thread' their way through a busy city. We are given an immediate sense of the everyday setting and the noisy street: 'Loud noons of cities'. This condensed image effectively conveys a realistic impression of the city-centre sounds at midday. Larkin adds drama to the scene by describing one 'Light glossy grey' ambulance suddenly coming to a 'rest at any kerb'. It is the immediate focus of attention. The poet fills in the dramatic scene with precise pictures of the various spectators. Women coming from the shops stop and stare. There is realistic detailed description of the 'smells of different dinners' and of the children who are innocently playing, 'strewn on steps or road'. However, Larkin's picture of the sick patient is the most convincing of all. 'A wild white face' staring up from the 'Red stretcher-blankets' suggests pain and fear. The vivid images create a compelling sense of the seriousness of what is happening.

EXAMINER'S COMMENT

As part of a full essay answer, this A-grade paragraph is firmly focused on how Larkin selects vibrant and energetic images to convey meaning and reinforce his themes. The quotations are effectively used to illustrate the poet's skill in creating key moments of drama surrounding the sudden arrival of the ambulance.

CLASS/HOMEWORK EXERCISES

1 How would you describe the dominant mood of 'Ambulances'? Using evidence from the poem, write a paragraph showing how Larkin creates this mood. (Model your answer on the sample paragraph above.)
2 Copy the table below into your own notes and fill in critical comments about the last two quotations.

Key Quotes	
They come to rest at any kerb	The ambulance (representing death) can come at any time. This is a central theme in the poem.
children strewn on steps.../ A wild white face	Typically, Larkin's evocative and detailed imagery is taken from everyday life.
the solving emptiness	Everyone must eventually face up to the reality of death. Assonant and sibilant effects add poignancy to the phrase.
They whisper at their own distress	
Unreachable inside a room	

The Trees

Philip Larkin

The trees are coming into leaf
Like something almost being said;
The recent buds relax and spread,
Their greennesss is a kind of grief.

Is it they are born again   5
And we grow old? No, they die too.
Their yearly trick of looking new
Is written down in rings of grain.

Yet still the unresting castles thresh
In fullgrown thickness every May.   10
Last year is dead, they seem to say,
Begin afresh, afresh, afresh.

'The recent buds relax and spread'

EXPLORATIONS

1   Larkin compares and contrasts the world of nature in 'The Trees' with the
     world of man. List one similarity and one contrast, and comment on their
     effectiveness. Support your views with reference to the poem.

2   'Like something almost being said'. In your opinion, what is almost being
     said? To whom and by whom is it being said?

3   'Begin, afresh, afresh, afresh.' Do you think this line is optimistic or full of
     false hope?

STUDY NOTES

'The Trees' was written in 1967 and forms part of the *High Windows* collection. At this point, Larkin's personal life had become complicated. His mother was suffering from the early stages of Alzheimer's. This adds a special resonance to the last line of the poem. Do you think that people often long to 'Begin afresh, afresh, afresh'?

Larkin deals with the classic theme of **transience** (passing time) in this lyric poem. The language in the opening stanza is harmonious and sombre, as long vowel sounds ('a', 'o' and 'u') announce the arrival of spring. The event is seen as inevitable; Larkin conveys the feeling that this has happened so often before. The mystery of the leaves' tentative arrival is suggested in the simile 'Like something almost being said'. We know it's going to happen, but we don't know how or why. It just does. Note the use of 'we' – this is a message for all of us. The verbs 'relax and spread' vividly convey the abundant covering of leaves on the former bare branches. But this rejuvenation of nature is not greeted warmly by the poet, who states that it is 'a kind of grief'. For whom is there sorrow? Man is unable to renew himself. Is the poet perhaps thinking of lost opportunities, what might have been? Or perhaps he is thinking of loved ones who are sick. The slow three-beat rhythm (iambic tetrameter) perfectly suits this lyrical meditation on the theme of decay and death.

In the second stanza, Larkin asks a rhetorical question to explore this thought further: 'Is it that they are born again/And we grow old?' The stark answer comes in the broken line 'No, they die too'. He does not flinch from the unpalatable reality of the **finality of all living things**. Time passes relentlessly and mercilessly, and the passage through time is recorded 'in rings of grain' in the tree trunks. The trees' appearance of renewal is just that – appearance, a 'trick'. The rhyme here (*cddc*) is pertinent: 'born again' rhymes with 'rings of grain', emphasising that their trick of renewal is exposed in the tree trunk.

Larkin's tone changes abruptly in the third stanza. **The energy and life** of the blossoming trees is celebrated in the metaphor 'unresting castles'. Spring's dynamic growth is shown in the compound word 'fullgrown' and in the assonance of 'unresting' and 'thresh'. Life springs back 'every May'. The trees, symbols of courage, are giving a message of hope to mankind as they seem to say, 'Last year is dead'. There is no use grieving over what is gone; concentrate on the future. The trees' exhortation is charged with urgency in the appeal 'Begin afresh, afresh, afresh'. Is this what was hinted at in the earlier phrase,

'Like something almost being said'? The vibrant rhetoric of spring demands that we seize the day. The life-force of the trees is sending out the hope-filled message: don't give up. Is this longing for life attractive but false? Which is the abiding message of the poem, the **vitality of life or the inevitability of death? Could it be both?**

ANALYSIS

Larkin was dismissive of his insights in this poem. He mocked 'The Trees' as 'awful tripe'. Do you agree or disagree with this view? Support your opinion with references from the poem.

SAMPLE PARAGRAPH

Larkin wrote of his 'astounded delight at the renewal of the natural world'. This lyric, with its theme of transience, emphasises this view, but also brings it a step further. Here is no attractive, false idea of renewal. The poet realises that the trees will, after renewing themselves year after year (unlike humans), eventually die. The abrupt broken line 'No, they die too' boldly states this fact. He calls their rejuvenation a 'trick', as if there is something false or deceitful in what they do. The passage of inexorable time is marked in the material, decaying world in 'rings of grain'. This is definitely not 'tripe', but genuine insight into the nature of things, however unsavoury. I feel his imagination is caught by the vitality and dynamism of the growing trees, which he describes as 'unresting castles'. The onomatopoeic 'thresh' captures this swaying movement and sense of being vibrantly alive. The concluding line, with its repetitive appeal to 'Begin afresh, afresh, afresh', seems to me to be a plea for hope. Life should be lived to the brim. So the voice of the trees/the poet is telling us to seize the day. I believe that Larkin was very wrong to be so dismissive of this lyric. Each new day brings with it the possibility of wonder.

EXAMINER'S COMMENT

This focused paragraph eloquently argues the merits of Larkin's poem. A clear viewpoint is established, detailing a range of points. Expression and vocabulary are impressive. The judicious use of quotation adds weight to the response. Grade A.

CLASS/HOMEWORK EXERCISES

1 Larkin said, 'When you've read a poem, that's it, it's all quite clear what it means.' Having read 'The Trees', would you agree or disagree with this view? Support your answer with reference to the text.

2 Copy the table below into your own notes and fill in critical comments about the last two quotations.

Key Quotes

The trees are coming into leaf/ Like something almost being said	This simile vividly shows the tentative arrival of the new growth on the trees and hints at the mystery of life.
Is it that they are born again/ And we grow old?	Larkin poses a rhetorical question, teasing out the difference between the fate of the trees and humans.
Their yearly trick of looking new	The word 'trick' suggests deception and double-dealing on the part of the trees, as they 'seem' to be rejuvenated each year. They appear to be defeating time.
Yet still the unresting castles thresh	
Begin afresh, afresh, afresh	

The Explosion

On the day of the explosion
Shadows pointed towards the pithead:
In the sun the slagheap slept.

Down the lane came men in pitboots
Coughing oath-edged talk and pipe-smoke,   5
Shouldering off the freshened silence.

One chased after rabbits; lost them;
Came back with a nest of lark's eggs;
Showed them; lodged them in the grasses.

So they passed in beards and moleskins,   10
Fathers, brothers, nicknames, laughter,
Through the tall gates standing open.

At noon there came a tremor; cows
Stopped chewing for a second; sun,
Scarfed as in a heat-haze, dimmed.   15

The dead go on before us, they
Are sitting in God's house in comfort,
We shall see them face to face –

Plain as lettering in the chapels
It was said, and for a second   20
Wives saw men of the explosion

Larger than in life they managed –
Gold as on a coin, or walking
Somehow from the sun towards them,

One showing the eggs unbroken.   25

'Fathers, brothers,
nicknames, laughter'

2 *pithead*: the top part of a mine.
3 *slagheap*: man-made hill formed
   from the waste of coal mining.
4 *pitboots*: heavy boots worn by
   miners.

8 *lark's eggs*: the eggs of the skylark,
   a native bird of England and
   Ireland.
10 *moleskins*: heavy material worn by
   working men.
15 *Scarfed*: wrapped up.

EXPLORATIONS

1 Does Larkin give a realistic picture of the working men? Choose two
   realistic details (images) that you found effective.
2 Would you consider this poem a religious poem? Why or why not?
3 Comment on the concluding image as a symbol of redemption.

STUDY NOTES

'The Explosion' documents a tragedy that can randomly happen to a
community, but it offers a consolation that is not present in Larkin's
other poems. The word 'explosion' brings to mind a loud bang,
destruction, dead bodies. What other words do you associate with the
word 'explosion'?

The **source** of this poem was a **documentary** Larkin watched on the coal-
mining industry. The poem gives an account of an underground accident in
which a number of miners lost their lives. Many of the miner's wives were
supposed to have seen visions of their husbands at the moment of the
explosion. Larkin also said, 'I heard a **song** about a mine disaster … it made me
want to write the same thing, a mine disaster with a vision of immortality at the
end … that's the point of the eggs.'

The poem **opens quietly as the scene is observed** in stanza one and we are gently led into the drama: 'On the day of the explosion'. Notice the word 'the'. This is a specific event that will affect specific people. The details give a premonition of disaster: 'Shadows pointed towards the pithead'. The alliteration of the explosive letter 'p' adds to the menace, as does the personification: 'slagheap slept'. The image of a sleeping monster that will wreak havoc if awoken is suggested. The alliteration of 's' emphasises the uneasy peace.

In **contrast**, along come the noisy miners, swearing and coughing in stanza two. An impression of proud, ordinary strong young men from the tough world of the mines is given in a few well-chosen details: 'pitboots', 'Coughing oath-edged talk and pipe-smoke'. The onomatopoeia in the line 'Shouldering off the freshened silence' gives an idea of their rough strength. They walk unknowing, but we know and this adds to the growing tension and suspense in the poem. **We are brought closer to the miners** in stanza three as we observe them playing about. One chases rabbits, but comes back with a 'nest of lark's eggs'. He 'shows' the eggs. These are men who are interested in and deeply respectful of nature. He 'lodged' the eggs in the grasses, where the mother bird could find them. We see the sensitivity in these tough men.

The miners are part of a **close-knit community**, as we learn in stanza four: 'Fathers, brothers, nicknames, laughter'. The poignancy is becoming unbearable for the reader as we realise all will be blown apart by the event that is about to occur. The 'tall gates' are waiting, 'standing open', almost like the gates of the underworld, inescapable. **These men meet their fate** in stanza five ('So they passed'). The language is almost biblical. The ending is becoming inevitable. Larkin records the accident calmly, without melodrama. Instead we are presented with the ripple effects of the explosion on nature: 'cows/Stopped chewing' and the sun 'dimmed' as it was supposed to have done at the crucifixion of Christ. Time stands still. The explosion only registered for a 'second'. This is in contrast with the world of the men, where nothing will ever be the same again. But the rescue and the grief are unmentioned. We are left to imagine the horror.

In the final part of the poem, (stanzas six to nine), **the focus is changed**. Now we are looking at the wives and their reactions to the deaths. The passage from the Bible is in italics, words of comfort, a certainty of resurrection: '*We shall see them face to face*'. The wives believe this so strongly that they have a glimpse of their husbands and sons 'for a second'. Notice the difference of the reaction of the wives and the animals. The women's lives are irrevocably changed, but the animals resume their grazing. This terrible tragedy is of no consequence to the world of nature. They are unable to explain this vision 'Somehow'. These men are as they were and also are now **transformed**, 'Larger than in life'. They are walking in brilliant light. The sun is now the blazing sun of eternity. They are 'Gold as on a coin', a pure and enduring metal. The rhythm is stately and formal, which suits the religious viewpoint.

The **poem ends on a note of affirmation**, with the potent image of the unbroken eggs suggesting the hope of resurrection, the continuity of life and the strength of the ties of love. The last line stands alone, separated from the eight other three-line stanzas. Larkin's scepticism is absent. He is moved by sympathy for these men and their families. As the poet has said (in 'An Arundel Tomb'), 'What will survive of us is love'. This is the last poem in his last collection of poetry. Is it being suggested that love triumphs over death? Is this a modern religious poem?

ANALYSIS

Write a paragraph on Larkin's use of memorable images in 'The Explosion'.

SAMPLE PARAGRAPH

Larkin captures the scene on the day of the explosion with a few well-chosen visual details. He alerts the reader to the possibility of disaster with the sinister image of the 'shadows' which 'pointed towards the pithead', almost as if they were arrows of destiny marking the target of the miners. The air of menace is further emphasised with the memorable image of the slagheap as it 'slept' in the sun. The personification suggests a sleeping monster that will cause chaos if woken up. The image of the 'tall gates standing open' appealed to me, as it suggested the entry of the men into death's kingdom. The long vowel sounds slow the line. Death does not know time. These vowels, 'a' and 'o', lend a stately, solemn rhythm to the phrase, which reminds me of a ceremonial funeral march. The final image, contained in the floating last line, 'One showing the eggs unbroken', is full of optimism and hope, as it reminds me of Easter and the Resurrection of Christ. The image reflects a rare moment when Larkin has a positive attitude towards a Christian afterlife. The little eggs suggest renewal, the beginning of a new era. Larkin has laid aside his cynicism. The poem ends on this memorable image of transcendence, making the poem a beautiful religious credo.

Philip Larkin

EXAMINER'S COMMENT

This is a succinct and well-controlled paragraph. The student has a close knowledge of the text and has clearly understood the task. The writing is fluent throughout and makes effective use of pertinent quotation. Grade A.

CLASS/HOMEWORK EXERCISES

1   Write a paragraph on how the structure of the poem helps Larkin communicate his theme effectively. (Look at the arrangement of the stanzas scene by scene on the page, the use of run-on lines, the placement of key words, the use of italics and the separate last line.)

2   Copy the table below into your own notes and fill in critical comments about the last two quotations.

Key Quotes

So they passed in beards and moleskins	The use of detailed images adds a strong visual quality and realism to the description of the miners.
Fathers, brothers, nicknames, laughter	Larkin recognises and admires the ordinary lives of this hard-working mining community.
At noon, there came a tremor	There are no details about the actual explosion. The tone is detached and the poet seems stunned by the event.
We shall see them face to face	
the eggs unbroken	

Cut Grass

Cut grass lies frail:
Brief is the breath
Mown stalks exhale.
Long, long the death

It dies in the white hours   5
Of young-leafed June
With chestnut flowers,
With hedges snowlike strewn,

White lilac bowed,
Lost lanes of Queen Anne's lace,   10
And that high-builded cloud
Moving at summer's pace.

'Lost lanes of Queen Anne's lace'

GLOSSARY

2 *Brief is the breath*: life is short (the Bible says: 'all the glory of man is as flowers of grass').

8 *strewn*: covered untidily.

10 *Queen Anne's lace*: cow parsley, a white wild flower with lace-like blooms.

EXPLORATIONS

1   This poem gives a picture of a rural landscape. What colour predominates? List three examples. What is the colour white usually associated with! (Innocence, weddings, funeral flowers, purity, etc.) In your opinion, why does Larkin use this colour?

Philip Larkin

2 In your opinion, what is the mood of the poem? Does it change or not? Give evidence from the text to support your view.

3 Write a paragraph giving your own personal response to this poem. Refer closely to the text in your answer.

STUDY NOTES

'Cut Grass' is a lyric dealing with a recurring theme in Larkin's poetry, passing time and death. Written in 1971, it appeared in his collection *High Windows*. It is a calm poem that Larkin saw as a 'succession of images'. His verdict was, 'I like it all right'. Yet it was written at the end of Larkin's life, when he was very bitter about the state of England ('what an end to a great country'). He was critical of socialism and immigrants: 'I have always been right wing ... I identify with certain virtues (thrift, hard work, reverence, desire to preserve).'

The Bible states that 'All flesh is grass'. The title of 'Cut Grass' echoes this classic theme implicitly as we are reminded of the figure of Father Time/Death with his scythe. All living things are mown down. The setting of this poem is a meadow that has been recently mown. 'Cut grass lies frail' suggests the **fragility and brevity of life** against the relentless approach of inescapable death. The word 'frail' almost seems to expire as its sound drifts away at the end of the first line of stanza one. The short, unpredictable life of the grass is eloquently captured in the alliterative phrase 'Brief is the breath'. Explosive 'b' sounds reflect the action of breathing in and out. This personification, continued in the verb 'exhale', implies the parallel between our tenuous hold on life and that of all living things. The full stop at the end of this line underscores the reality of death and its finality. In contrast to this, the first stanza runs on into the next stanza to emphasise the fact that death is endless; it is not subject to time: 'Long, long the death'.

Stanza two tells us when the grass in the meadow dies, just at the moment when all other things are growing profusely. The trees are beginning to come into leaf and the hedges are covered in foaming whitethorn, like snow ('snowlike strewn'). The alliteration and run-on lines suggest the abundance of nature. **Nature has the ability to renew itself**, as the compound word 'young-leafed' suggests. We wonder: can man renew himself? The assonance ('hours', 'flowers') adds a poignant, melancholy note to this stanza, as in the midst of life is death.

In the **third stanza**, this abundance continues as the succession of beautiful white images mirror each other: 'White lilac bowed' flows into frothy 'lanes of Queen Anne's lace'. This wild flower appears every summer in out-of-the way lanes throughout rural England. Is this poem also an elegy for a disappearing England? The alliteration of 'l' suggests the meandering, winding lanes of the countryside. Towering white clouds add to this picture of rural serenity, as they glide effortlessly by, 'Moving at summer's pace'. But all will die in their own time. **This elegy is like a lament or requiem**, its long vowel sounds suggesting the lingering of the bereaved, unwilling to let the dead go. The poet's tone is sympathetic, resigned to the inevitable.

Here is no Christian consolation, no exhortation to live life passionately. The two-sentence poem is divided into short, abrupt sentences at the start which showcase the harsh finality of death. The poem then moves into the long run-on lines of the second sentence, which is stately and dignified and is suitable for a lament. The regular rhyme scheme (*abab, cdcd, efef*) underpins the fact that time passes and death comes; it is unavoidable. **Larkin clearly valued traditional English poetry forms**, as he valued England.

ANALYSIS

Larkin said he wrote two kinds of poems, 'the beautiful and true'. Discuss this statement, referring to the poem 'Cut Grass'. Support your view with references from the poem.

SAMPLE PARAGRAPH

In my opinion, Larkin has indeed written a poem that resonates with truth. There is no escaping the sad finality of all human existence, 'Brief is the breath'. The poet does not give us any consolation either in this elegy. The real truth of human mortality floats in our consciousness as timeless and as inevitable as the 'high-builded cloud' floats in the sky on a summer's day. I also think this poem is beautiful, as the succession of idyllic images which are truly English are presented to us. The smell of cut grass is suggested in the evocative line 'Mown stalks exhale'. The abundance and generosity of nature is shown in the alliterative phrase 'hedges snowlike strewn'. But for me the real beauty of the poem lies in the musical writing. It reminds me of a song lyric. The assonance of long vowel sounds ('Long, long') and slender vowels ('White lilac') evoke long, lazy summer evenings that are quintessentially English. The melancholic phrase 'Lost lanes' seems to be lamenting a lost way of life, as well as death, as the 'l' sound lingers on the ear. Larkin is a superb craftsman. The gentle fading sounds of the words 'frail' and 'exhale' both disappear, as all individual existence does into the inevitability of death. The finality of death is punctuated sternly by the full stop after 'exhale'. The compound words 'young-leafed', 'high-builded' show the beauty of life. The regular rhyme scheme (*abab, cdcd, efef*) moves as effortlessly as the clouds 'at summer's pace'. Larkin expresses a classic, true theme in a beautiful way. Like him, I like this poem 'all right'.

EXAMINER'S COMMENT

This paragraph addresses the two elements of the question (beautiful and true). It shows a real appreciation of poetic technique. Fluent and varied expression, particularly the impressive vocabulary, merits a grade A.

CLASS/HOMEWORK EXERCISES

1 Larkin's poems show 'loneliness, emptiness and mortality'. Do you agree that this is true of 'Cut Grass'? Refer to the text in your answer.
2 Copy the table below into your own notes and fill in critical comments about the last two quotations.

Key Quotes

Cut grass lies frail	Life is short for all living things.
Mown stalks exhale	The long vowel sounds ('a' and 'o') slow the pace of the line, emphasising the inevitability of passing time.
It dies in the white hours/ Of young-leafed June	Contrast adds a poignant tone. The rest of nature is very much alive, as referenced by the compound word 'young-leafed'.
Lost lanes of Queen Anne's lace	
And that high-builded cloud/ Moving at summer's pace	

LEAVING CERT SAMPLE ESSAY

Q 'The appeal of Philip Larkin's poetry.'
Using the above title, write an essay outlining what you consider to be the appeal of Larkin's poetry. Refer to the poems by Philip Larkin that you have studied.

MARKING SCHEME GUIDELINES

Expect a clear focus on the appeal (or lack of it) of the poems by Larkin. Responses may concentrate on the poet's themes and/or style. Evidence of engagement/involvement with the work of the poet should be rewarded.

Material may be drawn from the following:
- The poet's distinctive personality; honesty, compassion.
- His observations of the ordinary, everyday world.
- Prominent themes: time, transience, love, death.
- Powerful visual images, metaphors, sound effects.
- Colloquial language, measured rhythm, controlled rhyme.
- Use of irony, dark humour, dry wit.
- Varying tones – optimism, nostalgia, disillusionment, etc.

SAMPLE ESSAY
(The Appeal of Larkin's Poetry)

1 *Philip Larkin has a reputation as a gloomy poet who sees nothing positive about the world around him. 'Writing about unhappiness is the source of my popularity' (Larkin). Yet he is still one of the most highly regarded poets of the twentieth century. His poems are memorable because they address everyday issues such as love, marriage and death. This is done through stories based on his own observations of the world around him. Best of all, he tackles these subjects in a fresh and honest way.*

2 *There is evidence in 'The Whitsun Weddings' that Larkin saw marriage in a very positive light. A wedding traditionally offered a chance for happiness. The poem has a narrative, colloquial quality that appeals to me. Larkin's insight into human behaviour is very interesting. It's as if we are listening to gossip. He witnesses several* newlywed couples boarding the train at each station, with their families waving farewell to them. At the beginning, he seems critical and cynical at what is going on, with 'the mothers loud and fat', 'An uncle shouting smut' and the 'jewellery-substitutes'. But this is the kind of honest criticism that makes the poem true to life. He even notes the sad aspects of weddings, where children leave the family home. This is suggested by the phrase 'The last confetti'. However, Larkin finally describes the 'arrow-shower ... somewhere becoming rain', a beautiful image clearly suggesting that there is hope for these couples.

3 The passing of time is a recurring theme in Larkin's poems. 'At Grass' takes a nostalgic look at another typical rural landscape where racehorses are quietly grazing. The poet creates a strangely calm scene with a cinematic image of the wide field. The two horses are imprecise figures far away in the distance: 'The eye can hardly pick them out'. The lines are slow moving and the punctuation holds up the pace: 'Then one crops grass, and moves about'. A strange sense of time passing is created with the use of dashes and the steady, even rhyme scheme. This forces the reader to closely observe what is being expressed, moment by moment. The attractive soft tone and gentle sounds are in keeping with the poem's wistful mood.

4 Larkin then draws in readers by giving us the history of these distinguished animals. They once won 'Cups and Stakes and Handicaps'. Short, snappy punctuation captures the tension and buzz of the racetrack. But all that glory and attention have now passed as they spend their final years in 'unmolesting meadows'. The mood of fulfilment brings the poem to a truly satisfying conclusion. Larkin contemplates what will happen when our 'fame' has ended. Will we all 'stand anonymous again'? What will happen to us when we are past our glory and our prime? The poet's tender sentiments illustrate his sensitive awareness of life's realities. However, like many of his poems, we can interpret the outlook as either positive or negative. For me, the poem is meaningful because it broadly celebrates life, but also regrets its passing.

5 What is interesting about Larkin's poems about death is that he openly writes about the one thing we all fear most. In 'Ambulances', Larkin begins looking at an ambulance's journey through a built-up town where the locals are busy getting on with their ordinary lives. But the ambulance is a reminder of how fragile life is. The poet's startling imagery reflects people's shock when they see this sick woman being stretchered out of her home. Her 'wild white face' is a reminder of how helpless and *fearful she is. People whisper 'Poor soul' but 'They whisper at their own distress'. What is impressive about Larkin is that he always gets to the truth. And the truth hurts. It's not that people don't feel sorry for the dying patient, it's more that they cannot really make sense of death.*

6 *Overall, there is an engaging sense of realism and energy about Philip Larkin's poems. He is honest enough to face up to universal fears while still feeling sympathy for ordinary individuals. I believe that Larkin isn't as cynical as he is made out to be. He celebrates life and relationships in poems such as 'An Arundel Tomb', where he concludes: 'What will survive of us is love'. There are many examples of where he is sympathetic to people (e.g. the victims in 'The Explosion') because they are powerless against fate. I am convinced that Larkin fully deserves his reputation and that his poetry will continue to appeal to readers.*

(approx. 750 words)

GRADE: A1		
P	=	15/15
C	=	13/15
L	=	13/15
M	=	5/5
Total	=	46/50

EXAMINER'S COMMENT

This is a good, personal response that is focused and well supported. The candidate displays a clear knowledge of Larkin's work. Quotations are accurate and successfully integrated into the general commentary. Despite some weaknesses, the essay is well organised, wide ranging and very confidently written. Grade A.

SAMPLE LEAVING CERT QUESTIONS ON LARKIN'S POETRY (45–50 MINUTES)

1   What impact did the poetry of Philip Larkin make on you as a reader? In shaping your answer, you might consider some of the following:
   • The poet's main themes.
   • Language and imagery in the poems.
   • Your favourite poem or poems.

2 Some critics have claimed that Larkin is 'one of the most sensitive and compassionate of poets'. Would you agree with this estimation of the poems by Philip Larkin on your course? Support your point of view by relevant quotation or reference.

3 If you were asked to give a public reading of some of Philip Larkin's poems, which ones would you choose? Give reasons for your choices, supporting them by reference to the poems on your course.

SAMPLE ESSAY PLAN (Q3)

If you were asked to give a public reading of Philip Larkin's poems, which ones would you choose? Give reasons for your choices, supporting them by reference to the poems on your course.

•	*Intro:*	Sense of audience expected; mention recurring themes that are still relevant and some interesting aspects of Larkin's style.
•	*Point 1:*	'Wedding-Wind' – adopts persona of new wife, concentration on joy, optimistic ending. We can appreciate this theme.
•	*Point 2:*	'The Whitsun Weddings' – train journey, ordinary experience, steady rhythm of train – poet reflects on newlywed couples at end.
•	*Point 3:*	'Ambulances' – imagery conveys graphic horror of violence and its indiscriminate nature.
•	*Point 4:*	'The Trees' – celebrates human resilience and courage in the face of certain death. Use of present continuous tense, sibilance, even rhyme scheme underlines this positive outlook.
•	*Point 5:*	'The Explosion' – illustrates how life can suddenly be disrupted by disaster. Vivid details convey the world of mining and the imminent dangers. Uplifting imagery.
•	*Conclusion:*	Larkin is a fine observer of ordinary lives/places, but he also challenges readers by exploring wider questions about life/death, sorrow/happiness.

EXERCISE

Develop one of the above points into a paragraph.

POINT 5 – SAMPLE PARAGRAPH

I feel that the poem 'The Explosion' is very much a description of a modern-day experience. After 9/11 and the London Underground Tube bombings, a working man returning home from work, unknowing that his life and those of his relatives will be disturbed by tragedy, strikes a deep fear in all of us. Do you feel safe in this modern world of random terrorism? The world of the miner is conveyed in a few well-chosen details, rather like close-ups on a TV news sequence: 'pitboots', 'in beards and moleskins'. After a day spent down the dusty mines, these miners were 'Coughing'. They are tough, their talk is 'oath-edged'. But the men are also part of a close-knit community: 'Fathers, brothers'. The personal angle, as the tabloids so often say, is given. They have 'nicknames', they are laughing. This adds to the poignancy of the scene. Then the focus is shifted to the aftermath of the tragedy. Again, a modern-day parallel strikes us. The people of London attended their memorial services for the dead and then returned to the Underground train stations. We marvelled at the courage of ordinary people under threat. So the wives of the dead drew comfort from 'We shall see them face to face'. The defiant human spirit is also shown in the uplifting image that ends the poem: 'One showing the eggs unbroken'. I am sure you will agree with the inclusion of this poem because it deals in such a true way with the unpredictability of life, a harsh fact, and the resilience of the ordinary man. These aspects of the tragedy become beautiful under the observant eyes of Larkin.

EXAMINER'S COMMENT

As part of a full essay answer, the student has written an impressive A-grade paragraph and gives a comprehensive explanation for the inclusion of 'The Explosion' in the public reading. Likening the poem to modern tragic events adds a compelling, unique dimension to the discussion. The response is well rooted in the text.

Last Words

'Larkin's poems are melancholy, melodious, disenchanted, bewitching, perfectly written and perfectly approachable.'

Seamus Heaney

'People marvelled that a poet they had never met could have spoken to them so intimately.'

Andrew Motion

'I want readers to feel yes, I've never thought of it that way, but that's how it is.'

Philip Larkin

'Out of the ash
I rise with my red hair
And I eat men like air'

Sylvia Plath   (1932–63)

Born in Boston, Massachusetts, in 1932, **Sylvia Plath** is a writer whose best-known poems are noted for their intense focus and vibrant, personal imagery. Her writing talent – and ambition to succeed – was evident from an early age. She kept a journal during childhood and published her early poems in literary magazines and newspapers. After studying Art and English at college, Plath moved to Cambridge, England, in the mid-1950s. Here she met and later married the poet Ted Hughes. The couple had two children, Frieda and Nicholas, but the marriage was not to last. Plath continued to write through the late 1950s and early 1960s. During the final years of her life, she produced numerous confessional poems of stark revelation, channelling her long-standing anxiety and doubt into poetic verses of great power and pathos. At her creative peak, Sylvia Plath took her own life on 11 February 1963.

PRESCRIBED POEMS (HIGHER LEVEL)

1 'Black Rook in Rainy Weather' (p. 386)

Plath uses the description of the rook to explore poetic inspiration and her joy when creative 'miracles' occur.

2 'The Times Are Tidy' (p. 391)

Disillusioned with the blandness of her times, this bitter social commentary contrasts the uneventful 1950s with the idealistic fairytale world of the past.

3 'Morning Song' (p. 395)

The poem records Plath's feelings after the birth of her daughter and focuses on the wonder of the mother–child relationship.

4 'Finisterre' (p. 400)

A highly descriptive poem dominated by disturbing themes of decay and death. Plath and her husband visited Finisterre on the north-west coast of France in 1960.

5 'Mirror' (p. 405)

The central themes are self-knowledge and ageing. In the first stanza, the poet is the mirror; in the second, she is the woman looking into it.

6 'Pheasant' (p. 409)

Another personal poem about man's relationship with nature. Plath believed that respect for life's natural order was vital.

7 'Elm' (p. 413)

An intensely introspective poem, rich in dark imagery and symbolism. The poet personifies the elm tree, giving it a voice.

8 'Poppies in July' (p. 418)

One of Plath's bleakest poems, contrasting the vitality of the poppies with her own exhausted longing to escape a world of pain.

9 'The Arrival of the Bee Box' (p. 422)

This narrative addresses several key themes, including power, freedom and oppression.

10 'Child' (p. 427)

In this short poem, Plath observes the innocence of childhood but is overcome by personal feelings of failure and hopelessness.

Black Rook in Rainy Weather

On the stiff twig up there
Hunches a wet black rook
Arranging and rearranging its feathers in the rain.
I do not expect a miracle
Or an accident   5

To set the sight on fire
In my eye, nor seek
Any more in the desultory weather some design,
But let spotted leaves fall as they fall,
Without ceremony, or portent.   10

Although, I admit, I desire,
Occasionally, some backtalk
From the mute sky, I can't honestly complain:
A certain minor light may still
Lean incandescent   15

Out of kitchen table or chair
As if a celestial burning took
Possession of the most obtuse objects now and then –
Thus hallowing an interval
Otherwise inconsequent   20

By bestowing largesse, honor,
One might say love. At any rate, I now walk
Wary (for it could happen
Even in this dull ruinous landscape); skeptical,
Yet politic; ignorant   25

Of whatever angel may choose to flare
Suddenly at my elbow. I only know that a rook
Ordering its black feathers can so shine
As to seize my senses, haul
My eyelids up, and grant   30

A brief respite from fear
Of total neutrality. With luck,

Trekking stubborn through this season
Of fatigue, I shall
Patch together a content   35

Of sorts. Miracles occur,
If you care to call those spasmodic
Tricks of radiance miracles. The wait's begun again,
The long wait for the angel,
For that rare, random descent.   40

'Hunches a wet black rook'

EXPLORATIONS

1   What is the mood of the poet? How does the weather described in the poem reflect this mood?

2   In your opinion, why do you think Plath sees light coming from ordinary household objects such as kitchen tables and chairs?

3   What do you think the final stanza means? Consider the phrase 'The wait's begun again'. What is the poet waiting for?

STUDY NOTES

'Black Rook in Rainy Weather' was written while Plath was studying in Cambridge in 1956. It contains many of her trademarks, including the exploration of emotions, the use of weather, colour and natural objects as symbols, and the dreamlike world. She explores a number of themes: fear of the future, lack of identity and poetic inspiration.

Stanza one begins with the straightforward description of a bird grooming itself, which the poet observes on a rainy day. But on closer inspection, the mood of the poem is set with the words 'stiff' and 'Hunches'. The bird is at the mercy of the elements ('wet') and there is no easy movement ('stiff'). **This atmospheric opening is dull and low key.** The black rook is a bird of ill omen. But the bird is presenting its best image to the world as it sits 'Arranging and rearranging its feathers'. Plath longed to excel in both life and art. If she were inspired, the rook would take on a new light as if on fire. But she doesn't see this happening. Even the weather is 'desultory' in the fading season of autumn. Poetic inspiration is miraculous; it is not ordinary. The world is experienced in a heightened way. Notice the long line which seems out of proportion with the rest as she declares that she doesn't expect any order or 'design' in the haphazard weather. The decaying leaves will fall with no ritual, without any organisation, just as they will. **This is a chaotic world**, a random place with no design, just as poetic inspiration happens by chance. It is also accidental, like the falling leaves. We cannot seek it, we receive it. It is active, we are passive.

After this low-key opening, the poem starts to take flight in stanzas three and four when the poet states: 'I desire'. Plath employs a witty metaphor as she looks for 'some backtalk' from the 'mute sky'. **She would like to connect with it.** It could happen on her walk, or even at home if she were to experience a 'certain minor light' shining from an ordinary, everyday object like a chair. The association of fire and light makes an ordinary moment special. It is 'hallowing'; it is giving generously ('largesse'). She is hoping against hope. Plath may be sceptical, but she is going forward carefully in case she misses the magic moment. **She must stay alert and watchful.** She must be 'politic', wise.

Stanzas six, seven and eight discuss poetic inspiration. Plath doesn't know if it will happen to her, or how it will happen. Two contrasting attitudes are at loggerheads: hope and despair. The rook might inspire her: **'Miracles occur'.** If she were motivated, it would relieve 'total neutrality', this nothingness she feels when living uninspired. Although she is tired, she is insistent, 'stubborn'.

The poet will have to 'Patch' something together. She shows human vulnerability, but she is trying. This determination is a different tone from the negative one at the beginning.

Literature was as important to Plath as friends and family. What she can't live without, therefore, is inspiration – a dark, passionless existence. **Depression** is an empty state with no feeling or direction, yet her view of creativity is romantic. It is miraculous, available only to a chosen few. 'The long wait for the angel' has begun. Notice the constant use of the personal pronoun 'I'. This is a poet who is very aware of self and her own personal responses to events and feelings. The outside world becomes a metaphor for her own interior world.

Plath uses both archaic language and slang as if reinforcing the randomness of the world. This is also mirrored in the run-on lines. All is haphazard, but carefully arranged, so even the extended **third-to-last line** stretches out as it waits for the 'random descent' of inspiration. In this **carefully arranged disorder**, two worlds are seen. One is negative: 'desultory', 'spotted', 'mute', 'dull', 'ruinous', stubborn', 'fatigue'. This is indicative of her own bleak mood. The other world is positive: 'fire', 'light', 'incandescent', celestial', 'hallowing', 'largesse', 'honor', 'love', 'shine'. Here is the possibility of radiance.

ANALYSIS

'Plath's poems are carefully composed and beautifully phrased.' Write a paragraph in response to this statement, illustrating your answer with close reference to the poem 'Black Rook in Rainy Weather'.

SAMPLE PARAGRAPH

Just like the rook, Plath 'arranges and rearranges' her words with infinite care to communicate the contrast between the dull life of 'total neutrality' which occurs when she is not inspired, when nothing sets 'the sight on fire'. I particularly admire how she artfully arranges disorder in the poem. This mirrors the chance of poetic inspiration. Long lines poke untidily out of the first three stanzas, seeking the 'minor light' to 'Lean incandescent' upon them. I also like how the lines run in a seemingly untidy way into each other, as do some stanzas. Stanza three goes into four, as it describes the chance of a light coming from an ordinary object, such as a kitchen chair, which is seen only if the poet is inspired. The alliteration of 'rare, random' in the last line mirrors the gift of poetic technique which will be given to the poet if she can receive the blessed benediction of poetic inspiration. 'Miracles occur'.

EXAMINER'S COMMENT

Close reading of the poem is evident in this original response to Plath's poetic technique. Quotations are very well used here to highlight Plath's ability to create disordered order. Grade A standard.

CLASS/HOMEWORK EXERCISES

1   In your opinion, has the poet given up hope of being inspired? Use reference to the poem in your answer.
2   Copy the table below into your own notes and fill in critical comments about the last two quotations.

Key Quotes

But let spotted leaves fall as they fall,/ Without ceremony	Decaying leaves drop as they will without any ritual to mark the event.
As if a celestial burning took/Possession of the most obtuse objects now and then	Poetic inspiration allows Plath to see the most ordinary things in a state of heightened awareness. They appear transformed into objects of beauty.
A brief respite from fear/Of total neutrality	A major concern of the poet is the distress of losing her inspiration.
If you care to call those spasmodic/ Tricks of radiance miracles	
that rare, random descent	

The Times Are Tidy

Unlucky the hero born
In this province of the stuck record
Where the most watchful cooks go jobless
And the mayor's rôtisserie turns
Round of its own accord.   5

There's no career in the venture
Of riding against the lizard,
Himself withered these latter-days
To leaf-size from lack of action:
History's beaten the hazard.   10

The last crone got burnt up
More than eight decades back
With the love-hot herb, the talking cat,
But the children are better for it,
The cow milks cream an inch thick.   15

'riding against the lizard'

GLOSSARY		
2 *province*: a remote place.		4 *rôtisserie*: meat skewer.
2 *stuck record*: the needle would sometimes get jammed on a vinyl music album.		7 *lizard*: dragon.
		11 *crone*: old witch.

EXPLORATIONS

1 What is suggested by the poem's title? Is Plath being cynical about modern life? Develop your response in a short paragraph.

2 Select one image from the poem that suggests that the past was much more dangerous and exciting than the present. Comment on its effectiveness.

3 Do you agree or disagree with the speaker's view of modern life? Give reasons for your answer.

STUDY NOTES

'The Times Are Tidy' was written in 1958. In this short poem, Plath casts a cold eye on contemporary life and culture, which she sees as bland and unadventurous. The poem's ironic title clearly suggests Plath's dissatisfaction with the over-regulated society of her day.

Do you think you are living in an heroic age, or do you believe that most people have lost their sense of wonder? Is there anyone in public life whom you really admire? Perhaps you despair of politicians, particularly when their promises sound like a 'stuck record'.

Stanza one is dominated by hard-hitting images reflecting how the world of fairytale excitement has disappeared. From the outset, **the tone is scornful and dismissive.** Plath believes that any hero would be totally out of place amid the mediocrity of our times. True talent ('the most watchful cooks') is largely unrewarded. The unexpected imagery of the 'stuck record' and the mayor's rotating spit symbolise complacent monotony and lack of progress, particularly during the late 1950s, when Plath wrote the poem. Both images convey a sense of purposeless circling, of people going nowhere. It seems as though the poet is seething with frustration at the inertia and conformity of her own life and times.

Plath's **darkly embittered sense of humour** becomes evident in **stanza two.** She laments the current lack of honour and courage – something which once existed in the world of fairytales. Unlike the past, contemporary society is compromised. There are no idealistic dragon-slayers any more. The worker who dares to stand up and criticise ('riding against the lizard') is risking the chance of promotion. The modern dragon – a metaphor for the challenges we face – has even been reduced to a mere lizard. Despite this, we are afraid of confrontation and prefer to retreat. The verb 'withered' suggests the weakness and decay of our safe, modern world. The poet openly complains that 'History's beaten the hazard'. Over time, we have somehow defeated all sense of adventure and daring. These qualities belong in the distant past.

In **stanza three**, Plath continues to contrast past and present. Witches are no longer burned at the stake. This might well suggest that superstition has disappeared, and with it, all imagination. The last two lines are ironic in tone, reflecting the poet's deep **disenchantment with the excesses of our consumer society**. The final image – 'the cow milks cream an inch thick' – signifies overindulgence. At one time, it was thought that supernatural forces could reduce the milk yield from cows.

The poet clearly accepts that **society has changed for the worse**. Children may have everything they want nowadays, but they have lost their sense of wonder and excitement. She laments the loss of legendary heroism. Medieval dragons and wicked witches (complete with magic potions and talking cats) no longer exist. Her conclusion is that life today is decidedly less interesting than it used to be. Unlike so much of Plath's work, the personal pronoun 'I' is not used in this poem. However, the views expressed are highly contemptuous and the weary, frustrated tone clearly suggests that Plath herself feels unfulfilled.

ANALYSIS

Write a paragraph on Plath's critical tone in 'The Times Are Tidy'.

SAMPLE PARAGRAPH

The tone of voice in 'The Times Are Tidy' is almost irrationally critical of modern life. Plath has nothing good to say about today's world as she sees it. The poem's title is glib and self-satisfied, just like the neatly organised society that Plath seems to despise. The opening comment – 'Unlucky the hero born/In this province' – emphasises this negative tone. The poet's mocking attitude becomes increasingly disparaging as she rails against the unproductive images of easy living – 'the stuck record' and 'the mayor's rôtisserie'. Plath goes on to contrast today's apathetic society with the more spirited medieval era, when knights in armour existed. The poet deliberately omits all the positive aspects of modern life and chooses to give a very one-sided view of the world. Plath ends on a sarcastic note, sneering at the advances of our world of plenty – 'cream an inch thick'. The voice here – and indeed, throughout the entire poem – is both sardonic and superior.

EXAMINER'S COMMENT

This A-grade paragraph demonstrates strong interpretive skills and is firmly focused on Plath's judgmental tone. The supporting references range widely and effectively illustrate the poet's critical attitude. Quotations are particularly well integrated and the management of language is assured throughout.

CLASS/HOMEWORK EXERCISES

1 Outline the main theme in 'The Times Are Tidy'. In your answer, trace the way the poet develops her ideas during the course of the poem.
2 Copy the table below into your own notes and fill in critical comments about the last two quotations.

Key Quotes

Unlucky the hero born/In this province	Plath is clearly disillusioned with the unheroic world in which she lives.
the mayor's rôtisserie turns/ Round of its own accord	The image of automation suggests how complacent and predictable life has become. Nothing seems to change.
History's beaten the hazard	Ironically, like the beasts of legend, excitement and romance have been crushed in these 'tidy' modern times.
But the children are better for it	
The cow milks cream an inch thick	

Morning Song

Love set you going like a fat gold watch.
The midwife slapped your footsoles, and your bald cry
Took its place among the elements.

Our voices echo, magnifying your arrival. New statue.
In a drafty museum, your nakedness   5
Shadows our safety. We stand round blankly as walls.

I'm no more your mother
Than the cloud that distills a mirror to reflect its own slow
Effacement at the wind's hand.

All night your moth-breath   10
Flickers among the flat pink roses. I wake to listen:
A far sea moves in my ear.

One cry, and I stumble from bed, cow-heavy and floral
In my Victorian nightgown.
Your mouth opens clean as a cat's. The window square   15

Whitens and swallows its dull stars. And now you try
Your handful of notes;
The clear vowels rise like balloons.

'The clear vowels rise like
balloons'

2 *midwife*: a person trained to assist
   at childbirth.
3 *elements*: primitive, natural,
   atmospheric forces.
9 *Effacement*: rub out, make
   inconspicuous, obliterate.

11 *pink roses*: images on the wallpaper.
18 *vowels*: speech sounds made
    without stopping the flow of the
    breath.

EXPLORATIONS

1 Comment on the suitability and effectiveness of the simile in line 1.
2 What is the attitude of the mother to the new arrival? Does her attitude change in the course of the poem? Refer to the text in your answer.
3 A metaphor links two things so that one idea explains or gives a new viewpoint about the other. Choose one metaphor from the poem and comment on its effectiveness.

STUDY NOTES

'Morning Song' was written in 1961. Plath explores the complex issues of the relationship between a mother and a child, celebrating the birth of the infant but also touching on deep feelings of loss and separation.

Do all mothers immediately welcome and fall in love with a new baby? Are some of them overwhelmed or even depressed after giving birth? Are parents often anxious about the new responsibilities a baby brings?

Plath wrote this poem after two intensely personal experiences, celebrating the birth of her daughter, Frieda, who was 10 months old when she wrote the poem, and shortly after a miscarriage. The poem is realistic and never strays into sentimentality or cliché. The title, 'Morning', suggests a new beginning, and 'Song' a celebration.

Stanza one describes the arrival of the child into the world in a strong, confident, rhythmic sentence announcing the act of creation: 'Love set you going'. The simile comparing the child to a 'fat gold watch' suggests a plump baby, a rich and precious object. The broad vowel effects emphasise the physical presence of the baby. The 'ticking' sound conveys action and dynamism, but also the passage of time. The child is now part of the mortal world where change and death are inevitable. At this moment of birth, the baby is the centre of attention as the midwife and parents surround her. But this is a cruel world, as we see from the words 'slapped' and 'bald'. The child is now part of the universe as she takes her place among the 'elements'. The verbs in this stanza are in the past tense – **the mother is looking back at the event**. The rest of the poem is written in the present tense, which adds to the immediacy of the experience.

Stanza two has a feeling of disorientation, as if the mother feels separated from the child now that she has left the womb. There is a nightmarish, surreal quality to the lines 'Our voices echo, magnifying your arrival'. Plath sees the child as a new exhibit ('New statue') in a museum. Commas and full stops break up the flow of the lines and **the tone becomes more stilted and detached**. The child as a work of art is special and unique, but the museum is 'drafty', again a reference to the harshness of the world. The baby's vulnerability is stressed by its 'nakedness'. The midwife's and parents' frozen response is caught in the phrase 'blankly as walls'. They anxiously observe, unsure about their ability to protect. This baby also represents a threat to their relationship as she 'Shadows' their safety. The child is perceived as having a negative impact on the parents, perhaps driving them apart rather than uniting them.

Stanza three catches the **complex relationship between child and mother**. Plath feels she can't be maternal ('no more your mother'). This is vividly shown in the image of the cloud that rains, creating a puddle. **But in the act of creation, it destroys itself and its destruction is reflected in the pool of water**. Throughout her life, the poet was haunted by a fear of her own personal disintegration and annihilation. Does she see a conflict between becoming a mother and remaining a writer? She also realises as the child grows and matures that she will age, moving closer to death, and this will be reflected in the child's gaze. The mood of this stanza is one of dislocation, estrangement and powerlessness. Notice how the three lines of the stanza run into each other as the cloud disappears.

In stanza four, the tone changes to one of intimate, maternal love as the caring mother becomes alert to her child's needs. The situation described is warm and homely – the 'flat pink roses' are very different to the chill 'museum' of a previous stanza. The fragile breathing of the little child is beautifully described as 'your moth-breath/Flickers'. **Onomatopoeia in 'Flickers' mimics the tiny breathing noises of the child**. The mother is anticipating her baby's needs as she wakes ('listen'). The breathing child evokes happy memories of Plath's seaside childhood ('A far sea moves in my ear'). The infant cries and the attentive mother springs into action. She laughs at herself as she describes the comical figure she makes, 'cow-heavy and floral'. She feels awkward as she 'stumble[s]' to tend her child, whose eager mouth is shown by a startling image ('clean as a cat's') as it opens wide to receive the night feed of milk.

The stanza flows smoothly over into stanza five, just as Nature flows to its own rhythm and does not obey clocks or any other man-made rules. Night becomes morning as the child swallows the milk and the window swallows the stars.

Sylvia Plath

Children demand a parent's time and energy. **The child now defines herself** with her unique collection of sounds ('Your handful of notes'). This poem opened with the instinctive, elemental 'bald' cry of a newborn, but closes on a lovely, happy image of music and colour, as the baby's song's notes 'rise like balloons'.

ANALYSIS

The poem opens with the word 'Love'. Is this poem about parental love or parental anxiety?

SAMPLE PARAGRAPH

This poem contains both as the tone varies from the confident assertion that 'Love' was the source of the child to the curiously disengaged tone of the second stanza, where the parents 'stand round blankly as walls'. The enormity of the event of the birth of their child into a harsh world, 'drafty museum', seems to overwhelm them, particularly the mother. In the third stanza, she declares that she is not the child's mother, and explores her feelings of annihilation through the complex image of the disintegrating cloud, which creates only to be destroyed in the act of creation. However, the poem ends on a positive, loving note as the attentive mother feeds her child on demand, listening to her baby's song 'rise like balloons'. This poem realistically deals with the conflicting emotions new parents experience at a birth.

EXAMINER'S COMMENT

The paragraph deals confidently with both attitudes in a well-sustained argument effectively using pertinent quotes. These references range widely over much of the poem and the expression is very well controlled. Grade A.

CLASS/HOMEWORK EXERCISES

1   Look at the different sounds described in the poem, such as 'slapped', 'bald cry', 'A far sea moves', 'The clear vowels rise', and comment on their effectiveness.
2   Copy the table below into your own notes and fill in critical comments about the last two quotations.

Key Quotes

The midwife slapped your footsoles	After a birth, the nurse slaps the child to make it cry and clear the mucus from its mouth and nose.
your nakedness/Shadows our safety	The baby's vulnerability is a threat to the parents' relationship.
cow-heavy and floral/In my Victorian nightgown	A slightly comic picture of a mother heavy with breast milk in a long, patterned, high-neck nightdress.
Our voices echo, magnifying your arrival	
And now you try/Your handful of notes	

Sylvia Plath

Finisterre

This was the land's end: the last fingers, knuckled and rheumatic,
Cramped on nothing. Black
Admonitory cliffs, and the sea exploding
With no bottom, or anything on the other side of it,
Whitened by the faces of the drowned.   5
Now it is only gloomy, a dump of rocks –
Leftover soldiers from old, messy wars.
The sea cannons into their ear, but they don't budge.
Other rocks hide their grudges under the water.

The cliffs are edged with trefoils, stars and bells   10
Such as fingers might embroider, close to death,
Almost too small for the mists to bother with.
The mists are part of the ancient paraphernalia –
Souls, rolled in the doom-noise of the sea.
They bruise the rocks out of existence, then resurrect them.   15
They go up without hope, like sighs.
I walk among them, and they stuff my mouth with cotton.
When they free me, I am beaded with tears.

Our Lady of the Shipwrecked is striding toward the horizon,
Her marble skirts blown back in two pink wings.   20
A marble sailor kneels at her foot distractedly, and at his foot
A peasant woman in black
Is praying to the monument of the sailor praying.
Our Lady of the Shipwrecked is three times life size,
Her lips sweet with divinity.   25
She does not hear what the sailor or the peasant is saying –
She is in love with the beautiful formlessness of the sea.

Gull-colored laces flap in the sea drafts
Beside the postcard stalls.
The peasants anchor them with conches. One is told: 30
'These are the pretty trinkets the sea hides,
Little shells made up into necklaces and toy ladies.
They do not come from the Bay of the Dead down there,
But from another place, tropical and blue,
We have never been to.   35
These are our crêpes. Eat them before they blow cold.'

'and the sea exploding'

GLOSSARY

1	*land's end*: literally 'Finisterre'; the western tip of Brittany.
3	*Admonitory*: warning.
10	*trefoils*: three-leaved plants.
13	*paraphernalia*: discarded items.
14	*doom-noise*: hopeless sounds.
19	*Our Lady of the Shipwrecked*: the mother of Christ prayed for sailors.
30	*conches*: shells.
31	*trinkets*: cheap jewellery.
36	*crêpes*: light pancakes.

EXPLORATIONS

1   Would you agree that this is a disquieting poem that is likely to disturb readers? Refer to the text in your answer.

2   There are several changes of tone in this poem. Describe two contrasting tones, using close reference to the text.

3   What does the poem reveal to you about Sylvia Plath's own state of mind? Use reference to the text in your response.

STUDY NOTES

'Finisterre' was written in 1960 following a visit by Plath to Brittany, France. As with many of her poems, the description of the place can be interpreted both literally and metaphorically.

The sea has always inspired poets and artists. It is at times welcoming, menacing, beautiful, peaceful and mysterious. Throughout her short life, Sylvia Plath loved the ocean. She spent her childhood years on the Atlantic coast just north of Boston. This setting provides a source for many of her poetic ideas. Terror and death loom large in her descriptive poem 'Finisterre', in which the pounding rhythm of storm waves off the Breton coast represents **Plath's inner turmoil.**

Stanza one opens dramatically and immediately creates a disturbing atmosphere. Plath describes the rocky headland as being 'knuckled and rheumatic'. In a series of powerful images ('the last fingers', 'Black/Admonitory cliffs', 'and the sea exploding'), the poet recreates the uproar and commotion of the scene. The **grisly personification** is startling, linking the shoreline with suffering and decay. There is a real sense of conflict between sea and land. Both are closely associated with death ('the faces of the drowned'). The jagged rocks are compared to 'Leftover soldiers' who 'hide their grudges under the water'. There is a noticeable tone of regret and protest against the futility of conflict, which is denounced as 'old, messy wars'.

Plath's **negative imagery** is relentless, with harsh consonant sounds ('knuckled', 'Cramped', 'exploding') emphasising the force of raging storm waves. The use of contrasting colours intensifies the imagery. As the 'sea cannons' against the headland, the atmosphere is 'only gloomy'. It is hard not to see the bleak seascape as a reflection of Plath's own unhappy state.

In stanza two, the poet turns away from the cruel sea and focuses momentarily on the small plants clinging to the cliff edge. However, these 'trefoils, stars and bells' are also 'close to death'. If anything, they reinforce the **unsettling mood** and draw the poet back to the ocean mists, which she thinks of as symbolising the souls of the dead, lost in 'the doom-noise of the sea'. Plath imagines the heavy mists transforming the rocks, destroying them 'out of existence' before managing to 'resurrect them' again. In a **surreal sequence**, the poet enters the water ('I walk among them') and joins the wretched souls who lie there. Her growing sense of panic is suggested by the stark admission: 'they stuff my mouth with cotton'. The experience is agonising and leaves her 'beaded with tears'.

Plath's thoughts turn to a marble statue of 'Our Lady of the Shipwrecked' in stanza three. Once again, in her imagination, she creates a **dramatic narrative** around the religious figure. This monument to the patron saint of the ocean should offer some consolation to the kneeling sailor and a grieving peasant woman who pray to the mother of God. Ironically, their pleas are completely ignored – 'She does not hear' their prayers because 'She is in love with the beautiful formlessness of the sea'. The feeling of hopelessness is all pervading. Is the poet expressing her own **feelings of failure and despondency** here? Or is she also attacking the ineffectiveness of religion? The description of the statue is certainly unflattering. The figure is flighty and self-centred: 'Her marble skirts blown back in two pink wings'. In contrast, the powerful ocean remains fascinating.

In the fourth stanza, Plath describes the local Bretons who sell souvenirs to tourists. Unlike the previous three stanzas, **the mood appears to be much lighter** as the poet describes the friendly stall-keepers going about their business. It is another irony that their livelihood (selling 'pretty trinkets') is dependent on the sea and its beauty. Like the statue, the locals seem unconcerned by the tragic history of the ocean. Indeed, they are keen to play down 'the Bay of the Dead' and explain that what they sell is imported 'from another place, tropical and blue'. In the final line, a stall-holder advises the poet to enjoy the pancakes she has bought: 'Eat them before they blow cold'. Although the immediate mood is untroubled, **the final phrase brings us** back to the earlier – and more disturbing – parts of the poem where Plath described the raging storms and the nameless lost souls who have perished at sea.

ANALYSIS

Write a paragraph on Sylvia Plath's use of detailed description in 'Finisterre'.

SAMPLE PARAGRAPH

The opening images of the rocks – 'the last fingers, knuckled and rheumatic' – are of decrepit old age. The strong visual impact is a regular feature of Sylvia Plath's writing. The first half of the poem is filled with memorable details of the windswept coastline. In her careful choice of descriptive terms, Plath uses broad vowels to evoke a pervading feeling of dejection. Words such as 'drowned', 'gloomy', 'rolled' and 'doom' help to create this dismal effect. The dramatic aural image, 'The sea cannons', echoes the roar of turbulent waves crashing onto the rocks. Plath's eye for close observation is also seen in her portrait of the holy statue – 'Her lips sweet with divinity'. The poem ends with a painstaking sketch of the Breton traders selling postcards and 'Little shells made up into necklaces and toy ladies'. The local people seem to have come to terms with 'the Bay of the Dead' and are getting on with life. Overall, the use of details throughout the poem leaves readers with a strong sense of place and community.

EXAMINER'S COMMENT

Quotations are very well used here to highlight Plath's ability to create specific scenes and moods through precise description. The examples range over much of the poem and the writing is both varied and controlled throughout. Grade A standard.

Sylvia Plath

CLASS/HOMEWORK EXERCISES

1   It has been said that vivid, startling imagery gives a surreal quality to 'Finisterre'. Using reference to the poem, write a paragraph responding to this statement.

2   Copy the table below into your own notes and fill in critical comments about the last two quotations.

Key Quotes

Admonitory cliffs, and the sea exploding/ With no bottom	Striking and dramatic images are a recurring feature throughout the poem.
Souls, rolled in the doom-noise of the sea	The poem is dominated by the underlying themes of fear, hopelessness and death.
They go up without hope, like sighs	Plath personifies the mists as the helpless souls of those who have been lost at sea.
Now it is only gloomy, a dump of rocks	
These are our crêpes. Eat them before they blow cold	

Mirror

I am silver and exact. I have no preconceptions.
Whatever I see I swallow immediately
Just as it is, unmisted by love or dislike.
I am not cruel, only truthful –
The eye of a little god, four-cornered.   5
Most of the time I meditate on the opposite wall.
It is pink, with speckles. I have looked at it so long
I think it is part of my heart. But it flickers.
Faces and darkness separate us over and over.

Now I am a lake. A woman bends over me,   10
Searching my reaches for what she really is.
Then she turns to those liars, the candles or the moon.
I see her back, and reflect it faithfully.
She rewards me with tears and an agitation of hands.
I am important to her. She comes and goes.   15
Each morning it is her face that replaces the darkness.
In me she has drowned a young girl, and in me an old woman
Rises toward her day after day, like a terrible fish.

'The eye of a little god, four-cornered'

GLOSSARY

1 *exact*: accurate, giving all details; to insist on payment.
1 *preconceptions*: thoughts already formed.
11 *reaches*: range of distance or depth.
14 *agitation*: shaking, anxious.

EXPLORATIONS

1   Select two images that suggest the dark, sinister side of the mirror. Would you consider that these images show an unforgiving way of viewing oneself?

2　What are the parallels and contrast between a mirror and a lake? Develop your response in a written paragraph.

3　Write your own personal response to this poem, referring closely to the text in your answer.

STUDY NOTES

'Mirror' was written in 1961 as Sylvia Plath approached her twenty-ninth birthday. In this dark poem, Plath views the inevitability of old age and death, our preoccupation with image and our search for an identity.

Do you think everyone looks at themselves in a mirror? Would you consider that people are fascinated, disappointed or even obsessed by what they see? Does a mirror accurately reflect the truth? Do people actually see what is reflected, or is it distorted by notions and ideals they or society have? Consider the use of mirrors in fairytales: 'Mirror, mirror on the wall, who's the fairest of them all?' Mirrors are also used in myths, such as the story of Narcissus, who drowned having fallen in love with his reflection, and *Through the Looking Glass* is a famous children's book. Mirrors are also used in horror films as the dividing line between fantasy and reality.

In this poem, Plath often gives us a startling new angle on an everyday object. The function of a mirror is to reflect whatever is put in front of it. **Stanza one** opens with a ringing declaration by the mirror: 'I am silver and exact'. This **personification has a sinister effect** in the poem as the mirror describes an almost claustrophobic relationship with a particular woman. The voice of the mirror is clear, direct and precise. It announces that it reports exactly what there is without any alteration. We have to decide if the mirror is telling the truth, as it says it has no bias ('no preconceptions'). It does not judge, it reflects the image received. The mirror adopts the position of an impartial observer, but it is active, almost ruthless ('I swallow'). It is not cruel, but truthful.

Yet how truthful is a mirror image, as it flattens a three-dimensional object into two dimensions? The image sent out has no depth. The voice of the mirror becomes smug as it sees itself as the ruler of those reflected ('The eye of a little god'). Our obsession with ourselves causes us to worship at the mirror that reflects our image. In the modern world, people are often disappointed with their reflections, wishing they were thinner, younger, better looking. But **the mirror insists it tells the truth**, it doesn't flatter or hurt. The mirror explains how it spends its day gazing at the opposite wall, which is carefully described as 'pink, with speckles'. It feels as if the wall is part of itself. This reflection is disturbed by the faces of people and the dying light. The passage of time is evoked in the phrase 'over and over'.

In stanza two, the mirror now announces that it is 'a lake'. Both are flat surfaces that reflect. However, a lake is another dimension, it has depth. There is **danger**. The image is now drawn into its murky depths. The woman is looking in and down, not just at. It is as if she is struggling to find who she really is, what her true path in life is. Plath frequently questioned who she was. Expectations for young women in the 1950s were limiting. Appearance was important, as were the roles of wife, mother and homemaker. But Plath also wanted to write: 'Will I submerge my embarrassing desires and aspirations, refuse to face myself?' The mirror becomes irritated and jealous of the woman as she turns to the deceptive soft light of 'those liars, the candles or the moon'. The mirror remains faithful, reflecting her back. **The woman is dissatisfied with her image**. In her insecurity, she weeps and wrings her hands. Plath always tried to do her best, to be a model student, almost desperate to excel and be affirmed. Is there a danger in seeking perfection? Do we need to be kind to ourselves? Do we need to love ourselves? Again, the mirror pompously announces 'I am important to her'.

The march of time passing is emphasised by 'comes and goes', 'Each morning' and 'day after day'. The woman keeps coming back. The mirror's sense of its importance is shown by the frequent use of 'I' and the repetition of 'in me'. As time passes, the woman is facing the truth of her human condition as her reflection changes and ages in the mirror. Her youth is 'drowned', to be replaced by a monstrous vision of an old woman 'like a terrible fish'. **The lonely drama of living and dying is recorded with a dreamlike, nightmarish quality**. There is no comforting rhyme in the poem, only the controlled rhythm of time. The mirror does not give what a human being desires: comfort and warmth. Instead, it impersonally reminds us of our mortality.

ANALYSIS

What is your personal response to the relationship between the mirror and the woman? Support your views with reference to the poem.

SAMPLE PARAGRAPH

I feel the mirror is like an alter ego, which is coolly appraising the woman in an unforgiving way. The mirror is 'silver'. This cold metal object is

Sylvia Plath

heartless. Although the mirror repeatedly states that it does not judge, 'I have no preconceptions', the woman feels judged and wanting: 'She rewards me with tears and an agitation of hands'. I think the relationship between the woman and the mirror is dangerous and poisonous. She does indeed 'drown' in the mirror, as she never feels good enough. Is this the payment the mirror exacts? The complacent mirror rules her like a tyrannical 'little god, four-cornered'. It reminds me of how today we are never satisfied with our image, always wanting something else, more perfect. Plath also strove to be perfect. This obsessive relationship shows a troubled self, a lack of self-love. Who is saying that the older woman is 'like a terrible fish'? I think the mirror has become the voice of a society which values women only for their looks and youth, rather than what they are capable of achieving.

EXAMINER'S COMMENT

In this fluent and personal response, the candidate has given a distinctive and well-supported account of the uneasy relationship between the mirror and the woman. Grade A answer.

CLASS/HOMEWORK EXERCISES

1 How are the qualities of terror and despair shown in the imagery of the poem?
2 Copy the table below into your own notes and fill in critical comments about the last two quotations.

Key Quotes

I have no preconceptions	The mirror states that it objectively reflects reality.
The eye of a little god, four-cornered	Plath's metaphor emphasises how this rectangular mirror considers itself very important.
Searching my reaches for what she really is	The woman looks deeply into the mirror at her reflection.
I am silver and exact	
in me an old woman/Rises toward her day after day, like a terrible fish	

Pheasant

You said you would kill it this morning.
Do not kill it. It startles me still,
The jut of that odd, dark head, pacing

Through the uncut grass on the elm's hill.
It is something to own a pheasant,   5
Or just to be visited at all.

I am not mystical: it isn't
As if I thought it had a spirit.
It is simply in its element.

That gives it a kingliness, a right.   10
The print of its big foot last winter,
The tail-track, on the snow in our court –

The wonder of it, in that pallor,
Through crosshatch of sparrow and starling.
Is it its rareness, then? It is rare.   15

But a dozen would be worth having,
A hundred, on that hill – green and red,
Crossing and recrossing: a fine thing!

It is such a good shape, so vivid.
It's a little cornucopia.   20
It unclaps, brown as a leaf, and loud,

Settles in the elm, and is easy.
It was sunning in the narcissi.
I trespass stupidly. Let be, let be.

'in its element'

GLOSSARY	1	*You*: probably addressed to Plath's husband.	13 *pallor*: pale colour.
	3	*jut*: extending outwards.	14 *crosshatch*: criss-cross trail.
	7	*mystical*: spiritual, supernatural.	20 *cornucopia*: unexpected treasure.
			23 *narcissi*: bright spring flowers.

EXPLORATIONS

1 Explain Sylvia Plath's attitude to nature based on your reading of 'Pheasant'.
2 Compile a list of the poet's arguments for not killing the pheasant.
3 Write a paragraph on the effectiveness of Plath's imagery in the poem.

STUDY NOTES

'Pheasant' was written in 1962 and reflects Plath's deep appreciation of the natural world. Its enthusiastic mood contrasts with much of her more disturbing work. The poem is structured in eight tercets (three-line stanzas) with a subtle, interlocking rhyming pattern (known as terza rima).

The poem opens with an urgent plea by Plath to spare the pheasant's life: 'Do not kill it'. In the first two stanzas, the tone is tense as the poet offers a variety of reasons for sparing this impressive game bird. She is both shocked and excited by the pheasant: 'It startles me still'. Plath admits to feeling honoured in the presence of the bird: 'It is something to own a pheasant'. The broken rhythm of the early lines adds an abruptness that heightens the sense of urgency. **Plath seems spellbound by the bird's beauty** ('The jut of that odd, dark head') now that it is under threat.

But the poet is also keen to play down any sentimentality in her attitude to the pheasant. Stanza three opens with a straightforward explanation of her attitude: 'it isn't/As if I thought it had a spirit'. Instead, **she values the bird for its graceful beauty and naturalness**: 'It is simply in its element'. Plath is keen to show her recognition of the pheasant's right to exist because it possesses a certain majestic quality, 'a kingliness'.

In stanza four, the poet recalls an earlier winter scene when she marvelled at the pheasant's distinctive footprint in the snow. The bird has made an even greater impression on Plath, summed up in the key phrase 'The wonder of it' at the start of stanza five. She remembers **the colourful pheasant's distinguishing marks against the pale snow**, so unlike the 'crosshatch' pattern of smaller birds, such as the sparrow and starling. This makes the pheasant particularly 'rare' and valuable in Plath's eyes.

The poet can hardly contain her regard for the pheasant and her tone becomes increasingly enthusiastic in stanza six as she dreams of having first a 'dozen' and then a 'hundred' of the birds. In a few **well-chosen details**, she highlights their colour and energy ('green and red,/Crossing and recrossing') and adds an emphatic compliment: 'a fine thing!' Her delight continues into stanza seven, where Plath proclaims her ceaseless admiration for the pheasant: 'It's a little cornucopia', an inspirational source of joy and surprise.

Throughout the poem, Plath has emphasised that the pheasant rightly belongs in its natural surroundings, and this is also true of the final lines. Stanza eight is considered and assured. From the poet's point of view, **the pheasant's right to live is beyond dispute**. While the bird is 'sunning in the narcissi', she herself has become the unwelcome intruder: 'I trespass stupidly'. Plath ends by echoing the opening appeal to spare the pheasant's life: 'Let be, let be'. The quietly insistent repetition and the underlying tone of unease are a final reminder of the need to respect nature.

It has been suggested that the pheasant symbolises Plath's insecure relationship with Ted Hughes. For various reasons, their marriage was under severe strain in 1962 and Plath feared that Hughes was intent on ending it. This interpretation adds a greater poignancy to the poem.

ANALYSIS

There are several mood changes in 'Pheasant'. What do you consider to be the dominant mood in the poem? Refer to the text in your answer.

SAMPLE PARAGRAPH

The mood at the beginning of 'Pheasant' is nervous and really uptight. Plath seems to have given up hope about the pheasant. It is facing death. She repeats the work 'kill' and admits to being shocked at the very thought of what the bird is facing. She herself seems desperate and fearful. This is shown by the short sentence, 'Do not kill it'. But the outlook soon changes. Plath describes the pheasant 'pacing' and 'in its element'. But she seems less stressed as she describes the 'kingliness' of the pheasant. But the mood soon settles down as Plath celebrates the life of this really beautiful bird. The mood becomes calmer and ends in almost a whisper, 'Let be, let be'. The dominant mood is calm and considered in the poem.

EXAMINER'S COMMENT

This is a reasonably well-focused response to the question. The candidate points out the change of mood following the first stanza. Some useful references are used to show the poem's principal mood. The expression, however, is flawed in places (e.g. using 'but' to start sentences). The standard is C grade overall.

CLASS/HOMEWORK EXERCISES

1   Plath sets out to convince the reader of the pheasant's right to life. Does she succeed in her aim? Give reasons for your answer.
2   Copy the table below into your own notes and fill in critical comments about the last two quotations.

Key Quotes

pacing/ Through the uncut grass on the elm's hill	Plath is a keen observer of the pheasant and uses details to capture its steady movement.
That gives it a kingliness, a right	Man's relationship with the world of nature is central to 'Pheasant'.
It is such a good shape	The poem contains many direct statements that reflect Plath's clear sense of appreciation.
I am not mystical	
It unclaps, brown as a leaf	

Elm

Sylvia Plath

For Ruth Fainlight

I know the bottom, she says. I know it with my great tap root:
It is what you fear.
I do not fear it: I have been there.

Is it the sea you hear in me,
Its dissatisfactions?   5
Or the voice of nothing, that was your madness?

Love is a shadow.
How you lie and cry after it
Listen: these are its hooves: it has gone off, like a horse.

All night I shall gallop thus, impetuously,   10
Till your head is a stone, your pillow a little turf,
Echoing, echoing.

Or shall I bring you the sound of poisons?
This is rain now, this big hush.
And this is the fruit of it: tin-white, like arsenic.   15

I have suffered the atrocity of sunsets.
Scorched to the root
My red filaments burn and stand, a hand of wires.

Now I break up in pieces that fly about like clubs.
A wind of such violence   20
Will tolerate no bystanding: I must shriek.

The moon, also, is merciless: she would drag me
Cruelly, being barren.
Her radiance scathes me. Or perhaps I have caught her.

I let her go. I let her go   25
Diminished and flat, as after radical surgery.
How your bad dreams possess and endow me.

Sylvia Plath

I am inhabited by a cry.
Nightly it flaps out
Looking, with its hooks, for something to love.　　　　30

I am terrified by this dark thing
That sleeps in me;
All day I feel its soft, feathery turnings, its malignity.

Clouds pass and disperse.
Are those the faces of love, those pale irretrievables?　35
Is it for such I agitate my heart?

I am incapable of more knowledge.
What is this, this face
So murderous in its strangle of branches? –

Its snaky acids hiss.　　　　　　　　　　　　　　40
It petrifies the will. These are the isolate, slow faults
That kill, that kill, that kill.

'I am terrified by this dark thing'

GLOSSARY

The wych elm is a large deciduous tree, with a massive straight trunk and tangled branches. It was once a favourite timber of coffin makers. Plath dedicated the poem to a close friend, Ruth Fainlight, another American poet.

1　*the bottom*: lowest depths.
1　*tap root:* the main root.

15　*arsenic*: poison.
18　*filaments*: fibres, nerves.
24　*scathes*: injures, scalds.
33　*malignity*: evil.
34　*disperse*: scatter widely.
35　*irretrievables*: things lost forever.
40　*snaky acids*: deceptive poisons.
41　*petrifies*: terrifies.

EXPLORATIONS

1 There are many sinister nature images in this poem. Select two that you find particularly unsettling and comment on their effectiveness.
2 Trace and examine how love is presented and viewed by the poet. Support the points you make with reference to the text.
3 Write your own individual response to this poem, referring closely to the text in your answer.

STUDY NOTES

Written in April 1962, 'Elm' is one of Sylvia Plath's most challenging and intensely dramatic poems. Plath personifies the elm tree to create a surreal scene. It 'speaks' in a traumatic voice to someone else, the 'you' of line 2, the poet herself – or the reader, perhaps. Both voices interact throughout the poem, almost always expressing pain and anguish. Critics often associate these powerful emotions with the poet's own personal problems – Plath had experienced electric shock treatment for depression. However, this may well limit our understanding of what is a complex exploration of many emotions.

The opening stanza is unnerving. The poet appears to be dramatising an exchange between herself and the elm by imagining what the tree might say to her. The immediate effect is eerily surreal. From the start, **the narrative voice is obsessed with instability and despair**: 'I know the bottom'. The tree is described in both physical terms ('my great tap root' penetrating far into the ground) and also as a state of mind ('I do not fear it'). The depth of depression imagined is reinforced by the repetition of 'I know' and the stark simplicity of the chilling comment 'It is what you fear'.

The bizarre exchange between the two 'speakers' continues in stanza two. The elm questions the poet about the nature of **her mental state**. Does the wind blowing through its branches remind her of the haunting sound of the sea? Or even 'the voice of nothing' – the numbing experience of madness?

Stanzas three and four focus on the dangers and disappointments of love – 'a shadow'. The tone is wary, emphasised by the comparison of a wild horse that has 'gone off'. The relentless sounds of the wind in the elm will be a bitter reminder, 'echoing' this loss of love 'Till your head is a stone'. **Assonance** is effectively used here to heighten the sense of hurt and abandonment.

For much of the middle section of the poem (**stanzas five to nine**), the elm's intimidating voice continues to dramatise a series of horrifying experiences associated with madness. The tree has endured extreme elements – rain ('the sound of poisons'), sunshine ('Scorched to the root'), wind ('of such violence') and also the moon ('Her radiance scathes me'). **The harsh imagery and frenzied language** ('burn', 'shriek', 'merciless') combine to create a sense of shocking destructiveness.

Stanzas 10 and 11 mark a turning point where the voices of the tree and the poet become indistinguishable. This is achieved by the seemingly harmless image of an owl inhabiting the branches, searching for 'something to love'. The speaker is haunted by 'this dark thing'. The **poet's vulnerability** is particularly evident in her stark admission: 'I feel its soft, feathery turnings, its malignity'. Plath has come to relate her unknown demons to a deadly tumour.

In the **last three stanzas**, the poet's voice seems more distant and calm before the final storm. The image of the passing clouds ('the faces of love') highlight the notion of rejection as the root cause of Plath's depression. The poem ends on a visionary note when she imagines being confronted by a 'murderous' snake that appears in the branches: 'It petrifies the will'. The scene of **growing terror builds to a hideous climax** until her own mental and emotional states (her 'slow faults') end up destroying her. The intensity of the final line, 'That kill, that kill, that kill', leaves readers with a harrowing understanding of Plath's paralysis of despair.

ANALYSIS

Do you think that 'Elm' has a surreal, nightmarish quality? In your response, refer to the text to support your views.

SAMPLE PARAGRAPH

I would agree that Sylvia Plath has created a very disturbing mood in the poem, 'Elm'. Giving the tree a speaking voice of its own is like something from a child's fairy story. Plath compares love to a galloping horse. The poem is mainly about depression and madness. So it's bound to be out of the ordinary. The speaker in the poem is confused and asks weird questions, such as 'Is it the sea you hear inside me?' She is obsessive and totally paranoid. Everything is against her, as far as she imagines it. The weather is seen as an enemy even, 'the rain is like arsenic' and 'sounds like poisons'. The end is as if she is having a bad dream with imagining a fierce hissing snake in the tree coming after her. This represents Plath's deepest nightmare, the fear of loneliness. The whole poem is surreal and confusing – especially the images.

EXAMINER'S COMMENT

This paragraph includes some worthwhile references to the poem's disturbing aspects. The points are note-like, however, and the writing style lacks control. Some of the quotations are also inaccurate. A C grade standard.

CLASS/HOMEWORK EXERCISES

1   What evidence of Plath's deep depression and hypersensitivity is revealed in the poem 'Elm'? Refer closely to the text in your answer.
2   Copy the table below into your own notes and fill in critical comments about the last two quotations.

Key Quotes

I know it with my great tap root	Through the 'voice' of the elm, Plath uses the tree metaphor to suggest her own depths of despair.
My red filaments burn and stand, a hand of wires	This image of suffering may relate to the poet's own experience of electric shock treatment for depression.
A wind of such violence/Will tolerate no bystanding	Many searing images in the poem suggest a world that has been wasted by nuclear conflict.
the atrocity of sunsets	
Its snaky acids hiss	

Poppies in July

Sylvia Plath

Little poppies, little hell flames,
Do you do no harm?

You flicker. I cannot touch you.
I put my hands among the flames. Nothing burns.

And it exhausts me to watch you   5
Flickering like that, wrinkly and clear red, like the skin of a mouth.

A mouth just bloodied.
Little bloody skirts!

There are fumes that I cannot touch.
Where are your opiates, your nauseous capsules?   10

If I could bleed, or sleep! –
If my mouth could marry a hurt like that!

Or your liquors seep to me, in this glass capsule,
Dulling and stilling.

But colorless. Colorless.   15

'You flicker. I cannot touch you.'

EXPLORATIONS

1   Examine the title, 'Poppies in July', in light of the main subject matter in the poem. Is the title misleading? Explain your answer.

2   What evidence can you find in 'Poppies in July' that the speaker is yearning to escape?

3   Colour imagery plays a significant role in the poem. Comment on how effectively colour is used.

STUDY NOTES

Like most confessional writers, Sylvia Plath's work reflects her own personal experiences, without filtering any of the painful emotions. She wrote 'Poppies in July' in the summer of 1962, during the break-up of her marriage.

The first stanza is marked by an uneasy sense of foreboding. The speaker (almost certainly Plath herself) compares the blazing red poppies to 'little hell flames' before directly confronting them: 'Do you do no harm?' **Her distress is obvious** from the start. The poem's title may well have led readers to expect a more conventional nature poem. Instead, the flowers are presented as being highly treacherous, and all the more deceptive because they are 'little'.

Plath develops the fire image in lines 3–6. However, even though she places her hands 'among the flames', she finds that 'Nothing burns' and she is forced to watch them 'flickering'. It almost seems as though she is so tired and numb that **she has transcended pain** and can experience nothing: 'it exhausts me to watch you'. Ironically, the more vivid the poppies are, the more lethargic she feels.

The uncomfortable and disturbed mood increases in the fourth stanza with **two startling images**, both personifying the flowers. Comparing the poppy to 'A mouth just bloodied' suggests recent violence and physical suffering. The 'bloody skirts' metaphor is equally harrowing. There is further evidence of the poet's overpowering weariness in the prominent use of broad vowel sounds, for example, in 'exhausts', 'mouth' and 'bloodied'.

In the fifth stanza, Plath's disorientated state turns to a distracted longing for escape. Having failed to use the vibrancy of the poppies to distract her from her pain, she now craves the feeling of oblivion or unconsciousness. But although she desires the dulling effects of drugs derived from the poppies, her **tone is hopelessly cynical** as she describes the 'fumes that I cannot touch'.

The mood becomes even more distraught in **lines 11–12**, with the poet begging for any alternative to her anguished state. 'If I could bleed, or sleep!' is an emphatic plea for release. It is her final attempt to retain some control of her life in the face of an overwhelming sense of powerlessness. Plath's **growing alienation** seems so unbearably intense at this point that it directly draws the reader's sympathy.

The **last three lines** record the poet's surrender, perhaps a kind of death wish. Worn down by her inner demons and the bright colours of the poppies, Plath lets herself become resigned to a 'colorless' world of nothingness. Her **complete passivity** and helplessness are emphasised by the dreamlike quality of the phrase 'Dulling and stilling'. As she drifts into a death-like 'colorless' private hell, there remains a terrible sense of betrayal, as if she is still being haunted by the bright red flowers. The ending of 'Poppies in July' is so dark and joyless that it is easy to see why the poem is often seen as a desperate cry for help.

ANALYSIS

'Poppies in July' is one of Plath's most disturbing poems. What aspects of the poem affected you most?

SAMPLE PARAGRAPH

'Poppies in July' was written at a time when Plath was struggling with the fact that her husband had deserted her. This affected her deeply and it is clear that the poppies are a symbol of this excruciating time. Everything about the poem is negative. The images of the poppies are nearly all associated with fire and blood. Plath's language is alarming when she compares the poppies to 'little hell flames' and also 'the skin of a mouth'. The most disturbing aspect is Plath's own unstable mind. She seems to be in a kind of trance, obsessed by the red colours of the poppies, which remind her of blood. I got the impression that she was nearly going insane in the end. She seems suicidal – 'If I could bleed'. For me, this is the most disturbing moment in the poem. I can get some idea of her troubled mind. Plath cannot stand reality and seeks a way out through drugs or death. The last image is of Plath sinking into a dull state of drowsiness, unable to cope with the world around her.

EXAMINER'S COMMENT

Overall, a solid B grade response which responds personally to the question. While the candidate dealt well with the disturbing thought in the poem, there could have been a more thorough exploration of Plath's style and how it enhances her theme of depression.

CLASS/HOMEWORK EXERCISES

1 Would you agree that loneliness and pain are the central themes of 'Poppies in July'? Refer to the text of the poem when writing your response.
2 Copy the table below into your own notes and fill in critical comments about the last two quotations.

Key Quotes

You flicker. I cannot touch you	The contrast between the poppies' energy and Plath's own passive state is a memorable feature of the poem.
And it exhausts me to watch you	Plath's overwhelming sense of despair is central to the poem.
Flickering like that, wrinkly and clear red	The vivid imagery used to describe the poppies is highly disturbing.
Where are your opiates, your nauseous capsules?	
If my mouth could marry a hurt like that	

The Arrival of the Bee Box

Sylvia Plath

I ordered this, this clean wood box
Square as a chair and almost too heavy to lift.
I would say it was the coffin of a midget
Or a square baby
Were there not such a din in it.   5

The box is locked, it is dangerous.
I have to live with it overnight
And I can't keep away from it.
There are no windows, so I can't see what is in there.
There is only a little grid, no exit.   10

I put my eye to the grid.
It is dark, dark,
With the swarmy feeling of African hands
Minute and shrunk for export,
Black on black, angrily clambering.   15

How can I let them out?
It is the noise that appalls me most of all,
The unintelligible syllables.
It is like a Roman mob,
Small, taken one by one, but my god, together!   20

I lay my ear to furious Latin.
I am not a Caesar.
I have simply ordered a box of maniacs.
They can be sent back.
They can die, I need feed them nothing, I am the owner.   25

I wonder how hungry they are.
I wonder if they would forget me
If I just undid the locks and stood back and turned into a tree.
There is the laburnum, its blond colonnades,
And the petticoats of the cherry.   30

They might ignore me immediately
In my moon suit and funeral veil.

I am no source of honey
So why should they turn on me?
Tomorrow I will be sweet God, I will set them free. 35

The box is only temporary.

'It is the noise that appalls me'

GLOSSARY

10 *grid*: wire network.
13 *swarmy*: like a large group of bees.
22 *Caesar*: famous Roman ruler.
29 *laburnum*: tree with yellow hanging flowers.

29 *colonnades*: long groups of flowers arranged in a row of columns.
32 *moon suit*: protective clothing worn by beekeepers; all-in-one suit.

EXPLORATIONS

1   How would you describe the poet's reaction to the bee box – fear or fascination, or a mixture of both? Write a paragraph for your response, referring to the poem.

2   Select two surreal images from the poem and comment on the effectiveness of each.

3   Would you describe this poem as exploring and overcoming one's fears and anxieties? Is the ending optimistic or pessimistic, in your opinion?

STUDY NOTES

'The Arrival of the Bee Box' was written in 1962, shortly after Plath's separation from her husband. Her father, who died when she was a child, had been a bee expert and Plath and her husband had recently taken up beekeeping. She explores order, power, control, confinement and freedom in this deeply personal poem.

The poem opens with a simple statement: 'I ordered this'. Straightaway, the emphasis is on order and control. The poet's tone in **stanza one** is both matter of fact and surprised: 'I was the one who ordered this', and also 'Did I really order this?' This drama has only one character, Plath herself. We observe her responses and reactions to the arrival of the bee box. Notice the extensive use of the personal pronoun 'I'. We both see and hear the event.

The box is described as being made of 'clean wood' and given a homely quality with the simile 'Square as a chair'. But then a surreal, dreamlike metaphor, 'the coffin of a midget/Or a square baby', brings us into a **nightmare world**. The abnormal is suggested by the use of 'midget', and deformity by 'square baby'. The coffin conveys not only death, but also entrapment and confinement, preoccupations of the poet. The box has now become a sinister object. A witty sound effect closes the first stanza, as 'din in it' mimics the sound of the bees. They are like badly behaved children.

Stanza two explores the **poet's ambivalent attitude to the box**. She is fascinated by it, as she is curious to see inside ('I can't keep away from it'). Yet she is also frightened by it, as she describes the box as 'dangerous'. She peers in. The **third stanza** becomes claustrophobic and oppressive with the repetition of 'dark' and the grotesque image of 'the swarmy feel of African hands/Minute and shrunk for export'. The milling of the bees/slaves is vividly captured as they heave around in the heat in an atmosphere of menace and oppression, hopelessly desperate.

We hear the bees in **stanza four**. The metaphor of a Roman mob is used to show how if they are let loose they will create **chaos and danger**. The assonance of 'appalls' and 'all' underline the poet's terror. The phrase 'unintelligible syllables', with its onomatopoeia and its difficult pronunciation, lets us hear the angry buzzing. Plath is awestruck at their collective force and energy: 'but my god, together!' Notice the use of the exclamation mark.

The poet tries to listen, but only hears 'furious Latin' she does not understand. She doubts her capacity to control them, stating that she is 'not a Caesar', the powerful ruler of the Romans, in **stanza five**. She regards them as 'maniacs'. Then she realises that if she has ordered them, she can return them: 'They can be sent back'. **She has some control of this situation**. Plath can even decide their fate, whether they live or die: 'I need feed them nothing'. She has now redefined the situation as she realises that she is 'the owner'. They belong to her.

The feminine, nurturing side of her now emerges as she wonders 'how hungry they are'. The stereotype of the pretty woman surfaces in the description of the bees' natural habitat of trees in **stanza six**. Plath thinks if she releases them, they would go back to the trees, 'laburnum' and 'cherry'. She herself would then merge into the landscape and become a tree. This is a reference to a Greek myth where Daphne was being pursued by Apollo. After begging the gods to be saved, they turned her into a tree.

Now she refers to herself in her beekeeping outfit of veil and boiler suit in **stanza seven**. She rhetorically asks why they would attack her, as she is not a source of sustenance ('I am no source of honey'). **She decides to be compassionate**: 'Tomorrow I will be sweet God, I will set them free'. She realises that they are imprisoned only for now: 'The box is only temporary'.

This poem can also be read on another level. The box could represent the poet's attempt to be what others expect, the typical 1950s woman – pretty, compliant, nurturing. The bees could represent the dark side of her personality, which both fascinated and terrified Plath. She has to accept this: 'I have to live with it overnight'. **The box is like Pandora's box**, safe when locked, but full of danger when opened. Although she finds this disturbing, she also feels she must explore it in the interests of developing as a poet. The references to the doomed character of Daphne and the 'funeral veil' echo chillingly. Would these dark thoughts, if given their freedom, drive her to suicide? The form of this poem is seven stanzas of five lines. One line stands alone, free like the bees or her dark thoughts. If the box represents Plath's outside appearance or body, it is mortal, it is temporary. Will the thoughts, if freed from the body, stop?

ANALYSIS

How does this poem address the themes of order and power? Write a paragraph in response. Support your views with reference to the text.

SAMPLE PARAGRAPH

The poem opens with a reference to order, 'I ordered this'. It is an assertion of power, a deliberate act by 'I'. Throughout the poem the repetition of 'I' suggests a person who consciously chooses to act in a certain way. 'I put my eye to the grid', 'I lay my ear to furious Latin'. It is as if the poet wishes to confront and control her fears over the contents of the box. This box contains live, buzzing bees, whose wellbeing lies in the hands of the poet.

'I need feed them nothing, I am the owner'. Although she realises that she is not 'Caesar', the mighty Roman ruler, she can choose to be 'sweet God'. She alone has the power to release the bees, 'The box is only temporary'. This poem can also be read as referring to the control a person exercises when confronting their innermost fears and desires. These thoughts can be ignored or faced. The person owns these thoughts and can choose to contain them or confront them. Plath feared her own dark side, but felt it should be explored to enable her to progress as a poet. For her 'The box is only temporary'.

EXAMINER'S COMMENT

This note-like response summarises parts of the poem that allude to order and power. However, it fails to address the question about the poet's approach to the central themes. There is little discussion about Plath's attitude to power. Grade C.

CLASS/HOMEWORK EXERCISES

1   How does Plath create a dramatic atmosphere in 'The Arrival of the Bee Box'?
2   Copy the table below into your own notes and fill in critical comments about the last two quotations.

Key Quotes

I have to live with it overnight/ And I can't keep away from it	The poet refers to the intense relationship she has with the box, which she cannot escape from.
With the swarmy feeling of African hands/Minute and shrunk for export	The bees are described as miniature African slaves who are imprisoned as they are sent off to another country.
I am not a Caesar	Plath admits that she would be unable to control these angry bees if released.
Tomorrow I will be sweet God	
The box is only temporary	

Child

Your clear eye is the one absolutely beautiful thing.
I want to fill it with color and ducks,
The zoo of the new

Whose name you meditate –
April snowdrop, Indian pipe,   5
Little

Stalk without wrinkle,
Pool in which images
Should be grand and classical

Not this troublous   10
Wringing of hands, this dark
Ceiling without a star.

28 January 1963

Sylvia Plath

'The zoo of the new'

GLOSSARY		
4	*meditate*: reflect.	7 *Stalk*: plant stem.
5	*Indian pipe*: American woodland flower.	9 *classical*: impressive, enduring.
		10 *troublous*: disturbed.

EXPLORATIONS

1   What was your own immediate reaction after reading 'Child'? Refer to the text in your answer.
2   Which images in the poem are most effective in contrasting the world of the child and the world of the adult?
3   Plath uses various sound effects to enhance her themes in 'Child'. Comment briefly on two interesting examples.

STUDY NOTES

> Sylvia Plath's son was born in January 1962. A year later, shortly before the poet's own death, she wrote 'Child', a short poem that reflects her intense feelings about motherhood.

The first line of stanza one shows the **poet's emphatic appreciation of childhood innocence**: 'Your clear eye is the one absolutely beautiful thing'. The tone at first is hopeful. Her love for the new child is generous and unconditional: 'I want to fill it with color'. The childlike language is lively and playful. Plath plans to give her child the happiest of times, filled with 'color and ducks'. The vigorous rhythm and animated internal rhyme in the phrase 'The zoo of the new' are imaginative, capturing the sense of **youthful wonder**.

In stanza two, the poet continues to associate her child with all that is best about the natural world. The baby is like the most fragile of flowers, the 'April snowdrop'. The assonance in this phrase has a musical effect, like a soft lullaby. Yet her own fascination appears to mask a deeper concern. Plath feels that such a perfect childhood experience is unlikely to last very long. Despite all her positive sentiments, what she wants for **the vulnerable child** seems directly at odds with what is possible in **a flawed world**.

Run-on lines are a recurring feature of the poem and these add to the feeling of freedom and innocent intensity. Stanza three includes two **effective comparisons**, again taken from nature. Plath sees the child as an unblemished 'Stalk' that should grow perfectly. A second quality of childhood's pure innocence is found in the 'Pool' metaphor. We are reminded of the opening image – the child's 'clear eye', always trusting and sincere.

The poet would love to provide a magical future for her young child, so that the pool would reflect 'grand and classical' images. However, as a loving mother, she is trapped between her **idealism** – the joy she wants for her child – and **a distressing reality** – an awareness that the child's life will not be perfectly happy. This shocking realisation becomes clear in **stanza four** and overshadows her hopes completely. The final images are stark and powerful – the pathetic 'Wringing of hands' giving emphasis to her helplessness. The **last line** poignantly portrays the paradox of the tension between Plath's dreams for the child in the face of the despair she feels about the oppressive world: this 'Ceiling without a star'. This dark mood is in sharp contrast with the rest of the poem. The early celebration has been replaced by anguish and an overwhelming sense of failure.

ANALYSIS

Do you think 'Child' is a positive or negative poem? Refer to the text in explaining your response.

SAMPLE PARAGRAPH

I think Plath's poem, 'Child', is essentially about a mother's inadequacy. The poet wants the best for her innocent son. Although the first half of the poem focuses on her wishes to protect him, this changes at the end. Plath starts off by wanting to fill the boy's life with happy experiences (bright colours and toys) and keep him close to nature. There are numerous references to nature right through the poem and Plath compares her son to an 'April snowdrop'. This tender image gave me a very positive feeling. Everything about the child is wonderful at first. He is 'absolutely beautiful'. This all changes at the end of the poem. The mood turns negative. Plath talks of being confined in a darkened room which has a 'Ceiling without a star'. This is in total contrast with the images early on which were of the bright outdoors. The poet was positive at the start. This has been replaced with negative feelings. The ending is dark and 'troublous' because Plath knows that her child will grow up and experience pain just as she has.

EXAMINER'S COMMENT

This paragraph addresses the question well and offers a clear response. The candidate effectively illustrates the changing mood from optimism to pessimism and uses apt quotations in support. The style of writing is a little note-like and pedestrian. A basic B-grade standard.

Sylvia Plath

CLASS/HOMEWORK EXERCISES

1   Write a paragraph comparing 'Child' with 'Morning Song'. Refer to theme and style in both poems.
2   Copy the table below into your own notes and fill in critical comments about the last two quotations.

Key Quotes

Your clear eye	The newborn child is innocent and is still unaffected by the corrupt world.
I want to fill it with color and ducks	The childlike language reflects the mother's desire to be part of her child's innocent world.
Stalk without wrinkle	Simple, memorable images typify Plath's sense of the child's perfection.
Not this troublous/Wringing of hands	
this dark/Ceiling without a star	

LEAVING CERT SAMPLE ESSAY

> **Q** **'Reading Sylvia Plath's poetry can be an uncomfortable experience.'**
>
> **Write a personal response to the above statement. Your answer should focus clearly on her themes and the manner in which she explores them. Support your points by reference to the poetry of Sylvia Plath on your course.**

MARKING SCHEME GUIDELINES

Reward responses that show clear evidence of personal engagement with the poems. The key term ('uncomfortable experience') may be addressed implicitly or explicitly. Candidates may choose to focus on the positive aspects of Plath's poetry. Allow for a wide range of approaches in the answering.

Material might be drawn from the following:
- Recurring themes of nature, disillusionment, transience, etc.
- Complexity of mother–child relationships.
- Contrasting images and tones.
- Startling and unusual language.
- The poet's life and how it links with her poetry.

SAMPLE ESSAY
(Reading Sylvia Plath's Poetry)

1 *The poetry of Sylvia Plath awakes a multitude of emotions in the reader, many of them disturbing. Plath's engulfing depression led her to take a view of the world that is alarming and often perverse. However, Plath's great understanding of life and love for her children led her to write poems that bring both joy and contentment to the reader. It is this diversity of approach that makes Plath one of the finest poets of the modern age.*

2 *Motherhood had a highly potent effect on Plath as a person. This is presented to the reader in the poem 'Morning Song', which is addressed to her daughter. She refers to her child with three words: 'fat gold watch'. This image suggests that the baby is valuable, to be treasured and praised. However, the image of a watch* may symbolise the dark undercurrent that time is passing, it is slipping away for both mother and daughter. This ambiguity exists in much of Plath's work and, when examined, may be a cause for distress and discomfort for the reader. The poet chooses to present the notion that her daughter is a work of art with the words 'New statue./In a drafty museum'. It is into this harsh world that her child will venture, a disturbing thought for both the poet and the reader.

3 The final image of the poem is of the birth of the baby herself trying a 'handful of notes'. The poet refers to the 'vowels' as they 'rise like balloons'. While the image seems to be a warm, content one, the image of a balloon seems to suggest something fragile, flimsy and transient. Even in her upbeat poems, Plath subtly presents disconcerting thoughts to the reader. The poem 'Black Rook in Rainy Weather' arises from the poet's feelings of contentment with life. She expresses this with the words 'I do not expect a miracle/Or an accident'. This inner peace leads the poet to rejoice in the mundane and urge us 'to let spotted leaves fall as they fall,/Without ceremony'. The poet becomes aware that 'Miracles occur' even if they are only 'spasmodic/Tricks of radiance'.

4 'Poppies in July' is undoubtedly one of the most disturbing poems by Plath. It deals with the horrors of her depression. The title seems to suggest a joyful image, but this could not be further from the truth. Plath refers to the poppies as 'little hell flames', seeing them as instruments which add to her suffering. Plath, it seems, would rather feel pain than feel nothing at all. She is horrified when she puts her hand 'among the flames' and 'Nothing burns'. Plath longs to find the poppies 'Dulling and stilling' and for everything to be 'colorless'. This poem gives a vivid description of how Plath feels choked by her destructive feelings. The depth of the poet's despair is evident in the troubling effect 'Poppies in July' has on the reader.

5 Plath explores a similar experience in 'Elm', which starts with the words, 'I know the bottom ... I know it with my great tap root'. The reference to a root suggests that the poet not only knew the lowest point, but draws her entire existence from that dark, hopeless place. We are told that Plath has 'suffered the atrocity of sunsets'. This hatred of something generally considered to be beautiful and joyous is a startling indication of the depth of her depression. Plath sees her sorrow as something that exists within herself – it is interior – and reveals that all day she feels 'its dark, feathery turnings, its malignity'. This horrifying image portrays the utter helplessness of the poet. It fills the reader with dread and fear, as Plath herself must have felt about her helplessness when she wrote the poem.

6 'Child' was written to Plath's son shortly before she died. She expresses the wish that life should not be 'this troublous/Wringing of hands, this dark/Ceiling without a star'. The absence of the star symbolises the absence of any hope. We get the sense that Plath will never manage to break free of this depression and it is this thought that horrifies the reader.

7 Even in poems that seem peaceful and loving, the echoes of Plath's depression exist as undercurrents. The explicit nature of her darker poems affects the reader deeply, revealing to them the horrors and terrible reality of utter despair. Few, if any, could read Plath's poetry and remain unchanged by it.

GRADE: A1		
P	=	15/15
C	=	15/15
L	=	13/15
M	=	5/5
Total	=	48/50

(approx. 740 words)

EXAMINER'S COMMENT

An impressive answer showing an excellent knowledge of Plath's poetry. The emphasis on the effect that the poems have on the reader is sustained throughout. Main points are well developed, often in great detail (e.g. in paragraph 2) and apt quotations are particularly well used. Apart from some repetition (paragraph 5), the overall expression is fluent and varied.

SAMPLE LEAVING CERT QUESTIONS ON PLATH'S POETRY (45–50 MINUTES)

1 'Introducing Sylvia Plath.' Using this title, write an article for your school magazine. Support your points by close reference to the prescribed poems by Plath that you have studied.

2 'Although Plath's poetry deals with intense experiences, her skill with language ensures that she is always in control of her subject matter.' Discuss this view, supporting your points with the aid of suitable reference to the poems by Plath on your course.

3 'Sylvia Plath's poems emerge from an unsettled world of anguish and personal torment.' Do you agree with this assessment of her poetry? Write a response, supporting your points with reference to the poems by Plath that you have studied.

SAMPLE ESSAY PLAN (Q2)

'Although Sylvia Plath's poetry deals with intense experiences, her skill with language ensures that she is always in control of her subject matter.' Discuss this view, supporting your points with the aid of suitable reference to the poems by Plath on your course.

•	*Intro*:	Identify the elements to be addressed – Plath's intensely disturbing themes and her innovative use of language.
•	*Point 1*:	Inner torment of 'Elm' presented through complex imagery and unsettling symbolism, allowing the reader to appreciate a nightmare world.
•	*Point 2*:	Contrast is effectively used in 'Poppies in July'. The speaker's deep yearning to escape is highlighted by the startling imagery of the flowers.
•	*Point 3*:	The depression in 'Black Rook in Rainy Weather' is also emphasised by conflicting images from nature and religion.
•	*Point 4*:	'Child' and 'Morning Song' express strong themes about intense relationships through her mastery of language.
•	*Conclusion*:	Many poems deal with extreme emotional states, but Plath's poetic technique never lapses.

EXERCISE

Develop one of the above points into a paragraph.

POINT 2 – SAMPLE PARAGRAPH

'Poppies in July' is an intense poem about Plath's desperation to escape from her unhappy world. It begins on a disturbing note. The speaker is troubled by the sight of poppies, which she calls 'little hell flames'. The references to hell and fire are developed through the rest of the poem, suggesting an extremely disturbed mind. The image of the red flames is both dramatic and terrifying – and typical of Plath's intense poetry. Readers can sense a standoff between the poppies and Plath herself. The flowers almost seem to mock the poet: 'You flicker. I cannot touch you'. Other images in the poem add to our understanding of the poet's deep pain – 'A mouth just bloodied' and 'fumes that I cannot touch'. Plath describes the poppies in a way that reveals her own troubled mental state. She is exhausted, almost beyond despair. We see her control of language when she contrasts the colour of the poppies with her own lifeless mood. We are left with a genuine sense of Plath's anguish. Unlike the blazing red flowers, the poet herself is 'colorless'.

EXAMINER'S COMMENT

This is a well-focused paragraph that concentrates on Plath's ability to use language in an inventive and controlled fashion. The contrast between the vivid appearance of the poppies and the poet's own bleak mood is very well illustrated. There is also a sense of engagement with the feelings expressed in the poem. A very good A-grade standard.

Last Words

'*Her poems have that heart-breaking quality about them.*'

Joyce Carol Oates

'*Artists are a special breed. They are passionate and temperamental. Their feelings flow into the work they create.*'

J. Timothy King

'*I am a genius of a writer; I have it in me. I am writing the best poems of my life.*'

Sylvia Plath

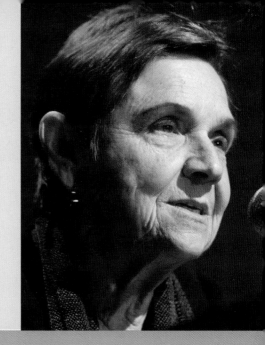

Adrienne Rich (1929–)

Adrienne Rich's most recent books of poetry are *Telephone Ringing in the Labyrinth*: *Poems 2004–2006* and *The School Among the Ruins: 2000–2004*. A selection of her essays, *Arts of the Possible: Essays and Conversations*, appeared in 2001. She edited Muriel Rukeyser's *Selected Poems* for the Library of America. In spring 2009, Norton published *A Human Eye: Essays on Art in Society*. She is a recipient of the National Book Foundation's 2006 Medal for Distinguished Contribution to American Letters, among other honours. She lives in California.

Adrienne Rich

PRESCRIBED POEMS (HIGHER LEVEL)

For copyright reasons, it has not been possible to include detailed study notes on the poetry of Adrienne Rich.

Aunt Jennifer's Tigers

Aunt Jennifer's tigers prance across a screen,
Bright topaz denizens of a world of green.
They do not fear the men beneath the tree;
They pace in sleek chivalric certainty.

Aunt Jennifer's fingers fluttering through her wool   5
Find even the ivory needle hard to pull.
The massive weight of Uncle's wedding band
Sits heavily upon Aunt Jennifer's hand.

When Aunt is dead, her terrified hands will lie
Still ringed with ordeals she was mastered by.   10
The tigers in the panel that she made
Will go on prancing, proud and unafraid.

GLOSSARY

1 *prance*: walk with exaggerated, bouncing steps.
1 *screen*: surface on which an image is formed; a movable structure used to conceal.
2 *topaz*: semi-precious stone, yellow or light blue.
2 *denizens*: inhabitants.
4 *sleek*: glossy; smooth; shiny.
4 *chivalric*: behaving in a courteous way.
6 *ivory*: hard, white bony substance that forms the tusks of elephants.
10 *ordeals*: painful or difficult experiences.

EXPLORATIONS

1 What aspects of Aunt Jennifer's character are revealed by Adrienne Rich's use of verbs in the poem?
2 This poem illustrates the power of a symbol. Comment on Rich's choice of symbols.
3 Do you regard the ending of the poem as positive or negative? Explain your answer with reference to the text.
4 'Rich challenges us with her ideas on relationships.' To what extent is this true in 'Aunt Jennifer's Tigers'?
5 Write your own personal response to the poem.

Adrienne Rich

CLASS/HOMEWORK EXERCISE

1   Copy the table below into your own notes and fill in critical comments about the quotations.

Key Quotes

Key Quotes	
Aunt Jennifer's tigers prance across a screen	
They pace in sleek chivalric certainty	
The massive weight of Uncle's wedding band	
her terrified hands will lie/ Still ringed with ordeals	
prancing, proud and unafraid	

The Uncle Speaks in the Drawing Room

I have seen the mob of late
Standing sullen in the square,
Gazing with a sullen stare
At window, balcony, and gate.
Some have talked in bitter tones,   5
Some have held and fingered stones.

These are follies that subside.
Let us consider, none the less,
Certain frailties of glass
Which, it cannot be denied,   10
Lead in times like these to fear
For crystal vase and chandelier.

Not that missiles will be cast;
None as yet dare lift an arm.
But the scene recalls a storm   15
When our grandsire stood aghast
To see his antique ruby bowl
Shivered in a thunder-roll.

Let us only bear in mind
How these treasures handed down   20
From a calmer age passed on
Are in the keeping of our kind.
We stand between the dead glass-blowers
And murmurings of missile-throwers.

GLOSSARY

Drawing Room: room where visitors are entertained.
1 *mob*: disorderly crowd.
2 *sullen*: unwilling to talk.
7 *follies*: foolish actions or ideas.
9 *frailties*: physical flaws or moral weaknesses.
12 *crystal*: clear and brilliant glass.
13 *missiles*: objects or weapons thrown or launched at a target.
16 *grandsire*: an old-fashioned word for grandfather.
16 *aghast*: overcome with amazement or horror.
17 *ruby bowl*: deep red glass bowl.
22 *in the keeping of our kind*: in the care and charge of people like us.
23 *glass-blowers*: people who make glass objects by shaping molten glass.

EXPLORATIONS

1   The voice in the poem belongs to the uncle. What type of man do you think he is? Consider what he says and how he speaks.

2   Choose two symbols or metaphors that are used in this poem and explain what you think each represents.

3   Do you think the formal structure of the poem suits its subject matter? Look at the layout, rhyme and rhythm of the poem.

4   What do you learn from the contrasting moods inside and outside the house?

5   'Poets draw on everyday events and experiences to make complex ideas accessible.' Discuss this statement with reference to 'The Uncle Speaks in the Drawing Room'.

CLASS/HOMEWORK EXERCISE

1   Copy the table below into your own notes and fill in critical comments about the quotations.

Key Quotes	
I have seen the mob of late	
These are follies that subside	
Certain frailties of glass	
To see his antique ruby bowl/Shivered in a thunder-roll	
We stand between the dead glass-blowers/ And murmurings of missile-throwers	

Power

Living   in the earth-deposits   of our history

Today a backhoe divulged   out of a crumbling flank of earth
one bottle   amber   perfect   a hundred-year-old
cure for fever   or melancholy   a tonic
for living on this earth   in the winters of this climate   5

Today I was reading about Marie Curie:
she must have known she suffered   from radiation sickness
her body bombarded for years   by the element
she had purified
It seems she denied to the end   10
the source of the cataracts on her eyes
the cracked and suppurating skin   of her finger-ends
till she could no longer hold   a test-tube or a pencil

She died   a famous woman   denying
her wounds   15
denying
her wounds   came   from the same source as her power

GLOSSARY			
2	*backhoe*: mechanical digger.	7	*radiation sickness*: illness caused by damaging radioactive rays.
2	*flank*: side.		
3	*amber*: orange-yellow colour.	8	*bombarded*: attacked.
4	*melancholy*: deep sadness.	11	*cataracts*: medical condition causing blurred vision.
6	*Marie Curie*: pioneering scientist.		
		12	*suppurating*: festering.

EXPLORATIONS

1 Briefly explain what you understand by the first line of the poem.
2 From your reading of the poem, what image do you get of Marie Curie?
3 How would you describe the tone in the final stanza? Refer to the text in your answer.
4 Write a paragraph on how this poem addresses the issue of power. Support your points with close reference to the text.
5 What impact did the poem 'Power' have on you? Refer closely to the text in your response.

Adrienne Rich

1 Copy the table below into your own notes and fill in critical comments about the quotations.

Key Quotes

Key Quotes	
Living in the earth-deposits of our history	
in the winters of this climate	
her body bombarded for years	
she could no longer hold a test-tube or a pencil	
a famous woman	

Storm Warnings

The glass has been falling all the afternoon,
And knowing better than the instrument
What winds are walking overhead, what zone
Of gray unrest is moving across the land,
I leave the book upon a pillowed chair   5
And walk from window to closed window, watching
Boughs strain against the sky

And think again, as often when the air
Moves inward toward a silent core of waiting,
How with a single purpose time has traveled   10
By secret currents of the undiscerned
Into this polar realm. Weather abroad
And weather in the heart alike come on
Regardless of prediction.

Between foreseeing and averting change   15
Lies all the mastery of elements
Which clocks and weatherglasses cannot alter.
Time in the hand is not control of time,
Nor shattered fragments of an instrument
A proof against the wind; the wind will rise,   20
We can only close the shutters.

I draw the curtains as the sky goes black
And set a match to candles sheathed in glass
Against the keyhole draught, the insistent whine
Of weather through the unsealed aperture.   25
This is our sole defense against the season;
These are the things that we have learned to do
Who live in troubled regions.

GLOSSARY		
1 *glass*: barometer.	15 *averting*: avoiding.	
7 *Boughs*: branches.	16 *elements*: weather.	
9 *core*: centre.	25 *aperture*: opening.	
11 *undiscerned*: unseen.		

EXPLORATIONS

1   Using reference to the opening stanza, comment on the way Adrienne Rich conveys the atmosphere as the storm approaches.

2   In your opinion, what does the poem suggest about people's attempts to control their environment? Support the points you make by quotation or reference.

3   Choose two images from the poem that you consider particularly interesting and briefly explain why you chose each one.

4   How would you describe the tone of stanza four? Support your opinion using reference to the poem.

5   Write your own personal response to 'Storm Warnings'. Refer closely to the text in your answer.

CLASS/HOMEWORK EXERCISE

1   Copy the table below into your own notes and fill in critical comments about the quotations.

Key Quotes	
The glass has been falling all the afternoon	
I leave the book upon a pillowed chair	
We can only close the shutters	
And set a match to candles sheathed in glass	
This is our sole defense against the season	

Living in Sin

She had thought the studio would keep itself;
no dust upon the furniture of love.
Half heresy, to wish the taps less vocal,
the panes relieved of grime. A plate of pears,
a piano with a Persian shawl, a cat   5
stalking the picturesque amusing mouse
had risen at his urging.
Not that at five each separate stair would writhe
under the milkman's tramp; that morning light
so coldly would delineate the scraps   10
of last night's cheese and three sepulchral bottles;
that on the kitchen shelf among the saucers
a pair of beetle-eyes would fix her own—
envoy from some village in the moldings...
Meanwhile, he, with a yawn,   15
sounded a dozen notes upon the keyboard,
declared it out of tune, shrugged at the mirror,
rubbed at his beard, went out for cigarettes;
while she, jeered by the minor demons,
pulled back the sheets and made the bed and found   20
a towel to dust the table-top,
and let the coffee-pot boil over on the stove.
By evening she was back in love again,
though not so wholly but throughout the night
she woke sometimes to feel the daylight coming   25
like a relentless milkman up the stairs.

1	*studio*: one-room studio flat with small kitchen and bathroom.	10	*delineate*: to show by outlining either in a drawing or by words.
3	*heresy*: judgement contrary to accepted opinion.	11	*sepulchral*: gloomy; melancholy.
6	*picturesque*: pleasant to look at; forming a picture.	14	*moldings*: decorative edging made of wood or plaster.
8	*writhe*: twisting movement of extreme pain.	19	*demons*: evil spirits; people who do something with great energy or skill.
		26	*relentless*: ongoing; merciless; without compassion.

GLOSSARY

EXPLORATIONS

1 'Living in sin' is not an expression often used today. What did this phrase originally mean? Has society's views on this matter changed? How?

2 Why do you think the poet uses both ordinary, everyday language and metaphorical language? Pick an example of each type of language that you found effective and give reasons for your choice.

3 Based on your reading of the poem, comment on the poet's use of contrast. Refer to the text in your answer.

4 It has been said that Adrienne Rich's poetry flows in more than one direction. To what extent is this true of 'Living in Sin'?

5 Write a personal response to this poem, referring to both its theme and the stylistic techniques employed. Support your answer with reference.

CLASS/HOMEWORK EXERCISE

1 Copy the table below into your own notes and fill in critical comments about the quotations.

Key Quotes	
Half heresy, to wish the taps less vocal	
A plate of pears, / a piano with a Persian shawl	
envoy from some village in the moldings	
jeered by the minor demons	
By evening she was back in love again, / though not so wholly	

The Roofwalker

—for Denise Levertov

Over the half-finished houses
night comes. The builders
stand on the roof. It is
quiet after the hammers,
the pulleys hang slack.   5
Giants, the roofwalkers,
on a listing deck, the wave
of darkness about to break
on their heads. The sky
is a torn sail where figures   10
pass magnified, shadows
on a burning deck.

I feel like them up there:
exposed, larger than life,
and due to break my neck.   15

Was it worth while to lay—
with infinite exertion—
a roof I can't live under?
—All those blueprints,
closings of gaps,   20
measurings, calculations?
A life I didn't choose
chose me: even
my tools are the wrong ones
for what I have to do.   25
I'm naked, ignorant,
a naked man fleeing
across the roofs
who could with a shade of difference
be sitting in the lamplight   30
against the cream wallpaper
reading—not with indifference—
about a naked man
fleeing across the roofs.

Adrienne Rich

EXPLORATIONS

1 Comment on the use of the poet's choice of adjectives in the first stanza. What do they suggest about the speaker's state of mind?

2 Look carefully at the poem's shape on the page. Can you suggest a reason for placing lines 13–15 on their own?

3 How do you respond to Adrienne Rich's use of metaphors in 'The Roofwalker'? Use quotation from the poem to support your views.

4 In your opinion, is there a definite conclusion reached at the end? Would you regard the poem as optimistic or pessimistic? Support your response with quotations from the poem.

5 What do you think the choice facing the speaker at the end of the poem is? Support your response with quotations from the poem.

CLASS/HOMEWORK EXERCISE

1 Copy the table below into your own notes and fill in critical comments about the quotations.

Key Quotes	
shadows/on a burning deck	
and due to break my neck	
A life I didn't choose/chose me	
a naked man fleeing/across the roofs	
sitting in the lamplight	

Our Whole Life

Our whole life a translation
the permissible fibs

and now a knot of lies
eating at itself to get undone

Words bitten thru words   5

meanings burnt-off like paint
under the blowtorch

All those dead letters
rendered into the oppressor's language

Trying to tell the doctor where it hurts   10
like the Algerian
who walked from his village, burning

his whole body a cloud of pain
and there are no words for this

except himself   15

GLOSSARY		
1	*translation*: interpretation.	9 *rendered*: turned into.
2	*permissible fibs*: acceptable untruths.	9 *oppressor's language*: words used
7	*blowtorch*: lamp for removing paint.	by tyrants.
8	*dead letters*: useless language;	
	undelivered mail.	

EXPLORATIONS

1   Comment on the effectiveness of the poem's title.
2   The poet mentions 'fibs' and 'lies' in the opening lines of the poem. What do you think she really means by this?
3   How would you describe the poet's tone in lines 3–7?
4   Write a paragraph in which you comment on Adrienne Rich's use of imagery in this poem. Support the points you make with close reference to the text.
5   Write your own personal response to 'Our Whole Life'.

Adrienne Rich

1 Copy the table below into your own notes and fill in critical comments about the quotations.

Key Quotes

Our whole life a translation	
a knot of lies/eating at itself to get undone	
All those dead letters/rendered into the oppressor's language	
Trying to tell the doctor where it hurts	
his whole body a cloud of pain	

Trying to Talk with a Man

Out in this desert we are testing bombs,

that's why we came here.

Sometimes I feel an underground river
forcing its way between deformed cliffs
an acute angle of understanding   5
moving itself like a locus of the sun
into this condemned scenery.

What we've had to give up to get here—
whole LP collections, films we starred in
playing in the neighborhoods, bakery windows   10
full of dry, chocolate-filled Jewish cookies,
the language of love-letters, of suicide notes,
afternoons on the riverbank
pretending to be children

Coming out to this desert   15
we meant to change the face of
driving among dull green succulents
walking at noon in the ghost town
surrounded by a silence

that sounds like the silence of the place   20
except that it came with us
and is familiar
and everything we were saying until now
was an effort to blot it out—
coming out here we are up against it   25

Out here I feel more helpless
with you than without you
You mention the danger
and list the equipment
we talk of people caring for each other   30
in emergencies—laceration, thirst—
but you look at me like an emergency

Adrienne Rich

Your dry heat feels like power
your eyes are stars of a different magnitude
they reflect lights that spell out: EXIT   35
when you get up and pace the floor

talking of the danger
as if it were not ourselves
as if we were testing anything else.

EXPLORATIONS

1   Comment on the effectiveness of the poem's title in relation to the themes addressed by the poet.

2   How would you describe the atmosphere in this poem? Refer closely to the text in your answer.

3   Choose two images from the poem that you found particularly effective. Comment on your choice in each case.

4   Based on your reading of lines 8–14, what was the couple's relationship like in the past?

5   How does the poem make you feel? Give reasons for your response, supporting the points you make with quotation or reference.

CLASS/HOMEWORK EXERCISE

1   Copy the table below into your own notes and fill in critical comments about the quotations.

Key Quotes	
Out in this desert we are testing bombs	
What we've had to give up to get here	
walking at noon in the ghost town	
Out here I feel more helpless/with you than without you	
Your dry heat feels like power	

Diving into the Wreck

First having read the book of myths,
and loaded the camera,
and checked the edge of the knife-blade,
I put on
the body-armor of black rubber   5
the absurd flippers
the grave and awkward mask.
I am having to do this
not like Cousteau with his
assiduous team   10
aboard the sun-flooded schooner
but here alone.

There is a ladder.
The ladder is always there
hanging innocently   15
close to the side of the schooner.
We know what it is for,
we who have used it.
Otherwise
it's a piece of maritime floss   20
some sundry equipment.

I go down.
Rung after rung and still
the oxygen immerses me
the blue light   25
the clear atoms
of our human air.
I go down.
My flippers cripple me,
I crawl like an insect down the ladder   30
and there is no one
to tell me when the ocean
will begin.

First the air is blue and then
it is bluer and then green and then   35

black I am blacking out and yet
my mask is powerful
it pumps my blood with power
the sea is another story
the sea is not a question of power   40
I have to learn alone
to turn my body without force
in the deep element.

And now: it is easy to forget
what I came for   45
among so many who have always
lived here
swaying their crenellated fans
between the reefs
and besides   50
you breathe differently down here.

I came to explore the wreck.
The words are purposes.
The words are maps.
I came to see the damage that was done   55
and the treasures that prevail.
I stroke the beam of my lamp
slowly along the flank
of something more permanent
than fish or weed   60

the thing I came for:
the wreck and not the story of the wreck
the thing itself and not the myth
the drowned face always staring
toward the sun   65
the evidence of damage
worn by salt and sway into this threadbare beauty
the ribs of the disaster
curving their assertion
among the tentative haunters.   70

This is the place.

And I am here, the mermaid whose dark hair
streams black, the merman in his armored body
We circle silently
about the wreck   75
we dive into the hold.
I am she: I am he

whose drowned face sleeps with open eyes
whose breasts still bear the stress
whose silver, copper, vermeil cargo lies   80
obscurely inside barrels
half-wedged and left to rot
we are the half-destroyed instruments
that once held to a course
the water-eaten log   85
the fouled compass

We are, I am, you are
by cowardice or courage
the one who find our way
back to this scene   90
carrying a knife, a camera
a book of myths
in which
our names do not appear.

GLOSSARY		
1 *myths*: ancient tales; folklore.	56 *prevail*: survive.
5 *body-armor*: wetsuit.	58 *flank*: side.
9 *Cousteau*: Jacques Cousteau (1910– 97), the famous French underwater explorer and documentary film- maker.	67 *threadbare*: worn; shabby.
	70 *tentative*: unsure; timid.
	70 *haunters*: divers who repeatedly explore wrecks.
10 *assiduous*: methodical; professional.	72 *mermaid*: mythical sea creature (part woman and part fish).
11 *schooner*: sailing ship.	
20 *maritime*: naval; related to the sea.	73 *merman*: male version of a mermaid.
20 *floss*: thread.	
21 *sundry*: varied; miscellaneous.	80 *vermeil*: precious metal; gilded silver or gold.
48 *crenellated*: having ridges or notches.	
49 *reefs*: outcrops of jagged rocks.	85 *log*: day-to-day ship's record.

EXPLORATIONS

1   What does the title of the poem suggest to you?

2   How would you describe the atmosphere in the opening stanza?

3   At one level, this poem is about exploring a shipwreck. In your view, what else is the speaker exploring? Refer closely to the text in your answer.

4   From your reading of the poem, what do you understand by the phrase 'threadbare beauty' (line 67)?

5   Write a paragraph on the poet's description of the underwater world. Refer closely to the text, commenting on the effectiveness of the language used.

CLASS/HOMEWORK EXERCISE

1   Copy the table below into your own notes and fill in critical comments about the quotations.

Key Quotes

Key Quotes	
The ladder is always there	
I crawl like an insect	
swaying their crenellated fans/between the reefs	
worn by salt and sway into this threadbare beauty	
a book of myths/in which/our names do not appear	

From a Survivor

The pact that we made was the ordinary pact
of men & women in those days

I don't know who we thought we were
that our personalities
could resist the failures of the race   5

Lucky or unlucky, we didn't know
the race had failures of that order
and that we were going to share them

Like everybody else, we thought of ourselves as special

Your body is as vivid to me   10
as it ever was: even more

since my feeling for it is clearer:
I know what it could do and could not do

it is no longer
the body of a god   15
or anything with power over my life

Next year it would have been 20 years
and you are wastefully dead
who might have made the leap
we talked, too late, of making   20

which I live now
not as a leap
but a succession of brief, amazing moments

each one making possible the next

GLOSSARY

1 *pact*: formal agreement.
18 *wastefully dead*: gone without
achieving.

Adrienne Rich

EXPLORATIONS

1 Consider the shape of the poem on the page. Is the fragmented order being used by the poet to say anything about life?

2 Why do you think the poet uses '&' between 'men' and 'women' in line 2? What does this suggest to you?

3 How would you describe the tone in 'From a Survivor'? Does it change at any point? Refer to the text in your answer.

4 Do you think the poem's ending is optimistic or pessimistic? Look at the absence of punctuation at the end. Why do you think Adrienne Rich chose to do this?

5 Write your own personal response to the poem.

CLASS/HOMEWORK EXERCISE

1 Copy the table below into your own notes and fill in critical comments about the quotations.

Key Quotes

Key Quotes	
The pact that we made was the ordinary pact	
Like everybody else, we thought of ourselves as special	
since my feeling for it is clearer	
Next year it would have been 20 years	
each one making possible the next	

SAMPLE LEAVING CERT QUESTIONS ON RICH'S POETRY

1 'Adrienne Rich's poetry is interesting both for its modern and universal themes and for its conventional and experimental use of language.' Discuss this statement with reference to the poems on your course.

2 'I like (or do not like) to read the poetry of Adrienne Rich.' Respond to this statement, referring to the poetry by Adrienne Rich on your course.

3 Do you consider the poetry of Adrienne Rich to be a 'succession of brief, amazing moments'? Consider this question in relation to the poetry of Adrienne Rich that you have studied on your course.

4 Adrienne Rich has said, 'The desire to be heard – that is the impulse behind writing poems for me.' Does Rich's poetry speak to you? Write your personal response to the poems of Rich that do/do not speak to you.

Last Words

'What is possible in this life? What does love mean, this thing that is so important? What is this other thing called "freedom" or "liberty" – is it like love, a feeling?'

Adrienne Rich

'Adrienne Rich's poems speak quietly but do not mumble ... do not tell fibs.'

W.H. Auden

'Formalism was part of the strategy – like asbestos gloves, it allowed me to handle materials I couldn't pick up barehanded.'

Adrienne Rich

Glossary of Common Literary Terms

alliteration:	the use of the same letter at the beginning of each word or stressed syllable in a line of verse, e.g. 'boilers bursting'.
assonance:	the use of the same vowel sound in a group of words, e.g. 'bleared, smeared with toil'.
aubade:	a celebratory morning song, sometimes lamenting the parting of lovers.
blank verse:	unrhymed iambic pentameter, e.g. 'These waters, rolling from their mountain-springs'.
conceit:	an elaborate image or far-fetched comparison, e.g. 'This flea is you and I, and this/Our marriage bed'.
couplet:	two successive lines of verse, usually rhymed and of the same metre, e.g. 'So long as men can breathe or eyes can see,/So long lives this, and this gives life to thee'.
elegy:	a mournful poem, usually for the dead, e.g. 'Sleep in a world your final sleep has woken'.
emotive language:	language designed to arouse an emotional response in the reader, e.g. 'For this that all that blood was shed?'
epiphany:	a moment of insight or understanding, e.g. 'Somebody loves us all'.
free verse:	unrhymed and unmetred poetry, often used by modern poets, e.g. 'but the words are shadows and you cannot hear me./You walk away and I cannot follow'.
imagery:	descriptive language or word-pictures, especially appealing to the senses, e.g. 'He was speckled with barnacles,/fine rosettes of lime'.
irony:	when one thing is said and the opposite is meant, e.g. 'For men were born to pray and save'.
lyric:	short musical poem expressing feeling.
metaphor:	image that compares two things without using the words 'like' or 'as', e.g. 'I am gall, I am heartburn'.
onomatopoeia:	the sound of the word imitates or echoes the sound being described, e.g. 'The murmurous haunt of flies on summer eves'.

paradox:	a statement that on the surface appears self-contradictory, e.g. 'I shall have written him one/poem maybe as cold/ And passionate as the dawn'.
persona:	the speaker or voice in the poem. This is not always the poet, e.g. 'I know that I shall meet my fate/Somewhere among the clouds above'.
personification:	where the characteristics of an animate or living being are given to something inanimate, e.g. 'The yellow fog that rubs its back upon the window panes'.
rhyme:	identical sound of words, usually at the end of lines of verse, e.g. 'I get down on my knees and do what must be done/And kiss Achilles' hand, the killer of my son'.
rhythm:	the beat or movement of words, the arrangement of stressed and unstressed, short and long syllables in a line of poetry, e.g. 'I will arise and go now, and go to Innisfree'.
sestina:	a six-stanza, six-line poem with the same six end words occurring throughout. The final stanza contains these six words. 'Time to plant tears, says the almanac:/The grand-mother sings to the marvellous stove/and the child draws another inscrutable house'.
sibilance:	the whispering, hissing 's' sound, e.g. 'Singest of summer in full-throated ease'.
sonnet:	a 14-line poem. The Petrarchan or Italian sonnet is divided into eight lines (octave) which present a problem o r situation. The remaining six lines (sestet) resolve the problem or present another view of the situation. The Shakespearean sonnet is divided into three quatrains and concludes with a rhyming couplet, either summing up what preceded or reversing it.
symbol:	a word or phrase representing something other than itself, e.g.' A tattered coat upon a stick'.
theme:	the central idea or message in a poem.
tone:	the type of voice or attitude used by the poet towards his or her subject, e.g. 'O but it is dirty'.
villanelle:	a five-stanza poem of three lines each, with a concluding quatrain, using only two end rhyming words throughout, e.g. 'I am just going outside and may be some time,/At the heart of the ridiculous, the sublime'.

ACKNOWLEDGMENTS

The author and publisher are grateful to the following for permission to reproduce copyrighted material:

The poems by Eavan Boland are reproduced by kind permission of Carcanet Press Limited;

'The Tuft of Flowers', 'Mending Wall', 'After Apple-Picking', 'The Road Not Taken', 'Birches', 'Out, Out–', 'Spring Pools', 'Acquainted with the Night', 'Design', 'Provide, Provide' from *The Poetry of Robert Frost*, edited by Edward Connery Lanthem. Copyright © 1916, 1928, 1930, 1934, 1939, 1969 by Henry Holt and Company, copyright 1936, 1944, 1951, 1956, 1958 by Robert Frost, copyright 1964, 1967 by Lesley Frost Ballantine;

The poems 'The Forge', 'Bogland', 'The Tollund Man', 'Mossbawn: Sunlight', 'A Constable Calls', 'The Skunk', 'The Harvest Bow', 'The Underground', 'Postscript', 'A Call', 'Tate's Avenue', 'The Pitchfork' and 'Lightenings viii' by Seamus Heaney are reprinted by kind permission of Faber & Faber Ltd;

The poems by Patrick Kavanagh are reprinted from *Collected Poems*, edited by Antoinette Quinn (Allen Lane, 2004), by kind permission of the Trustees of the Estate of the late Katherine B. Kavanagh, through the Jonathan Williams Literary Agency;

The poems by Thomas Kinsella, 'Thinking of Mr D.', 'Dick King', 'Mirror in February', 'Chrysalides', 'VI Littlebody' from *Glenmacnass*, 'Tear', 'Hen Woman', 'His Father's Hands', 'Model School, Inchicore' from *Settings*, 'VII' from *The Familiar* and 'Echo' from *Belief and Unbelief*, are taken from *Thomas Kinsella: Collected Poems*, Carcanet Press 2001 and reprinted by kind permission of Carcanet Press Limited;

The poems 'Wedding-Wind', 'At Grass', 'Church Going', 'An Arundel Tomb', 'The Whitsun Weddings', 'MCMXIV', 'Ambulances', 'The Trees', 'The Explosion', and 'Cut Grass' by Philip Larkin are reprinted by kind permission of Faber & Faber Ltd;

The poems 'Black Rook in Rainy Weather', 'The Times Are Tidy', 'Morning Song', 'Finisterre', 'Mirror', 'Pheasant', 'Elm', 'Poppies in July', 'The Arrival of the Bee Box' and 'Child' by Sylvia Plath are reprinted by kind permission of Faber & Faber Ltd;

'The Uncle Speaks in the Drawing Room', 'Our Whole Life', from *Collected Early Poems 1950–1980* by Adrienne Rich. Copyright © 1993 by Adrienne Rich. Copyright © 1967, 1963, 1962, 1961, 1960, 1959, 1958, 1957, 1956, 1955, 1954, 1953, 1952, 1951 by Adrienne Rich. Copyright © 1984, 1975, 1971, 1969, 1966 by W.W. Norton & Company, Inc. Used by permission of the author and W.W. Norton & Company, Inc. 'Aunt Jennifer's Tigers', 'Storm Warnings', 'Living in Sin', 'The Roofwalker', 'Trying to Talk with a Man', 'Diving into the Wreck', 'From a Survivor', 'Power', from *The Fact of a Doorframe: Selected Poems 1950–2001* by Adrienne Rich. Copyright © 2002 by Adrienne Rich. Copyright © 2001, 1999, 1995, 1991, 1989, 1986, 1984, 1981, 1967, 1963, 1962, 1961, 1960, 1959, 1958, 1957, 1956, 1955, 1954, 1953, 1952, 1951 by Adrienne Rich. Copyright © 1978, 1975, 1973, 1971, 1969, 1966 by W.W. Norton & Company, Inc. Used by permission of the author and W.W. Norton & Company, Inc.

The authors and publisher have made every effort to trace all copyright holders, but if any has been inadvertently overlooked we would be pleased to make the necessary arrangement at the first opportunity.